PADUA AND THE TUDORS

Portrait of Sir Henry Unton, artist unknown. By courtesy of the National Portrait Gallery, London

JONATHAN WOOLFSON

Padua and the Tudors

English Students in Italy,
1485–1603

James Clarke & Co Ltd
Cambridge

James Clarke & Co Ltd
P.O. Box 60
Cambridge
CB1 2NT

British Library Cataloguing in Publication Data:
A catalogue record is available from the British Library

First published in the U.K. by James Clarke & Co Ltd
First published in the U.S.A. and Canada by University of Toronto Press

ISBN 0 227 67942 3

For my father
and in memory of my mother

Contents

Acknowledgments

I thank the marquess of Salisbury for permission to quote from the Cecil Papers at Hatfield House; Andrew Thrush and the Trustees of the *History of Parliament* for permission to draw on unpublished draft biographies of MPs; and Ron Schoeffel and Barbara Porter of the University of Toronto Press for guiding this work to publication.

Grants and research fellowships from the Central Research Fund of the University of London, the Gladys Krieble Delmas Foundation, and the Society for Renaissance Studies have enabled me to conduct research in Padua, Venice, Bologna, and Rome. My greatest debt in this respect is to the British Academy, whose award first of a Major Postgraduate Studentship, and then of a Postdoctoral Fellowship, has made the completion of this work possible. During the writing of this book and the doctoral thesis on which it is based I have been privileged to work in two unique and contrasting institutions, St Mary's University College, Strawberry Hill, and the Warburg Institute of the University of London. I have learned so much from the people who work in these places, especially from Christopher Durston, J.B. Trapp, Nicholas Mann, Jill Kraye, Susan Doran, and my former supervisor David Chambers. I also wish to thank Edward Chaney, Andrew Gregory, James McConica, Robert Goulding, Tania String, Emilia Veronese Ceseracciu, Paul Hammer, John Guy, Miriam Skey, Peter Denley, and Tom Mayer for their help. For all her encouragement I am deeply grateful to Rita Maria Comanducci. Thanks are inadequate for what my father, Mark Woolfson, has done for me. His steadfast support has helped to sustain me through thick and thin. This book is dedicated to him and in loving memory of my mother, Helen Woolfson.

Abbreviations

AAU	Padua, Archivio Antico dell'Università di Padova.
ACV	Padua, Archivio della Curia Vescovile di Padova.
AGA, 1501–50	*Acta graduum academicorum Gymnasii Patavini, ab anno 1501 ad annum 1550*, ed. E. Martellozzo Forin (Padua, 1969–72).
AGA, 1601–5	*Acta graduum academicorum Gymnasii Patavini, ab anno 1601 ad annum 1605*, ed. F. Zen Benetti (Padua, 1987).
AO	*Alumni Oxonienses: The Members of the University of Oxford, 1500–1700*, ed. J. Foster (Oxford, no date).
ASP, AN	Padua, Archivio di Stato di Padova, Archivio Notarile.
BAV	Vatican City, Biblioteca Apostolica Vaticana.
BL	London, British Library.
BRUO	A.B. Emden, *A Biographical Register of the University of Oxford, A.D. 1501–40* (Oxford, 1974).
Cal. SP Dom. Eliz.	*Calendar of State Papers, Domestic, of the Reign of Elizabeth*, ed. R. Lemon (London, 1865–72).
Cal. SP For. Eliz.	*Calendar of State Papers, Foreign, of the Reign of Elizabeth*, ed. J. Stevenson et al. (London, 1863–1950).
Cal. Ven.	*Calendar of State Papers Relating to England in the Libraries of Venice and Northern Italy*, ed. R.L. Brown (London, 1864–97).

CE   *Contemporaries of Erasmus: A Biographical Register of the Renaissance and Reformation*, ed. P. Bietenholz (Toronto, 1985–7).

CWE   *The Collected Works of Erasmus* (Toronto and Buffalo, 1974–.).

DNB   *Dictionary of National Biography*, ed. L. Stephen and S. Lee (Oxford, 1921–2).

EH   *The English Hospice in Rome, The Venerabile,* Sexcentenary Issue 21 (1962).

HMC   Historical Manuscripts Commission.

LP   *Letters and Papers, Foreign and Domestic, of the Reign of Henry VIII,* ed. J.S. Brewer, J. Gairdner et al (London, 1862–1910).

LPL   London, Lambeth Palace Library.

PRO   London, Public Record Office.

QSUP   *Quaderni per la storia dell'Università di Padova.*

STC   *A Short-title Catalogue of Books Printed in England, Scotland and Ireland and of English Books Printed Abroad, 1475–1640,* ed. A.W. Pollard and G.R. Redgrave, 2nd ed (London, 1986).

PADUA AND THE TUDORS

Introduction

[handwritten: 1222]

The university of Padua was one of Europe's great centres of learning in the pre-modern period. Located in northeast Italy about twenty miles from Venice, the Paduan *studium* was officially founded in 1222 as a result of a student migration from the university of Bologna. In the *[handwritten: √]* course of the following century it came to be recognized as a 'universitas scholarium,' that is, as a self-governing, legal corporation of *[handwritten: term]* scholars, protected by Padua's civic authorities. From 1260 its statutes were codified, and from 1264 its chancellor, who was always the bishop of Padua, conferred academic degrees by the pope's sanction. *[handwritten: 1264]*

Before the period dealt with in this study, the *studium* had already succeeded in attracting many important intellectual figures, including a number of early humanists, the pioneers of the Renaissance classical revival: in the fourteenth century these numbered the poet laureate *[handwritten: Date]* Albertino Mussato and the jurist Baldo degli Ubaldi, the physicians *[handwritten: P's]* Pietro d'Abano and Giovanni Dondi d'Orologio, and the humanists Giovanni da Ravenna and Pier Paolo Vergerio the Elder. In the fifteenth *[handwritten: 1400's]* century (by which time there were two universities at Padua, one of law and one of arts and medicine) its luminaries included the jurists Giason del Maino and Filippo Decio, the physicians Jacopo della Torre, Ugo Benzi, and Michele Savonarola, the philosophers Paolo Veneto and Gaetano da Thiene, and the humanists Gasparino Barzizza, Vittorino da Feltre, and Demetrius Chalcondylas.

Crucially for this study, Padua had a long tradition of welcoming *[handwritten: ✳]* foreign students and professors. In the fifteenth century its alumni included Nikolaus Cusanus, Conrad Peutinger, and Hartmann Schedel from Germany; the Czech humanist Protasius of Czernahora; the Hungarian János Vitéz; the Pole Jan Ursinus; the Greeks Joannes

Argyropoulos and Joannes Laskaris; and the Englishmen John Tiptoft, John Free, and Peter Courtenay.

However, in the period dealt with here – the late fifteenth and sixteenth centuries – as a result of the patronage of the Republic of Venice, which had conquered Padua in 1405, the *studium* enjoyed its golden age. In this period, under the impact of Andreas Vesalius, Realdus Colombus, Fabricius ab Acquapendente, and others, Paduan medicine dominated the field in Europe. As a result of the work of Nicholas Copernicus and Galileo, the *studium* developed a reputation for science and mathematics. Through thinkers such as Pietro Pompanazzi, Francesco Piccolomini, Giacomo Zabarella, and Francesco Patrizi its philosophy became famous. By the presence of Pietro Bembo and Sperone Speroni its humanists were esteemed. Through the work of Marco Mantova Benavides, Tiberio Deciani, and Antonio Burgos its juristic thought was respected. And, in this period an even greater number of foreigners came to study in the *studium*. Germans (of which there were several hundred) included Joachim Mynsinger, Joachim Camerarius, and Kaspar Hoffman; Frenchmen Michel de l'Hopital, Émile Perrot, and Jean Coras; Poles Jan Kochanowski and Jósef Struś; Hungarians János Sámboky, Stefan Báthory (later king of Poland), and Andreas Dudith; Portuguese Damião de Goes; Spaniards Antonio Augustín; Swiss Caspar Bauhin; and Greeks Manuel Pigas.

For Englishmen, too, Padua continued to offer a considerable lure in this period. Its dozens of English alumni included statesmen, soldiers, and ambassadors such as Francis Walsingham, Robert Bertie, and Henry Wotton; churchmen such as Cuthbert Tunstall and Reginald Pole; humanists such as Richard Pace, Thomas Starkey, Richard Morison, and Thomas Wilson; and physicians such as Thomas Linacre, John Caius, and William Harvey.

That Padua was of some significance for the cultural, intellectual, and political life of England has long been recognized.[1] The careers at Padua of a few of the most famous English students have been investigated, and some indication is available of the impact that they had on English medicine, humanist studies, and political thought. In this book these subjects are reconsidered and some others are discussed in addition; and English students have been more closely investigated and their experiences reassessed in both an institutional and individual context. The general aim has been to provide a closer and more comprehensive prosopographical and intellectual study of the subject than has hitherto been attempted. Many pages that follow address not only the question of why English students went to Padua and what they did there, but the more complex issues of cultural transmission and reception, of how their experiences had an impact on Tudor life and thought. I will argue that Padua influenced England in profound, enduring, and sometimes surprising ways.

Furthermore, what isolated studies of famous Paduan alumni or of limited periods within the sixteenth century have not yet shown is the sheer number of English visitors to this Italian city in the era of Renaissance, Reformation, and Counter-Reformation. The biographical register, which has formed the basis of my interpretations and which is included here as an appendix, establishes that the Paduan *studium* was the most favoured foreign destination for English students in the period between 1485 and 1603. Certainly no other Italian universities compare to Padua for numbers of Englishmen.[2] Particularly instructive is the experience of Bologna, a centre whose English constituency probably outnumbered Padua's until the beginning of the sixteenth century.[3] The combined effect of the city's restoration to the papacy in 1506 and Henry VIII's break with Rome was to reduce English numbers dramatically.[4] Even those Italian universities which had had lower records of English attendance up to the fifteenth century were subject to similar experiences in the sixteenth century. Only Padua, the university city of the last Italian state to remain truly autonomous from imperial influence after 1530 – and a state which was famous for its religious toleration – continued to attract numerous Englishmen. In the wider European context universities such as Louvain, Leiden, and Basle all welcomed English students in this period, sometimes in large numbers: none of them sustained so continuously an English community comparable in size to Padua's.[5] By demonstrating in the biographical register – blow by blow, as it were, and for the first time – just how many alumni of Oxford, Cambridge, and the Inns of Court went to Padua, I hope also to show how seriously educational travel in general needs to be taken as an historical phenomenon.

The aim of the prosopographical approach is to view English students at Padua in their entirety, to assess changes in their social complexion over a long period, and to set English experience in its proper Paduan context. Inevitably there has been a problem of institutional definition, of describing the actual make-up of the *studium* of Padua and its membership. This has been rendered more difficult by fragmentary and miscellaneous sources, many of them hitherto unexplored for this subject. The complexity of this situation will take some explaining and I do this in chapter 1. But in attempting to provide as multifaceted a picture as possible of the English experience in Padua, I have opted for broad and inclusive criteria in the biographical register.

In fact I have attempted to include here all Englishmen known to have been in Padua, regardless of whether or not explicit documentary evidence demonstrates that they were students. The incomplete nature of records relating to formal study in the city has precluded the possibility of a narrowly defined institutional work, and at the same time other extant evidence suggests that much study was carried on informally. There was no princely court in Padua, no state government, no embassies, no major mercantile centre, no large garrisons of soldiers or sites of military and strategic importance. Besides the *studium* and related places of learning such as schools, academies, and religious houses, Padua housed some family *palazzi*, civic and ecclesiastical buildings, and some extraordinary works of art which – with the exceptions of the supposed tomb of the mythical founder of Padua, the Trojan Antenor, and the supposed home of the ancient historian Livy[6] – go largely unremarked by English visitors; some religious shrines noted by three English pilgrims early in the sixteenth century;[7] and some baths just outside the city, whose medicinal properties were tried out by a few English gentlemen.[8] Beyond the world of learning, the most we usually hear of the city of Padua in this period from its English visitors is that it had good air and was well supplied with victuals and, crucially, that it was near to Venice, a city which was important in all the ways that Padua was not. In other words, Padua was out and out a university city – 'the *studio* was the heart and soul' of Padua, as one of its Venetian governors wrote in 1547, and without it the city 'would be a dead body'; 'Without the *studio* Padua would not be Padua,' wrote another in 1549.[9] Its magnetism for Englishmen in this period largely resulted from its cultural, academic, and intellectual excellence. For dozens of Englishmen known to have been present there the documentary evidence for their activities tells us this much explicitly; for most of the others, it may also be inferred that they were studying there in some form or other, whether they were learning Italian, or being taught under private tutors, or were gathered into informal intellectual circles, or collecting intelligence for the English government, or dropping in on university lectures, or formally enrolled in the universities. There were many reasons for visiting Padua in the Tudor period – Henry Wotton did so in 1591 to escape the temptations afforded by the courtesans in Venice[10] – and these reasons are explored here. But even the most unlikely people – the forty-one-year-old Peregrine Bertie, Lord Willoughby d'Eresby, or the fifty-five-year-old Henry Fitzalan, earl of Arundel, for example – show some signs of contact with the intellectual life of the city or with its seat of learning.

There was, nevertheless, an institution at the heart of the *studium* which gives some definition to the English experience at Padua – the English 'natio' or nation, a statutory entity within Padua's law university which is explored in chapter 1. The interest of the nation's history is that it lies on the borderline of two cultural worlds, that of England and of Italy, and its development reflects an ongoing dialectic between purely local and English conditions; it was in the nature of this institution to be at the very heart of Anglo-Italian relations in the sixteenth century. It also operated in a context which was unusually multinational; Padua remained a cosmopolitan centre whose university life followed patterns determined by the nations much later than in other Italian universities. 'More students of forraine and remote nations doe live in Padua, then in any one University in Christendom,' observed Thomas Coryat in 1608.[11] Indeed in few sixteenth-century contexts does English experience appear so thoroughly European as it does here; even allowing for its special features and history, the Paduan *studium* remains something of a microcosm of the European life of this period.

The historically urgent questions of how and to what extent England's culture was drawing on Europe's in the early modern period thus inform much of my research. Nowhere is this more the case than for Roman civil and canon law, a neglected field in the history of Anglo-Italian relations and one in which Padua reveals itself as something of a 'missing link' in two respects. The English attendance at Padua's law university helps to explain how the law of the Catholic church could continue to operate in English ecclesiastical courts after its teaching had been banned in the post-Reformation English universities. It likewise suggests an explanation for the wider dissemination of civilian thought and practice in the later sixteenth century at a time when civilian teaching at the English universities attracted few students. Furthermore, as I argue in chapter 2, the very traditional and antihumanist flavour of Padua's law school may have provided far more of a fillip to an ethic of civic activism and political service in England than Italian 'civic humanism.'

'Civic humanism,' a modern, catch-all term, has been used to describe a certain Renaissance political consciousness which draws on ancient Greek and Roman sources; it has far too often been conjured as the thing which sixteenth-century Englishmen acquired from Italy. It is hoped that a more detailed look at one Italian context will help to define the nature of English experience in Italy more accurately and suggest some new answers. I believe that just as legal education offers a more viable source for a civic ethic in England than 'civic humanism,' so the study of medicine and natural philosophy at Padua, discussed here in chapter 3, suggests a source for a broad strain in English humanism which could inform the intellectual experience not only of a physician such as Thomas Linacre but also of a political thinker like Thomas Starkey. Medical historians have already demonstrated the centrality of England to the European medical renaissance.[12] In this study Padua is the vehicle of an attempt to relate English medicine and natural philosophy to the mainstream of English cultural life and to suggest their importance to Tudor intellectual history.

The categories by which these two chapters have been divided are intended to be truthful to the Paduan context, where the law university was a separate institution from the university of arts and medicine, and where law and medicine were the higher faculties. Nearly all English students at Padua had already received some education at Oxford and Cambridge when they arrived in the city and possessed a grounding at least in the trivium – grammar, rhetoric, and dialectic. It was to law and medicine, and to a certain extent to natural philosophy, that they turned in Padua.

These chapters thus attempt to treat Padua on its own terms and to challenge some entrenched Anglo-Saxon assumptions about the Italian Renaissance. The absence of a chapter on theology likewise reflects the lesser importance accorded to the subject in Padua compared to the English universities, although some qualifications must be made here. Although not as favoured a subject as law or medicine, theology could be studied in the arts university; lectures in theology were offered and a separate college of professors of theology examined candidates for doctorates in the subject.[13] The tradition of medieval Oxford philosophy was carried to Padua by the Scotist theologian Thomas Penkenth, who nevertheless returned to England in 1480, before the period treated here.[14] Religious changes in England during the reign of Edward VI threw up two more students of theology at Padua.[15] And three English seminary priests from the English College in Rome studied theology in the city in the Elizabethan period.[16] They are, however, a small detail in the broader picture.

Erasmian humanism and Italian spiritualism were more significant influences on the religious orientations of English students at Padua in this period, and these are discussed in chapter 4. This chapter deals with humanism in general and confirms it as the eclectic phenomenon described by recent studies.[17] Although humanistic approaches thoroughly penetrated Padua's university of arts and medicine, much of the ideological import of humanist thinking was transmitted on a more personal level. For more than three decades the source of inspiration here was the Paduan philosopher Niccolò Leonico Tomeo. He encouraged the study of ancient Greek and Latin texts among his many English students and introduced them to values which stressed the educational and social importance of humanist studies. The fortuitous survival of Leonico's letter collection with its English addressees has determined a more strictly textual approach in this chapter.

Chapter 5 returns more fully to the English background, pursuing those many Englishmen who went to Padua in the wake of the dramatic religious, political, social, and cultural changes of the sixteenth century. Though in some senses on the margins of Paduan intellectual life, English tourists and exiles were a product of social and educational changes in Padua and in England; they made important contributions to the English view of the contemporary Italian world, and were inspired by the Italian example to help create an English vernacular culture. The English intelligencers who, at the end of this period, reported from Padua to the English government on foreign affairs and on the movements of English outlaws are a testimony to important changes in England's view of its situation in Europe.

My attempts both to capture the richness of this subject and to assess its significance – rather than merely to describe it – have thus led to discussions of Paduan and English educational, medical, and legal institutions; of theoretical and applied aspects of English, Italian, and European law, medicine, natural philosophy, and humanism; and of the changing nature of English travel. There are also here extensive discussions of Tudor political thought and action, though I have tried to resist the tendency to relate every manifestation of culture and thought to issues of politics and power, or at least to deal only with those manifestations for which such a relationship can be established. The reductionism sometimes involved in this approach can give a depressingly one-dimensional impression of Tudor experience which does not accord with the reality as I see it. What I hope emerges instead is a broad study or series of studies on the theme of the Tudor experience in Padua. The Italian impact on England was invariably complex, and this could not be more true of the particular subject investigated here. It is intended that a wide-ranging approach is historically faithful to what was a multifaceted and changing phenomenon.

1

The English Nation at Padua

Padua was 'an universitie famous for lawe and phisicke, frequented by all nations, who have a consul whom they change each yeare, during which time those of the same nation are obliged to obey.' Thus wrote an anonymous English observer at the end of the sixteenth century.[1] The English nation was one of the twenty or so primary components of Padua's university of law, and enjoyed a continuous institutional life from the fourteenth to the eighteenth centuries.[2] (There was no English nation in the university of arts and medicine.) The 'natio Anglica' was never one of the larger nations, and its social and cultural functions were limited. But through the nation English participation in the law university was more important than might be expected from English numbers. This was due to the history of the university itself, in which two inter-related features are outstanding: the extent to which institutional identity was based on nationhood, and the fact that the university was student-controlled. In order to explain the position of the English nation in the sixteenth century, it is necessary to describe how these features came about.[3]

For the historical development of the Bolognese *studium* and those universities, especially the Paduan, which replicated its organizing principles, foreignness was an essential component of institutional identity. There had been places of higher learning in Bologna before the *studium*, Europe's oldest, emerged in the late-twelfth century. But the unique feature of this 'universitas scholarium' depended on the fact that it was a scholarly community composed entirely of foreigners. In their formative periods the Bolognese 'universities' or nations, responding to psychological and religious, as well as social and legalistic needs, thus manifested themselves as communities of Englishmen (the oldest

identifiable community, dating to a period before 1180); Germans;
Tuscans and Lombards; Provençales; Italians; and Romans and Campa-
nians (the latest, existing from about 1217).[4] The early nations emerged
independently from each other and then underwent a process of association and amalgamation, so that by the middle of the thirteenth
century there were two universities at Bologna, each with its own rector:
an ultramontane university, whose members came from north of the
Alps, and a cismontane, whose members came from south of the Alps.
This process excluded students with Bolognese citizenship well into the
Renaissance; this may also explain one of the most significant features
of the Bolognese *studium*, the exclusion of professors from membership
of the universities, for most if not all of them were originally of
Bolognese origin.

The extent of the privileges claimed by the universities in Bologna led
to a series of conflicts with the *comune*. This caused the first migration
to Padua in 1222 and the reaffirmation at Padua of the privileges and
principles worked out in Bologna. It was a community defined by its
foreignness, and confirmed as such by successive migrations from
Bologna in 1260–2 and in the early fourteenth century, each of which
had the effect of consolidating student liberties and introducing the
contemporary Bolognese example. The Paduan statutes of 1260 established ultramontane and cismontane universities a few years after
Bologna had adopted this organization, and the four earlier Paduan
universities, the French, German, Italian, and Provençale, were to be
encompassed within these two.[5] In 1331 the Paduan statutes explicitly
named Bologna as their organizational model, and it is from these
statutes that the structure of the law university as it is found in the
fifteenth and sixteenth centuries emerges, a single university comprising
cismontane and ultramontane nations, including the English.[6] There
were still two rectors in the fourteenth century, but the rulings of the
ultramontane rector took precedence in cases where the rectors issued
contradictory orders; the ultramontane university was the cismontane's
'mater' and 'magister.'[7] Furthermore, ultramontane electoral domination
of the university council was helped by the fact that the German nation
had two votes rather than the usual one.[8]

Each nation annually elected a *consiliarius*, who represented the nation
to the university and also formed collectively the university's executive
council under the rector. Students matriculated into their nations, and
their names were then reported to the *massarius* by the *consiliarii*.[9] Just
as the corporate trappings of the university – its seals, oaths, statutes,

privileges, and officials – had been borrowed from contemporary organizations such as the guild, so the nations replicated many of the
guilds' functions, at least in intention: care of the sick, provision of
funerals, arbitration between students, and help for the poor.[10] The 1331
statutes of the law university mention the statutes of individual nations
in the context of the fixing of the nations' separate feast days.[11] But such
statutes are not extant; it may be that the mushrooming of endowed
collegiate societies at Padua from the second half of the fourteenth
century reflects the financial inability of the nations to fulfil these
functions properly.[12] Certainly by this period the political independence
of the nations had been compromised by the consolidation of the university as a whole. Students' oaths of obedience were made to the
rector, and in practice he would intervene above the heads of *consiliarii*
to discipline them.[13] The identity of the university as a community of
foreigners, however, remained intact. Paduan citizens were officially
excluded both from the university and from the salaried professorships
(although the latter prohibition was frequently ignored).[14]

From the early fifteenth century a single rector was elected to govern
the university, alternating annually between an ultramontane and a
cismontane. But in the course of the century the rector's political
influence was reduced. The expense of the office was deterring candidates from coming forward, and this resulted in the election only of a
vice-rector in some years and of a Venetian or a Paduan in others.
Internal power, no doubt, devolved onto the *consiliarii,* but the reduced
authority of the rector was also the result of Venetian paternalism after
the Republic's conquest of Padua in 1405.[15] Despite the presence by this
time of Paduan and Venetian students at the university, they were still
denied real corporate electoral or political power on account of the *a
priori* claims of their citizenship.[16] Only Venetian students who concealed
their citizenship were able to claim full student privileges, a matter of
repeated concern to the Venetian Senate.[17] Indeed in the sixteenth
century new nations were created, reinforcing the cosmopolitanism of
the university in a period in which the student composition of the other
European universities was becoming more indigenous.[18] The international make-up of the student population at Padua had been helped by
the creation, on the initiative of the early Renaissance ruler of Padua,
Francesco da Carrara, of a separate university of arts and medicine,
which had emerged by the end of the fourteenth century with its own
rector and statutes. Arts students before this time had been incorporated
into the law university where, however, they had had no rights of

representation. Two traces of this subordination remained in the fifteenth century in the right of appeal by artist students to the jurist rector for sentences pronounced by the artist rector, and in the ceremonial investiture of the artist rector by the jurist rector.[19]

Imitating the Bolognese model, the universities continued to exclude professors, whose conditions of employment were to a large extent determined by student ballot, and who formed their own professorial organizations: the 'Sacred' colleges. These colleges enjoyed special rights confirmed by the Paduan civic authorities, the Republic of Venice, and papal bulls, all of which were enshrined in their statutes. Election to these organizations was not open to all professors, though in the course of the sixteenth century membership was expanding.[20] Most professors during the fifteenth century were not Paduan citizens, but pressure to admit more citizens continued and resulted in the creation of 'third ordinary' chairs by the middle of the fifteenth century, which were reserved for Paduans. Much of this pressure must have come from the colleges themselves, whose members not only comprised the chief degree-granting body for the university but also included local medical practitioners and advocates who were not salaried professors.[21] The Venetian Republic also wanted to reserve the right to appoint professors without reference to the student ballot, although from the late 1470s they excluded Venetians from the major lectureships to avoid politicizing the *studium*. For most of the fifteenth century, despite a number of appointments having been imposed by Venice, students had retained the right to determine the distribution of salaries and to elect professors nominated by the three *trattatores*, Paduan citizens appointed by Venice to represent it to the university. Only in 1479 was the first ordinary chair in medicine excluded from the student ballot. And only in 1503 was this exemption extended to professors of law who had been teaching at the *studium* for more than five years. However, these student privileges were rapidly removed on the reopening of the *studium* in 1517 after the war of the League of Cambrai. For the rest of the century students retained the right to elect only recent graduates to minor lectureships, paid for by the university itself.[22] Hence, for an English example, 'Guidonus anglicus' and 'Gulielmus anglicus' were elected by the university to the minor lectureship of the 'schola universitatis iuris civilis' in 1519 and 1520 respectively, each with a salary of twenty florins.[23]

Meanwhile, after 1517 the Paduan *trattatores* were replaced by Venetian *riformatores*, and this had the effect of strengthening Venetian involvement in the *studium*. From the middle of the sixteenth century *consiliarii* were able to appeal above the head of the rector to the *riformatores* or even to the *podestà* of Padua (the Venetian governor of the city), and professors and *riformatores* had a hand in the design of statutes. Venetian power was also strengthened by the ever-increasing waves of Venetian students. Venetians had been studying at Padua since the fourteenth century and constituted a nation in the 1331 law statutes. In 1406 and 1407 the Republic had forbade the development of *studia* at Vicenza and Treviso, and at the same time compelled students from the Veneto (Venice's Italian dominion) to study at Padua on penalty of a fine, unless they wished to study north of the Alps. However, Venetian student representation in the university was undermined by the application of the 'ius supplendum.' This was the rule by which inquorate nations were not permitted to elect their own *consiliarius*, and instead he would be elected by the rector and other *consiliarii*. Because of its special situation the Venetian nation, whatever its size, was considered by statute to have been inquorate in every year.[24]

Internal governance of the university continued to function in this period but students were becoming divested of real power. The squabbles between nations, which constituted much of the university's internal political life, seem counterproductive, and national assertiveness had its own part to play in the undermining of student independence. The acts of the German nations, for example, record their repeated appeals to the arbitration of the Venetian authorities for university decisions that went against their interests. Venetian intervention was often activated by international conflict, some of it violent, which thrived as a result of the nation-based structures of the universities as well as because of that freedom which students still did enjoy to govern their own affairs. This conflict was viewed as unacceptable misconduct and irresponsibility.[25] On the other hand, any embryonic sense of nationalism would have found a haven in these politics. Furthermore, ultramontane superiority was seen as essential to the character of the university; when new nations did come into being, it was as much in order to preserve this electoral superiority in council as to respond to demands for democratic representation by any groups of students. The printed statutes of 1551 explain some of this.[26] Here, representation by nations rather than by numbers of students, the rule that ultramontane nations must in all situations be represented by ultramontane students, and the ultramontane nations' quorum of three as against the cismontanes' quorum of six are presented as virtues explicitly intended to maintain the ultramontane political interest.[27]

Nevertheless, in the larger picture the balance of power had swung not to northern Europe but to Venice. A large number of ducal letters – instructions issued by the Doge – are recorded in the 1551 statutes, granting privileges and prohibitions, making and enforcing decisions. They locate for us the perceived authority in the middle of the sixteenth century; indeed they have become a source of institutional identity.[28] This demonstrates what other documents confirm: in the first half of the sixteenth century the university rapidly adjusted itself to Venetian paternalism. Venetian prestige, Venetian influence, and above all Venetian money were welcomed. Venice endorsed the contemporary student structure even while in practice changing its relationship to its external environment. Much interference – the settling of disputes, advice on statutes, payment of salaries to rectors – was intended to revitalize the original system. Venice also went to remarkable lengths to protect ultramontane groups, especially Germans, from ecclesiastical censure in connection with their Protestantism.[29] In sixteenth-century Padua, discontent with Venetian rule mostly manifested itself within groups excluded from the running of the university – students and patricians from Venice itself and native Paduans.[30] Venice was, after all, instrumental in maintaining the greatness of the Paduan *studium*, by seeking out famous teachers and offering them considerable salaries.[31] That the 1551 and 1562 statutes of the law university were drawn up by Paduan professors of law on the instructions of Venice is indicative of the balance of power at this time. Antonio Riccoboni, another Paduan professor, was the first historian of the *studium*. His failure to make any institutional distinction between professors and university rectors in his work of 1598, *De Gymnasio Patavino*, seems to reflect a new reality; both, after all, were in the pay of Venice by this period.

At the same time new or revived centres of student social life were also diluting the cohesiveness of the universities. In the sixteenth century colleges continued to flourish.[32] More significantly, the separate institutional life of some of the nations underwent a revival. The expense of matriculation, the required length of study, and the degree examination with its enormous cost and, in the second half of the sixteenth century, declaration of Catholic faith would have deterred some students from officially joining the universities. The new cultural and educational tourism of the European nobility encouraged more informal and briefer attendance at the universities, study under private tutors of music, mathematics, and Italian, and visits to the Paduan academies for other subjects not offered at the *studium*, or to Paduan schools of riding and swordsmanship. Some foreign students had enough wealth and prestige to penetrate the elitist literary circles of Paduan and Venetian aristocrats and Florentine exiles. The *studium* itself was only one of several foci of student life in the sixteenth century.

These developments had a considerable effect on the complexion of the English nation in the city, but to understand how, we must be sensitive both to developments in English society in this period and to the changing nature of the extant records. Whether or not changes in the social composition of the English universities in the Elizabethan period were so extensive as to warrant the term 'educational revolution' (which has long been a subject of debate), it seems self-evident from the sources that the population of England was rising in that period, that more people described themselves as gentlemen than had done so before, that more could afford to send their sons to the universities, and that consequently there were more gentlemen in higher education.[33] It is not a great surprise, then, to find that larger numbers of gentlemen travelling to Padua began to alter the social complexion of the English nation from the late 1540s and start to feature in the records of the university of law as English *consiliarii*.[34] Particularly striking is the attendance at Padua of successive generations of gentle or noble families such as the Paytons, the Berties, the Carews, the Friars, the Clements, the Masons, the Sackvilles, the Cecils, the Untons, the Wilsons; of brothers such as the Brookes, the Dennys, the Foxes, the Cavendishes, the Saviles, the Huses, the Haringtons, the Hobys, the Parrys, and the Manners; and of close networks of gentlemen related by marriage such as John Ashley, Francis Walsingham, William Godolphin, John Coke, Arthur Throckmorton, the Carews, and the Dennys; John Pelham and William Morley; Gilbert Talbot, Henry Gray, Henry Leonard, Henry Cavendish, and Richard Baker; Edward de Vere and the Berties; Henry Neville and Henry Killigrew; and Roger Manners and Philip Sidney. Nevertheless, many of these gentlemen, and of these the more wealthy and influential, had little or nothing to do with the university as far as we can tell. Some, such as Thomas Hoby in 1548, Edward Unton in 1563, Philip Sidney in 1573–4, Nicholas Faunt in 1581, and Samuel Foxe in 1585, were tourists and may have looked in on some lectures. Others were political and religious exiles, awaiting a return to England, or were on their way to European centres of Protestantism during the reign of Mary, or centres of Catholicism during the reign of Elizabeth. In fact for most of this period, the majority of English students enrolled in either the law university or the arts university were pursuing vocational studies with a view to careers in law or medicine, the church or government, and many of these came from the middle or lower ranks of society.

This pattern is repeated for noblemen. Francis Russell, earl of Bedford, was an exile for religion in Padua and Venice around 1555; he had nothing to do with the university. Nor did Thomas Sackville (soon to become Lord Buckhurst), in Padua in 1563, or Henry Fitzalan, earl of Arundel, in Padua in 1566, or Edward de Vere, earl of Oxford, in Padua in 1575, or Edward Lord Zouche, in Padua in 1592. Reginald Pole, the cousin of Henry VIII and the only determined student among this group, was taught by a retired Paduan professor, but there is otherwise no evidence of a formal connection of his with either university. Before the 1590s, only the nobleman Edward Courtenay, earl of Devon, seems to have been a member of the law university, though this becomes salient only on his death: it was on the orders of the rector that the German nation in its entirety attended his funeral in October 1556.[35] But Courtenay was far more a political and religious exile than a serious student.[36]

For information about involvement in the Paduan university of law, we must rely to a large extent on the unpublished acts of the law university. As will become clear in the discussion below, this source only provides names on a regular basis for nations' *consiliarii*, not for their entire membership. For Englishmen this situation only changes for the period 1591–8, when the university's matriculation register becomes available, listing names of matriculants and their identifying features. Sixty-five Englishmen matriculated in this period – a considerable number – and many of these were gentlemen or noblemen; for the more obscure of them this can be established from their earlier admissions to Inns of Court, or from being described as the sons of gentlemen, or as commoners, in their earlier matriculations at Oxford or Cambridge. The better-known include Edward Cecil, the grandson of Lord Burghley; Peregrine Bertie, Lord Willoughby d'Eresby; Roger Manners, earl of Rutland; Thomas Sackville, the son of Lord Buckhurst; Henry Leonard, the son of Baroness Dacre; and Thomas, Baron Gray of Wilton.[37] The matriculation list seems to suggest then that the English nation was dominated by gentlemen and noblemen by the 1590s.

But this source must be treated with caution. English students who emerged from Padua with medical degrees, or who in any case we know to have been studying medicine, feature in this law university's matriculation register from 1594.[38] This suggests that the register is not to be taken as the record of serious students of law. Although most of the gentlemen in the list were young men who would have undertaken some studies in the city, the appearance of the forty-one-year-old Peregrine Bertie suggests that this was not the reason for matriculating. In fact we know that Bertie, a leading military commander and statesman, was in Padua for the recovery of his health. His subscription here – and consequently that of the others – is surely explained by the fact that members of the university enjoyed the protection of the Venetian government against prosecutions for heresy by the ecclesiastical authorities. Comparing the numbers on the matriculation list with information available in the university's acts seems to confirm this. Though the acts supply few names other than *consiliarii*, they do record the numbers of Englishmen (without their names) who elected their *consiliarius* annually. It is striking that significantly more names feature every year on the matriculation register than appeared at the annual electoral meetings.[39] This suggests that many matriculants were in Padua for only short periods, and also that many of them did not have real electoral status in the law university because they were not recognized as, or did not consider themselves to be, serious students. In other words, for this latter group we must continue to rely on the names of *consiliarii* in the university acts in this period, though for serious students of law even this begins to become a doubtful source from at the latest 1600, when William Harvey, without question a student of medicine, was elected the English nation's *consiliarius* in the law university.[40]

In short, what the matriculation register testifies to is the extent of the late Elizabethan vogue for tourism and for educational travel, not for serious courses of study, and not for an English nation dominated by gentry and nobility. And interestingly, in the fact that English names appear in this register for religious reasons, there is a curious parallel with Oxford, where the motivation for keeping closer and more accurate lists of students – which are the main source for higher numbers there in the Elizabethan period – was the enforcement of religious orthodoxy.

These considerations have a bearing on the nature of the English nation in comparison with other nations. It is clear that the German nation, for example, gained power and prestige from the high standing and wealth of its members. Its extra vote in the university council – an ancient privilege – could give it the casting vote in the election of rectors or, when other nations were inquorate and the election was by the 'ius supplendum,' of other *consiliarii*.[41] This and the number of

German students available to take on these positions explain continued German domination of the university even in the face of cismontane numerical superiority. Furthermore, by the sixteenth century the German nation had won the permanent right to have one of its members elected *consiliarius* of the Bohemian nation by the 'ius supplendum' when that nation was inquorate, as it frequently was. In 1553 the German *consiliarius*, Siegfried Pfintzing of Nuremburg, recorded how, by his own diligence, he had negotiated the same right for the English and Scottish nations, and had hopes of winning the Burgundian nation as well. As he notes, with the two votes of the German rector this would give the German nation a total of eight votes on a council of twenty-two nations and twenty-five votes. He records this so that his successors should know it and strive to conserve the authority of the nation.[42] The acts of the university testify to the short-term success of this policy. Before 1553 the majority of students acting as English *consiliarii* when the English nation was inquorate were Provençale or Burgundian, though there were also some Spaniards, Greeks, Poles, Hungarians, Bohemians, Piedmontese, Tridentines, and even Veronese.[43] But from 1553 until a new influx of English students in 1555, all four non-English *consiliarii* elected by the 'ius supplendum' were Germans.[44] This kind of influence had a real impact on the choice of teachers and on the nature of the curriculum because the Venetian authorities were forced to listen to the German nation's demands about these matters, a fact which points to the seriousness with which many German students pursued their studies in the university of law.

The wealth of the German nation's membership also brought the money required to sustain an elaborate institutional life. In 1553 the German nation split into two and from this year artists and legists had their own separate statutes, acts, matriculation registers, libraries, seals, festivals, and officials.[45] According to the only extant document on the matter, it was primarily social conflict that had brought about this division: the more aristocratic law students had been denigrating and bickering with the lesser-born students of arts and medicine, and both sides decided that divorce was the only solution.[46]

Tensions like these are not evident in the English nation. Despite the social changes from the 1540s mentioned above, most English members of either university were from lower down the social scale and would have had little surplus money for the nation. They were financially dependent on parental support, patrons, or collegiate fellowships from Oxford and Cambridge. Thomas Starkey and William Harvey, for example, owed their educations in part to their fathers,[47] Thomas Goldwell to his father and to the archbishop of Canterbury,[48] Henry Coles to Dr William Knight,[49] Richard Pace to Thomas Langton,[50] John Friar to Edward Foxe,[51] Hugh Turnbull to Anthony Huse,[52] Nicholas Faunt to Anthony Bacon,[53] Simeon Foxe to Sir Robert Cecil,[54] and John Clement and John Mason to Henry VIII.[55] Edward Wotton, John Chamber, John Caius, and Henry and Thomas Savile were among those financed by their Oxford and Cambridge colleges.[56] Reginald Pole, initially at least, had a comfortable stipend from Henry VIII, and then presumably the income from his ecclesiastical benefices and Oxford fellowship. He helped a number of English students at Padua through his hospitality, including Starkey, George Lily, Michael Throckmorton, and Henry Coles. For those with insufficient funds, Padua could be expensive. As Francis Davison at Lucca wrote unsubtly to his father in 1596, 'whosoever, being a traveller, will feed his eyes and his mind, must starve his purse.'[57] Over a dozen of Richard Morison's letters from Padua beg Pole, Starkey, or Thomas Cromwell for money to finance his studies in the 1530s. Pole did help him, as did Thomas Winter, who gave him a doublet, while Coles, John Friar, and Throckmorton lent him money.[58] For Morison, entering Thomas Cromwell's service resolved his financial difficulties as much as it consummated his career ambitions.[59]

The budget of the *studium* of Padua was usually the highest of any university in Italy, and consequently the Paduan degree came at a prohibitive price. In 1572 it was said to cost more than fifty *scudi*, as compared to just under that figure at Bologna, around thirty-four at Siena and twenty-eight at Ferrara.[60] For the period from 1485 to 1603, the records of twelve degrees awarded to Englishmen by one of the Paduan colleges are extant, ten in medicine or philosophy and medicine and two in law.[61] The record of John Orphinstrange's examination in civil law in 1555 is the only one which breaks down his expenses. Orphinstrange paid eight *soldi* to the suffragan bishop (degrees were awarded by the bishop of Padua in his palace), eighty *lire* and twelve *soldi* to the prior and his twelve assistants, four *lire* to the 'punctatores,'[62] two *lire* and ten *soldi* to the college of jurist doctors, six *lire* and sixteen *soldi* to the notary, and sixty-two *lire* and ten *soldi* to the 'orators,' amounting to a total of 156 *lire* and sixteen *soldi*.[63] Students borrowed from each other to cover the expense. In 1505 the English law student John Lupus lent Nicholas Beysell of Liège twelve ducats so that he could pay for his degree examination in medicine.[64] The 'wandering scholar' could be a prosaic and indigent figure; although there is evidence of sixteenth-century Paduan students moving to different Italian universities in order to attend the lectures of particular professors, the prospect of cheaper degrees may have mattered as much.[65] This is probably true for John Clement, whose degree came from Siena; perhaps it was also a consideration for Robert Fisher, William Walter, Laurence Huse, and John Pelham, each of whom spent time in Padua but graduated at Bologna; for Richard White, who graduated at Pavia; and for Thomas Wilson, who graduated at Ferrara.[66]

There were two other possibilities for English students at Padua. One was to apply for a 'grace,' which enabled a student to take his degree examination free of charge. In 1525 Edward Wotton received his doctorate by these means, on account of his poverty and distance from home.[67] So too did Paul Rutland in 1531 and Thomas Bill in 1533.[68] These, however, were students of medicine; among English students of law, only John Le Rous is recorded as having received the same benefit.[69]

Another option was to receive the doctorate from one of Padua's many counts palatine. These were permitted to award degrees in their own homes as representatives of the civic authority and with imperial endorsement. Some members of the doctors' colleges – who were, in conjunction with the Paduan bishop, the 'official' examiners and bestowers of degrees – cooperated in degree examinations by count palatine by acting as promoters and examiners; indeed a member of the college of jurists, Marco Mantova Benavides, was himself created a count palatine and proceeded to award his own degrees. There was less fanfare and formality in the degree by count palatine and it was consequently cheaper and quicker – but less prestigious – than the 'official' route.

By supplicating for the degree by count palatine, it may have been easier to avoid a declaration of Catholic faith, the scope of which expanded after the promulgation of Pius IV's bull of 1564, 'In Sacrosancta.'[70] Before 1564 only candidates supplicating for a degree in theology were required to swear to an oath, but afterwards it was a requirement of all supplicants; hence John Le Rous took the oath for his degree in law in 1571,[71] as did Joseph Webb for his in philosophy and medicine in 1603.[72] (The universities, being student controlled, did not require a declaration of religious orthodoxy of matriculants, unlike Oxford and Cambridge in this period.)[73] Vigorous protests against this obligation by the nations under the leadership of the Germans were a continuous feature of this period; indeed in 1565 German students threatened an *en masse* migration from Padua for this reason. Not only were Protestants motivated to object on principle; Catholics from Protestant countries feared persecution at home for swearing to such an oath, which would have appeared on their doctoral diplomas. Venetian anxieties not to alienate the foreign community at Padua led to concessions. When a German rector who refused to take the oath was unanimously elected to the law university in 1565 – for the papal bull's requirement also extended to high officials in the university – the *podestà* of Padua, Niccolò da Ponte, prevaricated and let the matter pass.[74] In 1587 the Venetian government promised the Germans protection from ecclesiastical persecution in exchange for their guarantee that they would not publicly display manifestations of religious heterodoxy. From 1616, a decade after the papal interdict against Venice, the Paduan bishop could be circumvented where necessary through the award of degrees in arts and medicine 'by the authority of Venice.' In 1635 law degrees were available by the same means.[75] This may have been an attempt to stem the tide of degrees by count palatine, of which the Venetians disapproved, for the Venetian authorities had attempted to ban such degrees in 1612.[76]

It is difficult to generalize about the significance of degrees by counts palatine, especially because, for the second half of the sixteenth century, dozens of them may remain undiscovered in Padua's notarial archive.[77] We know that many Catholic students also chose the option, and a number of records show that students swore the oath of Catholic faith in the home of the count palatine as they would have done in the bishop's palace; perhaps for these students the low cost was what mattered. In the 1580s some seminary priests from the English College in Rome sought or acquired Paduan doctorates in theology by these means, but the college authorities and the English Jesuits disapproved, and this route was effectively closed by Pope Clement VIII's decree of 1597, which required these men, on pain of excommunication, to study for eight years before supplicating for the doctorate.[78] There is some evidence for English participation in the protests against the declaration of faith in 1566 and 1610. And in 1591, Archbishop John Whitgift claimed that the English law student Henry Hawkins, who had 'heard, read, disputed and conferred with the chief lawyers of our time,' would have taken a doctorate at Padua 'if the oath of the pope's supremacy and to all the articles of the Tridentine Council had not hindered and stayed him.'[79] Nevertheless, the majority of extant degrees awarded to Englishmen by counts palatine after 1564 include such a declaration. The record of John Hart's doctorate in both laws, awarded in 1574 by Marco Mantova Benavides, states that Hart took the oath as required by the bull of Pius IV.[80] (The same formula is found in the record of the degree of the Scottish student John Russell, awarded by Marco Mantova in the same year.)[81] The Englishman William Clement's doctorate in medicine, awarded in 1599 by Sigismondo Capodilista, also mentions the oath.[82] So too does the doctoral certificate of the medical student Samuel Turner, awarded by a count palatine in 1611.[83] Among Englishmen who took degrees by count palatine, only the medical students Edward Benedict (in 1601) and Thomas Hearne (in 1602) evaded it, Benedict swearing loyalty instead to the family of Capodilista as representatives of the emperor.[84] William Harvey's doctorate in philosophy and medicine of 1602 is an interesting hybrid. The notarial record in Padua is identical to the formal certificate which he took home with him and which is now in the library of the Royal College of Physicians in London, except that in the former he is recorded as swearing to the oath, whereas this is missing from the latter. On the reverse of the notarial copy, the notary has recorded that he deliberately excluded the oath from the certificate, 'pro convenientibus respectibus dicti domini Gulielmi': Harvey evidently asked him to leave it off.[85] For Jews there remained an unequivocal incentive for seeking out this kind of degree after 1564, for the papal bull was understood to apply only to those who belonged to a Christian confession.[86] But for Englishmen the evasion afforded by recourse to count palatine seems to have been more of a reality before 1564. Hence in 1550 George Dudgeon and Hugh Turnbull were each awarded doctorates in theology from the count palatine Transalgardo Capodilista.[87] In a letter to the privy council Peter Vannes, the English agent in Venice, explained how recourse to Capodilista had enabled Turnbull and Dudgeon to evade the declaration, the consequences of which they feared on their return to Edwardian England; it should be stressed that Turnbull and Dudgeon, like many of their successors at Padua in the Elizabethan period, were Catholics.[88] Only with the creation of degrees 'by the authority of Venice' did an evasion like this become possible again: in 1622 John Bastwick was awarded a Paduan degree in medicine by what was known as the 'collegio veneto artista.'[89]

I have suggested that wealth and high social standing sometimes disinclined Englishmen to join either university. Poverty and religion could also act as disincentives to pursuing a degree. These factors had a negative impact on the development of the English nation. The law university's record by nation of numbers of students electing *consiliarii* and *electionarii* in any one year, tabulated on pp 26–7 for years when the English nation was quorate, reveals the English as a fairly small constituency.[90] The meaning, uses, and limitations of the information on this table must now be assessed.

The nations' meetings recorded in the acts elected the *consiliarius* and *electionarius*. (The *electionarius* was an official concerned only with casting his nation's vote in the annual election of rector. In the English nation *consiliarii* and *electionarii* were the same people in most years.) The *consiliarius* of the English nation was elected by the 'ius supplendum' in the following years: 1502, 1506, 1517, 1524, 1529–32, 1536–7, 1539–49, 1553–4, 1572–5, and 1586. This indicates that for these years which predate 1550, there were less than four Englishmen in the nation, and after 1550 less than three; in 1550 the new statutes of the university reduced the number of students which constituted an ultramontane quorum.[91] For example, we know there were two English law students at Padua in 1506 – Robert Spencer and Robert Wingfield. Wingfield's associate at Padua of this period, Demit Selley, may also have been a student of law, but either way the nation would not have been quorate. However, the year 1538 is an exceptional case, when only two Englishmen were present but the nation was judged to be quorate; this year features on the table and the case is discussed below. Likewise in the year 1582 the English election is not recorded as by the 'ius supplendum,' though only two voters were present.[92] And finally it should be noted that the electoral record from 1596 begins to show regularly some elections by the 'ius supplendum,' but others where the national attendances were zero. The reasons for this remain unclear, but it may be an indication that university politics – and its records – were not being taken quite so seriously by this period.

Even in those years when the nation was inquorate and election was by the 'ius supplendum,' Englishmen sometimes took precedence as candidates for the *consiliarius*. Hence an Englishman was elected English *consiliarius* by the 'ius supplendum' in the years 1502[93] and 1549,[94] whereas in 1586 the English candidate, John Froso, lost the election by the 'ius supplendum' to a German, Peter Swidich.[95] Ad hoc elections of *consiliarii* of individual nations often took place in the course of a year for any number of reasons. However, the acts of the university recorded the size of nations on only one occasion during the year, when all nations' *consiliarii* were being elected. This was generally in August, prior to the election of the rector and the ballot for lecturers, and the figures recorded on the table are for these occasions (though in the course of many individual years the English nation had more than one *consiliarius*.) An exception is 1508, when all the nations elected their officials together in both January and July.

The acts of the law university commence in 1498 and no full record of events before that year exists. This is also true for the period during the war of the League of Cambrai and its aftermath, from 1509 to 1516, when effectively the university ceased to function. The incomplete information for 1500 and 1518 probably reflects the fact that the records were, respectively, relatively new and just recommencing after a long break. Henry Style was elected English *consiliarius* in 1518, but it is not clear from the acts whether or not the nation was quorate in this year, and no figures either for the English nation or for any other nation were recorded. Although the acts are extant, electoral figures are not recorded for the years 1498–9, 1501, 1503–5, 1535, 1550, 1585, 1590, 1595, and 1601, whereas for 1507 the figures are recorded but not the nations to which they correspond. Hence, for example, we know that John Boxall was English *consiliarius* in 1550, but we do not know whether or not the nation was quorate. No figure for the English nation was recorded in 1563, although we know the nation was quorate. In 1503 we know that two English students of law were present in Padua, Robert Fisher and Arthur Coo, but neither is recorded as *consiliarius*, although Fisher had been *consiliarius* in 1499. In the years 1587–9, 1591, 1598–1600, and 1602–3, only elections by the 'ius supplendum' are recorded, and the English nation is not among them. Finally, records for the years 1519–23, 1526–8, 1569–71 and 1578–9 are more or less missing altogether.

Besides these gaps in the evidence, how reliable are the figures which are recorded? For most of this period no matriculation records are extant for most of the nations, the exceptions being the German one, which commences in 1546,[96] and the Polish, which commences in 1592. The university's matriculation record is extant – though not continuously – from 1591 and, as discussed above, records English names from that year until 1598. The gaps for most of this period, then, preclude the possibility of verifying the electoral record by systematically matching it to names. Where this can be attempted for the English nation in the 1590s, I have already argued that there is a discrepancy which suggests that the status of matriculants within the university should be treated with caution. Furthermore, from the 1560s there is a decline in the standard of record-keeping in the university acts. As the table shows,

The English nation in context: electoral figures for the Law University for years in which the English nation was quorate

| Nation/ | | Jan. | July | | | | | | | | | | | | | |
Year	1500	1508	1508	1533	1534	1538	1551	1552	1555	1556	1557	1558	1559	1560	1561	1562
Germany				20	53	54	85	108	90	89	72	55	76	80	12	44
Bohemia	S	S	S	S	S	S	S	3	S	S	31	4	S	5	4	S
Poland	S	S	S	16	9	10	S	5	S	6	14	14	14	11	14	40
Hungary		S	9	S	3	4	13	11	S	3	4	4	S	S	S	4
Provence		8	9	14	14		8	12	5	3	4	3	7	14	4	3
Burgundy		7		14	16	21	18	7	12	4	6	12	4	5	S	3
England		7	9	26	4	2	6	5	3	9	13	11	5	3	3	4
Spain		18		S	3		S	S	S	3	4	S	S	S	S	S
Ultramarine	S	S	S	6	8		8	8	10	16	23	8	7	16	S	10
Scotland	n/a	n/a	n/a	n/a	4	S	S	S	S	S	S	S	S	S	S	S
Rome	34	28	7	13	23		15	15	12	14	12	12	34	40	40	50
Sicily		17	12	S	5	8	S	6	S	S	S	S	6	10	10	30
Ancona		8	9	13	15		9	10	3	S	S	20	17	21		30
Lombardy	39	36	43	67	39	104	48	60	21	46	125	25	39	110	8	45
Milan	10	17	21	12	17	35	21	18	7	14	33	46	80	60	20	50
Tuscany		10	18	10	19	8	8	8	7	10	20	6	8	17	6	17
Treviso		50	25	8	64		40	11	32	90		18	129	S	12	100
Friuli		21	15	7	12		10	13	13	19		9	22	10	8	10
Dalmatia	S	9	8	7	7		4	5	S	S	S	S	S	7	9	15
Piedmont	n/a	n/a	n/a	n/a	13		10	9	11	S	S	12	8		8	15
Genoa	n/a	n/a	n/a	n/a	n/a	n/a	n/a	n/a	n/a	n/a	n/a	n/a	n/a	n/a	n/a	20

1563	1564	1565	1566	1567	1568	1576	1577	1580	1581	1582	1583	1584	1592	1593	1594	1596	1597
161	200	151	80	90	60	57	18	65	90	80	100	68	30	19	30	10	300
S	3	12	S	5	S	4	3	3	7	10	13	20	4	7		7	10
12	16	3	8	9	32	10	3	10	16	20	13	6	6	15		7	16
S	S	S	S	S	5	4	5	6	2	6	7	8	S	S		S	3
9	12	20	S	7	4	8	3	15	16	21	7	15	20	20		0	4
9	36	3	6	4	8	8	3	10	34	13	10	S	20	10	6	0	6
	10	6	6	6	8	8	3	4	8	2	7	10	4	8	4	5	6
3	S	S	S	S	S	S	S	S	S	S	2	S	S	S	S	S	S
8	20	17	14	20	37	3	5	6	7	5	6	4	2	3	4	8	9
S	S	S	S	S	S	S	S	S	S	S	S	S	5	4	3	S	S
36	50	95	7	10	40	S	S	S	6	6	10	9	5	7	4	7	0
26	40	61	33	25	20	S	S	S	S	4	7	6	1	4	S	S	S
50	30	80	50	25	20	S	9	6	11	7	6	6	S	8	4	0	3
60	100	151	85	122	30	10	12	10	12	15	12	8	S	11	14	8	7
60	60	9	20	15		11	S	12	11	19	10	8	S	4	8	7	0
62	50	23	20	20	25	6	4	6	7	13	7	9	S	S		4	0
50	30	70	90	40	70	10	6	25	19	18	25	15	20	10	6	2	0
7	S	15	15	14	65	S	S	10	20	8	9	9	6	3	8	6	0
6	6	6	6	10	6	S	S	7	7	5	3	10	4	12	4	0	0
12	S	S	10	S	12	S	S	S	3	S	12	18		6	3	S	0
30	20	9	12	S	10	4	4	S	S	S	4	S			3	0	S

the notary from that period was inclined to round up numbers to the nearest ten, and is probably more reliable for smaller, more easily countable, figures. There are further degenerations in record-keeping in the 1580s and 1590s. Moreover, it is important to remember that these figures record numbers of students attending particular electoral meetings, rather than numbers in the university as a whole. As in student politics today, apathy on the one hand and political manipulation on the other may have had an impact on the numbers recorded. This partly explains quite large fluctuations in size in consecutive years.

For the English nation, it is important to know whether these figures include students of arts and medicine. The status of these students is mysterious because there was no statutory English nation in the arts university; they may have matriculated into the arts university's ultramontane nation.[97] If this is so, however, they seem never to have become officials of the nation or the university, since they do not appear in its extant acts.[98] One English student of medicine, James Gomund, matriculated in the German artists' nation in 1599, but overall it is more likely that English students of arts and medicine belonged to the English law nation, just as German arts students until 1553 belonged to the German law nation, an institutional legacy of the single university of the fourteenth century which would have been perpetuated by national cohesion. This makes sense of the sixteenth-century student's manuscript description of the *studium* which includes an English nation among the artists; it would otherwise flatly contradict all else we know.[99]

There were certainly a number of Englishmen with (nonmedical) 'arts' interest who were members of the law university, and even became the English nation's *consiliarius*.[100] Nevertheless, no English students of medicine or Englishmen who emerged with a degree in philosophy and/or medicine definitely feature in the acts of the law university until 1600, when William Harvey was elected the English nation's *consiliarius*.[101] It may be concluded, then, that for most of the sixteenth century such students would not have been permitted voting rights in the English nation and are not included in these figures.

The litigious nature of university politics, the determination to follow statutory proprieties, and the pursuit of personal and political vendettas functioned to both obstruct and create constitutional irregularities. Two examples of the former will suffice. In the run up to the election of rector in 1534 Henry Coles was accused, among other things, of not being a student of law – an accusation which other evidence does not contradict – and he lost his right to vote in the nation.[102] In 1547 Francis

Peto was disqualified as English *consiliarius* because he had been a student for less than two years, and his place was taken by a Burgundian.[103]

A larger conflict involving two Englishmen illustrates the relentlessness with which political opponents sought to undermine the electoral power of the opposition. In May 1538 Nicholas Bigod was elected English *consiliarius* by his twin brother Peter. Stephanus Bochart, a Burgundian student later to become rector, opposed them, claiming that they were not English but French; he suspected in Nicholas Bigod's election a covert attempt to strengthen the Provençale interest in the university. This would have been particularly resented since Burgundians were often able to fill the office of English *consiliarius* by the 'ius supplendum.' Since Bochart successfully stood for rector of the university in August of the same year, he probably already realized that control of the English nation could have an important electoral impact upon his candidacy. Bochart argued that even if the Bigods were Englishmen, two members of a nation did not constitute a quorum; election of the English *consiliarius* should be by the 'ius supplendum' unless more Englishmen could be found. The matter was taken to the *podestà* of Padua. In his hearing it was contended that the onus was on Bochart, as the accuser, to prove that the brothers were not English. Since there were no other Englishmen in the city at this time to vouch for them, this could not be done. Matriculation records were consulted, and it was found that the Bigod brothers did not appear in them in any guise. Since this was irregular, the brothers sought a special dispensation from the rector to be admitted to the university and to represent the English nation. The rector first insisted that they take an oath in which they would swear to being English. This they did. The rector also ruled that two members of an ultramontane nation could elect one of them as *consiliarius*. All objections having been overcome, Nicholas Bigod was confirmed as English *consiliarius*.[104]

In the summer of 1538, Bochart continued to accuse the brothers of hiding their true identities, bringing in another scholar, the Brescian Onofrio de Madiis, to testify that the common belief among students was that the Bigods were French. Further witnesses against the Bigods claimed that their parents had been English, but had emigrated to France many years ago, where the brothers were raised and educated. On this accusation, the *podestà* again summoned the brothers, who admitted that they had lived in Bourges for about fifteen years. They contended, however, that until the age of five they had been brought up in an (unnamed) village four or five miles from London. They confessed that they knew no English, but argued that they had forgotten it, having lived in France for so long. After many more French and Italian testimonies they won their case, and Nicholas was confirmed as English *consiliarius* until August 1538, when he swapped places with his brother. But within a day of his election, Peter Bigod petitioned the rector to absent himself from the university for a month, and neither brother surfaces in the acts again.[105]

A quorum of two was exceptional; in 1545 the English nation had two members but the Burgundian Franciscus de Plainchamp was elected their *consiliarius* by the 'ius supplendum.' The table records a more perplexing figure at the other end of the numerical scale. Twenty-six students of the English nation are recorded as having elected Cosimus Passerius as English *consiliarius* in August 1533. This was the first time the English nation had been quorate for a number of years; indeed only in May 1533 the Frenchman Joannes Maiaco had been elected English *consiliarius* by the 'ius supplendum.' Twenty-six voters was the nation's highest figure for the century, and in 1533 it was second in size only to the Lombard nation.

It is tempting to suppose that only developments of great political import could have swelled English (and Scottish) numbers so dramatically within a matter of months, and indeed such developments present themselves – the first stages of the Henrician Reformation. Might these numbers attest to a Henrician exile in the wake of the early Reformation, just as figures during the Marian and Elizabethan periods also show a swelling on account of religious and political exiles?

Some members of the English nation in this period, who were associated in Padua with Reginald Pole, did indeed become a part of the embryonic opposition to Henry VIII (though it is questionable whether they can be described as such as early as 1533). While it would have been surprising if Pole himself had joined them in the English nation, we know that Thomas Starkey, George Lily, Henry Coles, and Michael Throckmorton, two of whom chose permanent exile in Italy with Pole, were law students at Padua in 1533. One Richard Notur emerges in the acts of the law university in the following year, so may also be numbered among the twenty-six. Other law students at Padua in 1533 included Richard Morison and Bartholomew Bainham. Thomas Goldwell, John Mason, and Thomas Winter were also in Padua, probably in the law university. Four named law scholars are described as Scotsmen in 1534. These may have been members of the English nation in the previous year (prior to the creation of a separate Scottish nation). Given the position of arts students discussed above, it seems unlikely that the medical students John Friar and Thomas Bill should be added to the list. Even if they are included, this tentative and hypothetical exercise yields only seventeen names.

It remains near to inconceivable that English and Scottish numbers could have swelled so suddenly in 1533 and contracted just as quickly in 1534. A more credible explanation is that, although some of the more likely Englishmen mentioned above should be counted in the number, more members of the English nation in 1533 were in fact Piedmontese.

This possibility emerges from events of March 1534, when two new nations were created, a Scottish nation in the ultramontane camp and a Piedmontese in the cismontane. The 1551 statutes of the university claim that the Piedmontese nation was formed in order to end the long controversy between Piedmontese and ultramontanes, and the Scottish nation was created to maintain the electoral preponderance of the ultramontanes in this event. Since the Piedmontese had previously been members of one of the ultramontane nations (usually the Provençale), they were allowed to fill the vacancy of an ultramontane *consiliarius* every other year by the 'ius supplendum' if their own nation was inquorate.[106] Returning to the twenty-six voters of the English nation in the previous year, we note that they elected not an Englishman as *consiliarius* but a Piedmontese, Cosimus Passerius. He had been Provençale *consiliarius* in 1530, an event which had precipitated a conflict between Provençale and Piedmontese students.[107] Between 1530 and 1533, then, a number of disenfranchised Piedmontese students were 'a people in search of a nation.' The fact that the electoral figure of the new Piedmontese nation in 1534 was fourteen while simultaneously the English figure plummeted from twenty-six to four confirms that a transfer of personnel took place from the English nation to the Piedmontese nation between 1533 and 1534. The attempts by two Provençale students to undermine the English nation in 1534 shows that it had again become a small and easily manipulated constituency.

Although the primary motive for creating the Scottish nation was to maintain the balance between ultramontane and cismontane nations, its emergence implies that there was an available Scottish constituency in the English nation in 1533 which would be able to form a new nation. The members of the Scottish nation in 1534 were Bernardus Grivellus, Claudius Brocard, Ugetus Arnuldus, and Georgius Onis: each is unequivocally described as 'scotus.'[108] Yet notarial documents from Padua confirm the evidence of other sources in proving that two of these, Grivellus and Brocard, were in reality Frenchmen.[109] The irresistible conclusion is that the Scottish nation was created by a fraud perpetrated by French students. Indeed this charge emerged at the time but was rapidly dismissed; its first *consiliarius*, Claudius Brocard, was accused of being a Frenchman masquerading as a Scot.

After 1534 the Scottish nation remained inquorate until 1592. In the interim other nations, especially the Provençale and German, jockeyed to control it. And in 1603 its *consiliarius* was an Englishman, Simeon Foxe, the son of the martyrologist John Foxe. The English were permitted to occupy this position on account of the recent accession of James VI of Scotland to the English throne.[110] If the Reformation had any impact on English numbers in this period, it was not in swelling the size of the nation in 1533 but in keeping it small for the remainder of the 1530s and throughout the 1540s; Henry VIII's ban on the teaching of canon law at the English universities had a catastrophic impact on the law faculties of Oxford and Cambridge.[111] Smaller levels of recruitment in England directly affected English numbers in Padua. Hence in 1551 the statutes of the Paduan law university suggest that Piedmontese students, in years when their own nation is inquorate, could join the English nation, there having been no Englishmen in the university 'for many years.'[112] The evidence suggests that in fact the Piedmontese did not go on to fill English places. Both the English and the Piedmontese nations became quorate in 1551 and 1552. The Piedmontese nation remained quorate in 1553 and 1554, allowing the Germans to gain control of the English nation, which had become inquorate in these two years. By the time the Piedmontese nation was inquorate again, in 1556 and 1557, another influx of Englishmen rendered the English nation quorate. And so it remained at least for another decade.

From about the middle of the sixteenth century some of the nations began to develop a stronger cohesion and institutional identity, which is expressed in a variety of ways. From the 1540s *consiliarii* were beginning to celebrate their offices with the coats of arms which still adorn the hall and court of the original university building.[113] In this period appeared the first English arms, those of the *consiliarius* Robert Poyntz, dating from 1564.[114] Lists of Hungarian doctorates commence in 1575 and a book of expenses of Hungarian students dates from 1552.[115] Just as German influence in the university came to be articulated through demands for religious tolerance, so the Polish nation was strengthened through the attempts of the Catholic church to use it to promote the Catholic interest in religiously divided Poland.[116] An *Accademia Padovana dei Polacchi* existed between 1556 and 1559 and in the same period an *Hospitium Polonorum* was established. Conflict between Germans and Poles after the papal bull of 1564 followed confessional patterns. By the 1590s, when Polish *matricula* and *acta* commence, the nation conscientiously excluded Protestants from its membership.[117]

These developments are of great interest in the wider European context. We are witnessing in microcosm that sense of national cohesiveness which has long been said to have emerged from confessional strife in the sixteenth century. For the English case, there is little evidence of a thriving institutional culture. Independent of the university's matriculation register, matriculation lists of English students do not begin until 1617, and an English bedel surfaces only in that year. A library was not formed until 1649.[118] There are instances, however, of English assertiveness within the university. On one occasion, an attempt to undermine the electoral influence of the English nation through accusations against its members can be shown to have been ideologically motivated.

The background to this event is the attempt by the Frenchman Jean Coras to be elected as Provençale *consiliarius* in August 1534, by removing the electoral power of his opponents in the nation.[119] Accusations against members of the university, intended to disenfranchise them, were a normal aspect of university politics and took place in most years. The university prescribed an exact procedure for this and a list of admissible reasons for disqualification.[120] What makes the accusations of 1534 remarkable is their extent, the proportion of them that are concerned with moral shortcomings or religious heterodoxy, and the fact that they reveal the Provençale nation as deeply divided.

Coras, only around twenty years old in 1534, was already establishing a reputation as a jurist. His doctoral defence at Padua in 1536 was legendary; it was said that he had successfully defended one hundred legal propositions. On his return to his native Toulouse he became a professor of the university, then a judge in the Toulouse *parlement*. In 1560, the year that his most important legal work, the *Tractatus de iuris arte*, was published, he acted as a judge in the celebrated trial of Martin Guerre.[121] He died in 1572, lynched by a Catholic mob in Toulouse in the aftermath of the St Bartholomew's Day massacres.[122] It is not clear from external evidence whether or not by the early 1530s he was already the dedicated follower of Calvin he later became. But the charges of heresy levelled against him at Padua, discussed below, conform to the chronology of his movements; his arrival in Italy in 1534 coincided exactly with the escalation in prosecutions against heretics in France, which forced the flight of Calvin himself in the same year.

Coras set off the conflict in July 1534 by accusing the Provençale *consiliarius*, Perinetus de Reviliascho, of keeping a whore. Reviliascho, the provost of Avignon and a protonotary apostolic,[123] denied the charge, but witnesses, including the Frenchmen Jacobus Gallien and Franciscus Gymnasius, confirmed his guilt. Reviliascho countered by accusing Coras of being a heretic, a charge expanded on by another Frenchman, Gerard Servientis, who claimed Coras had been banished from Toulouse for his heresy. Coras initially answered that he was a good Christian, but Servientis then accused him of not receiving the Eucharist and of not attending confession. Coras swore an oath to the effect that he did receive the Eucharist, prompting Servientis to alter the charge, claiming now that Coras had not paid his dues to the university. It was proved that he had paid, and so Coras survived the accusations while Reviliascho was deprived of his vote.[124]

Coras then brought charges against other members of the Provençale nation. He successfully accused Ludovico Malamort and Johannes Podio of blasphemy.[125] Gerard Servientis, now a candidate against Coras for the position of Provençale *consiliarius*, brought accusations against some of Coras's Provençale supporters. He claimed that Claudius Rabot owned 'illicit' and 'magic' books,[126] that Carolus Precontal had not paid his university dues,[127] and that Petrus Panizza had not acquired his doctorate within the statutory time limit.[128] He accused Coras's colleague in the accusations against Reviliascho, Jacobus Gallien, of hitting a student and of blasphemy.[129] He accused another associate of Coras, Franciscus Gymnasius, of keeping a 'concubine' and of having been excommunicated for assaulting a clergyman.[130] Coras, avenging himself on Servientis, accused him of keeping a 'concubine,'[131] but it was not proved, and in the election of Provençale *consiliarius* on 1 August, Coras lost to Servientis.[132]

In the same period Coras, in alliance with Gymnasius, began accusations against Englishmen. Presumably they realized that the English nation, now dramatically reduced in size after the departure of the Piedmontese and Scots, could be easily undermined. The five accusations of Coras and Gymnasius in July 1534 were directed against Henry Coles, George Lily, Richard Morison, and Richard Notur (and against the candidate for Scottish *consiliarius*, Claudius Brocard).[133] Only the substance of the charges against Coles and Brocard emerges in the acts – that Coles was not a scholar and did not know how to respond in law, and that he had not paid his dues to the university[134] (it was ruled that by the following day Coles had to prove that he had paid), and that Brocard was not a Scotsman but a Frenchman and was proceeding fraudulently.[135] Before the election of English *consiliarius*, only Richard Notur is recorded as having lost his vote.[136] Nevertheless, in the election on 1 August, four voters are recorded as having chosen Richard Morison as their *consiliarius*.[137]

The accusations did not stop there: Gymnasius now attempted to influence the election of rector. Twelve days after Morison's election, Gymnasius asserted that a conspiracy was afoot to block the election of a French rector. Richard Morison was involved, and Gymnasius accused him of attending a secret 'conventicle' which met in the church of San Firmo to orchestrate the conspiracy. When asked to swear that he had not been there, Morison refused and thus lost his vote and counsellorship.[138] A week later and before a new English *consiliarius* could be elected, Gymnasius was able to renew the charges against Lily, Notur, and Coles. Simultaneously he made accusations against members of the Scottish nation, Arnuldus, Grivellus, and Claudius Brocard. The university bedel summoned these to answer the charges, but only the French pretenders Grivellus and Brocard attended. The others were automatically denied their votes.[139] Thus the new English *consiliarius* was a Polish student elected by the 'ius supplendum' on 22 August.[140]

Perhaps by this time apathy had set in among the English students of law. With so few of them it would have been difficult to withstand the relentless politicking of Coras and Gymnasius. When English numbers were larger, however, the nation's rights were asserted more energetically. For example, the right to elect a representative was argued in 1563, after George Vastopolis of Chios had been elected by the 'ius supplendum.' Anthony Fortescue explained to the university that although the English election meeting had been quorate, it had been abandoned in uproar. Vastopolis was now willing to resign to make way for a new English *consiliarius*. This was agreed, and in the new election Robert Poyntz became *consiliarius*.[141]

An incident in 1559 is another example of the same phenomenon, but it also shows how, typically in this period, nations' rights were asserted at the expense of the rector's prerogative and with the cooperation of the Venetian authorities. Henry Denny was elected *consiliarius* by eleven voters of the English nation in August 1558. The eldest son of Sir Anthony Denny, he was an exile for religion whom Thomas Hoby had encountered in Padua in August 1554 with his two brothers and their probable tutor John Tamworth. In the interim he had been a student at Basle with Francis Walsingham, and had become a friend of Heinrich Bullinger.[142] In December 1558 or January 1559, in the middle of his term of office, he left Padua, probably because of the accession of Queen Elizabeth the previous November, but apparently on the (almost certainly false) pretext of a death in the family.[143] Although he was replaced by George Acworth, another *consiliarius*, 'Dominus Princeps Bisutius,' objected in council on 13 January that this had not been done according to the rules. In the first place Denny had not sought the permission of the rector to leave the university, and had not made arrangements for his replacement although he knew he did not intend to return. Furthermore, while the new election should have taken place three days after notice of it was affixed to the doors of the university, it in fact took place ten days later. Bisutius thus proposed that the election of Acworth should be annulled and a new *consiliarius* be elected by the 'ius supplendum.' Acworth contended that the original election should be considered valid or, if a new election were to be called, at least the nation itself should be given the opportunity to choose its *consiliarius*. The election of Acworth himself had not taken place on the required third day after notification because it had still not been clear whether Denny intended to return or not, and only became so after letters of his were received in Padua. The matter was put to a vote of the *consiliarii*, and Acworth's election was invalidated by a majority of twelve.[144]

This would have ended the dispute had the English and their supporters not appealed to the Venetian authorities. Three days later the *podestà* of Padua, Niccolò da Ponte, presided over a meeting at which Adriano Polcastro, *consiliarius* of the Trevisan nation, Johannes de Gualdo, and some English scholars objected that the statutes had not been adhered to in this English reelection by 'ius supplendum,' without the three days' prior announcement and the participation of the nation itself. Despite the counterarguments of Celso de Duchis of Brescia, da Ponte ruled in their favour. Elections were held, and Francis Alford became English *consiliarius* on 18 January.[145]

Not all material in the university acts relating to Englishmen involves their conflicts with other nations. Students also took on conciliating roles. In 1569, for example, John Page was appointed a 'judge of the opposition,' one of the officials who was charged with determining the validity of accusations and citations against student voters, prior to the election of a rector.[146] In 1561 Anthony Fortescue, at the beginning of his lifelong residence in Padua, was appointed to intervene in the infamous conflict between two professors in the arts university, Carlo Sigonio and Francesco Robortello. From November 1561 the two rivals were meant to be lecturing concurrently, but sessions were suspended because they were squabbling over the same lecture hall. Sigonio was offered an alternative hall by the law students, where the law professor Tiberio Deciani also lectured. Fortescue and another student, Ludovico Gambara, were deputized to approach Sigonio. They were instructed to assure him that the hall was suitable since other humanists, including Romolo Amaseo, also used it. Sigonio accepted the offer.[147]

Besides acting as *consiliarii* and *electionarii*, students took on other university offices. John Pelham, for example, was elected one of the two ultramontane *syndici* in 1556. It was an important position, for the syndics represented the university in any litigation and advised the rector on the legality of his activity.[148] Three years later John Voley formed part of a committee of eight *consiliarii* who were to present the *rotulus* of elected lecturers to the Venetian Senate. In 1561 the Venetian Senate ordered the revision of the statutes of the law university and appointed four law professors to undertake this: Jacobo Filippo Portio, Marco Mantova, Girolamo Torniello, and Tiberio Deciani. The university, in order to assent to the revisions, was required to supply students to oversee the task. Fortescue was one of four *consiliarii* thereby elected.[149] In 1567 Edward Bichier was one of the university's delegates who paid traditional respects to the Venetian Senate after Easter.[150] In 1579 Claudius Sotor became vice-rector.[151]

We have no English testimony independent of the acts which could tell us what the participants made of their activities, how seriously they took the university's politics, and what motivated them. And this is a significant lack, given how unusual this kind of politics was in an English context. No equivalent organizations in England – and certainly not the English universities – offered this level of political involvement to such young men. As so many students at Padua went on to positions of political influence in their own countries, it may not be entirely anachronistic to see the law university as a kind of school of politics, like student unions today. Taken in isolation, the record surely cannot tell the whole story, and perhaps the impression that these politics were sometimes counterproductive, vicious, or merely trivial is a false one. At least the continued vitality of the university's internal life in the age of Venetian domination is a measure of the extent to which the ancient 'Bolognese model' of university organization had been preserved at

Padua into the sixteenth century as nowhere else. And if student power had been undermined in some areas, the German nation came to ensure its continuation in others. The fundamental connection between twelfth-century Bologna and sixteenth-century Padua lies in the continued importance of national identities as the organizing structure of student life. Nevertheless, university politics engaged a relatively small number of English students, and for the others, the nation provided a social base and institutional framework for study in the city. These studies are explored in the chapters which follow.

2

Students of Law

The examples of participation in the law university described in chapter 1 elucidate an aspect of Paduan university life from a particular national perspective. They are also, however, suggestive for that area of English intellectual history which has been grappling for decades with the difficult relationship between English humanism and political action.

The problematic directions into which the historiography had strayed were revealed in two important essays by Alastair Fox in 1986.[1] Fox showed how differences between the intellectual outlooks of English humanists had been obscured, and men who were not humanists at all had been included in their number, by an 'excessive, and sometimes exclusive, reliance on extrinsic rather than intrinsic evidence.'[2] Humanists all over Europe have been defined in this period in relation to their commitments to that cycle of classical learning which was known in the Renaissance as the *studia humanitatis* (especially grammar and rhetoric) and also to other aspects of the classical textual heritage. In England such commitments have been ignored or have gone unnoticed. Instead, as Fox also pointed out, anyone who had been involved in politics or demonstrated 'civic concern' and also had a literary or theoretical turn of mind was taken to have possessed the qualities of a humanist.[3]

Fox's alternative model is not without its problems, but his argument on this point is worth reiterating because is has not been heeded. Recently Thomas Linacre has been considered 'rather overrated' as a pioneer.[4] Yet Linacre was probably the only Englishman up to the 1520s to have attained a level of classical erudition which is comparable to his Italian contemporaries.[5] Furthermore, it was an applied erudition, not merely existing, for example, in a reputation forged through friendship with Erasmus: he was responsible for new translations of Galen which reached a considerable European audience and which had a major role in the sixteenth-century transformation of European medicine. Indeed either in the field of medicine or outside of it, no Englishman's philological efforts were *more* pioneering. But although a royal servant, Linacre was a grammarian, translator, and physician. He was not influential in the political life of his times, and this explains his continued marginalization. The dominant historiographical tradition has not been concerned to describe humanism on its own terms, but rather to trace the intellectual origins of what Geoffrey Elton called 'the age of reform,' that period of government initiative associated with the reign of Henry VIII. And this in turn has allowed for the primacy in English historiography of what many historians of European humanism would regard as only one of a number of consequences of the humanist movement: the elevation of political engagement and anthropocentric values.

Some of the semantic confusion generated by such different understandings of the term – and leading in turn to such improbable mongrels as 'civic humanism' – disappears if we heed the testimony of contemporaries. Thomas Starkey, for example, that arch-'civic humanist' of Tudor England, identified the intellectual wellsprings of his political activism in a different – and less elusive – field than 'humanism': 'bycause my purpos then was to lyve in a polytyke lyfe, I set my self now thes last yeres past to the knolege of the cyvyle law, that I myght therby make a more stabyl & sure jugeme[n]t of the polytyke order and customys usyd amonge us here in our cu[n]tery ...'[6] This statement has often been quoted because it is unusually self-conscious about 'the politic life' as an option for Henrician Englishmen. But that the 'civil law' was a suitable preparation for this life has hardly been explored. Yet at least by Englishmen like Starkey who studied at Padua, his statement about the civil law is replicated, and makes him more representative than any 'civic humanism' which is attributable to him. George Acworth, for example, wrote that he studied at Padua because the civil law – unlike the barbarous common law – retained for him some of the intellectual integrity of the humanistic subjects he had previously studied at Cambridge but was more useful than them; the civil law, claimed Acworth in a patronage-seeking letter to Archbishop Reginald Pole, strove to make people good citizens.[7] Richard White located the source of his dissatisfaction with Marian Oxford in the fact that it was 'addicted' to 'arts and doctrine' whereas he was destined to help the commonwealth. He had been urged to study the civil law with a view to attaining a post in the 'supreme court of civil doctors' and as an ambassador to foreign nations. Hence his plan to study the civil law for ten years at the best universities in Christendom to know the peoples and their customs, languages, and laws. The supplication of the Paduan alumnus Henry Hawkins for a law degree at Cambridge was supported by Archbishop Whitgift in 1591 because his legal studies abroad meant that 'his service may be very profitably employed in public matters.'[8] A significant number of other Englishmen in the sixteenth century attended the Paduan law school, and emerged from it to become political counsellors, privy councillors, diplomats, and secretaries, and advocates in the conciliar and ecclesiastical courts of the Tudor polity. If any class of Englishmen in the sixteenth century can be said to have comprised the 'civil service,' it was the civil lawyers: political service was their *raison d'être*.[9] A solid historical quantity with its own texts and methods, the civil law as studied by Englishmen at Padua may help bridge the explanatory gap between Tudor thought and political action.[10]

One of the reasons for this is that the Paduan law school itself was steeped in an ethic of political counsel. For the student university the activities of some English student counsellors – the *consiliarii* and other officials – in advising the rector and in university decision-making have already been described. But this legalistic student counselling only aped the more important professional activities of Paduan teachers of law.

The Paduan college of jurists was more than a degree-awarding body. Comprising Paduan advocates as well as professors of canon and civil law, it acted as a court of appeal for Paduan citizens, for the citizens of Cattaro in Dalmatia, and for other *terraferma* communities under Venetian control such as Bassano, as well as for other Italian communities such as Trent and Ravenna.[11] Its legal advice was sought by the Venetian government, while its individual members sometimes acted as official legal counsellors for the Republic.[12] The prestige of its judgments is suggested by its role as a validator of the legal decisions of other jurists, magistrates, and jurist colleges in Italy; the Roman *Rota* and jurist colleges at Lucca, Bologna, and Pavia each sought the endorsement of the Paduan college for their own judgments during the sixteenth century.[13] As a source of interpretation of European law, the college of jurists provided judgments for other princes and governments of Christendom on a wide variety of issues. For example, in 1551 Philip, landgrave of Hesse, sought the college's opinion on whether he was entitled to benefit from his territories while he was a prisoner of Charles V.[14] Ercole II, duke of Ferrara, sought a judgment in 1561 on whether he and his ambassadors took precedence over the duke of Florence and his ambassadors.[15] In 1579 Ranuccio Farnese, through his uncle the duke of Parma, sought a judgment on the validity of his candidature for the Portuguese crown.[16]

Henry VIII's consultation in 1530 of Padua among other foreign universities on the question of his marriage to Catherine of Aragon is another example. This initiative has sometimes appeared as little more than a series of cynical attempts to bribe the universities in an attempt to put pressure on the pope to grant a dispensation; this charge was levelled at the time and seems accurate for some parts of the process.[17] But from the point of view of Paduan law professors, Henry's action was but one of many by foreign princes who approached them through agents and ambassadors, offering appropriate payment for a judgment of legal and political import. Acting on fixed procedures, the college frequently debated such issues and offered written pronouncements on them, although by the sixteenth century judgments to foreign princes required the prior approval of the Venetian government.[18] The anticlerical temper of the Paduan college of jurists may have inclined it to favour Henry because the question it was asked to resolve, of whether the pope had power to dispense with the Levitical impediments, necessarily impinged on the question of the extent of ecclesiastical and papal jurisdiction. Indeed the king's agent in Padua reported in 1530 that he had persuaded a majority in the college to support him. However, the matter was inevitably complicated by the interests of the emperor. Inasmuch as the civil law was imperial law, imperial opposition to the annulment of Henry's marriage may have neutralized the intellectual force of that law's claims for an extensive monarchical prerogative, and Charles V himself, the nephew of Catherine of Aragon, directly applied pressure on Paduan professors to remain silent or support his cause. The Venetian government expressly forbad involvement for fear of the emperor, an order that was widely ignored but which nevertheless explains the ultimate failure of the college to come to a corporate judgment. Henry's agent at Padua, Richard Croke, wrote of the college of jurists in November 1530: 'as yet there is nothing done *collegialiter* ... All the college would gladly determine with your highness, wer[e it not for] fear of the Senate which hath commanded the contrary.'[19] (The college of theologians at Padua did produce a judgment in the king's favour.)[20] Attempting to evade the Venetian veto, John Stokesley and Croke approached members of the jurist college individually for their own judgments, with some positive results. The episode demonstrates that legal judgments by individual jurists, often ending up in the published volumes of *consilia* which form a large proportion of Paduan jurists' professional printed output, cannot be completely separated from the process of collegiate judgment. The writing of such counsels for private payment seems unusual in an English context but was an almost routine aspect of professional activity at Padua. Indeed far from seeing it as mercenary, Paduan jurists in Henry's case defended their activity against the politically interested Venetian government on the principle of a professional obligation to all and any paying clients.[21]

The possibility must remain that Paduan jurists such as Pietro Paolo Parisio and Marco Mantova Benavides, those who defied Venice in offering written counsels in favour of Henry VIII, had an impact on the thinking of the king or his advisors. The extent and nature of competing legal jurisdictions was the subject of a great deal of civilian thought,[22] and it is certain that Paduan jurists drew on the civil law in their discussions of Henry VIII's case. Recent research has predated the conception of a caesaro-papal position by Henry's advisors to 1530 at the latest, the year in which a body of manuscript materials was compiled, the so-called *Collectanea satis copiosa*, which seems to have formed the intellectual basis of the break with Rome, and which is to be distinguished from works simply intended, on theological and canon law grounds, to establish the invalidity of Henry's marriage to Catherine of Aragon and the invalidity of the pope's dispensation for that marriage.[23] It has been suggested that the intellectual case is confirmed by the political act; the consultation of the universities was in itself an attack on the pope's power to judge such issues.[24] It is not yet clear whether any of the material in the *Collectanea* was derived directly from the main texts of the civil law, the *Corpus iuris civilis*, and its accumulated glosses and commentaries, as some of it certainly was from canon and English common law sources. But the medieval English legal authority Bracton, himself heavily civilian, was quoted to argue that any state which did not acknowledge a superior was an empire.[25] Henry himself invoked Justinian in 1531 and 1533 as an authority for the emperor's right to legislate in ecclesiastical matters.[26] Edward Foxe's *De vera differentia* of 1534 makes use of the same authority in the same way.[27] Other writings of the period show clear civilian influence: 'Collections out of the civell and cannon laws against churchmen that defame Princes' must surely date from the 1530s.[28] The issue of civilian influence on the royal supremacy is fundamental to an understanding of that much-debated question of whether England was in danger of a 'reception' of Roman law in the Henrician period. Edward Surtz's research into Paduan opinion on the affair shows that in Italy as in England the wider implications for papal power and the narrower technical issues were addressed in 1530 simultaneously.[29] Further research may yet reveal a link between thinking on the king's 'great matter' at this time on the continent and the development of royal policy after 1530. There are admittedly powerful political reasons for expecting the civil law not to have been convenient for the case in England. Civilian and canonist legal practitioners were the same people there, the advocates of the ecclesiastical courts, and had been subject to intense common law criticism for years, reaching its culmination in the 'Reformation Parliament' of 1529 and the fall of Thomas Wolsey: Henry pursued his annulment on the back of these events. For present purposes, Henry's consultation of Paduan jurists demonstrates the practical nature of their professional work and the particular vision of the lawyer's vocation which underlay it, a nature and vision which manifest themselves even in an English context.

To what extent was this 'ethic of counsel' informed by 'legal humanism'? Pending further research into this question, any answer has to be provisional.[30] Traditional legal studies at the beginning of the sixteenth century depended on a historical conception of jurisprudential development which stretched back four hundred years. It began with the late eleventh- and twelfth-century recovery of the *Corpus iuris civilis*, the texts of ancient Roman legal maxims and legislation which the Emperor Justinian had originally gathered in the sixth century. In later medieval Europe these became the central texts of the civil law. They underwent a process of explication by the so-called glossators and postglossators until the fourteenth century. Their successors, the so-called commentators, building closely on their work, set about adapting the *Corpus iuris civilis* to the conditions of early modern Europe, thus creating a European law known generally as the *ius commune* (not to be confused with the English common law); continental jurisprudence thus developed an important applied aspect.

By the fifteenth century, traditional legal science depended on this accumulation of explications of the *Corpus iuris*. With its own technical methodology and vast literature, traditional academic law had become a closed intellectual system. As such it was a ripe target for standard humanist attacks. In fact these had begun in the fourteenth century with Petrarch, who sought a jurisprudential interest in the Roman law as it had existed before Justinian. In the fifteenth century, Lorenzo Valla and Maffeo Vegio criticized linguistic inelegance and barbarity in the law, attacking the style not only of their contemporaries but of the authorities upon whom they depended, especially the fourteenth-century authorities Bartolus and Baldus. Humanist philology was first systematically applied to the *Corpus iuris* by Angelo Poliziano, who completed a collation towards the end of the fifteenth century of the standard text of the *Digest* and the older but unused Florentine manuscript of it owned by Lorenzo de'Medici. Guillaume Budé continued the philological explication of the legal texts in his *Annotationes in Pandectas*, printed in 1508. These early 'legal humanists' were humanists first and foremost, applying a philological method to legal texts in much the same manner as humanists in the same period – and sometimes the same humanists – were turning their attentions towards other technical texts which were central to the classical heritage. None of them were professors of law and their impact on legal studies in the short term was probably limited.

Ulrich Zasius and Andrea Alciati were professors of law active in the middle of the sixteenth century who engaged more fully with their traditional contemporaries. They challenged the medieval authorities Baldus and Bartolus on their own terms, by using philological methods to arrive at new interpretations of the legal meaning of the *Corpus iuris*. In their work a new historical conception of the law is detectable: the *Corpus iuris* remains the central text of the law, but understanding and interpreting it depends on setting its component parts in their own different legal and historical contexts, rather than on viewing it through the accumulated wisdom of a medieval exegetical tradition. Later members of this school such as François Hotman were, perhaps, 'legal antiquarians' rather than legal humanists, turning these methods towards the recovery of old French law. Indeed the later sixteenth-century French 'historical' school of law became 'an exercise in historical understanding designed to bolster the claims of local customary law against supposed imperial legal uniformity, seen as a threat to the indigenous institutions of the French nation.'[31]

The *mos gallicus* is a term that predates this French antiquarian movement, emerging in the 1550s. It was particularly associated with that school of humanistic thought pioneered in the circle of Andrea Alciati at Bourges in central France, while its supposed obverse, the *mos italicus*, the traditional jurisprudence which relied heavily on the work of Bartolus, continued to flourish in Italy. *Mos gallicus* and *mos italicus* were in reality polemical terms which are useful only to define ends of a wide scale. Most legal scholars belonged in the hazy middle ground; despite the occasional trading of insults, many humanistic jurists (especially those who themselves were legal practitioners) continued to respect the Bartolist school. This is true, for example, of Alciati himself,[32] and of his pupil Boniface Amerbach.[33] And as 'legal humanism' was a broad and pluralistic movement, so Bartolists could pick and choose what they found of value in it.

Although influenced by humanism in certain ways, the Paduan school of law remained a Bartolist school for the whole of the sixteenth century; but this did not diminish its enormous prestige, even among humanists themselves. The student of Alciati, Viglius Zwichem van Aytta, reported to Erasmus in the early 1530s that he was abundantly satisfied by the professors of civil law at Padua, despite their unfamiliarity with more humane letters.[34] The French legal humanist Jean Coras remembered his teacher at Padua in the same period, Franceschino Curzio, with devotion.[35] Alciati himself pursued friendly scholarly relations with members of the school.[36]

Literary and humanistic preoccupations can be readily detected in the cultural lives of several of the most important Paduan jurists. Marco Mantova Benavides is a significant case, because he was the most famous jurist of sixteenth-century Padua and the most long-standing, and because the number known of students who fell under his sway is formidable.[37] For English students at Padua exact pedagogical relationships have been difficult to uncover, but Mantova outnumbers other Paduan jurists in his three known English students, John Orphinstrange, John Le Rous, and Richard White.[38] It is likely that there were in fact more. Mantova was devoted to Italian letters. He was the author of *Della eloquenza*, three *novelle*, and the *Discorsi sopra i dialoghi di M. Speron Sperone*, a work which, with its hyperbolic praise for the rhetorical abilities of Speroni, locates Mantova in the mainstream of Paduan vernacular extramural culture. Although his membership of Speroni's Accademia degli Infiammati is not proven, he was a friend of many members, as well as of earlier Paduan luminaries such as Pietro Bembo, Trifone Gabriele, and Lazzaro Bonamico.[39] Mantova's antiquarianism suggests a point of contact between his humanism and legal learning. One of the most formidable of Paduan collectors, he owned not only pictures and many hundreds of books, but also antique statuary and coins; Guillaume Budé's coin collection had formed the point of departure for his discussion of money in antiquity and its relevance to contemporary legal injustices in his *De asse et partibus eius*. Mantova's antiquarian strain seems to have had an impact on his student Richard White. White went on to become Regius Professor of Civil Law at Douai and an historian of, among other things, ancient Roman legal institutions. White's *Aelia Laelia Crispis* of 1568, an interpretation of an ancient inscription found near Bologna, includes a letter to Mantova.[40] It is also clear that Mantova's legal writing was influenced by the humanist preoccupation with literary elegance. Whereas many of Mantova's legal commentaries were cast in a simple question and answer form, his *De concilio* belongs to the genre of *cinquecento* dialogue in its attempt at realistic characterization and discourse, and it even includes an attack on the Bartolist fondness for piling up citations. Mantova's *Epitoma virorum illustrium qui vel scripserunt, vel iurisprudentiam docuerunt in scholis* of 1559 fails to include Budé or Poliziano, but celebrates Alciati, who is credited with having invented a new form of legal writing, along with Azzo, Baldus, and Bartolus.[41]

Guido Panciroli, a central figure in Paduan law in the second half of the sixteenth century, also taught Richard White and probably also Henry Hawkins,[42] and knew Reginald Pole, who commended the English law student Thomas Clement to him.[43] The friend of the humanist and printer Paolo Manuzio, Panciroli demonstrated a more fully developed legal antiquarianism than Mantova, which seems to have owed much to the example of Alciati. His works include histories of ancient Roman institutions and civil, legal, and military officials, as well as a topographical description of the ancient city and an account of its buildings.[44] He also wrote a commentary on Tertullian's *De oratione*,[45] and the humanistic *Thesaurus variarum lectionum utriusque iuris*,[46] but was perhaps most well known for his *History of Memorable Things Lost*, an 'encyclopaedic' collection of historical curiosities and *miscellanea*.[47] His *De claris legum interpretibus libri quatuor* was as ecumenical in its sympathies as Mantova's *Epitoma*.[48]

Other Paduan jurists with an English connection participated in this broad cultural movement. One of the doctoral promoters of John Le Rous and Richard White, Tiberio Deciani, was, like Mantova, a vernacular *literato* and humanist, and a collector of coins and pictures.[49] Two other promoters of John Le Rous – Jacobo Menochio and Giovanni Cieffalo – were friends and correspondents of the Florentine humanist Pietro Vettori.[50]

All of these may have influenced English students at Padua in various ways: private friendships and private teaching may have sustained interests which went beyond the curricular bounds of the *studium*.

Indeed there is evidence to suggest that English students of law exploited the wider cultural *ambiente* of the city. If Cuthbert Tunstall was a student of law, as seems likely, his intellectual interests in Padua nevertheless included Aristotelian natural philosophy.[51] Although he had been a *consiliarius* of the law university in the early 1530s, Richard Morison's correspondence from Padua makes no mention of legal studies at all. He apparently spent his time on the Greek texts of Aristotle,[52] and read Euripides and Aristophanes with another English law student, George Lily. Morison promised to return to England skilled in Greek, philosophy, and theology. Although from England Thomas Starkey advised him to read the books of 'old lawyers,' the remaining record of Lily's studies has him reading Sophocles, Xenophon, and Plutarch, and attending the lectures of the celebrated humanist Giovan Battista Egnazio in Venice.[53] To judge by the books later owned by their contemporary at Padua, Henry Coles, he too was interested in humanistic subjects, a fact which perhaps explains why he was cited in the law university for not being a student of law.[54] The audience at Padua for John Cheke's readings of Demosthenes' *Three Orations* in 1554 almost certainly included some formal students of the law university.[55] Possibly one of these, Francis Walsingham, himself a *consiliarius* of the university, is recorded as having purchased a clavichord in the city.[56] The interests of Richard White and his circle in the 1560s were also wide-ranging.[57] And in the later Elizabethan period there is in Edmund Bruce a *consiliarius* of the English nation whose interests lay wholly in the 'arts' fields of astronomy and mathematics.

Nevertheless, the extent to which all of this influenced the substantive content of Paduan jurisprudence is questionable. Students required a practical training in the law for future careers as advocates and magistrates, while professors, in their roles as consultants, were already engaged with the law as it was applied. These were inevitably forces for conservatism in methods of interpretation. The sixteenth-century *ius commune* was largely the creation of the commentators. Inasmuch as jurist opinion mattered in court, a body of legal wisdom accumulated over hundreds of years could not simply be thrown overboard. As Donald Kelley has explained, what was important for an applied system like this was the understanding of the 'spirit of classical forms' rather than the letter of classical texts.[58] Analogical interpretation fostered by argument and disputation did violence to the original meaning of these texts but was a necessity for applying them a millennium after they had been compiled.[59] Literary and philological accuracy and historical fact were subordinate to legal principles as already developed in a long line of commentaries on the *Corpus iuris civilis*.[60] Thus Padua remained a centre for the printing of endless commentaries and *consilia* in the traditional mode, even authored by such humanistic lights as Mantova and Panciroli. The Bartolist system already had its own methodological and philosophical rationales and its own historical line of development. Jurists refused to regard law as subordinate to philosophy, rhetoric, or grammar: concepts like justice and natural law allowed them to elevate legal studies to the status of the supreme science.

Furthermore, legal practice in sixteenth-century Europe witnessed the penetration of university-educated jurists into the law courts. In the long term this, more than 'legal humanism,' would signal the demise of those types of legal writing characteristic of the *mos italicus*: judgments made in court came to be regarded as worthy of the published record, because they were now the decisions of men learned in the law. Ultimately judicial precedent itself would be seen as more authoritative than the citing of sources and of juristic opinions which had initially rendered these judgments important. The type of legal writing emerging from the judgments of the medieval Avignonese and Roman *Rota* and the fifteenth-century *Decisiones* of the Grenoble *parlement* and Neapolitan *Sacro Regio Consiglio* would thus transplant the *consilia* and *responsa* of individual jurists working outside of the courts, a development whose early progress in later sixteenth-century Padua may be witnessed by the increase in extant collegiate rulings of the jurists. Itself a classical revival of sorts, this, more than the 'historical school of law,' would transform European jurisprudence.[61] In the short term, though, it meant that Bartolist law was becoming more important to the regulation of European societies in the sixteenth century, a phenomenon most clearly seen in Germany, the provenance of a large number of Paduan law students.[62] All of this tended to insulate Bartolist law from humanistic influences.[63]

At Padua this insulation was bolstered by a degree of curricular rigidity in the law university. There is a danger that institutional and statutory models may obscure a more fluid situation. The extramural cultural interests of Paduan jurists was evidently one area where they met 'artists' on equal terms. There are also cases of cross-fertilization between the two universities. For example, Pietro Francesco Zino delivered his *De legum et iuris laudibus oratio* at the opening of the law university in 1548, a year after he had become professor of moral philosophy in the university of arts and medicine.[64] Nevertheless, generally speaking, the institutional situation must have militated against such tendencies. The university of arts and medicine had a monopoly over the teaching of subjects such as logic, dialectic, and moral and natural philosophy, each of which had been susceptible to humanistic transformation, and which had the potential for being related to legal study. Padua's most famous humanists belonged on that side of the divide which elevated medicine rather than law to the status of the supreme art.[65] This may explain the almost complete absence of writings emanating from Padua in this period on legal dialectics, such a conspicuous feature of French and German legal thought in this period. Indeed almost no textbooks on subjects propaedeutic to the law were written by Paduan jurists,[66] although students at the university must have made use of works from elsewhere and some alumni became legal dialecticians.[67] Presumably Paduan jurists restricted their discussions of method and interpretation to commentaries on the relevant parts of the *Corpus iuris* such as the last title of the *Digest*, 'De verborum significatione.'[68] This would have accorded with the way lectures were organized. Law lecturers were obliged to keep to a fairly rigid preordained program of commentaries on the main legal texts of civil and canon law.[69] One suspects that in this instance the greater student power at Padua in comparison with other universities served to maintain the status quo for much longer. Professors had reason to be in fear of students who still had some influence over their contracts and salaries. For their part, students knew that they would be examined for their doctorate on four, arbitrarily chosen *puncta taxata*, passages from the *Corpus iuris* which teachers were obliged to cover in their lectures.[70] It was for this reason that still in the sixteenth century the rector of the law university had students clandestinely planted in lecture halls to report to him on whether or not the professors were keeping to their briefs.[71] Predictably for a city whose culture was steeped in remembrances of the ancient world, it was the antiquarian strain of 'legal humanism,' already observed in the work of Guido Panciroli, that penetrated the Paduan law school more successfully than the dialectical, but only at a late stage; it is represented in the establishment of a lectureship on the *Pandects* in 1578.[72]

Crucially for the English context, where notions of counsel were concerned, Paduan law swam directly against the tide of the new movement. Almost since the beginning of the revival of Roman law, jurists had had to defend their commentaries on the *Corpus iuris* because of the embarrassing fact that in the *Corpus* itself Justinian had expressly forbidden interpretations of his laws. Indeed the *Corpus* was compiled in order to sweep away the confusion which had emerged from the proliferation of legal interpretations.[73] In the sixteenth century the charge of generating confusion was also directed against the genre of legal *consilia* and *responsa* by one of the central figures of 'legal humanism,' Andrea Alciati, in the last book of his *Parergon iuris*.[74] Alciati objected to the legal bias which inevitably emerged from such *consulti*. Academic freedom was compromised by the giving of academic opinions to interested parties at a price. Both sides of an argument were rarely discussed in full in each case. The progress of juridical science was obstructed by the failure of the genre to allow for a philological – and hence more impartial – approach to the main legal texts. The proliferation of such works led to confusion among students of law because of this bias, and neglect of teaching duties amidst the unseemly rush towards clients and printers.

It was the professor of criminal, then of civil, law at Padua, Tiberio Deciani, who responded to Alciati's charges in his *Apologia pro iuris prudentibus adversus dicta per Alciatum Parergon lib. XII cap. ult.*, appended to his own three volumes of *Responsa*, in 1579.[75] Deciani is of some significance to the Paduan school of law in the sixteenth century. Himself a graduate of the school, he went on to become an important political and diplomatic figure of his native Udine, before being appointed to the recently instated chair of criminal law at Padua in 1548. Both the new chair and his appointment to it betray a Venetian initiative which resulted from anxiety that the law university was not attracting as many students as the university of arts of medicine, and that its professors were not the most prestigious. In addition, German students at Padua had apparently petitioned for lecture courses specifically on the criminal law. In 1532 the emperor had promulgated the *Constitutio criminalis carolina*, which explicitly advised the courts to consult academic jurists on points of criminal law.[76] Whereas the medical school's sixteenth-century success rested to a large extent on the new humanistic tendencies of its medical teachers, Deciani's prestige at this stage in his career resulted from political rather than philological experience. Soon after his appointment to the chair of criminal law Deciani was commissioned by the Venetian *riformatori* to revise the statutes of the law university. By the time of the publication of his *Responsa* he held both the first ordinary chair of civil law at Padua and the office of *consultore* in law to the Venetian government.

His *Apologia* is a comprehensive historical and contemporary survey of the role of counsellor which argues passionately that *consilia* reflect the reality of the law better than more academic types of treatises like commentaries. Its historical perspective is a reminder that 'legal humanists' did not have a monopoly over historical views of the law, but it does differ from the philological approach in stressing the continuity rather than the 'otherness' of past legal institutions down to contemporary times and in justifying contemporary practice by reference to the past. Thus the origins of the contemporary legal counsellor are traced back to the consuls of ancient Rome, and the potential conflict of interest between teaching and counselling, identified by Alciati, is resolved by reference to the first ancient public teacher of law, Tiberius Coruncanius, who was also a consul.[77] For Deciani the contemporary doctorate in law conferred not only a *ius docendi* but also a *ius responden-di*. To Alciati's charge that teaching duties are neglected by writers of counsels, Deciani asks, 'Cannot a farmer cultivate arable, vines, olives and fruit all at the same time? ... Was not Michelangelo the prince not only of painters, but also of sculptors and architects?'[78] The importance of the applied aspect of law to Deciani is brought out by his observation that many judges do not understand elegant Latin, so it is important that *responsa* are written in a plain style. He accuses Alciati of not having wished to print his *consilia* because he knew this, had written them accordingly, but feared compromising his humanistic reputation by publishing inelegant work. But 'like women,' writes Deciani, 'justice and equity are more pleasing unadorned.'[79]

To measure the influence of all of this on England is rendered difficult by the lack of surviving evidence. Only a few teacher–student relationships are documented. Besides those described above, we know that Richard White was also taught by Girolamo Torniello, John Hart by Georgio Gregelio, and Edward Maners by Bartolomeo de Urbino.[80] But there is nevertheless a quantitative case for suspecting the impact of Paduan law on sixteenth-century England to have been considerable. Documentary survival in the Paduan archives is more favourably disposed towards the institutional study of the law university than the university of arts and medicine. While the acts of the law university survive almost continuously from 1498, those of the university of arts and medicine are extant for only a handful of years during the period treated here. Furthermore, since English arts and medicine students at Padua had no national corporation they are, until the late sixteenth century, largely invisible in official university documents. It is partly for these reasons that English law students known by name at Padua far outnumber those of arts and medicine. The electoral figures of the

English nation shown in the table on pp 26–7 add some unknown law students which significantly increase the ratio in favour of lawyers.

Almost certainly we do not know of all English students of arts and medicine. There may have been an element of 'natural selection': given Padua's reputation for medical studies and the expense of a period spent there, probably only the most promising students ever went. The impact of Padua itself – the kudos attached to claiming her as an alma mater and a medical training that in its sophistication went well beyond anything available in Oxford and Cambridge – would have been important determinants of success back in England. This may explain why most of those medical students from Padua whose names are extant in English sources were foremost in their field in England. But it is more likely that these were simply the ones who have left us documentary traces of their activity.

There are difficulties enough in defining the professional parameters of civil and canon lawyers, but it is clear that their situation and status were wholly different.[81] This was partly because they practised in institutional settings where regular record-keeping was normal – the courts – while the medical practitioner saw to his private patient; and partly because civil and canon lawyers had a single institutional home in the heart of London – Doctors' Commons – which, being a social and educational organization rather than, like the College of Physicians of London, a regulatory one, encompassed large numbers of university-educated legal practitioners whose names are inscribed in its registers.[82]

Nevertheless, in terms of attendance at Padua, a quantitative pattern emerges across the Tudor age, which in very broad terms is reliable. English attendance at the university of arts and medicine was rising in the early Tudor period, reaching a peak in the 1520s and 1530s, after which it declined sharply, picking up again only in the late 1580s. The pattern of attendance at the law university is almost the reverse of this, declining in the 1530s but rising again quite significantly in the mid-Tudor period, before declining again slightly in the last two decades of the sixteenth century. This has most to do with educational opportunities in England. Henry VIII banned the study of canon law in 1535 but the ecclesiastical courts, the mainstay of any doctor of law, continued to practise it because successive Tudor governments failed to produce an alternative code of law for the *ecclesia Anglicana*. When the survival of the ecclesiastical courts became more certain, from the middle of the sixteenth century, it made sense to acquire a doctorate in the civil law – a requirement for practice in the higher ecclesiastical courts –

somewhere; Padua's school of law had the advantage of not being run down like the English law faculties, as well as offering lectures in canon law. But with the innovations, bequests, and foundations of Linacre and others in the 1510s and 1520s, medical study in England became easier; more medical students stayed at home. Conversely, it was the institutional contrast between medical and legal practice which accounted for the more conspicuous impact of Paduan students of medicine on English society than those of law. Physicians – notably Thomas Linacre and John Caius – innovated in what was, relatively speaking, an institutional and intellectual vacuum, while lawyers returned home to a web of complex political, financial, intellectual and institutional interests.[83]

Civil and canon law – the type of law taught at Padua – was not the most important type of law studied and practised in England. The vast majority of English legal practitioners belonged to a different profession, that of the common lawyers. At least until the middle of the Elizabethan period, most of them had no university education but learnt their craft in the Inns of Court in London and practised in common law courts, encountering their civilian cousins only in some of the 'prerogative' or conciliar courts. Likewise the common law operated on different principles and procedures to the civil and canon laws.

Until recently a delineation of the two systems would have been a straightforward matter: England was renowned for being different in its law.[84] Recent work has rendered the picture much more complex, with several historians approaching the subject from a range of perspectives, detecting similarities between English and continental law. Most important among these is John Baker, who suggests that both systems were in the process of exchanging similar sources of legal authority in the sixteenth century, moving from a reliance on jurisprudence, that is legal learning, to judicial precedent.[85] There is also some evidence that the two systems shared some of the same sources: a certain amount of Roman law can be shown to have influenced the English common law in its formative, medieval period, and there are some twelfth- and thirteenth-century cross-currents in the English legal writers Glanvill and Bracton, both of whom were being read by common lawyers in the early Tudor period.[86]

Furthermore, civil and canon laws were known in England from the practice of the ecclesiastical courts, for it is becoming clearer than ever that Roman canon law continued to be a vital force in post-Reformation English church courts. And however much that law had been modified by English decisions and local customs, this did not stop practitioners from finding a range of continental legal writings of use. R.H. Helmholz has uncovered a large number of English canon law praxes, epitomes, treatises, and reports of court decisions in manuscript, mainly emerging in the last quarter of the sixteenth century, which demonstrate this continued use by English civilians of contemporary continental canonist and civilian jurisprudence of a traditional kind.[87] A recent study of Cambridge libraries shows the lasting and clear predominance of *mos italicus* literature, as well as the continued influx of works of the canon law, and especially continental praxes, procedural works, and works of legal reference and method.[88] Some of these were the kind of material which one Cambridge law student in the 1570s and 1580s, Gabriel Harvey, closely annotated, as has recently been shown, with the ultimate goal of becoming a civilian advocate.[89] A study of one York civilian has shown how extensively both his legal practice and his own published treatises drew on contemporary European civilian thought.[90] And a case from the Court of Arches, the most important provincial court of the Archbishop of Canterbury, dating to 1601 shows how, ironically, that court continued to be dependent on medieval canon law in some of its work, even when the Council of Trent had reformed practice on the continent.[91] What is striking here is how few humanistic legal works from Europe were found to be relevant to the English situation. Despite the trumpeting of 'legal humanism' by Sir Thomas Smith in his inaugural oration as Regius Professor of Civil Law in Cambridge in 1542, it was mainly the common lawyers at the end of the Elizabethan period, not the civilians, who identified with the concerns of the lawyers of the French historical school.[92] As far as civilians are concerned, it fits in with the general picture that the most famous civilian working in England in the Tudor period, Alberico Gentili, was also Europe's most vitriolic polemicist against the French method.

These findings and their chronologies are reflected in patterns of recruitment to the church courts. The major ecclesiastical courts were relatively successful under Elizabeth, adding to the civilian opportunities afforded by Chancery and the other equity courts which are discussed below. The ecclesiastical courts were no doubt enjoying their share of the massive increase of litigation in that period.[93] Whereas the Court of Arches received its lowest number of admissions of advocates in the 1530s and 1540s, numbers of practitioners rose steadily from the 1550s to the end of the century.[94] Admissions to Doctors' Commons show a more constant rate, but were rising in the 1560s and 1570s, despite the fact that the organization only barred non-civilian members in 1570;[95] civilian numbers there were certainly rising after that year and probably before it as well. A career as an advocate of the Arches was the mainstay of many Paduan-educated lawyers because advocacy there required a doctorate in law and could be lucrative. Furthermore, since the Henrician Reformation and particularly the suppression of appeals to Rome, positions in the ecclesiastical courts had been open to laymen.[96] Among English students at Padua, Cuthbert Tunstall represents the pre-Reformation type of church lawyer who was fully absorbed into the ecclesiastical hierarchy: he was appointed chancellor of the archbishop of Canterbury in 1509 and commissary of the Prerogative Court of Canterbury in 1511.[97] In the same period three other members of Doctors' Commons from Padua, Robert Birch, Henry Style, and Gamaliel Clifton, were probably advocates of the Arches.[98] Three Paduan-educated lawyers enjoyed the patronage of Archbishop Reginald Pole in the ecclesiastical courts during the reign of Mary: Pole appointed his contemporary at Padua, Henry Coles, dean of the Arches,[99] and he appointed John Orphinstrange and Laurence Huse as advocates there.[100] Orphinstrange also worked in the archidiaconal court of the diocese of London. Under Elizabeth, John Gardiner, George Acworth, Matthew Carew, Thomas Wilson, and Edmund Wyndham became advocates of the Arches.[101] In the same period Coles was briefly a commissary of the Prerogative Court of Canterbury, which dealt with testamentary matters; William Drury became commissary for the Faculties in 1562 (the office of the archbishop of Canterbury which oversaw dispensations previously granted by Rome) and a judge in the Prerogative Court of Canterbury in 1575; while George Acworth was appointed a judge in the Prerogative Court in Ireland.[102] A number of these men were also active in other aspects of ecclesiastical justice and administration, for example as members of courts of high commission, as deans, or as archdeacons; Cuthbert Tunstall for most of his career was a bishop. It should also be noted that this pattern of recruitment to the ecclesiastical courts conforms quite closely in its chronology both to the number of law graduates at Oxford and to the electoral figures of the English nation at Padua, tabulated above. In particular, both of these show a dramatic drop in numbers in the 1530s and 1540s before picking up again in the 1550s.[103]

Although the church courts employed the majority of Paduan-educated lawyers, men who worked in the church courts also worked in other courts. Tunstall, Carew, Huse, Orphinstrange, and Drury were also masters in Chancery, Wilson was a master and judge in the Court of Requests, Tunstall was active in Star Chamber and participated in the 1510s in a tribunal to settle piracy claims. Other ecclesiastical lawyers worked in courts tied closely to the royal council or privy council. Tunstall was a privy councillor active in Star Chamber and also on the king's council in the north (as was Drury). Wilson was also a privy councillor. The overlap between ecclesiastical and secular administrations is of particular interest in the case of Chancery, in ways which will now be explored.[104]

Chancery originated as a court of appeal from the other central law courts to the 'aequitas' of the king. In the Middle Ages this English principle of equity was very similar to the continental principle and probably drew on the same sources in the *Corpus iuris*, possibly mediated through Glanvill and Bracton, and certainly made use of Aristotle's definition of equity in the *Nichomachean Ethics*. This last was still quoted in the sixteenth century with the result that equity was seen, as on the continent, as a corrective in individual cases to the inflexibility of the law.[105] Chancery therefore needs to be identified with those other central courts which remained tied to the royal prerogative in the sixteenth century and whose procedures were at least implicitly equitable: Star Chamber, whose personnel was the king's council meeting in its judicial capacity, with the addition of two chief justices from the common law courts; the Court of Requests, whose personnel was predominantly civilian; and the local councils.[106] And all these should be distinguished from those courts which also grew out of the king's council but which by this period had become the backbone of the common law itself: the Court of King's Bench, whose appeal function rested only on technical disputes about legal procedure rather than on principles of 'conscience' or 'equity';[107] the Exchequer of Pleas, which nevertheless had developed a minor equity side to its work by the end of the sixteenth century; and the Court of Common Pleas. The 'aequitas' of the king in Chancery was delegated to the chancellor, who for a century and a half, until Sir Thomas More, had been an ecclesiastic and frequently a doctor of both laws. Thomas Wolsey, who was only the first of these, gave Chancery a bad name among some common lawyers by applying equity in ways which were seen as idiosyncratic and personal and therefore arbitrary – as opposed to being based on natural law and reason – but his Chancery – and his Star Chamber – witnessed a massive rise in business because the procedural flexibility of these courts enabled the victory of legal suits that would have failed in the common law courts. As a result, King's Bench and Common Pleas continued their precipitate decline.

Legal historians generally distinguish between the equity courts and the common law courts, but reveal an intense reluctance to admit to civilian influences. Both for English and European courts, the issue has been confused by a problematic distinction between substantive law and court procedure. This is not the place to rehearse that debate, but only to suggest that in terms of legal principles, court personnel, and procedure, each of which will be dealt with briefly in turn, there is reason to believe that the civil law had an impact on the equity courts.

Equity was originally a Greek and Roman concept which passed into both the *Corpus iuris civilis* and the *Corpus iuris canonici*, and nearly all medieval chancellors were civil and canon lawyers; therefore, there is every reason to believe that Chancery's central principle of equity was a Roman one.[108] In fact in sixteenth-century Europe the principle of equity came to be associated especially with canonist and Bartolist thinkers, because equity favoured judicial discretion and a free and extensive interpretation of the written law.

It was these varieties of continental legal thought which we find most prominent in England in the Tudor period, and the masters in Chancery, those with Paduan educations and the others, continued to be educated in these types of law. Including the Master of the Rolls, there were usually twelve masters at any one time and their main job was fact discovery, to gather and prepare material relating to particular law suits for the consideration of the chancellor or his deputy in Chancery, and to advise on procedure.[109] At some point in the sixteenth century, as a result of the vast increase in the business of the court, they also acquired some of the judicial functions of the chancellor himself. For a number of reasons – especially the archival distribution of surviving records and the fact that historians of the church courts tend not to be the same people as historians of the secular courts – the extent to which Chancery masters in the sixteenth century were absorbed into the ecclesiastical legal establishment has gone unnoticed. But a cursory examination of their careers shows a common pattern of long periods of service in the major ecclesiastical courts followed by appointments in Chancery, a pattern which begins in the 1470s and which is firmly established by the reign of Henry VIII.[110] Of the eighty-two masters in Chancery from the start of his reign to the end of the Tudor period, only about twenty did not have civil or canon law doctorates. Of the other sixty or so masters, we know that fifty-eight were members of Doctors' Commons, and of these at least fifty-four were probably advocates of the Arches. Between their dates of admission to Doctors' Commons and their appointments in Chancery there is an average gap of ten years, suggesting that Chancery was a top job for ecclesiastical lawyers. These men were active in other aspects of ecclesiastical justice and administration: twenty-four sat on courts of high commission, thirteen were archdeacons, eight were bishops' chancellors. And ten, incidentally, worked in the Court of Requests. It was only in the late sixteenth and seventeenth centuries, a period for which the civil lawyers have been more intensively studied, that common lawyers began to capture the masterships in Chancery, the first such one being William Lambarde in 1597. But even in this period civilian masters remained active. The Paduan alumni Laurence Huse and Matthew Carew, who had practised as advocates of the Arches before their appointments to Chancery for three and four years respectively, were two of the most active masters in the 1590s. In fact if the survival of court records accurately reflects the distribution of court business, for certain years in the 1590s these two monopolized the masters' reporting activities.[111]

For the Tudor period, the civilian fortunes of Chancery may be examined a little more closely. Chancellors Morton and Warham (1487–1515) were both archbishops and doctors of law in the fifteenth-century mould. Chancellor Wolsey was not a doctor of law, and common lawyers have been shown to have been active in his Chancery, though crucially not as Chancery masters but as the representatives of litigants.[112] In fact common lawyers were the most vocal group to criticize Wolsey's methods, accusing him of ignorance, contempt of the law, and arbitrary judgments. The appointment of Sir Thomas More as his successor in 1529 may partly represent an attempt to appease the common lawyers, but his cultural milieu suggests a lurch back to the old style of chancellor: More was a diplomat, royal servant, and member of Doctors' Commons. However, More's successor, Sir Thomas Audley, was, like him, a common lawyer, with Thomas Cromwell becoming Master of the Rolls, the head of the masters in Chancery. All three effectively diffused much of the common law opposition to Chancery.

Nevertheless, the fortunes of the civil law in Chancery improved again from the 1540s and the chancellorship of Sir Thomas Wriothesley, the first in a new wave of non–common law chancellors that extended from 1544 to 1558. Historically, it may have resulted from Henry VIII's banning of the study of canon law in 1535, which potentially created a group of doctors educated in civil but not in canon law, and hence not practically qualified to work in the ecclesiastical courts. In the decades of religious uncertainty, from the 1530s to the 1550s, Chancery was a principle means by which the civilian tradition survived in England. It was initially achieved through deliberate government patronage of civilians, the first major step in this direction being Henry VIII's establishment of Regius Professorships of Civil Law at Oxford and Cambridge in 1540. The first Cambridge incumbent was Sir Thomas Smith, whose 1542 inaugural oration recommended Chancery work as one of the principal career opportunities for civilians.[113] Wriothesley continued the trend, as did that autocratic patron of classicism and of English travel in Italy, Protector Somerset:[114] in 1547 a group of students from the Inns of Court petitioned the Lord Protector to curb the civilian jurisdiction of Chancery, because civilians were determining 'weighty causes of this realm' not according to the common law, but according to the civil law or their own consciences.[115] By the Elizabethan period, masters in Chancery were almost exclusively civilians despite the fact that – or perhaps precisely because – chancellors themselves had ceased to be so; this fact is attested to in John Stow's *Survey of London* and in Richard Robinson's *A brief collection of the queenes majesties most high and most honourable courtes of record*.[116] This is what gave ideological colour to the common law attack on Chancery in the late sixteenth century. Francis Alford, a civilian with a Paduan education but not himself a master, seems to have been involved in the campaign to defend Chancery masters from common law attack in this period.[117] In 1596, the Paduan alumnus Matthew Carew defended the masters against the criticism of charging exorbitant fees with an explicit reference to what was permitted in the civil law.[118] His nephew George Carew, who had also been a visitor to Padua, wrote a treatise defending the masters in Chancery at around the same time. His work, *A Treatise of the Maisters in Chauncerie*,[119] deserves quotation because it is explicit about the civil law: 'And albeit for performance of most of the service ... the knowledge of the common lawe bee most requisite, yet undoubtedlie it was not withowt great ground of reason, that auntientlie men skilfull in the civill and canon lawes hav bene chosen to supplie somme of the places.'[120] Carew proceeds with an historical survey of the main areas of law dealt with in Chancery before concluding: 'All which, seinge they are to bee expedited, not in cours of common lawe, but in cours of civill or cannon lawe, it was necessarie to assist the lord chauncellor with some learned in those lawes; and the distribution and dispensation of prohibitions and consultations, was alsoe more aptlie committed to those of the chauncerie, whoe understood bothe lawes, then it cann be exercised by those that are cunning in the secular lawe onely ...'[121] Thus Chancery rested on Roman law principles and underwent a 'reception' of civilians in the fifteenth and sixteenth centuries. If the procedures cannot be judged as inherently Roman, they were at least quite clearly not common law procedures and were within the European mainstream, a hybridity expressed by Richard Robinson's formulation for this court in around 1592: 'this Court may well be called officina iuris civilis Anglorum.'[122] Sir Thomas Smith, admittedly not an impartial observer, went further, contrasting 'English' trial by jury with civilian trial by judge, and observing that the Chancery proceeded by written bill rather than by writ and oral pleadings, in his *De republica Anglorum* of 1565: 'And in this court the usual and proper form of pleading of England is not used, but the form of pleading by writing which is used in other countries according to the civil law; and the trial is not by twelve men, but by the examination of witnesses as in other courts of the civil law.'[123]

Smith's distinction between written and oral pleading is of only limited usefulness, since oral pleading was in decline in the common law courts.[124] But behind the description is a useful distinction between the common law procedure, whereby the issues at stake in any one case were successively reduced by debate in court to a single issue at law, which was the issue decided by a lay jury, and the equity courts' procedure in which the trial was at all times in the hands of professional lawyers, there was no lay jury, the full facts of the case could be tried by the judge after witnesses were called to the court by subpoena, and the set-piece adversarial trial was avoided because information on the cases was usually gathered piecemeal and discussed in the absence of the litigants. This opportunity to try a case in all its facets gave equity its value and relevance in England, and it cannot be a coincidence that Chancery emerged just at the time when central secular courts on the continent drawing on Romano-canonical procedure were coming into being, also moulded by personnel with civilian educations. In terms of procedure trial by jury as opposed to trial by judge, and, for a time, oral pleadings as opposed to subpoena and written bills, seem to distinguish the common law from conciliar and equity law.

The careers of Paduan-educated civilians in England confirm that this division between jury courts – the common law courts – and other courts delineates the realm of civilian penetration of English law. No Englishmen educated at Padua worked in the common law courts which employed the writ system, oral pleadings, and trial by jury unless they also had an Inns of Court education. On the other hand, Paduan lawyers can be shown to have been active in most of the other courts. In addition to those mentioned above, John Boxall was a master in the Court of Requests and was active in Star Chamber, and Robert Chaloner was a member of the king's council in the north; Thomas Savage, who studied at Padua in the early 1480s, became chancellor of the earldom of the March.[125] But the work in these courts of Paduan-educated lawyers is also explicable in terms of the closeness of the relationship between the courts and the government itself. Civilians with a Paduan education were particularly close to government as the monarch's councillors: John Boxall, Francis Walsingham, Cuthbert Tunstall, and Thomas Wilson all served on the king's council or the privy council.

A final field of activity described by both Sir Thomas Smith and Richard White as the particular task of civilians tied them even more closely to the state – diplomacy.[126] This was a burgeoning field of activity throughout the Tudor period and the advantages of an education in the civil law were obvious for an ambassador. Not only was the civil law spreading across Europe, but the *Corpus iuris civilis* also specified a particular area of law which was considered universal to all states and governed relations between nations, the *ius gentium*. In England the emergence of the civilian High Court of Admiralty shows a recognition of the inadequacy of the common law for governing relations between England and foreigners, although this did not stop the usual jurisdictional disputes concerning, for example, which courts should handle the prosecution of pirates. For a diplomatic education, Padua was particularly advantageous. An education abroad was an education in foreign customs, languages, and institutions; Padua and nearby Venice were remarkably cosmopolitan cities. Furthermore, while Padua could teach 'civil science,' Venice, famed for the perfection of her constitution, was herself a lesson in statecraft.[127]

Consequently Englishmen with a Paduan education were prominent as diplomats. Thomas Savage and Cuthbert Tunstall exemplify the pre-Reformation type of ambassador drawn from the church, whom Richard Morison, in a treatise to be discussed below, wanted displaced. Savage, who had been a rector of the law university at Padua in 1481–2, became successively dean of the Chapel Royal, bishop of Rochester, bishop of London, and archbishop of York. He was a royal envoy to Spain in 1488, attended the conference at Boulogne in 1490, and negotiated a commercial treaty for England at Riga in 1498. Tunstall, successively bishop of London and Durham, was at Padua from about 1497 to 1501, and was employed on diplomatic missions from the 1510s to the 1540s. He was ambassador to Charles V (Charles of Ghent) at Brussels in 1515–16 and in Spain in 1519–20 and 1525–6. In 1527 he helped Wolsey negotiate the Treaty of Cambrai and in 1546 he was an ambassador to France. But laymen with a Paduan legal education were also employed as diplomats in this period. Robert Wingfield undertook successive diplomatic missions to the Emperor Maximilian from 1507 to 1516, was an envoy to Charles V (Charles I of Spain) in 1517, and was ambassador to Charles again from 1521 to 1526. Richard Morison benefited from Protector Somerset's realization of the value of civilians as diplomats. In connection with his plan to establish civil law colleges at the universities, Somerset wrote to Bishop Ridley in 1549, 'And we are sure ye are not ignorant how necessary that study of civil law is to all treaties with foreign princes and strangers.'[128] Morison was sent to negotiate with the Hanseatic towns in 1546 and was ambassador to Charles V from 1550 to 1553.[129] The trend continued under Elizabeth. Thomas Wilson was ambassador to Portugal in 1567–8 and to the Netherlands from 1574 to 1577. Richard Spencer was sent on a mission to the duke of Parma in 1588 and was commissioner in The Hague in 1607–8. William Drury, though himself never an ambassador, was consulted on international law in 1571 by Elizabeth I concerning the rights to diplomatic immunity of Mary Stuart's conspiratorial ambassador, the bishop of Ross. Henry Hawkins acted as the earl of Essex's intelligence agent in Venice in the 1590s.

Paduan-educated civilians were not only councillors but counsellors. Two treatises, both offering counsel to the king concerning English law, came from the pens of the Paduan alumni Thomas Starkey and Richard Morison. The fate of these works has generally been interpreted as evidence that England was not in danger of a 'reception' of Roman law in the Henrician period. Starkey's recommendation of a complete transfer to the civil law went unheeded, while Morison's proposal for the codification of the common law in Latin fell on equally deaf ears. Furthermore, neither of these men became lawyers even of the civilian variety. Their work has thus tended to be seen as manifestations of an irrelevant and inconsequential English humanism, but this is not the full story.

There are indeed humanistic elements in their work.[130] Starkey's background, analysed in more detail in chapter 3 below, was in the humanist milieu of late 1510s Oxford. In the 1520s he was a student of natural philosophy in Padua and a friend of Reginald Pole and Niccolò Leonico Tomeo. His *Dialogue between Pole and Lupset*, written between about 1529 and 1532, contains a recommendation that England 'receive' the civil law. An explicit link is made between the barbarity of the common law and injustice in the common law system: 'These hungry advocates and cormorants of the court study much to delay causes for their lucre and profit ... but it is also a fault in the order of the law, and in policy. For this is sure: if it were well ordered, justice should not be so defeated.'[131] The law is 'over-confuse. It is infinite, and without order or end.'[132] This lets in the cunning of self-serving serjeants and judges. Law French is 'ignominious, and dishonour to our nation, forasmuch as thereby is testified our subjection to the Normans':[133]

Who is so blind that seeth not the great shame to our nation, the great infamy and rot that remaineth in us, to be governed by the laws given to us of such a barbarous nation as the Normans be? Who is so far from reason that considereth not the tyrannical and barbarous institutions infinite ways left here among us, which all should be wiped away by the receiving of this which we call the very civil law – which is, undoubtedly, the most ancient and noble monument of the Romans' prudence and policy, the which be so writ, with such gravity, that if Nature should herself prescribe particular means whereby mankind should observe her laws, I think she would admit the same.[134]

The *Dialogue* reveals a profound respect for the civil law. This suggests that Starkey's study of it at Avignon in 1532 and at Padua from 1532 to 1534 was important to him for the 'politic life,' the reason he gave for studying it in his patronage-seeking letter to Thomas Cromwell.[135] Early in the *Dialogue* Starkey writes that the 'natural seeds and plants of virtue,' that is, natural law, are maintained and set forward by man in the 'civil law, for because they be as means to bring man to the perfection of the civil life. Without the ordinance of these laws, the other soon will be corrupt, the weeds will soon overgrow the good corn.'[136] Although later in the *Dialogue* the common and civil laws are clearly called by these names, it is interesting to note that here Starkey goes on to write that the 'law civil,' meaning the civil law which he has just described, is variable from place to place and that, although it emerges from natural law, one is only bound to obey the laws in the place where one is. It seems here that Starkey is seized by the anxiety to include English law in his account, obscuring his meaning by deploying terms such as 'civil ordinance.'[137] Nevertheless, the common law was never called the civil law, though it was sometimes called 'municipal law'; from what Starkey writes later, his belief in the *Corpus iuris civilis* and his disillusionment with both the common law and the English court system are clear. This is confirmed here by the fact that this very distinction between natural law and civil law derives from the *Digest*, a part of the *Corpus iuris civilis*, itself drawing on the *Institutes* of Gaius and Ulpian.[138]

However, in the context of Starkey's wider aims for reform, his 'civilianism' partly emerges as the consequence of a conservative desire to undermine the increasing royal and ecclesiastical prerogatives and to reconstitute the nobility in their proper governmental role.[139] He suggests that young noblemen be educated in the civil law, and proposes a council to regulate the rule of the king, presided over by the constable.[140] This revival of the position of constable has important historical resonances; the last holder of the title, Edward Stafford, duke of Buckingham, was executed by Henry VIII in 1521, suspected of heading a conspiracy of nobles to overthrow the king. It is no coincidence that the interlocutor to propose this measure in the *Dialogue* is 'Pole,' who in real life was Buckingham's cousin.[141] Although Buckingham was not able to exercise the supervisory role of this position under Henry, it may be relevant that the constable traditionally presided in the High Court of Chivalry, a court which regulated the bestowal and holding of coats of arms and which was staffed by civilians.[142]

On English law itself, Starkey regrets the increasing centralization of the system, complaining of the removing of law suits out of their shires of origin to the Westminster common law courts by the writ system, and from these courts to Chancery and the 'higher council' by 'injunction.' He believes that the king's prerogative is far too 'weak' a 'thread' to ensure the easing of sentences which are generally over-harsh in the law itself. Likewise in canon law Starkey believes that the power of the pope is excessive: 'the pope hath no such authority to dispense with general laws made by the Church,' a sentiment which would have pleased Henry VIII were it not equated with *his* power: 'wherefore in the abuse thereof is no less detriment to the law of the Church than is to the common law here of our country by the prerogative of the prince.' The appellation of ecclesiastical suits to Rome is disparagingly equated with the removal of common law suits to London.[143]

Although the *Dialogue* was being written from about 1529 to about 1532, around the period when Starkey commenced his studies in civil law, there are strong civilian sentiments in it. It seems likely therefore that they were incorporated during a late rewriting. Furthermore, given that Starkey and Morison were contemporaries and friends at Padua during the 1530s, there is every reason to believe that they discussed the idea of 'reception' with each other. Their specific proposals are far from identical, though they echo each other on a number of points. But the strong belief in the political efficacy of 'civil science' is common to both.

What evidence remains of Morison's studies at Padua locates them in the fields of Greek literature, philosophy, and theology. Although Morison was something of a political operator in the law university in 1534 and the English nation's *consiliarius* in the same year, no evidence remains of his legal studies.

Morison's *A Perswasion to the Kyng that the laws of the realme shulde be in Latin*, a work full of interest for the history of the 1530s, also contains humanistic elements.[144] The proposal to encode the English laws in Latin comes from a conviction that Latin is more copious than English and more suitable for the law.[145] Justice for Morison depends on the 'scientific' systemization of the law, which requires the 'knowlage of other sciences and artes liberall' on the part of lawyers; these sciences and arts themselves require a knowledge of Latin.[146] The subjects Morison has in mind are logic,[147] rhetoric,[148] philosophy,[149] and 'goddes laws.'[150] This more than echoes the calls of many continental 'legal humanists,' 'ius civile in artem redigere,' to reduce the civil law to an art, a preoccupation which emerges directly from Cicero's *De oratore*. Indeed, Morison quotes from *De oratore* at length on precisely this issue.[151] He makes an explicit link between the ignorance, barbarity, and confusion of lawyers on the one hand and their greed and corruption on the other:

By reason that the laws be not in the Latin tongue the lawyers, making the only end of their studies an increase of riches, a heaping together of possessions which they get by the practice thereof, never give themselves to the study of good laws but, as much as in them is, flee the same because they would serve nothing but their private profit. How many be there in so great a multitude that can with great study, without help of other learned men, make an oration? What speak I of orations, that require diverse kinds of learning? How many is there among them that can expound in English any piece of a good Latin oration and answer to the parts of it? To come somewhat higher, how many are among them that cannot make a deed or a plea in their own Latin, but are forced to draw it first in their French, and after to cause their clerks to turn it into Latin? ... good lawyers be so abhorred among this sort of lawyers, that when they prepare any young man given to good learning, desirous therewith to have the knowledge of the laws, they will earnestly persuade him to forget and leave his old study, as though good lawyers and the law could not agree in one person.[152]

Morison frequently quotes from the storehouse of classical historical *exempla* to underline his points. An implicit exhortation to Henry VIII not to go to war but to look after the commonwealth at home is couched in terms of praise for the king for doing just that. He is compared to Theompompus, who 'desired not to increase his dominion in quantity but in quality, to adorn it with good laws, to establish his subjects in virtue and honest living' rather than the conquering Alexander the Great; the former's achievements lasted longer than the latter's.[153] The Lacedaemonians are praised for their careful overseeing of their population.[154] Old Testament typology is wielded in praise of Henry VIII in the same way as it had been used by Henrician propagandists from the mid-1530s;[155] for Morison Henry is a latter-day Moses, leading the English people out of the bondage of the latter-day Pharaoh, the bishop of Rome. Intriguingly, Morison's humanism leads him to a strongly historical sense of both the English and the Roman law, on which his argument ultimately depends. For Morison the *Corpus iuris civilis* is not an absolute and unchanging body of rules, but the text resulting from an historical event which Henry is now exhorted to re-enact for his own times; just as all rulers have instilled into the youth of their realms anything which they desired to be continued, 'So did the noble Emperor Justinian, who out of his whole laws caused the elements to be taken out and rules to be made purposely.'[156] Justinian is a historical example rather than a legal authority, whom Morison deploys to challenge hidebound conservatism. To those who argue that if the task of common law codification was possible, 'our forefathers' would have done it, he replies: 'Many things every man knoweth they did, which might have been better undone; and many things they omitted which with great praise they might have committed ... Those laws that we now call civil, before the Emperor Justinian's time were as much dispersed and as far out of order as ours be. Nevertheless, you see that he brought them into great certainty, digested them in order, made thereof an act, insomuch that the books thereof for the good order and certainty be called Digests, that is, set in order and certainty.'[157]

Whereas Starkey was prepared to countenance complete Romanization, Morison's combination of anxiety about the barbarousness of

English institutions and patriotic Protestant pride for distinctively English forms anticipates much writing of the Elizabethan period:[158]

If it were so possible and so easy to frame and bring the Roman laws to an art and certainty, how much more possible and easy is it to bring ours into a certainty and into the Latin tongue? The same reason, the same law of nature that was among the Romans is among us. Our laws, although they differ in form and handling, be made of that matter that their laws be. And as it be not impossible for an Italian tailor, but easy, to make of an English cloth an Italian cloak, or for an English tailor to make of an Italian velvet an English gown, so is it not impossible but easy to turn the matter of the civil laws into ours, and yet in no point change any of ours. There is nothing hard but where good will lacketh.[159]

Morison's tract is hardly a technical treatise on the law. Indeed it is his detachment from the intricacies of both systems that enables him to pass so freely between the two;[160] it would be asking too much of the evidence to trace his unsophisticated brand of 'legal humanism' directly back to Padua, especially since the date of his treatise is not completely clear.[161] It is obvious, nevertheless, that Italy in a general sense provided him with his comparative perspective and historical equipment, both of which are so evident in his other writings as well. It may also be that his vision of the political role of lawyers, like Starkey's, derived from the Paduan law school. One of the reasons behind the proposed Latin codification of the law is that lawyers should be more useful to the commonwealth:

If lawyers were forced to study the Latin tongue, as they could not but do if the laws were once written in that tongue, then within short time through knowledge of other arts, whereunto they might easily attain, they then should be able to serve your majesty at home in things pertaining to your realm, they should then be able to perceive what things annoyed and what should further your graces commonwealth, they should then be meet to serve your highness in foreign and outward causes, meet to be your ambassadors, which office your grace of necessity now oftentimes is constrained to commiss to bishops and doctors who be chiefly ordained to preach and teach God's word, for lack of laymen learned to exercise that office, whereby their duty resteth undone, and a great number of your poor subjects for lack of teaching be ignorant in the knowledge of God, in their duty of obedience to him, your Grace and your laws.[162]

In this respect it is interesting to consider the political consequences of this characteristically civilian credo. Morison was not alone among English students of the civil law in adapting himself more quickly than some common lawyers or theologians to the changes of the 1530s, and the considerable prerogative allowed to the prince in civilian thought may have something to do with this. It is striking in this connection to compare his writings in this period with those of Stephen Gardiner, a learned English civilian who was quicker than many of Henry's bishops in adjusting to the Reformation. While Gardiner wrote his *De vera obedientia*, Morison wrote *A Lamentation in which is showed what ruin and destruction come of seditious rebellion* and *A remedy for sedition*. Obedience to the prince was the touch word of all three tracts.[163]

Starkey, with doctorates in theology and arts and close ties to Reginald Pole, was a more complex figure whose accommodation to the Cromwellian regime remained uneasy.[164] And while Morison's tract was presented to the king, Starkey's was not; an altogether more idiosyncratic and less opportunistic work than the *Perswasion*, the *Dialogue*'s advocacy of the civil law was part of an attack on all those developments in English law which were likely to make 'reception' a possibility. Morison was already the successful servant of the king when he framed his *Perswasion*, unlike Starkey when he wrote the *Dialogue*. Thus, rather than Starkey's bolder and more sophisticated proposal, Morison's treatise, on the one hand, and its ultimate rejection, on the other, are the realistic boundaries within which English law's relationship to the civil law may be described for the 1530s. It is not surprising that civilian forms were being urged on a monarch of a both reformist and highly autocratic temper. The enormous powers of royal prerogative potentially granted to the monarch in the *Corpus iuris civilis* were in some senses anticipated in Chancery and Star Chamber under Wolsey. The most conspicuous feature of legal development in the Henrician period is of new courts, some of them staffed by civilians, not tied to common law procedures. Common reason and natural law, the bases of both the English and Roman systems, according to Morison, were particularly associated with equity; when the common lawyer Christopher St German had argued for the identity of the common law courts and equity courts a few years before Morison, he had resorted to the same principles.[165] Systematization and centralization of government were in the air in the 1530s. Furthermore, two of Morison's proposals came much nearer to being introduced than has hitherto been noticed. Some time between 1534 and 1547 Henry VIII established a 'royal commission' to inquire into the state of the Inns of Court and to propose reforms. The resulting report suggested a new Inn in which the existing system of legal education would be supplemented with, among other things, the teaching of Greek and Latin, works of classical rhetoric and political philosophy, French, and the sending of students on foreign embassies.[166] Nothing came of this, but Henry did extend his patronage to civilians in his 1540 endowment of Regius Professorships at the universities. Protector Somerset was even more sympathetic to them, involved in an unsuccessful attempt to establish separate colleges of civil law at the universities. It is a measure of how far English law had changed by the 1530s that Morison was able to frame his proposals at all.

However, in England civil and canon law went hand in hand in the sense that the civilians were primarily the advocates of the ecclesiastical courts. In these circumstances, the Henrician revolution of that decade was undertaken with the aid of common lawyers in parliament determined to undermine the jurisdictional power of the ecclesiastical courts. This, and the crisis of Henry's divorce, may have temporarily deflected attention away from the inadequacies of the common law itself.[167] Moreover, inasmuch as this revolution emphasized the jurisdictional self-sufficiency of the realm of England as an empire, the civil law's autocratic edge was blunted by the fact that it was the law of the Holy Roman Emperor. Furthermore, the civil law had long been associated in England with foreign tyranny and as such it is questionable how useful it was to a country in the process of cultural self-definition. As Donald Kelley has pointed out, this particular brand of chauvinism extended well back into the Middle Ages.[168] *Magna Carta* and various statutes of Edward III associated an Englishman's freedom with the common law. In the later fifteenth century Sir John Fortescue's *De laudibus legum Angliae* condemns French law – identified mistakenly here as the civil law across the board – as unjust and brutal. Padua has a special place in this story. According to the Florentine bookseller Vespasiano da Bisticci, prior to the execution of John Tiptoft, earl of Worcester, in 1470, the crowds demanded his death because he had introduced the brutal 'law of Padua' into England.[169] Even the civilian Sir Thomas Smith's 1565 distinction between the 'usual' common law procedures used in England and the civilian procedures of Chancery 'used in other countries' can be read both ways. The chauvinism reached its height in the seventeenth century, when the civil law also acquired a reputation for being sinisterly popish.[170] A succession of Catholic exiles who studied the civil law at Padua during the reign of

Elizabeth undoubtedly exacerbated that reputation. By the 1570s, even Francis Alford and William Drury, Marian exiles and law students at Padua in the 1550s, apparently could not throw off the popish taint of the civil law.[171] When finally a printed and widely accepted work of systematization of English common law principles did come, this book, Sir Edward Coke's *Institutes* of 1609, was to be viciously anticivilian in tone and suffused with an insular antiquarianism.[172]

If Paduan law was pragmatic, then the English civilians it produced were even more so.[173] While Matthew Carew, William Drury, Richard Morison, Thomas Starkey, Henry Coles, John Orphinstrange, Francis Alford, Edmund Wyndham, and Thomas Wilson all partook of the intellectual life of the civil and canon laws in their various ways, no documented tradition of civilian thought in the universities or canonist thought in the church seems to have been implanted from the Paduan school of law. Those few Paduan alumni who returned to Oxford or Cambridge stayed there only for short periods. William Drury, for example, Regius Professor of Civil Law at Cambridge from 1559, left the university in 1561 to become an ecclesiastical advocate and administrator. Religious factors exacerbated this tendency. Drury's successor as Regius Professor was William Soone, who had been *consiliarius* of the English nation at Padua in 1558–9 and had become a doctor of both laws by 1561. Would his principles permit, Soone wrote from Cologne in 1575, he would prefer Cambridge to a kingdom; by then he had been an exile for thirteen years, working as a professor of law at Louvain, a cartographer in Antwerp, and an administrator in the Papal State.[174] Two other Englishmen made substantial contributions to continental legal thought but remained abroad in the Elizabethan period. Jerome Sapcot, active in the Paduan law university in the 1560s and 1570s and 'addicted' to the Pandects according to his friend Richard White, was still in the Veneto when his *Ad primas leges Digestorum de verborum et rerum significatione* was published in Venice in 1579. White himself returned to England in 1568 after three years in Padua, but had emigrated to Douai by 1570, where he became Regius Professor of Law, rector of the university, a count palatine, and a priest. His considerable published output included works of legal antiquarianism and studies of the canon law, but it is not known whether even his history of Britain had an English readership.

With their competence in the law of the church and other civilian courts, experience of foreign countries, and knowledge of foreign languages, of 'civil science,' and European law, there is ample evidence to suggest that Paduan-educated civilians were of value to the Tudor government and church. While never reaching the numbers of common lawyers, the number of civilians was increasing in the sixteenth century, a trend reflected in numbers attending the law university at Padua. Towards the end of this period, canonical and civilian thought of a strongly Bartolist flavour was able to put down more solid roots in England, and this no doubt equipped civilians to survive the series of crises after 1640, which would nevertheless leave them in a permanently weakened state.[175] By helping to sustain the civilian presence in England, Padua played an important part in ensuring civilian survival. But civil lawyers' vulnerability in English society in the seventeenth century was the consequence of their lack of institutional and professional independence in an era of ever-hardening professionalization; of religious and intellectual cosmopolitanism in an era of Protestant insularity and national self-definition; and of an ethic of royal and government service in an era of parliamentarianism. Inasmuch as Padua had a hand in fostering all of these qualities, in the long term it cannot be said to have helped English civilians achieve the kinds of intellectual strength, institutional unity, and political power which were themselves features of Paduan jurist culture.

3

Students of Medicine and Natural Philosophy

When John Chamber left Oxford in 1503 to study medicine in Padua, the anonymous registrar of Merton College noted that Padua was 'a most famous university for all humane studies,' and that Chamber was going there to devote himself to the works of 'Avicenna, Galen, and other physicians.'[1] For much of the following century Paduan medicine and natural philosophy would exert a profound influence on English humanist studies and Aristotelianism.

This influence has been recognized only in the most fragmentary of ways. Despite the examples of Thomas Linacre, John Caius, and William Harvey, academic medicine tends to be consigned to the specialist periphery by historians of 'mainstream' cultural and humanistic studies. On the continent the historiographical gulf between medicine and Renaissance humanism is only now beginning to be bridged. By re-examining the English experience at Padua, this chapter sets out to show that also in England medicine and natural philosophy had a central importance in humanist learning.

The sixteenth-century Paduan *studium* was renowned above all for its medicine, and before the end of the fifteenth century it had begun to absorb that movement in the field pioneered by Niccolò Leoniceno in Ferrara and now usually described as 'medical humanism.'[2] Medical humanism was primarily an attempt to reconstruct the original words of the ancient Greek medical sources, especially of Hippocrates and his interpreter Galen, and of the chief source of ancient natural philosophy, Aristotle; to make their writings available, in Greek and in new Latin translations, to medical students, as the essential first step towards a reformed and academically moderated medical practice; and to challenge the position in academic medicine held by medieval Arabic interpreters of the Greek tradition, especially Avicenna.[3] Because of the therapeutic importance of medical simples in ancient medicine, and because of Galen's emphasis on the educational value of dissection, especially as revealed in his newly discovered work *De anatomicis administrationibus*, the movement also ushered in at Padua a vogue for botany and anatomical studies which would have far-reaching effects in the mid- and late-sixteenth century.

However, the intellectual appeal of Renaissance Galenism was broader than this. It equipped the student not only with medical knowledge, but also with an ideology based on Galen's example, medical philosophy, and powerful rhetoric of what it was to be a physician. Galen's physician believed in the value of experience, observation, and travel, and in the cumulative progress of medical knowledge; Galen repeatedly attacked physicians for their slavish adherence to received wisdom. But crucially, his physician was also a philosopher, drawing eclectically on rational deduction as well as experience. The title of a work of his was translated into Latin by Erasmus as 'Quod optimus medicus sit quoque philosophus,'[4] a sentiment which came to embody Galenic medicine in the sixteenth century. It was reflected in the curricular structure of the northern Italian universities, where natural philosophy was medicine's propaedeutic and where academic physicians were socially and economically superior to philosophers. It was known in England, where Richard Pace claimed that medicine was philosophy's first and foremost companion[5] and Linacre had the words 'Opus non medicis modo, sed et philosophis oppido quam necessarium' printed on the title page of his Latin translation of Galen's *De temperamentis*.[6] Later in the sixteenth century this unity of theory and practice was to break down, with challenges both to the substance of Galenic medicine itself and to the curricular continuum of philosophy and medicine in the universities. Andreas Vesalius, though heavily indebted to Galen, attacked elements of Galenic anatomy and physiology on the basis of his own observations in the 1540s; Paracelsus's criticism of Galen in the 1560s was launched from a philosophical perspective; Francesco Patrizi in the 1580s was questioning the usefulness of an Aristotelian education for physicians.[7] Indeed from this period the anatomy spawned by Galenism was perhaps beginning to offer a challenge to Aristotelian natural philosophy as the basis for medical study.[8] But in the first half of the century, when the ideological contest was primarily between Hellenists and Arabists, the philosophical integrity of this academic field, which claimed as its central aim the saving of lives, must have been one of its chief attractions to English humanists reared in an intellectual *milieu* whose leading lights were to become stranded between the competing ideologies of the active and contemplative lives.[9] In this period, when the advocates of Galen were winning the field against the advocates of Avicenna, a significant number of English medical students frequented the Paduan *studium*, propelled there by a small group of patrons and scholars of the new learning, mainly in Oxford.[10] In the late sixteenth century and in the early seventeenth century, a more critical and less philological approach to ancient texts in Padua, combined with more sophisticated anatomical studies, would attract a second wave of English students including William Harvey, the discoverer of the circulation of the blood.

Medicine in medieval universities was associated with arts faculties, and Oxford and Cambridge in the fifteenth and sixteenth centuries were dominated by arts students.[11] Yet few of them seem to have proceeded to the study of medicine. In Oxford this in part may be ascribed to the separate existence of a medical faculty, which may have suffered for its isolation, for the record of the association between arts and medicine reveals itself in a negative light: the medical faculty had no bedel of its own and had to rely on the services of the arts bedel.

Even within the period of a new and ultimately successful attempt to encourage the study of medicine in Oxford, Emden's *Biographical Register of the University of Oxford* shows at a glance how few medical degrees were awarded between 1501 and 1540, and for the fifteenth century it has been calculated that only about fifty medical doctorates were awarded as opposed to five hundred theology doctorates.[12] Part of Oxford's prestige in theology must have stemmed from numerous early endowments which encouraged the study of the subject. Although Oxford's earliest statutes, dating from before 1350, made provision for a doctoral degree in medicine connected, as on the continent, with the granting of licences for the practice of medicine, there were in reality few opportunities for the study of the subject. Such permissive legislation was different in kind to the institutional incentive of a bequest. Only two colleges founded before 1500, New College and Magdalen, mentioned medicine in their statutes, but also in the permissive sense of allowing two and three scholars respectively to be studying medicine at any one time, with the agreement of the fellows. In Cambridge the foundation statutes of King's College (1440) permitted two fellows to study medicine. Other colleges allowed one or two students to study medicine without the formal recognition of the founding statutes, but there is little evidence for many students doing so. All Souls College, Oxford, Linacre's *alma mater*, may be typical in this respect: six of its students are known to have studied medicine during the fifteenth century, but only one is known to have proceeded to a doctorate while still a member of the college.[13] The availability of medical writings in Oxford and Cambridge paints a slightly more optimistic picture and suggests that on an informal level an interest in medicine was increasing throughout the fifteenth and sixteenth centuries.[14] Five of the All Souls students mentioned above donated medical works to the college.[15] In Oxford in 1520, the bookseller John Dorne sold approximately fifteen medical books, about half of them by Galen. On the other hand, this represents a tiny proportion of the works listed in his day-book.[16]

One of the difficulties in maintaining an active teaching faculty in medicine seems to have been that Oxford was not a rich urban centre with a plentiful supply of patients, nor was it adjacent to one. Inevitably, university-educated physicians tended to gravitate to London, and the continuity of teaching was sometimes jeopardized. The university registers show this to have happened on a number of occasions, when there was an insufficient number of medical examiners or an absence of a regent doctor for the granting of medical degrees. As late as 1536, upon the establishment of a regius chair in medicine, the royal commissioners could describe the leaders of Oxford medical teaching as blind men.[17]

In Italy, on the other hand, scholar-physicians held a central place in society, so that for a university town like Padua, with its rich Venetian hinterland of noble patients, long history of medical study, and tradition of civic participation, the number of medical graduates was considerable. The majority of arts students were studying for doctorates in arts and medicine and, on becoming doctors, would be called 'philosophus et medicus.' All the senior chairs in the arts university were medical ones, the chief degree-granting body of the arts university was the college of physicians and philosophers, and the only subject which came near in prestige and importance to medicine was its ancillary and propaedeutic, natural philosophy.

The cosmopolitanism of medical studies at Padua was ensured by the increasing involvement of the Venetian authorities in the running of the *studium*. The Venetians maintained the bar on native Paduans from holding major lectureships and extended it to Venetians as well. This meant that the senior chairs were all filled by outstanding figures from other universities, within Italy or from elsewhere. The incentive to teach in a prestigious university such as Padua was heightened by large salaries. The importance of Venice as a centre of European trade and travel no doubt encouraged this cosmopolitanism; Padua was above all accessible, and known to Englishmen whose country had long enjoyed a tradition of study there and warm relations with Venice. In short, given medicine's centrality in Padua, it would be surprising to find no English students there enjoying its rich medical resources, in terms of books, teachers, camaraderie, and prestige.[18] One of the most important of these students was Thomas Linacre.

Linacre's Italian period is well known. After studies with leading humanists in Florence and Rome, he gained a Paduan degree in medicine in 1496, and from then until his return to England in 1499 was associated with the Aldine 'academy' in Venice. The paucity of the sources for this period of Linacre's life make it impossible to know when and how he was impelled to seek a medical degree, although it has been argued that the existence of several All Souls physicians in the years prior to his departure to Italy suggests that this ambition may be go back to before 1487.[19] On the other hand, both of his teachers in Florence, Angelo Poliziano and Demetrius Chalcondylas, participated in the development of 'medical humanism,' Poliziano by searching for and working on manuscripts of Galen, and by translating Hippocrates' *Aphorisms* with Galen's accompanying commentary, and Chalcondylas by translating Galen's *De anatomicis administrationibus*, the first Latin version which came to be printed.[20] It also seems likely that Poliziano taught Pliny's *Natural History* to Linacre,[21] and it is possible that Linacre met Niccolò Leoniceno in Florence. The latter had stayed in the city some time before 1492 on Poliziano's invitation; Linacre was there with Poliziano from about 1487 to 1490.[22] But it may also have been that Linacre was directed to medicine only after beginning his studies in Padua.

Chalcondylas's interest in the Greek medical corpus may have a significant bearing on the development of Greek studies at Padua, for the university's Greek renaissance began with his appointment to the first chair in Greek there in 1463.[23] In Linacre's time, the holder of this chair was Lorenzo Cretensis ('il Cretico'), perhaps Linacre's most likely teacher at Padua; a comment which suggests that Linacre was taught by Niccolò Leonico Tomeo, the first Paduan professor to lecture on the Greek text of Aristotle, is unreliable. Linacre is linked to other professors at Padua through the record of his degree examination in arts and medicine. The most reputable physician among his 'promotores' on this occasion – though not a particularly humanistic one – would have been Gabriele de Zerbis, who held the first ordinary chair in medical theory from 1494 to 1505. He published four medical works (on gerontology and anatomy) and a volume of *Quaestiones metaphysicae*.[24] The others were Nicoletto Vernia, who held the first ordinary chair in natural philosophy and initiated the Paduan debate on the immortality of the soul, which would have been raging while Linacre studied there;[25] Giovanni dell'Aquila, holder of the first ordinary chair in practical medicine from 1491 to 1506;[26] Pietro Trapolino, author of *De humidi radicali*, holder of the first ordinary chair in medical practice from 1494 to 1504 and the second ordinary chair in medical theory from 1506 to 1517;[27] Lorenzo Noale;[28] Giovanni ab Asta; and Niccolò Teatino.[29]

The beginnings of a rise in medical interests in England coincided with Linacre's return there at the turn of the century. For example, Oxford's first public lectures in medicine were delivered in 1504 by Andrew Alazard, a physician from the university of Montpellier. But more developments can be ascribed to Linacre himself. He was appointed royal physician in 1509; there is a tradition that he lectured publicly at Oxford in 1510; and his eight printed translations of Galen between 1517 and 1524 gained him a reputation across Europe. His activity in founding the College of Physicians of London and his bequest of medical lectureships to the universities of Oxford and Cambridge during the same period both reflect his importation into England of Paduan practice. Indeed the opening section of the College of Physicians' 1518 charter refers explicitly to the Italian precedent[30] and this imitation runs throughout the charter's organization of the college. Beyond these formal aspects, it is clear that Linacre was attempting to structure the place of physicians in society in such a way that the medical profession would acquire power and prestige, discipline, and regularization along Italian lines.[31] Likewise his lecture courses were divided into junior lectures on the theory of medicine drawn from Galen and senior lectures on the practice of medicine, as in Padua. And more generally, the realization that the lack of medical teaching in the English universities was due to the absence of a 'substantial and perpetual lecture' must have been inspired by the success of regular lectureships at Padua.[32]

Furthermore, among Linacre's closest associates an awareness of the medical component in the new learning is evident. Bishop Richard Fox's foundation of 1517, Corpus Christi, became Oxford's most humanistic college, providing for public lectureships in humanity, Greek, and theology; the leading offices of the college were to be a president and vice-president, as in the College of Physicians founded in the following year. Corpus Christi was the first college to set aside a fellowship for a medical scholar and to exempt him by statute from the necessity of taking religious orders; the college's statutes also provided the opportunity for the study of ancient languages in Italy. Corpus's first president, the commentator on Pliny John Claymond, was a friend of Linacre's to whom the physician wrote one of his few extant letters, and Fox was a patient of Linacre's to whom Linacre dedicated a copy of his translation of Galen's *De sanitate tuenda* in 1518; the dedicatory letter encouraged Fox to maintain his health the Galenic way so that he could accomplish his great design: by this he presumably meant the success of the new college.[33]

The statutes of Cardinal Wolsey's college likewise permitted the study of medicine and provided for a public lecturer on the subject.[34] Linacre was also Wolsey's physician; he wrote a letter of dedication to him with his *De sanitate tuenda*, and had printed a dedication to him at the front of his rendering of Galen's *De pulsum usu* in 1522. Finally, the only non-physician noted among the petitioners for the College of Physicians in Henry VIII's letters patent was Wolsey.

More theoretical perceptions of the utility of humanistic medical studies were also current amongst Linacre's humanist associates. For example, in the oration in praise of Greek studies delivered in around 1519 by Richard Croke, Cambridge University's first reader in Greek, the perceived connection between Greek studies and medicine is very explicit:

Medicine urges me on and bids me to speak out against those unskilled in Greek, as she is about to exact a bitter punishment from them, who have so often turned her precepts, invented for mortal health, to its destruction, and have taken it so far that just as they once approved of her after good trial, now they condemn her before any experience, as if she were a butcher and executioner, with the many savage burnings and cuttings which those are accustomed to practise who have never read Galen, Hippocrates, Aeginetes or Dioscorides in the way in which these can be understood, that is in Greek. With their back-slidings into barbarism and their too credulous belief in the delusions of translators, it is their fault that today the men of this most noble profession appear to be experimenting with our lives and to be learning at the peril of humanity.[35]

Beyond Linacre himself other Englishmen with a Paduan education participated in this medical revival. As already mentioned, the extant university records of English students of arts and medicine in Padua are very unsatisfactory and as such admit to few certainties. Inevitably the English medical students known to have studied at Padua are those who reached the top of their profession on their return to England and have thus left other documentary traces of their activities. But these individuals are of considerable significance. Physicians with a foreign degree comprised a tiny elite of medical practitioners in England.[36] The extant record suggests that those with a Paduan degree were more numerous than those with medical degrees from other foreign universities. Furthermore, they were successful in finding influential and prestigious patients and appointments in the centres of English courtly and medical life, and especially in the College of Physicians.

The first of these after Linacre is John Chamber, who gained his MD in Padua in 1505. Chamber's Paduan degree is unsurprising in light of Merton College's unusually vigorous tradition of medical education; as the college's annals have demonstrated, Chamber went to Padua specifically for medical purposes. He went on to become a royal physician and it was probably in this capacity that he first met Thomas Linacre, together with whom he was a founder of the College of Physicians in 1518. Chamber was president of the Barber-Surgeons' Guild of London at its incorporation in 1541, and was represented as such in Holbein's painting of the granting of the charter by Henry VIII. His only known writings form part of a collaborative manuscript pharmacopoeia of plasters, lotions, and unguents compiled with three other royal physicians, Doctors Butts, Cromer, and Agostini.[37]

In the 1520s, after the closure of the Paduan *studium* during the Venetian wars, English students in Padua included one 'Adrianus Britanus,' who graduated in medicine in April 1525,[38] and, perhaps also dating from this period, the 'Augustinus Paitonus medicus' to whom John Leland wrote one of his *encomia*, commenting on his and Linacre's time in Padua.[39] But the most significant evidence of English medical activity associated with the Paduan *studium* in this period emerges from the printing of the *editio princeps* of the Greek Galen by the Aldine press in 1525. In the prefatory letter to the fifth volume, addressed to the chief editor Giovan Battista Opizo, the head of the Aldine press, Andrea Torresani, mentions the editorial help of four Britons: 'Clementus,' 'Odoardus,' 'Roseus,' and 'Lupsetus.'[40]

The origins and influence of the publication have been investigated,[41] and yet a question mark hovers over the most salient fact for the purposes of this discussion: how did it come to pass that four out of the five editorial assistants on one of the most ambitious undertakings of the Aldine press and one of the major events in the history of the Galenic revival came from England? With problems of identification excepted, this is an easier question to answer from the English perspective than it is from the Italian, for all four English editors emerge in Italy directly from humanist Oxford.

John Clement was one of the first pupils at St Paul's School under its first master, William Lily (whose son stayed in Padua in the 1530s and from 1548 became the most important transmitter of the English humanist heritage to an Italian readership). Thomas More took Clement into his household in about 1514 as a servant-pupil and then as tutor to his children. Clement's abilities in Greek are attested by the fact that in 1516 or 1517 he was teaching the language to John Colet.[42] In 1518 he was appointed Cardinal Wolsey's first reader of rhetoric and humanity, residing in Corpus Christi until 1520, at which date, according to More, he had given himself up entirely to the study of medicine.[43] An early friendship with Reginald Pole and, perhaps on the part of both Pole and Clement, an early interest in medicine, are suggested by More's 1518 letter to both of them, thanking them for acquiring a medical prescription for More.[44] There is an obvious connection between Clement's commencement of medical studies in 1520 and his arrival in Padua two years later, since both took place in the context of an *alma mater* which expressly encouraged the study of the subject.[45] Moreover, the record of Henry VIII's grant to Clement to study 'ultra mare' in 1525–6 demonstrates that the king himself was interested in the promotion of medical studies.[46] This may well have been under the influence of Linacre, Wolsey, Fox, or More, although the king's employment of several foreign physicians, including the Italians Agostino de'Agostini and Balthasar Guercie, suggests an awareness on his part of the superiority of European and especially Italian medicine.[47] In any case, it is of the greatest significance that of the royal scholars sent abroad in the 1520s, one was a physician.[48] In the event, Clement's MD of 1525 was acquired from Siena,[49] although he was in the Veneto in that period. Not only does his identifiable work on the Aldine Galen suggest so, but a letter of Niccolò Leonico Tomeo's to Reginald Pole has him delivering a copy of More's *Utopia* to Leonico's house in Padua.[50] While in Italy Clement was acquainted with Christophe de Longueil and Andrea Navagero,[51] and collected a large number of Greek works and Latin translations, some of them Aldine and many of them works of medicine and natural philosophy, including a manuscript of Galen later used by his friend

John Caius.[52] His subsequent career is well known, and follows a pattern already suggested by the careers of Linacre and Chamber. He was admitted a fellow of the College of Physicians in 1528 and became its president in 1544, and was also appointed physician to the king.[53]

Thomas Lupset was another pupil of St Paul's who went on to Pembroke Hall in Cambridge. It has been conjectured that he went with Richard Pace to Italy in 1515, but he was definitely studying in Paris in 1517, where he supervised the printing of More's *Utopia*. In 1520 he succeeded Clement as Wolsey's reader in humanity in Oxford, residing from 1519 to 1522 in Corpus Christi College. He arrived in Padua in 1523, possibly as tutor to Wolsey's illegitimate son, Thomas Winter, and became a member of Pole's household there. Although Lupset was not moving in such a determinedly medical world as Clement, his experience of seeing Linacre's translation of Galen's *De sanitate tuenda* through the press in Paris in 1517 would have been useful in his work on the Aldine Galen.[54] That he is mentioned separately from the other English 'centuriones' in the preface to the Aldine Galen may suggest that his capacity on the project was different to that of the other three English medical students (although as it happens, our knowledge of specific contributions to the work among these Englishmen is limited to the emendations of John Clement).[55]

Two likely identifications have been presented in the secondary literature for 'Odoardus,' but it is now clear that the name refers not to David Edwardes but to Edward Wotton, whose presence in the Veneto in 1525 is recorded through his MD examination at Padua in that year, witnessed by Thomas Starkey, Nicholas Wilson, Roger Smith, Robert Chaloner, and Robert Birch. In 1521 Wotton had become the first reader in Greek at Corpus Christi College, although in the same year Bishop Fox made him a *socio compar* of Corpus, giving him leave to travel in Italy for three or five years, primarily to study Greek.[56] Wotton was admitted a fellow of the College of Physicians in 1528, was president from 1541 to 1543, and was appointed physician to Henry VIII and Princess Mary. His friendship with Pole is attested by the fact that he looked after Pole's financial affairs during the period of Pole's absence from England.[57] He later achieved a Europe-wide reputation for his work of zoology, *De differentiis animalium*, printed in Paris in 1552.[58] His identity with the 'Odoardus' of the Aldine Galen is clinched by his testimony that Georg Agricola had been a friend and familiar of his.[59]

The two possibilities for the identity of 'Roseus' – William Rose and Anthony Rose – have also been reduced to one by Vivian Nutton.[60]

William Rose, as a fellow of Oriel College, shares with the others an Oxford provenance, and in an epigram dedicated to him by John Constable and published in 1520 he is praised as 'philosophus, astrologus et medicus.'[61] Notices of him in Oxford cease in 1521 and he died in Rome in 1525.[62] He has been linked to the figure on whom Thomas More based his pseudonym, Guilielmus Rosseus, for his *Responsio ad Lutherum* of 1523.[63] By the time of Ro. Ba.'s *Life of Sir Thomas More* of 1599, he has been transformed into a 'mad companion that then wandered in italie and for the manner of his behaviour was well knowne of most men.'[64]

The humanist associations of these Englishmen are therefore clear. All four came from Oxford, and three of them were members of Oxford's new humanistic foundation, Corpus Christi. But a few extant biographical details suggest that at least three of these Englishmen were in the Veneto for the specific purpose of studying medicine. As mentioned above, Rose was already being called 'medicus' by 1520, while still in Oxford, and Clement had given himself up entirely to medicine by the same year. Lupset never went in the same direction, his commitments remaining in the fields of education, classical scholarship, moral philosophy, and patristic theology. For Wotton the evidence is less clear, but it is likely that an interest at least in natural philosophy was stimulated in him by John Claymond, with whom he would have had long association, first as a schoolboy of Magdalen College School, then as an undergraduate, BA (1514), and fellow (1516) of Magdalen College, of which Claymond was then president. Claymond wrote an extensive commentary on Pliny's *Historia naturalis*, which was one of Wotton's sources in his *De differentiis animalium*.[65]

It is very likely that it was Thomas Linacre who advanced their participation on the Aldine Galen. Linacre's association with Bishop Fox and Corpus Christi College has already been mentioned. A further connection between Linacre, Corpus Christi, and English students in Padua is suggested by the fact that some time between 1518 and 1520, Reginald Pole was taught by Linacre.[66] Pole himself is said to have resided in the lodgings of the president of Magdalen College, John Claymond,[67] was present at the founding ceremony of Corpus Christi in 1517, when its first president, the same Claymond, was appointed, and was made a fellow of the college, *in absentia*, in 1523.[68] In 1521 Christophe de Longueil wrote to Linacre from Padua to thank him for a gift brought to him from England by Reginald Pole and remarked on Linacre's hospitality to him in England the previous year.[69] Moreover, in the 1520s Linacre and Niccolò Leonico Tomeo were in correspondence. Finally, connections can be established between Linacre, on the one hand, and Lupset and Clement, on the other. Clement, for example, had dealings with Linacre in the latter's capacity as the executor of William Grocyn's will, and was a trustee of two of the properties acquired by Linacre for the endowment of his Oxford lectureship.[70] According to More, Linacre had praised Clement for the standard of his lecturing in Oxford.[71] As mentioned above, Lupset had been present at the printing of Linacre's Galen in Paris in 1517. Given these connections, perhaps the later high profiles of both Clement and Wotton in the College of Physicians represented the fulfilment of some kind of obligation to Linacre.

Furthermore, we know that during the last years of his life one of Linacre's preoccupations was the systemization and secure foundation of medical activity in England. His impulses in this direction, the founding of the College of Physicians and the bequest of medical lectureships to Oxford and Cambridge, were designed to ensure a high standard of native medicine responsible to a professional body and the opportunities for Englishmen to study the corpus of medical learning. In the meantime, the low standard of medical education in England would have rendered foreign training, in Linacre's view, an obvious necessity. He died in October 1524, in the midst of business concerning the Cambridge lectureship. Torresani acquired the licence to publish the Greek Galen from the Venetian authorities in June of the same year.[72] There was time, therefore, for Linacre to have advanced English medicine through the Aldine Galen. He was in an excellent position to do so, having been a member of Aldo's household in the 1490s, during the formative period of Venetian Hellenism.

The Aldine publications with which Linacre was associated were the *editio princeps* of the Greek Aristotle (1495–8) and the 1499 edition of pseudo-Proclus's *Sphaera*, which Linacre himself had translated for Aldo.[73] In the preface of the Aristotle edition, Linacre is praised for his erudition only lines before Aldo states the intention of bringing out a complete edition of Galen.[74] In the preface to the *Sphaera*, Aldo celebrates Linacre as exemplifying British participation in the great endeavour of renewing learned arts and letters in Italy. Since barbarous letters first came into Italy from Britain, 'the wound will be healed by the very spear that inflicted it.'[75] In the 1525 Galen edition, Linacre is again commemorated by Andrea Torresani as a member of Aldo's household and a devotee of Galen. Could this recollection of the Englishman rest on more than his European reputation or Andreas's thirty-year-old memories? Little is certain about Linacre's life, but we do know that after his return to England he maintained contact with two ex-Aldine academicians, Girolamo Aleandro and Ambrogio Leone di Nola.[76]

The scholarly reception of the Aldine Galen was equivocal. Praise of the achievement of making all of Galen's work available in Greek was mixed with condemnation of philological standards. Erasmus was a vehement critic. His complaint that Torresani had produced the work on the cheap by not hiring a truly scholarly editor implies a slur on the philological capacities of all the editors and makes the English participation seem like little more than cheap labour.[77] Giovanni Manardi, Niccolò Leoniceno's successor at the *studium* of Ferrara, found the Greek codex 'ubique erroribus maculatus.'[78] Georg Agricola, who by 1529 had written his own emendations to the text,[79] failed to mention his own participation in the project when noting that of 'quorundam Anglorum' in his *Bermannus*.[80] Arguing backwards, it is tempting to suppose a perverse fulfilment of Linacre's educational initiatives in the failings of the Aldine Galen. Might not these failings have resulted from the shortcomings of the English medical humanist education which Linacre may have hoped to put right precisely by sending these Englishmen to the Aldine press? In the late 1510s teachers of Greek in England were few and embattled. In 1517 William Latimer had resisted the urgings of More and Erasmus to undertake to teach Greek to Bishop Fisher, arguing that to make real progress in the subject Fisher should send for an Italian.[81] In the following year Oxford Graecists were lampooned by More's 'Trojans.'[82] Croke's two orations on Greek studies, probably delivered to the university of Cambridge in 1519, are defensive in tone.[83] But with the establishment of the Corpus lectureships it is difficult to find similar evidence for the 1520s, and in any case Wotton and probably Rose, Clement, and Lupset had been in Italy for four, three, and two years respectively before the Aldine Galen was printed.[84] Furthermore, the European reputations of Wotton, Clement, and Lupset as Greek scholars were, or came to be, extraordinarily high. Agricola, for example, thought Clement the most promising of the new generation of medical humanists, an opinion which could only have been formed from time spent with him at the Aldine press.[85] Moreover, as Vivian Nutton has established, there were other reasons for the Aldine Galen's shortcomings, such as the limited number of manuscripts used despite the availability of others in the area.[86] If employees of the Aldine press worked as long hours as Erasmus suggested in his satire of the firm, the colloquy 'Opulentia sordida' of 1531, then Clement's story of wax dripping onto a part of the copy while the printer took a nap is wholly credible.[87] This huge and expensive project was evidently rushed.

The attraction of Paduan medicine to Englishmen, however, continued. In the 1530s English medical students at Padua included Paul Rutland, who gained a medical degree in 1531,[88] and Thomas Bill, who gained his MD in 1533 and became a physician to Henry VIII and Edward VI, attending the Princess Elizabeth in 1549. In 1543 he was elected censor and councillor of the College of Physicians.[89] John Friar was another Cambridge MA who was poached by Wolsey for his new Oxford college in 1525 and studied medicine in Padua from 1533, gaining his MD there in 1536.[90] Friar was made a fellow of the College of Physicians in the year in which he graduated and held a number of its offices until he became president in 1549–50. He was considered both an outstanding Graecist and physician,[91] and was the author of a Latin translation of Hippocrates's *Aphorisms*, written in verse as an *aide de memoire*, presumably for students who were expected to master this basic medical text.[92] This period of English medical study culminates with John Caius, later the founder of Gonville and Caius College, court physician, long-time president of the College of Physicians, and formidable hunter of Galenic texts and emendator of the Galenic corpus. He was studying for a medical doctorate in Padua from 1539 to 1541.[93] After Caius gained his doctorate, he held one of the Paduan chairs of philosophy from 1542 to 1543, lecturing on the Greek text of Aristotle, and went on to forge numerous contacts on manuscript-hunting expeditions throughout Italy. In Padua the 'promotores' for his doctoral examination were Giunio Paulo Crasso, Girolamo de Urbino, Odo de Odis, Francesco Frigimelica, and Ludovico Pasino.[94] He shared a house in the city with the great anatomist Andreas Vesalius, and recalled the leading Galenist of his age, Giovan Battista da Monte, as his teacher,[95] and Realdus Columbus – the successor of Vesalius in Paduan anatomy – as his colleague.[96] In the philological element of medical humanism Caius brought Linacre's tradition full circle. In his *De libris propriis*, a bibliographical autobiography consciously written in imitation of Galen's book of the same name, Caius associated himself with the cumulative work of emendation pursued by his predecessors Linacre and personal friend John Clement.[97] Galen's works remained canonical at Padua, but Caius's English successors there did not share his zeal for medical philology.

Despite the fact that on Caius's initiative his Cambridge college, Gonville and Caius, permitted medical fellows to study abroad,[98] in the decades following his own sojourn in the city the number of English medical students at Padua was small, partly as a consequence of both new opportunities for studying the subject in England and the rise of other European centres of medical study. This pattern also reflects a general shift away from humanistic study and 'arts' subjects and towards law and informal studies of contemporary Italian life and letters among English students at Padua. The Reformation also had its part to play in limiting English attendance. Other than the possible student of medicine Henry Knolles, until the late 1580s there are only a few certainties after Caius. One is the botanist and physician William Turner, though the importance of his time in Padua in the early 1540s may be doubted; his experiences at Bologna and Ferrara were clearly more significant for him. Another is Gilbert Scheneus, a friend of Richard White in Padua in the early 1560s. A third is Robert Persons, who briefly studied medicine in Padua in 1574, before going to Rome and joining the Society of Jesus.[99] His companion George Lewkenor probably also studied medicine at Padua at the same time. Thomas Friar, the son of John Friar, was a Catholic exile who gained a Paduan doctorate in medicine in 1570.[100] Edward Ratcliffe possibly spent some time in Padua in the early 1580s before acquiring a doctorate in medicine from the university of Orleans. And there is a somewhat mysterious John 'Froso,' who was in Padua around 1586.

Edward Jordan's acquisition of a Paduan medical doctorate in around 1591 inaugurated a much more intensive and extremely productive period of English medical study in Padua, and one in which Cambridge colleges, reversing the earlier trend, are more conspicuous patrons than Oxford ones.[101] Jordan went on to write two scholarly medical works. One, *A brief discourse of a disease called the suffocation of the mother*, first printed in 1603, argues from ancient and contemporary medical authorities that possession by evil spirits can be explained by natural causes in the body; it draws heavily on Italian physicians, including the Paduan professors Alessandro Benedetti, Vettore Trincavello, and Alberto Bottono, the last of whom was teaching at Padua while Jordan was a student there.[102] Jordan's other work was a technical treatise on English baths, *A discourse of natural baths and mineral waters*. In Jordan's involvement in the College of Physicians of London a typical career path can be discerned, though as late as 1595 the college would only give him licence to practise on condition that he study works by Galen and Hippocrates. Jordan was admitted a fellow of the college in 1597, just as a number of other English students were studying or about to study medicine in Padua. These include John Frear, who was present in Padua in 1595 and acquired his doctorate there in 1610, William Clement, who acquired his degree in 1599, Thomas Hearne and William Harvey, who acquired theirs in 1602, Matthew Lister, also present in Padua in that year, and Simeon Foxe, who was present in Padua from 1601 and gained his degree there probably in 1604. Each of these was admitted to, and all but one held high office in, the College of Physicians, Foxe becoming its president. Others went on to careers in England in other contexts. Joseph Webb, who acquired a Paduan degree in arts and medicine in 1603, became a Latin grammarian. Peter Mounsel, present in Padua in 1602, was appointed Professor of Physic at Gresham College in London in 1605. Joseph Lister, in Padua in 1597, went on to practise medicine in York. A significant number of these combined a period in Padua with visits to Leiden and Basle. Other English students of medicine do not resurface in English contexts: Nicholas Calwoodley, who gained his Paduan medical doctorate in 1597, died abroad in around 1622; James Gomund, described as a lover of medicine on his matriculation in Padua in 1599, disappears from view altogether, as does Edward Benedict, who acquired his doctorate in medicine in 1601.[103]

The writings of the Gonville and Caius College fellow William Harvey and the large secondary literature on him testify to the importance of Padua for his work, and also provide us with the most comprehensive picture of the type of medical teaching that he and these other English students experienced.[104] One of the strongest features of his education at Padua, and one which already had an illustrious tradition there when he arrived was anatomy. By his own testimony, Harvey's most important teacher in this context was Fabricius ab Acquapendente, who had been responsible for the establishment of Padua's anatomical theatre in 1594 (the first ever permanent one), and whom Harvey considered an inspiration for him second only in authority to Aristotle himself. It is more than likely that Harvey attended Fabricius's dissections. Fabricius wrote on two of the central subjects of Harvey's later work, the cardiovascular system and animal generation, in both cases reassessing the writings of Aristotle on these subjects. And he was working on the venous valves while Harvey was in Padua, publishing his *De venarum astiolis* there in 1603.[105]

Aristotle in general was central to Harvey, though historians have disagreed about what his Aristotelianism consisted of, to what extent it represented a turning away from Galen, and how critical it was of the philosopher himself. Some historians see Harvey as heavily indebted to

Aristotle's method and discussions of method, whether this be to his teleology and logic of proof[106] or to his appeal to sense perception as a final authority.[107] Some have emphasized the extent to which Aristotle's animal books offered a body of knowledge which was both useful for Harvey and an inspiration for further research,[108] others the extent to which Aristotle's conception of the soul was drawn on by Harvey.[109] While there is consensus that Harvey preferred Aristotle to Galen, differences of emphasis on this point also remain, some historians detecting a critical but creative use of Galen's methodology and doctrine in Harvey, others seeing him as basically anti-Galenic.[110]

Certainly it is clear that the older views of Harvey as a proto-mechanist and an anti-Aristotelian were wrong-headed:[111] Harvey stands at least as much at the end of a Renaissance tradition as he does at the beginning of the 'Scientific Revolution.' For Charles Schmitt, for example, Harvey was 'the last major innovator in science who adhered so closely to the spirit of Aristotelian philosophy and who benefited so directly from the peripatetic tradition.'[112]

In all the debates about Harvey's work, a range of professors at Padua have been seen as mediators. From before his period in Padua there are Vesalius, Giovan Battista da Monte, and Giacomo Zabarella,[113] while potential teachers of his include Francesco Piccolomini,[114] Cesalpino,[115] Giulio Pace,[116] Cesare Cremonini,[117] Thomas Minadous, and Julius Casserius, the last three of whom are cited in his works, and the last two having acted as 'promotores' at his doctoral examination.[118] While there is general consensus – not least because Harvey says so himself – that Fabricius as an inspirer towers over these, it is also worth mentioning that John Aubrey added to the names of Harvey's teachers at Padua Eustachio Rudio; though Aubrey is generally unreliable, his mention of Rudio is unusual and consequently worthy of consideration, especially as Rudio was indeed teaching in Padua in Harvey's period there and wrote, among other things, on the heart and blood.[119]

While very little specific information is extant on the education of Harvey's compatriots in the Paduan medical faculty, what we do have shows a strong identity of interests with his studies there. A striking example is the record of medical texts chosen for Joseph Webb to be examined on in April 1603. They cover two of Harvey's central concerns, referring to a passage from Aristotle's *De anima*, I.3.2, on the movement of things and on the movement of the soul, and from Avicenna's *Canon*, 1.1.4, on Galen's and Avicenna's views on the importance of the blood as a body fluid.[120] What this and Harvey's medical education at Padua confirm is the extraordinary and ongoing vitality of the Aristotelian tradition there and also the centrality of natural philosophy. Consequently, it was not only career physicians at Padua who benefited from the university's medicine-oriented culture. The following discussion considers the interests of those English students who drew on Paduan medical and natural philosophical thought in contexts which were not themselves medical.

Henry Cuffe is one such student from around Harvey's time. A pupil and colleague of Henry Savile's in Oxford in the late 1570s and 1580s, Cuffe had been appointed Regius Professor of Greek in 1590, later became a client of the earl of Essex, and was implicated in his rebellion. Like a significant number of other members of the Essex circle, Cuffe matriculated at Padua in 1597. In 1600 he wrote a work of natural philosophy which was printed posthumously in 1607 as *The differences of the ages of man's life*. It is impossible to establish a precise relationship between this philosophically eclectic work – which draws on Plato, Aristotle, Galen, the hermetic writers, Averroes, Avicenna, Paracelsus, and Ficino – and Cuffe's studies in Padua, but the relationship itself is surely embedded in the work; this is strongly suggested by Cuffe's long discussions of issues such as the question of the eternity of the world and the mortality of man, and the physiological and humoural conditions which contribute to human longevity. All of these were central preoccupations of the Paduan school of arts and medicine. Among Englishmen such interests can be detected earlier in the century as well. Though his own humanistic output was not in the field of science, Richard Pace, a student at Padua from around 1498 to 1501, at Ferrara under Niccolò Leoniceno in 1508, and afterwards a friend of Thomas Linacre,[121] articulated the medical humanists' standard case for Greek studies in his humanistic *De fructu qui ex doctrina percipitur*:

But O you young men who intend to be physicians, be sure that you study Greek as well as Latin. For all the sciences in which the Romans wrote something flowed from the fountains of Greece, and this one especially. So you'll hardly be able to understand anything about it if you don't know Greek. If you disregard it, you'll be one of those physicians who literally get away with murder.[122]

At Padua Pace was one of a large number of Englishmen to be taught by the philosopher Niccolò Leonico Tomeo, who inspired a considerable

English interest in medicine's propaedeutic, natural philosophy. While Leonico and his wider significance for English students at Padua will be discussed in chapter 4, it is worthwhile to point out here his own interest in medicine and natural philosophy and the ways in which this interest may have been transmitted to his English students. The determining event in this respect is Leonico's famous appointment in 1497 as Padua's first lecturer on the Greek texts of Aristotle's medical and philosophical works, an appointment which, coming from the Venetian Senate, was probably connected to the Aldine publication of the Greek Aristotle in these years. Contemporary recollections of this event suggest that it was the determining moment in his career and in the history of Greek studies at Padua, elevating as it did the intellectual thrust of humanistic Hellenism to the institutional level, and preparing the ground for the replacement of the medieval tradition of Aristotelian science.[123] Leonico's publications included Latin translations and commentaries of Aristotle's *Parva naturalia* dedicated to Pace,[124] the first book of Aristotle's *De partibus animalium*,[125] Aristotle's *De animalium motione* and *De animalium incessu*,[126] and his own *Quaestiones naturales*,[127] works regarded as remarkable for the lucidity of their humanistic style, faithfulness to the original texts, and reversion to Greek commentators such as John Philopponus and Alexander of Aphrodisias.[128] To these works can probably be added his edition of a translation of Galen's *De puero epileptico*, published posthumously.[129] Leonico's *Dialogi*, dedicated to Reginald Pole and printed in Venice in 1524, contain a medical discussion which draws on Galen, Paolo d'Egina, Dioscorides, Theophrastus, and Pliny and which insists on the importance of a purified Greek and Latin style for the reclamation of the classical medical heritage. Leonico shared these interests with the major personalities of his intellectual environment; together with Pietro Bembo and Andrea Navagero, he is recorded as having attended the lectures of the Spanish philosopher Johannes Montesdoch on Aristotle's *De caelo*, at Padua in 1523.[130]

Richard Croke's testimony of 1530 that Leonico taught Linacre at Padua is almost certainly negated by the air of unfamiliarity between the two men which emerges from Leonico's letter to Linacre of 1524.[131] Nevertheless, Croke was certainly right when he mentioned William Latimer and Cuthbert Tunstall as two other of Leonico's students.[132] In the later correspondence between Leonico and Latimer, it is noted that the two Englishmen had attended Leonico's lectures on the *Parva naturalia*.[133] Since Latimer and Tunstall arrived in Padua in 1497 or after – whereas by then Linacre was with the Aldine press in Venice – the chronology of their relationship suggests that the origins of Leonico's three decades of inspiration of English scholarship reside in his 1497 appointment. Most of Leonico's broader humanistic, Platonic, literary, and patristic interests emerged in a later period; in the late 1490s he was primarily – though not exclusively – a teacher of Greek and of Aristotelian natural philosophy. This suggests that the interests of Latimer and Tunstall in his teaching were also primarily philosophical, and represent a redirection from the scholastic Aristotelianism to which they would have been exposed in Oxford and Cambridge. While the evidence for Tunstall's and Latimer's period in Padua tends to be miscellaneous and fragmentary, Aristotelian interests feature in both of their early intellectual biographies. For example, on the evidence of Latimer's letter to Aldo Manuzio of 1498, P.S. Allen suggested that Latimer as well as Linacre may have taken part in producing the great Aldine edition of Aristotle which appeared between 1495 and 1498.[134] He links this to a more credible possibility from an authoritative source, George Lily, son of the early Tudor humanist William Lily, that Linacre, Grocyn, and Latimer planned a Latin translation of the complete works of Aristotle which never came to fruition.[135] One of the two books which Latimer borrowed from the Vatican Library in 1510 contained the *Ethics* of Aristotle;[136] Leland's *encomium* to Latimer also suggests Aristotelian interests.[137] Finally, Leonico's testimony to one of Latimer's Italian friendships while in Padua, with the Brescian humanist and professor Domenico Bonomini, may suggest medical or natural philosophical interests on his behalf. In the process of telling Latimer about his newly published *Dialogi*, Leonico mentions that the medical dialogue, 'De Alica,' is dedicated to Latimer and conducted with Bonomini, with whom Latimer had been very friendly.[138]

Tunstall's connections with both Leonico and Aldo likewise suggest an interest in Aristotelian philosophy, a suggestion confirmed by the books in Tunstall's library[139] and his own later compendium of the *Nichomachean Ethics*. Tunstall's friends at Padua included the law students Antonio Surian and Jerome Busleyden, but also the physician Giovanni Pietro da Mantova, father of Marco Mantova Benavides.[140]

In the second phase of English humanism in Padua in the 1520s, Leonico was closely associated with two of the editors of the Aldine Galen. In a letter of Leonico's to Reginald Pole in 1524, 'Clemens noster' had visited Leonico's house bearing a copy of More's *Utopia*. His intimate correspondence with Lupset dates from the same period. In one letter Lupset supplies him with a name he had evidently requested, that

of the president of Corpus Christi College, himself a natural philosopher.[141] Furthermore, indications of exchanges of texts between Leonico
and the Aldine press suggest a discreet involvement by Leonico in the
project of the Aldine Galen. In a letter to Reginald Pole of 1524 Leonico
claimed to have reread the works of Galen which related to philosophy,
a rereading which, he says, made him realize just how good Plato and
Aristotle were.[142] It has been suggested that Leonico might have acquired
these manuscripts of Galen from the library of the medical humanist
Niccolò Leoniceno and that he subsequently passed them on to the
Aldine press for use on their edition.[143] Leonico had done this before: a
Bessarion volume of Ammonius, Simplicius, and Philopponus commen-
taries on Aristotle was only retrieved from Leonico after thirty years by
Pietro Bembo, the librarian of the St Mark's library. In the interim
Leonico had leant the manuscript to Aldo for the 1504 edition of
Philopponus.[144]

Natural philosophy engaged other English members of Leonico's
circle in the 1520s. The scanty record of the studies of his most
important English student, Reginald Pole, has Pole reading some of
Aristotle's *libri naturales* with Leonico.[145] Moreover, if Pole is the author
of the *Vita Longolii* as seems likely,[146] he was certainly aware of
Christophe de Longueil's interests in botany and zoology, for the *Vita*
records Longueil's travels around Europe to identify and verify the
plants and fishes described in Pliny's *Natural History*.[147] Furthermore, in
1522 Pole came into possession of Longueil's library, which went on,
after Pole's death, to enrich the humanistic holdings of New College and
Corpus Christi College, Oxford. Longueil's collection contains a number
of important medical books, including works by Celsus and translations
of Galen by Niccolò Leoniceno.[148] Pole's huge collection of Greek
manuscripts includes a number of commentaries on Aristotle's *libri
naturales* in which Alexander of Aphrodisias, the authority on whom
Leonico drew so extensively, is strongly represented, although it is not
clear precisely when Pole acquired these.[149]

Another friend of Leonico's was Thomas Starkey, who was probably
in Padua from 1523 to 1526 and again from circa 1532 to 1534. He is a
more interesting case in the analysis of the Paduan medical impact on
Englishmen because his subsequent life and writings have to a large
extent determined historians' perceptions of Padua's contribution to
English humanism in this period. The earliest examination of Starkey's
work in the light of his Paduan experience was by Gordon Zeeveld in
his *Foundations of Tudor Policy* of 1948. This work attempted to establish

the continuity of English humanism in the period after the execution of Thomas More through an examination of Pole's crisis over the royal divorce and supremacy, the drift to Cromwell of some of Pole's friends in the 1530s, and the intellectual content of their work as Cromwellian servants. Among the latter was Thomas Starkey. According to Zeeveld, Starkey emerged out of the rich intellectual environment of Pole's Paduan household, turned against Pole under the pressure of the polarization engendered by the royal divorce, and in the process evolved, in his writings, the Anglican *via media*. This line was more or less the orthodox one until the publication in 1989 of Thomas Mayer's *Thomas Starkey and the Common Weal*. Mayer's infinitely more sophisticated and detailed analysis of the Paduan milieu led him to present Starkey's intellectual formation in Padua in the 1520s and his resulting *Dialogue between Pole and Lupset* mainly in terms of his contact with Italian 'civic humanists' or his exposure to their ideas.[150] For Mayer, Starkey was 'the most Italianate Englishman of his generation and among the most eager importers of Italian concepts in the sixteenth century.'[151]

This approach is problematic, based as it largely is on inferences drawn from Starkey's better documented political activities of the 1530s. It assumes that the 'politic life' was long an ambition for Starkey; his *Dialogue* represents a landmark in his personal political maturation. But while the *Dialogue* indeed betrays the influence of contemporary Italian republican, and especially Venetian, thought, there is no evidence whatsoever that during Starkey's years in Padua in the 1520s he had any contact with any of the political thinkers who were in the city, nor indeed with anyone with a demonstrable political orientation of any kind. It is asking far too much of the evidence to guess that his friendship with Pole provided Starkey with an entry into 'civil' or 'civic' society, as Mayer would imply. With some few exceptions, the record suggests that Pole's Italian friends had little or no acquaintance with other Englishmen in Padua.[152] This is not surprising: Pole himself was feted by Erasmus, Bembo, the pope, and the doge, but he was a cousin of the king of England.[153] Starkey, the relatively humble doctoral student, had no such credentials, and one would surely expect to find him not among the great and the good, but among other students or teachers of his chosen subject. In any case, none of Pole's Italian friends comprised Padua's 'civic humanists,' whatever criteria may be employed to identify this group. Indeed it would be difficult to find a more disengaged crew than Pietro Bembo, Trifone Gabriele, Romolo Amaseo, Giovanbattista Cibò, and Ermete Stampa.

The fact that Starkey was probably not in Padua for as long as Mayer has suggested and left soon after gaining his doctorate mitigates further against both Mayer's hypothesis of a substantial exposure to Paduan 'civic humanism' and his suggestion that the *Dialogue* was written almost immediately after Starkey's first Paduan sojourn. Mayer's supposed departure date for Pole of 1528 is based on undated letters of Pole's to Romolo Amaseo which have been misdated by the editors of *Letters and Papers of the Reign of Henry the Eighth*.[154] The last of these letters is written from England; it mentions the Sack of Rome and invites Amaseo to teach at Wolsey's new Oxford college, so must be dated in or after 1527. But the second letter was sent from Padua to Bologna and dated in *Letters and Papers* as 1528. In this letter Pole hopes to arrange a meeting between Amaseo and the 'English ambassador' – surely a reference to Pace, Pole's close friend – and to have letters delivered by Marmaduke Waldby. Yet Marmaduke's movements in Italy are traceable only to the period 1524–6, Pace had left Italy in the summer of 1525, while Amaseo was not installed at Bologna until 1524. The letter must have been written within these two years.[155] Furthermore, the correspondences of Erasmus, Bembo, and Leonico incontrovertibly prove that Pole left Padua in August or September 1526. In a letter of Bembo's of July of that year, he is still in Padua, but by October, according to John Botzheim, he had already left Constance; by May 1527, according to Germanus Brixius, 'apud suos Anglos vivat.'[156] Mayer believed that Starkey left Padua with Pole, and this still seems possible: he had got what he had come for by 1525 – a doctorate – and in 1529 was to be found with Pole in Paris.[157] Leonico's letter to Starkey of April 1529 records the receipt of a letter from Starkey from London dated November 1528 and complains that this had been the first letter from Starkey for a long time, implying that Starkey had been out of Padua for a long time.[158] Furthermore, a royal payment to a Thomas Starkey as one of the king's 'officers in Wales,' noticed by Herrtage, would have him back in England by as early as 1526.[159]

How, then, did Starkey come to write his political tract? This question requires an examination of the evidence relating to Starkey in the 1510s, 1520s, and 1530s, including the *Dialogue* itself.

What little evidence remains of Starkey's career in Oxford locates him, tentatively at least, within the ambit of the Oxford humanists of the late 1510s. He had been a bachelor and master of Magdalen College, and had come to the attention of Cardinal Wolsey, who appointed him a pro-proctor of the university in May 1522, together with Laurence

Barbar.[160] Barbar was a fellow of All Souls College to whom Thomas Linacre, in his capacity as executor of the will of William Grocyn, had given forty shillings in 1520. As a doctor of theology Barbar wrote to Wolsey in 1525 requesting an appointment as a Wolsey lecturer in philosophy.[161] Only one fact remains on record about the intellectual content of Starkey's academic activities at Oxford, and it is a significant one: as a Regent Master from March 1521 he lectured for one year on natural philosophy.[162]

Starkey's resignation as pro-proctor in October 1522 is the last evidence of his presence in Oxford, making it possible for him to be both the unidentified Thomas whom Lupset mentioned in a letter to Erasmus as being in Constance in April 1523 and the 'other Thomas' whom Leonico asked after in a letter to Pole of June 1524.[163] By 1525 Starkey was recognized in Padua as 'artium doctor,' which suggests the likelihood that he had gone there in 1523 to pursue a doctorate in arts under the inspiration and/or patronage of Magdalen College or Wolsey or both.[164] But no record of his degree examination survives, and it seems quite possible that he was not in Padua continuously in these years and even acquired his degree elsewhere – in Siena, for example, like John Clement.

Starkey's only documented connections in the Veneto during this period are Pole, Lupset, Edmund Harvel (the English merchant resident in Venice), and Leonico; the other Englishmen with whom Starkey witnessed Wotton's MD examination together with, of course, Wotton himself; and, possibly, John Clement and Giovan Battista Opizo.[165] Of these, only Harvel seems to have recognized and encouraged any active political ambitions in Starkey, although this was later, in 1531.[166] Any possible community of interests between Starkey and Wotton, Leonico, Clement, and Opizo has to be located, on the other hand, within the fields of natural philosophy and medicine. Opizo, for example, wrote to Starkey with a list of medical remedies for Pole, but recommending that Clement treat him.[167] That Starkey maintained contact with these four after his first Paduan period suggests that these interests were ongoing, as does his friendship with the English medical student John Friar, which must date from Starkey's second Paduan period, circa 1532–4. Due to a mistranscription it has been hitherto overlooked that Starkey, together with Friar, witnessed the doctoral examination of the English medical student Thomas Bill in 1533.[168] In 1535 Friar wrote to Starkey in London with news of a conflict which had blown up amongst the Paduan doctors of medicine.[169] Another friendship dating from Starkey's stay in Avignon in 1532 was with the physician Hieronymus Lopis. He wrote to Starkey in Padua, probably in 1533, demanding news of Pole's health and the quality of the air.[170] Other English students at Padua in the early 1530s also demonstrated natural philosophical interests.[171] Finally, in a bid for employment by Thomas Cromwell in 1534, Starkey provided his own account of what he was doing in Padua in the 1520s, a testimony which accords with all the documentary evidence listed above:[172]

I shal brevely show unto you the ordur, processe & end of al my studys. Fyrst here in Oxforth a grete p[ar]te of my youthe I occupyd myselfe in the study of phylosophy, joynyng therto the knolege of both tongys, bothe Latyn & Greke, and so aftur passyd over in to Italy, whereas I so delytyd in the co[n]te[m]pla-tyon of natural knolege, wherin the most p[ar]te of me[n] lettryd ther occupye themselfys, that many tymys I was purposyd to ... spend the rest of my lyfe holly therin, tyl at the last movyd by chrystyan charyte, phylosophy set apart, I applyd my selfe to the redyng of holy scrypture, jugying al other sciente knolege not applyd to some use & profyt of other to be but as a nauyte, wherfor in the study of holy letturys c[er]tayn yerys I spent, after the wych bycause my purpos then was to lyve in a polytyke lyfe, I set my self now thes last yeres past to the knolege of the cyvyle law, that I myght therby make a more stabyl & sure jugeme[n]t of the polytyke order & custumys usyd amonge us here in our cu[n]tery.[173]

This letter has to be contrasted with the account of his life supplied by Starkey in the dedicatory letter of the *Dialogue* addressed to Henry VIII and probably written in 1535.[174] In that account, there is no study of natural philosophy and a greater emphasis on policy, but here Starkey has deliberately and clearly simplified and distorted his biography – for example, he has conflated his two Italian periods – so that it was consonant both with the aims of the *Dialogue* and with the perceived qualities required for royal service of a political nature.

From other information it is clear that the letter to Cromwell is a more reliable account of Starkey's career than the letter to Henry VIII. The theological spell he describes is hinted at by the period that Starkey, together with Pole, spent in the Charterhouse at Sheen in 1531, and more firmly established by the fact that Starkey had a doctorate in theology by that year, although it is not exactly clear when he had turned away from the study of 'natural knowledge.' Probably it was several years before, because he was already a doctor of arts by 1525, because he says he spent 'certain years' studying holy letters, and because from 1532 to 1534 Starkey was studying law in Avignon and Padua, from which university he returned to England with his third doctorate, in both laws. The impact of Paduan law on Starkey's political thought in the early 1530s and its implications for the place of civil law in Tudor England have already been surmised. What is pertinent for the present discussion is that here, even in a letter which was a bid for a 'politic life,' Starkey recalls that most of Italy's *literati* are natural philosophers, and that not only was he absorbed in that subject in his early Italian years, but that at that time he had no intention of substituting this interest for a more political orientation.

Where does all this leave the *Dialogue*? Its secular, anthropocentric thrust and reformist pragmatism seem to point towards the influence of Italian thought, and some of the more specific suggestions for social and political reform are further testimony to the ubiquity of the Venetian political myth. In the opening discussion between 'Pole' and 'Lupset' on the active and contemplative lives, the overwhelming necessity of political participation emerges decisively triumphant by virtue of the fact that the reticent 'Pole' is entirely converted by 'Lupset's' arguments. At the beginning, it was 'not all sure' for 'Pole' whether 'the perfection of man' lay in 'administration of the matters of the common weal' or in the 'knowledge of things.'[175] But at the end of the discussion he declares:

Master Lupset, you have bound me now; I have no refuge further to flee. Wherefore I promise you I shall never pretermit occasion nor time of helping my country, but ever, as they offer themself, I shall be ready to my power ever to apply and endeavour myself to the maintenance and setting forward of the true common weal.[176]

This echoes Harvel's exhortation to Starkey to leave the monastery and teach men 'quam sit humaniter vivendum,' and contrasts powerfully and perhaps deliberately with the doubt-ridden and fantastical results of the same discussion in a work which was circulating among Starkey's acquaintances in Padua in the 1520s, More's *Utopia*. The message conveyed, of the superiority of the active life, and the means by which it is achieved, a dynamic dialogue in which personal transformation is effected through the application of reason by way of discussion, seem the very stuff of contemporary Italian letters. Structurally, this clears the way for the remaining 'action' of the *Dialogue*, in which the two participants develop their proposals for social and political reform. However,

the methodology by which this is allowed to develop is wholly dependent on another element of Starkey's writing to which insufficient
attention has been given: the repeated use of medical analogies and the
structural deployment of the body politic metaphor to explain and
describe political action and to develop political concepts.[177]

'Pole' and 'Lupset' agree that their first task is to describe the perfect
commonwealth, for which, borrowing from Aristotle, 'Pole' argues that
they must first discover what constitutes the wealth of each individual.
'Lupset' protests that the interests of the individual and the community
are often in conflict, but 'Pole' argues that this is only the case when
individuals become excessively self-interested, as at present. In this case,
he continues, it is necessary for 'politic persons' to intervene to correct
their 'blindness and oversight ... like as physicians now be necessary in
cities and towns, seeing that men commonly give themself to such inor-
dinate diet, whereas if men would govern themself soberly by temperate
diet, then physicians were not to be required.'[178] After describing the
three qualities that comprise the individual's happiness – strength,
health, and beauty of the body; an abundance of worldy things; and a
virtuous soul – the body politic metaphor is used for the first time to
smooth the deductive transition from the individual to the communal:

like as in every man there is a body and also a soul in whose flourishing and
prosperous state both together standeth the weal and felicity of man so likewise
there is every commynalty city and country, as it were a politic body, and
another thing also resembling the soul of man, in whose flourishing both
together resteth also the true common weal, this body is nothing else, but the
multitude of people the number of citizens in every commynalty city or
countrey, the thing which is resembled to the soul, is civil order and politic law
administered by officers and rulers ... like as the weal of every man sounderly
by himself riseth of the three principal things before declared, so the common
weal of every country city or town sembably riseth of other three things
proportionable and like to the same ...[179]

The strength, health, and beauty of the body politic correspond to a
plentiful number of people, an absence of physical disease, and a
balance of the body's parts, 'for this body hath his parts which resemble
also the parts of the body of man.'[180] The parts are the heart (the ruler),
head (ministers), hands (craftsmen and warriors), and feet (ploughmen
and tillers).[181] A little further on 'Pole' develops the idea of a body
balanced in its parts by referring to the Galenic humours, sanguine,

melancholy, phlegmatic, and choleric. These, he suggests, resemble the three Aristotelian types of political organization, rule of the prince, rule of a group of wise men, and rule of the people, inasmuch as one of them may predominate without endangering the health of the body; different types of political organization may suit different communities, although, he adds, 'as of physicians the sanguine complexion is judged of other chief and best for the maintenance of health of the body, so the state of a prince, whereas he is chosen by free election most worthy to rule, is among the other chief and principal judged of wise men for the maintenance and long continuance of this common weal and politic rule in any commonalty.'[182]

The next task of 'Pole' and 'Lupset' is to diagnose the ills of the present 'politic body,' for, as 'Pole' argues, 'it avails physicians little to know the perfect state of the body, if they cannot judge of the sicknesses and diseases of it.'[183] The first specific complaint is consumption, or a 'certain slenderness, debility and weakness' in the politic body which is associated with shortage of population. Here Starkey has added in another ink in the margin the Latin medical term he was thinking of, 'tabes in corpore,' and below in a third ink the Greek term for a paucity of people, 'ὀλιγανθρωπια.'[184] The next complaint is dropsy, or the imbalance of the humours and an excess of ill humours, corresponding to the burden of too many negligent and idle people. Here Starkey has added in a marginal note the Greek medical term for this condition, 'πληθωρὶα.'[185] Next is palsy, excessive preoccupation with making and procuring things for vain pastimes and pleasures;[186] and then pestilence, want of agreement between the different estates.[187] 'Pole' proceeds to describe shortcomings in the strength and beauty of the body politic, and then diagnoses diseases of specific parts of the body. The head, for example, has a frenzy, in that the rulers and officers impulsively and irrationally pursue their 'vain pleasures and foolish fantasy';[188] idle ploughmen, labourers and craftsmen are responsible for gout in the hands and feet.[189] There is a further list of illnesses of the soul.

Finally, the interlocutors propose solutions to each problem in turn, 'forasmuch as the process of our communication hitherto is but of littel or no value, except we find out convenient remedies prudently to be applied to such sores and diseases in our politic body.'[190] The methods by which this is to proceed are taken first from nature, supplying the body politic with its necessities and adornments as nature first forms the body, and then providing it with 'politic governance' as nature gives the body a divine soul; and second from 'the general rule of expert physicians in curing bodily diseases as much as we can ever observing, that is first to insearch out the cause of the diseases without the which the applying of remedies little availeth.'[191] Consumption – the population dearth – is caused by people not procreating, and the remedy is the development of various legal inducements to matrimony.[192] Dropsy – idleness – is caused by young people being brought up to expect and seek an easy life, and is to be cured by the legal requirement for every child from the age of seven to learn a craft or attend a school; idle adults should be banished from the cities. Palsy – the procuring of vain things for other men's pleasure – has the same cause and is to be remedied by similar means. Pestilence – different parts of the body in conflict with each other – is remedied by equitable justice by rulers, clearly defined tasks and duties, and the banishment or execution of seditious persons.[193] And so on.

Mayer has demonstrated that a good deal of discreet borrowing of Italianate and Venetian political concepts was taking place in the *Dialogue*. Paduan jurisprudence was also a component in Starkey's 'civic' outlook. But it is also the case that the medical analogy is the most conspicuous facilitator of Starkey's thinking about political reform and political transformation.[194] The metaphor of the body politic itself was, of course, unoriginal. It has a long medieval history and classical antecedents in Plato's *Laws*[195] and in Aristotle's conception of the state as natural and organic in his *Politics*. As early as the twelfth century, the idea is fully developed in John of Salisbury's *Policraticus*, and he claims to have drawn on the *Institutio Trajani*, a work which he attributes to Plutarch.[196] More significantly, the early fourteenth-century physician Marsilius of Padua draws on the Aristotelian conception and extends it to the use of specific medical analogies in his *Defensor pacis*, a work which, with its attack on papal power and advocacy of wide political representation, has frequently been taken as one of Starkey's major sources.[197] And it is not difficult to find contemporaries of Starkey employing the metaphor, especially in an Italian context, for example, Machiavelli and Donato Giannotti.[198] But the attention to specifically medical diagnostic and prescriptive detail in Starkey's work is still striking, and in this perhaps he most resembles among his contemporaries another Englishman, a naturalist and a physician, also with Italian experience, William Turner. Like Starkey, Turner in his *Spiritual physik* of 1551 identifies specific diseases in the body politic and their – in this case, Protestant – remedies: palsy (unlearnedness), dropsy (excessive consumption by the nobility), romish pox acquired by spiritual fornication (Catholicism), leprosy (social upstarts).[199]

In these terms then, the healing of man the microcosm represented a blueprint for the healing of the common weal. This suggests that Starkey's 'civic humanism' was neither as 'modern' nor as intellectually detached from the 'medical humanism' of his naturalist friends as the historiography implies. In this sense Starkey too partook of what Vivian Nutton has called the 'Linacre tradition,' an approach to medicine which was characterized by classical theory and social reform. Its credo emerges in Sir Thomas Elyot's riposte to critics who accused him through the publication of his *Castel of helthe* of setting himself up as a physician: 'Truly if they will calle him a phisition, which is studiouse about the weale of his countray, I witsaufe they so name me.'[200] Indeed the flurry of medicine-related activities in England around 1517 and 1518, the Corpus fellowship, Linacre's foundation of the College of Physicians, and others, was surely in part a social response to the serious outbreak of the sweating sickness in those two years. Andrea Ammonio died from it, Reginald Pole was sick with it,[201] and Thomas More, if himself not afflicted, was taking precautions against it.[202] With the exception of Linacre – protected, presumably, by his superior knowledge of the Greek Galen – all the most important patrons of English medicine, Bishop Fox, Cardinal Wolsey, and Henry VIII, were affected. Advanced English thinkers in this period saw themselves as putting their learning to good use, not only in terms of healing the social and political ills of their country, but also in terms of healing the physical illnesses of at least their country's more privileged members. For a number of those impelled to the Paduan university of arts and medicine, these two motives embodied a single and coherent intellectual ideal.

4

Humanists

Chapter 3 has suggested ways in which the medical humanism and humanistic natural philosophy of the Paduan *studium* influenced English intellectual life and medical practice. But the English humanism which emerged from Padua was more broadly based than this alone suggests. From the 1490s to the 1530s, a significant number of Englishmen pursued interests within this wider dimension, and their intellectual and social activity is given a particular coherence by the centrality in English circles of Niccolò Leonico Tomeo, whose letter collection documents the nature of their milieu.

For its size and range of correspondents, this collection – MS Rossiano 997 in the Biblioteca Apostolica Vaticana – is a central record of English humanism in Padua and a key text in the history of cultural exchange between early Tudor and Italian scholarship. We do not have evidence of visits to Padua for John Colet, William Grocyn, and William Lily, and they had left Italy before Leonico's appointment as public lecturer at Padua on the Greek text of Aristotle in 1497. But Leonico corresponded with every other leading English student of the new learning who ventured into Italy.[1] A crude count of letters in the manuscript – excluding those to Italian correspondents and unidentified addressees – gives some indication of Leonico's epistolary range: there are five letters to William Latimer, one to Thomas Linacre, four to Cuthbert Tunstall,[2] seven to Richard Pace,[3] two to Thomas Lupset, one to Thomas Starkey, and twenty-four to Reginald Pole.[4] The manuscript records a further three letters sent to Leonico by Englishmen, two from Pole and one from Lupset. Leonico was personally acquainted with other Englishmen in northeast Italy: Marmaduke Waldby, later a chaplain to Cardinal Wolsey; John Clement, the medical student; the otherwise mysterious 'Mauritius,' an English student at Padua in the mid-1520s; Richard Croke and Bishop Stokesley, Henrician agents;[5] and Edmund Harvel, the English merchant resident in Venice. And he corresponded with Englishmen lacking in Italian experience: Francis Poyntz, the translator of Cebes,[6] and Thomas More.

Leonico should therefore figure centrally in any account of the cultural relations between England and Italy from the end of the fifteenth century until his death in 1531, but hitherto he has hardly done so. Cardinal Francis Gasquet's *Cardinal Pole and his Early Friends* brought Leonico's letter collection to scholarly attention as early as 1927. But this work was itself unenlightening and inaccurate, stringing together some very free translations with a rather misleading narrative. Two subsequent plans to publish the complete correspondence apparently proved abortive.[7] More recently Daniela De Bellis has thoroughly reconstructed some of Leonico's social and intellectual relationships, partly from the manuscript, but Leonico in his Anglophile incarnation still deserves more attention than he has received.[8]

Niccolò Leonico Tomeo was born in Venice in 1456 to Epirote Greek parents, studied under Demetrius Chalcondylas at Florence and Milan, and graduated in arts at Padua in 1485.[9] He was at the forefront of a major Hellenic renaissance at Padua which also featured Chalcondylas, Lorenzo Cretensis, and Alessandro Zeno (who were the successors to Chalcondylas in the chair of Greek grammar at Padua), Leonico's friend and probable student Lazzaro Bonamico, and Marcus Musurus. This proceeded in tandem with extramural developments at Venice: Bessarion's influential bequest of Greek manuscripts to the Republic, the publishing of the major Greek classics by Leonico's associate Aldo Manuzio, the Manutian 'Academy,' and the Hellenic interests of young Venetian patricians such as Pietro Bembo, Andrea Navagero, and Marin Sanudo, all of them friends of Leonico.[10] Indeed from around 1504 Leonico taught Greek in one of the public schools in Venice, but he returned to Padua in 1506 and remained there for the rest of his life. During the closure of the Paduan universities during the wars of the League of Cambrai, he gave himself over to the study of Plato and Aristotle[11] and was to become known as much for his Platonic writings as for his interpretations of Aristotelian natural philosophy. For Erasmus, whom he may have met in Padua in 1509, Leonico was, with Bembo, one of the 'lights' of the age, noted particularly for these Platonic studies.[12]

Leonico blamed ignorance of Aristotelian science on human cupidity, which, within the curricular structure of Padua's universities, led men to seek careers in the more financially rewarding fields of law and medicine.[13] The subordinate status of natural philosophy and Leonico's Platonism may help explain why his cultural milieu is not comprehended by the Paduan *studium* alone. His chair was an extraordinary one which seems to have lapsed after 1504. He apparently took little interest in the affairs of the *studium* and features nowhere as a promoter in the acts of Paduan students' doctoral examinations. He was not a member of the college of philosophers and physicians, where the latter group tended to hold sway. Leonico's teaching of English students in the 1520s was a private affair and, at least from the Paduan point of view, unofficial. Despite the assumption that he was appointed as Reginald Pole's teacher by the Venetian Republic, no evidence for this exists, and the links between Leonico and Tunstall, Pace, and Latimer in the 1520s strongly suggest that the initiative came from England. Furthermore, Leonico received not only gifts from his former English students in this period, but also monetary payments (although the evidence is not explicit about the reason for this).[14] The only clear evidence of the Venetian government's intervention in the relationships between Leonico and his English students is the order to the *podestà* of Padua in 1522 that Leonico should accompany the English ambassador Pace from Padua to Venice, and that it should seem to Pace that this was a spontaneous act on Leonico's behalf.[15]

Although friendly with university luminaries such as Romolo Amaseo and Domenico Bonomini, Leonico's cultural identity should also be considered in the light of his friendships with the religious reformers (*spirituali*) Gasparo Contarini, Giacomo Sadoleto, and Gian Matteo Giberti: a manuscript version (though not the printed edition included in Leonico's *Opuscula*) of Leonico's translation of the pseudo-Aristotelian *Quaestiones mechanica* contains a dedicatory letter to Contarini;[16] Giacomo Sadoleto was a correspondent of Leonico and features as an interlocutor in one of his *Dialogi*;[17] Leonico wrote to Giberti in 1528 requesting a copy of Chrysostom's commentary on St Paul's *Epistles*, which was edited by Giberti.[18] Leonico's passion for art, his Platonism, and his interest in the vernacular found outlets in his association with Pietro Bembo, the spirit of whose Paduan *otium* resonates into Leonico's correspondence.[19] Notwithstanding a quip about tyrants attributed to Leonico in Castiglione's *Cortegiano* and his appearance in Giannotti's *Libro della repubblica de'Viniziani*, there is little evidence in his life and works of political ambition or opinion.[20] The comments about public affairs in Leonico's correspondence tend to be conventional, though he shows an insatiable thirst for 'news,' especially in the period around

1524 and 1525, a time during which he also requested from Pole a copy of the new Aldine edition of Cicero's *Letters to Atticus*.[21] If in these respects Leonico, the earliest known Italian reader of More's *Utopia*, was a Hythlodaean,[22] he was also a prolific editor, translator, and commentator of the Aristotelian scientific corpus, as outlined in chapter 3. Besides these works, his probable translation of Galen, and his own medical and natural philosophical works, he also translated Ptolemy's *Inerrantium stellarum significationes* and, as mentioned above, the *Quaestiones mechanica*.[23] His translation of Proclus's commentary on Plato's *Timaeus* and his own *Dialogi* add Platonic and neoplatonic elements to his work;[24] in the tradition of Bessarion and Pico della Mirandola, Leonico was a syncretist whose project was to demonstrate the essential concordance of the two Greek philosophers and their schools.

By no means was every element in this eclectic cultural profile transmitted to Leonico's English students. Little of his artistic and antiquarian sensibility, for example, seems to have rubbed off on them. That Tunstall's coin collecting may have been inspired by Leonico's is a speculation for which there is no real evidence.[25] That Pole had artistic interests in this period as he certainly did later is a possibility: Marcantonio Michiel noted that a marble relief of the Judgment of Solomon, commissioned by Battista Leone, was given by Leone to 'an English bishop,' usually identified as Pole.[26] Yet the identification of Pole remains problematic: he was only consecrated as a bishop on becoming Archbishop of Canterbury in 1556, about four years after Michiel's death. Identifying him as the 'English bishop' requires us to believe in the improbability that the generally accurate Michiel wrote 'bishop' for 'cardinal' and that he saw the terracotta model for the relief in or after 1536, the year Pole was raised to the cardinalate, eight years after Leone's death.[27] But the identification of Pole might be taken as read were it not for the fact that an earlier Paduan alumnus and a probable inspirer of Pole's studies in Padua *was* an 'English bishop,' Cuthbert Tunstall. The possibility that he was the recipient of Leone's gift hints at an axis in this network of Anglo-Paduan relationships for which there is no further evidence;[28] but as suggesting an English visual sensibility inspired by Leonico or other Paduan collectors and antiquarians this material is disappointing.

As suggested in chapter 3, in the first phase of English humanist activity in Padua (the 1490s and 1500s), it was Aristotelian philosophy that was the main intellectual bond between Leonico and his students Tunstall and Latimer. This obviously did not preclude the development of other interests later; both were noted for theological preoccupations in the wake of the rise of Erasmus and the Reformation. Indeed Latimer may have helped Erasmus with revisions of his New Testament, as Tunstall certainly did.[29] Moreover, Tunstall was subsequently known as a Hebraist, though the evidence for him having studied Hebrew in Italy, or indeed for any real mastery of the language, is not overwhelming; no contemporary tribute to Tunstall as a classical linguist makes mention of his Hebrew.[30]

But the fruits of Tunstall's early studies with Leonico may be glimpsed in his compendium of the *Nichomachean Ethics* and in his mathematical work of 1522, *De arte supputandi*.[31] (It should also be remembered that Tunstall was probably a student at the law university in Padua.) At the same time the collection of books donated to Cambridge University by Tunstall in 1529, the majority of them bought in Italy, testifies to an extremely wide-ranging interest in the classical Greek heritage. To volumes one and four of the Aldine *editio princeps* of the Greek Aristotle and an Aldine commentary on Aristotle by Johannes Philopponus can be added a large collection of Greek grammars including works by Theodore Gaza and Apollonius, the *editio princeps* of the Greek Homer, and works by Herodian, Herodotus, and Ulpian.[32] It has recently been suggested that the large inventory of books in British Library MS Additional 40676 represents Tunstall's library in the early 1550s: the positive evidence for this is not sufficient to make it a certainty, though equally there is little evidence to rule it out. The collection records one of the largest of extant private libraries from sixteenth-century England and is very wide-ranging intellectually. Built up over a lifetime, this library contains some works printed in Italy, which may have been brought back from there by Tunstall.[33]

While Latimer, Tunstall, and Linacre were fundamental in encouraging the second wave of Anglo-Paduan humanists in the 1520s, Pace's intellectual career actually spans the two phases.[34] Pace's patron Thomas Langton, bishop of Winchester, sent him to Italy in the mid-1490s, and he remained a student in Padua, Bologna, and Ferrara until 1509, when he entered the service of Cardinal Bainbridge, Langton's nephew and Henry VIII's envoy to the papal curia. At Bologna Pace was taught by the humanist and Greek scholar Paolo Bombasio, who later sent the manuscript of Pace's *De fructu qui ex doctrina percipitur* to the Froben press at Basle and provided the work with a prefatory letter. At Ferrara Pace studied with the medical humanist Niccolò Leoniceno and met Erasmus there, who understood him to be collecting material for a book of classical allegories. He also knew there the Ferrarese humanist Celio Calcagnini.[35] Calcagnini's later support for Henry VIII in his 'great matter' was apparently stimulated by Pace's praise for the king.[36] While in Venice Pace is said to have delivered an oration in praise of Greek studies in 1504,[37] and in Padua he was helped in this subject by Latimer and Tunstall and taught by Leonico.[38] In 1519 Pace succeeded John Colet as dean of St Paul's and in the following year was appointed lecturer in Greek at Cambridge, a post which he apparently never took up. He translated a series of treatises of Plutarch which were published at Venice in 1523 and dedicated to Tunstall. His *De fructu* was a wide-ranging, anecdotal survey of humanistic studies.

Pace's diplomatic missions in the 1520s were the occasion of a renewed intimacy with Leonico, underscored on the one hand by the arrival in Padua of Leonico's new English students Reginald Pole and Thomas Lupset, and on the other by Leonico's revived contact with Tunstall and Latimer in England.[39] Their correspondence in this period reveals Leonico's considerable esteem for Pace as a humanist following Pace's translation of Plutarch,[40] but the majority of Leonico's letters contain political news of relevance to Pace's diplomatic activity. A vivid series of accounts of the Italian wars and the wider European conditions underpinning them between May 1524 and February 1525 while Pole, Pace, and Lupset were apparently in Venice, Trent, and somewhere near Pavia, also reveal the increasing deterioration of Pace's health, perceived as a consequence of the stresses of his political activity.[41] In a letter to Pace of 29 January 1524, Leonico advises him to remove himself as far as possible from 'prisons' and 'swords' and to relearn through humane letters a gentler lifestyle.[42] After February 1525, Pace became seriously ill and he was permitted to return to England, where he lived until 1536. Pace's significance for the English circle of Leonico in the 1520s was mainly diplomatic; highly regarded by the government of the Venetian Republic, Pace both advanced Leonico's publishing career in Venice and represented there the interests of Reginald Pole.[43]

In a wider sense, Pace's political activity reproduces a pattern already evident among early Tudor humanists. Like Tunstall, More and Colet, Pace's work as a philologist and teacher was unsustained and intermittent. This is a reflection of both the lack of institutional opportunities for serious humanists in England and the heights in government service to which this tiny group of talented intellectuals could climb. Although by the 1520s there is no doubt that the broader Erasmian programme had become an important component of the educated Englishman's outlook, dedicated scholars of Greek language and literature remained, and continued to remain, few and far between. This is not particularly surprising. Contemporaries found Greek a difficult language to master, and the succession of Latin and vernacular translations emerging from Europe in the sixteenth century would increasingly render the necessity of learning the language a thing of the past. From this perspective the encouragement afforded to Reginald Pole by Tunstall, Linacre, and Latimer to pursue humanistic studies in Padua in the 1520s, and the small group of privileged young Englishmen who gathered there around Pole, reflect the failure of Greek studies to take much more solid institutional root in England than they had in the 1490s.[44]

In the context of the English uses of Padua, the 1520s and early 1530s thus continue to represent a period in which humanistic and Greek studies were predominating themes, and this renewed and more intense period of Leonican inspiration reveals the continued dependence of English humanism on Italian sources. Most English members of the Leonico circle in this period knew Erasmus and may even be considered a part of his extended European *familia*, but their activities in Padua also complicate the picture of a supposed 'translatio studii' from south to north which Erasmus's rising influence and reputation are sometimes said to epitomize. Furthermore, unlike the earlier Paduan sojourns of Tunstall, Linacre, and Latimer, it is not as easy to tie the interests of Anglo-Paduans in the 1520s so completely to ancient Greek science, and hence to oppose them to 'Erasmian' or 'Christian' humanists. Christian piety and the works of the early church fathers preoccupied at least two of the central figures of this Paduan group, Thomas Lupset and Reginald Pole, and religious themes likewise began to reorientate Leonico's intellectual activities in this period, perhaps under the influence of his students and of Erasmus himself, certainly under the influence of Contarini, Giberti, and Sadoleto. Not a trained theologian, Leonico was, nevertheless, responsible for writing the positive determination of the Paduan college of theologians on the king's 'great matter' and for persuading the members of the college to subscribe to it.[45] All of this suggests that while Erasmus energized English humanism and influenced its agenda, this only impelled English humanists back to Padua. In Padua, meanwhile, Italian humanists were increasingly turning to Erasmian priorities.

The focus of Leonico's English circle in the 1520s was the household of Pole, the nobleman and cousin of the king, who had been raised in an educational atmosphere redolent of humane studies at Magdalen

College and Corpus Christi College, Oxford.[46] Magdalen was Oxford's most humanistically progressive college until the foundation in 1517 of Corpus Christi by the probable Magdalen alumnus, Bishop Richard Fox. The two colleges were closely associated through an interchange of personnel and Corpus Christi's direct imitation of the Magdalen statutes. Significantly, the president of Magdalen, John Claymond, was also Corpus Christi's first president and Pole had been a witness to the official foundation of the college on 5 March 1517.[47] Pole's Corpus connection continued: in 1523 he was joined in Padua by ex-Corpus resident Thomas Lupset and in the same year he himself was nominated a fellow of the college by Bishop Fox.[48] Leonico's characteristic interest in English letters is suggested by a brief 1525 correspondence between him and Lupset in which Claymond's name is passed on to him.[49]

In a letter to Erasmus commending Pole in 1525, Lupset mentions Thomas Linacre and William Latimer as Pole's teachers, and Latimer was also noted as his teacher by Ludovico Beccadelli, Pole's later friend and first biographer.[50] These, then, provide the surest evidence of a continuity of aims and ideals in English attendance at Padua between the 1490s and the 1520s, although the departure of Pole for Padua in 1521 was probably a more complex occasion than this alone suggests.[51]

Pole's generosity to fellow Englishmen made him, between 1521 and 1526, the focus of an English circle at Padua which comprised at different times Thomas Starkey, Thomas Winter, John Clement, Marmaduke Waldby, his closest companion Thomas Lupset, and probably also Nicholas Wilson, Edward Wotton, Robert Birch, and Robert Chaloner. Pole's social position afforded him recognition by the Venetian government[52] and entry into Italian circles unprecedented by any former English student. His friends and acquaintances included Jacobo Roccabonella, in whose house he seems to have lived,[53] Pietro Bembo, Trifone Gabriele,[54] Romolo Amaseo,[55] Marco Mantova Benavides,[56] Gian Matteo Giberti,[57] Giovanbattista Cibò,[58] Gaspare Stampa,[59] and almost certainly Peter Martyr,[60] Flaminio Tomarozzo, Giacomo Sadoleto,[61] Marcantonio Flaminio,[62] Francisco Bellino,[63] Rodolfo Pio di Carpi,[64] Jan Laski,[65] and Giovan Battista Casali.[66]

Probably Pole's most important foreign friendship in this period was with the Flemish humanist Christophe de Longueil. Famed for his Ciceronianism, Longueil had visited England in 1519 after being hounded out of Rome for his oration attacking the Romans. He was a friend of Pietro Bembo, his chief defender in Rome, and Linacre, Pace, Sadoleto, Navagero, and Leonico.[67] He lived in Pole's house in Padua from 1521 until his early death the following year. In a letter from there to his former host in Padua, Stefano Sauli, Longueil praised Pole's learning and judgment but complained that he was taciturn. The letter also describes his daily routine in Pole's house; his reading included Thucydides and Cicero and one of his companions was Flaminio Toma-rozzo.[68] In 1555 Marco Mantova, commending to Pole his nephew, who was to visit England in the service of the Venetian ambassador, recalled Longueil as Pole's 'servitore' in Padua. In a last letter to Pole, Longueil bequeathed to him his library.[69] It seems probable that the *Vita Longolii*, printed with his letters in 1524, was Pole's first published work.[70]

The surviving evidence of Pole's studies in this period suggest an eclectic humanistic education. The only specifically documented studies of his with Leonico are of Aristotle's *Topics* and *libri naturales*,[71] but mention of Leonico's *Dialogi* in their correspondence also implies reading of a more Platonic orientation; indeed the dedicatory letter of the work to Pole suggests that Pole first encouraged Leonico to publish them.[72] We do not know what Pole may have studied with his other Paduan teacher, Battista Leone. Leone was a philosopher particularly renowned as an interpreter of Aristotle,[73] and Greek manuscripts surviving from his library suggest broadly similar interests to those of his friend Leonico.[74] More literary and stylistic preoccupations are suggested by Pole's reading in 1525 of Bembo's *De imitatione*.[75]

The only other source reflecting on Pole's intellectual interests in this period derive from his library. The most certain group to have belonged to him in this period (but presumably only indirectly reflecting his own tastes) were the books bequeathed to him by Longueil, a large collection of classical and neo-classical Greek and Latin works.[76] Scientific and philosophical works are well represented, but there are also editions of Cicero's orations and rhetorical works annotated in Longueil's hand; these were obviously key classical texts for Pole and his friends.[77] Although it is unlikely that all of Pole's other extant manuscripts were purchased in Italy in these years, a letter to Erasmus of 1527 suggests that he and Lupset had brought a large collection of manuscripts back to England in the previous year, and it is known also from Erasmus's correspondence that Pole purchased a manuscript of Chrysostom in around 1524.[78] Of the Greek manuscripts in New College, Oxford, that may have belonged to Pole, there are several grammatical or rhetorical texts, a handful of historical and literary classics, half a dozen texts of Aristotle, about twenty separate Aristotelian commentaries, and one theological work. Of the manuscripts in this collection which definitely belonged to Pole, one certainly and others probably post-date the 1520s, but mounting evidence suggests that some were copied for him in the exact period under consideration.[79] Besides the works of natural philosophy mentioned above, there are two manuscripts comprising commentaries on the *Nichomachean Ethics*;[80] Theodore Gaza's *De arte grammatica* probably also belonged to Pole.[81] The vast majority in this group are theological and patristic works, including about a dozen Chrysostom texts.[82] The patristic orientation is obviously significant in the light of Pole's later vocation; Longueil had also displayed a religious commitment from which emerged his oration against Luther,[83] Clement and Lupset had inherited similar preoccupations from their connection with Erasmian humanism,[84] and Leonico's religious sympathies were directed precisely towards that group of Italian reformers with whom Pole would be so closely identified during his later career in papal service.[85]

Ludovico Beccadelli described a revolution in Pole's thinking when he returned to the Veneto from England in 1532 'tutto volto alli studi sacri,'[86] while John Friar wrote in 1535 that Pole was undergoing a great change, 'exchanging man for God';[87] this change is usually understood to have been a consequence of the crisis of conscience engendered by Henry VIII's divorce.[88] But the evidence that Pole was amassing a library of patristic texts in the mid-1520s suggests the need for some revision of this chronological scheme. Pole's ambivalence towards the king was almost certainly older than Henry's matrimonial difficulties,[89] and it may be that an ecclesiastical vocation had been his ambition all along; indeed his mother, the countess of Salisbury, asserted exactly this in a desperate letter to Pole of 1536 pleading with him to recant his opposition to Henry VIII.[90] This also makes sense of Pole's eagerness, in 1524 and 1525, for an introduction to Gian Matteo Giberti and through him to the pope.[91] What is certainly clear is that the amassing of these manuscripts in the 1520s is testimony to a commitment to Greek learning and a precocious erudition of which contemporaries were fully aware.[92]

Taken together, Leonico's letters demonstrate a certain vision of social life which formed an important component of this humanistic activity. Humanistic studies are emphatically not a solitary pursuit, but undertaken communally among like-minded friends. Indeed 'amicitia,' that most neo-classical of social virtues, to a large extent sustains and lies behind the ideological rationale of the humanism in this circle. Most of Leonico's letters are not merely intended to convey information, but are vehicles and tokens of love and remembrance. 'News' is not only of the affairs of the world, but portrays an intensely personal and sometimes mundane private life. The style is sometimes elliptical, hyperbolic, or merely formulaic. 'Meaning' resides in the 'event' of the letter itself and in the friendship and sense of common endeavour which it betokens. Hence the failure of Leonico's correspondents to write back evinces an angry response from him.[93] As Leonico wrote to Thomas Starkey, only through letters can friends separated by large distances 'enjoy' and 'see' each other: not writing violates the laws of friendship, whereas letters are tools for navigating the distance between men.[94] Closely following classical and Renaissance ideas about letter-writing, Leonico's letters are 'conversations with absent friends.'[95]

Overlaying this but elaborating the same general point is the exchange of gifts which went on within this correspondence.[96] Even those that were plainly utilitarian served a further function; Latimer's gift of a horse to the septuagenarian philosopher frequently reminds Leonico of Latimer, and becomes known as the 'canterio latymeriano.'[97] The grace with which Leonico forbore the animal's sickness on arrival in Italy is in sharp contrast with his anger and hurt at the presentation of a lame horse by Henry VIII's agents at the time of the king's 'great matter,' the horse representing not so much a gift as payment for services rendered. Leonico sent Latimer a clock in return, since there was no chiming clock where Latimer lived. It is a token of Leonico's love and is in place of a 'going-home present' (*apophoretus*), as if the two men had been talking together over a meal. This was precisely the role which clocks had played in Erasmus' colloquy, 'Convivium religiosum,' where they are intended to encourage the recipients to use their time well. Here, perhaps, Leonico is reminding Latimer of their friendship which has endured despite the passage of many years.[98]

Books served a fundamental purpose among learned friends and seekers of friendship.[99] Leonico's pretext for writing to Thomas Linacre and Thomas More is to send them his publications in the hope of receiving one of theirs in return;[100] it may be that the cramp rings which Leonico received from Francis Poyntz, delivered by hand by Pole, were Linacre's gesture of response. Poyntz was a member of the king's inner circle, a trustee of the Knight Rider Street property acquired by Linacre for the College of Physicians, and a translator of a work attributed to Cebes, the associate of Socrates, into English.[101] Leonico wrote to Linacre in January 1524 and Leonico replied to Poyntz in August of the same year; perhaps by this time Linacre, who was to die in October, was too ill to write to

Leonico himself. Their communication at this period may also be connected with Linacre's inspiration of English participation on the Aldine Galen of 1525.

Cramp rings were the characteristic token of the royal physician's friendship, although it is interesting that in the learned atmosphere of these circles two former recipients rather denigrated the gifts. Guillaume Budé, whose rings from Linacre had been blessed by the king as a charm against spasms, wrote to Linacre that he had handed them out among the wives of his friends, making probably satirically high-sounding claims for their curative properties as he did so.[102] Christophe de Longueil, who had known Linacre in England and whose rings were delivered to him in Padua by Pole, accepted them as a 'monument' of their friendship, but complained that from a 'homo philosophus' he would rather have received a letter.[103] To underline the upbraiding, Longueil sent Linacre a letter and a book in return. But Leonico's rings, also blessed by the king, completely delighted him, essentially because he took them as tokens and catalysts of love and friendship between himself and Poyntz. Inverting the pejorative force of Longueil's contrast between 'gold' and 'letters,' Leonico gives thanks to Poyntz, 'who desired, not through words but through works, to count me among your friends.'[104]

Through John Clement Leonico seems to have received from More the copy of *Utopia* which he had requested, an event which sets the scene for a piece of conventional epideictic letter writing addressed to Pole.[105] It is appropriate the work should have been delivered by Clement; he features briefly in the letter to Peter Gillis which prefaces *Utopia* as disputing More's recollection of Hythlodaeus's account of the geography of the island. He is also noted for his precocious ability in Latin and Greek. He had been present with More on the 1515 embassy to Bruges when the work was conceived. (Tunstall, incidentally, was also central to the genesis of *Utopia*, having been More's colleague on the same embassy and a friend of Gillis, as mentioned at the beginning of *Utopia*. According to More, Tunstall had read and approved of *Utopia* by the following year. A copy of the work belonging to him is extant.)[106] Leonico's letter is the first known Italian response to *Utopia* and one of the earliest pieces of writing on the work not to be included in the apparatus of the printed versions of *Utopia* itself.[107]

However, the letter consummately fails in any direct way to add to our understanding of *Utopia*'s contemporary 'meaning,' for it is full of rhetorical hyperbole and cliché, particularly disappointing from a student of Plato: *Utopia* delighted Leonico and went beyond his many expectations;[108] he does not know what to praise the most, the fertility of the idea, the admirable felicity of invention, the elegant style or grace of eloquence, or again the breadth and dignity of the matter itself; the republic of Utopia seems to be neither in matter, laws, nor merit outdone by those described by the ancients; if only it were not fiction but real history, so that in some place a true republic of philosophers may be found.

This letter represents an act of homage to a central figure of the Pole and Leonico circle. As such, it strongly suggests that *Utopia*'s contemporary reception can only be understood in the context of the ideological paraphernalia generated by Erasmus and More and their circles in order to pave the way for the work.[109] In the case of Leonico, the ideology of Erasmian humanism seems to have generated an entirely positive, but rather formulaic, response. Perhaps Leonico's most revealing comment is that the book was 'iocundissimus.'[110] Then again, only one of Leonico's letters records philosophical profundities:[111] generally the letters are *gestures* towards a common intellectual and social identity, as classical letters often were.

When Leonico sends Tunstall his commentaries on the *Parva naturalia*, it is as a testimony of his remembrance of him, and so that Tunstall should be reminded of Leonico whenever he reads them.[112] The dedicatory letters in Leonico's printed works and which also feature in his letter collection serve the purpose of creating an illusion of intimacy and personal immediacy. Like the attempts at realistic characterization and conversation worked into Leonico's *Dialogi*, his letters try to generate the fiction of a real human presence or presences, an endeavour which is perhaps characteristic of humanistic letter writing in general, drawing as it does on rules of classical rhetoric intended for the 'live art' of speaking.

This is demonstrated in particular in his letter to Pole describing a debate in Pietro Bembo's garden on the relative merits of Latin and the Italian vernacular.[113] The letter is redolent with recognizable cultural tropes; indeed the extent to which Leonico's impression of Bembo's *ambiente* adheres to the one created by Bembo himself is remarkable. The scene is set by Bembo's return from business in Rome to the 'honestum otium' of his Paduan villa. Leonico mentions the rivulet which ran through the garden, next to which Bembo, toga-clad, was to be depicted in a coin designed by Valerio Belli in the early 1530s.[114] Precisely the same location had been used for Bembo's first published work, the dialogue *De Aetna,* and was also to be used in the dialogue of Donato Giannotti, *Libro della repubblica de'Viniziani* (1526). At his villa Bembo's friends come to pay their respects, among them Giovan Antonio Marostica and Christophe de Longueil. These two begin a dispute about the vernacular – praised by Marostica – and Latin – praised by Longueil. Marostica asks Bembo, the famed master of both tongues and the author of the dialogue *La prosa della volgar lingua,* written very near the time of this event, to judge between them, but Bembo fears that his own reputation will be compromised by taking sides. Leonico suggests that each contestant prepare a longer speech on the merits of each language, and Bembo assents to judge these. The letter ends at the point when Longueil is about to make his case for Latin.

Thus the letter as we have it is curiously unfinished. Perhaps Leonico intended or wrote a 'sequel' letter or told Pole orally what happened. But the main interest of this piece is that it is both a letter and a dialogue, creating the fiction of live presence doubly; both the letter writer and the interlocutors at Bembo's villa are 'made to speak.' As a hybrid, then, it is revealing about both 'humanistic' social life and Renaissance dialogues. Since the dialogue was described in a private letter, there seems no doubt that some such conversation on this subject and among these individuals at Bembo's villa took place; learned conversation was central to this social milieu. In the absence of a classical theory of dialogue writing, this letter may confirm the importance of real social situations to Renaissance dialogues.

By these means Leonico's letters purvey the belief in a way of learned living for which friendship, conversation, and letters themselves were extremely important. It is likely that some of the letters, particularly those to Reginald Pole, had an educational function, and were intended as models of eloquent Latin correspondence. But these features also reinvigorate for sixteenth-century humanism the social charge of the term *humanitas* as found, for example, in such classical authors as Aulus Gellius, who says that it is sometimes defined as a 'readiness to help' and a 'goodwill shown to all men.'[115] In terms of the ideological coincidence of serious Greek studies and *amicitia,* that is, of the sociability of a humanism which purported to be for its own sake, this phase in the history of English students at Padua was not repeated in the sixteenth century. Leonico had written to Edmund Harvel in 1524 about his fondness for learned Britons, freely admitting it but not knowing its cause,[116] but his later relations with Englishmen became soured during the missions of Stokesley and Croke to the Veneto on behalf of Henry VIII in 1530. Leonico became caught up in the more mercenary aspects of the event at the same time as some of his earlier English friends were apparently forsaking him. In the year that Leonico secured the Paduan theologians' support for the annulment of the marriage of Catherine of Aragon, he also wrote to Tunstall complaining bitterly of receiving no letters from him, probably not realizing that Tunstall was Catherine's legal counsel.[117] At the same time Leonico was furious at his treatment by Henry's agents, who had paid him for his services with a lame horse, and he threatened to denounce the king in his forthcoming book, *De varia historia*.[118] This was a hint of what the English Reformation might do to Anglo-Italian intellectual relations. Although Pole himself succeeded in persuading the Paris theologians to support Henry in the same period, within six years Pole had definitively rejected the schismatic English polity and chosen permanent exile in Italy, and from the English side a black cloud fell over him and the Englishmen who stayed with him.

Among these Englishmen were Michael Throckmorton and George Lily, English students at Padua in the early 1530s. Tunstall and Pace, the last major surviving 'early Tudor humanists' after the executions of More and Fisher, came to terms with the royal divorce and supremacy. Pace endorsed the illegality of the king's first marriage as early as 1530,[119] while Tunstall came round in the early 1530s. In 1536 he wrote an attack on Pole's *De unitate*; it was printed in London in 1560 as *A letter written by Cuthbert Tunstall late Bishop of Durham and John Stokesley sometime Bishop of London ... to R. Pole Cardinall, being then at Rome.* Richard Morison, who knew Pole at Padua around 1534, returned to England to become one of the most effective and vitriolic Henrician propagandists against him. Thomas Starkey managed briefly to accommodate himself to the Henrician regime, but his association with Pole eventually caught up with him, and he was attainted for treason posthumously in 1539.

No Italian Anglophile emerged to replace Leonico, though George Lily, Richard Morison, and probably Henry Coles and Thomas Goldwell pursued Greek studies in Padua in the years immediately following his death,[120] as did John Caius in the early 1540s. Through Caius Padua made a small contribution to the debate in England about Greek pronunciation and may have influenced English architecture, but his studies largely bore fruit in the field of medical humanism.[121] In 1581 the Oxford astronomer Henry Savile was able to extend his interests in ancient Greek mathematical works in Padua through his association with the Paduan *erudito* Giovan Vicenzo Pinelli. Pinelli, owner of one of the largest private libraries in Europe, was also acquainted with Edmund Bruce, Richard White, Henry Wotton, and Savile's pupil Henry Cuffe, with whom he worked on manuscripts of the Byzantine bibliographer Photius. Thomas Savile continued his older brother's philological and scientific work with Pinelli in 1589;[122] by this period Padua clearly had an outstanding reputation for the study of mathematics and astronomy, noted, for example, by Fynes Moryson, which had attracted Edmund Bruce, and which would culminate in the work of Galileo.[123] But in their interest in the philological dimension of the Greek scientific heritage, the Savile brothers and Cuffe are unusual in an English context. More generally Greek had taken its place behind other preoccupations by this period. In 1574, for example, Philip Sidney considered studying Greek at Padua but was discouraged by his mentor Hubert Languet, who believed it would be too difficult and time-consuming and not particularly suited to a gentleman of Sidney's high position. (Languet on the other hand endlessly recommended to Sidney the advantages of acquiring good friends.)

The Paduan setting of John Cheke's disquisitions on Demosthenes' *Three Orations* in the mid-1550s suggests a hardly more serious commitment to Greek studies among English students at Padua.[124] First, Cheke was merely continuing a series of lectures which he had begun in Cambridge before the accession of Mary. Second, in the context of the Marian exile this work may have assumed a hardly concealed political function, as did Thomas Wilson's English translation of the *Orations*, which presents an implied parallel between the tyrant Philip of Macedon and Philip II of Spain; Wilson's work had been inspired by Cheke's. Furthermore, the work of Wilson and probably of Cheke was one of explicating and translating the text for an English-speaking audience rather than of using it as a tool for Greek teaching or for restoring its textual purity. Finally, nobody other than Englishmen is recorded at Cheke's lectures and all the Englishmen were Marian exiles.[125] The conclusion that this episode was largely conditioned by the experience of political and religious exile rather than by the kind of disinterested humanism characteristic of the Leonico circle seems irresistible. By the 1550s, then, the English uses of Padua had already undergone a fundamental change, a change, it must be noted, which coincided with the movement in English attendance at Padua away from the arts university and towards the law university. This change is the theme of the next chapter.

5

Exiles, Tourists, and Intelligencers

Even before the Marian exile, Padua functioned as a place of refuge. In the case of Reginald Pole, Italy was to become the focus of an alternative set of values, beliefs, and ways of living, but the immediate circumstances of his arrival there in 1521 suggest that the city was a convenient respite from an angry king. For his visit to Padua, as for the whole of his previous education, Pole was dependent on the benevolence of Henry VIII, but from 1518 his family encountered problems in their relationship with their royal cousin. In this year Wolsey began to raise the king's suspicions against Edward Stafford, duke of Buckingham, the Poles' cousin from the Stafford line and the greatest magnate in the land.[1] Much is still unclear about this episode, but in any case it ended in Buckingham's trial and execution in May 1521. Both at the time and subsequently Wolsey was seen as the main instigator of the movements against Buckingham, and it is a conversation between Wolsey and Buckingham in 1516 which links the Staffords and the Poles. Apparently Wolsey had recommended a marriage between Buckingham's son, Henry Lord Stafford and the daughter of the earl of Shrewsbury. Buckingham liked the match in principle, but Shrewsbury complained that the dowry being asked was too large.[2] Buckingham thus turned his attentions to Ursula Pole, daughter of the countess of Salisbury, Reginald's sister. Indentures were drawn up in October 1518 and the marriage of Ursula and Henry took place in February 1519. It linked two of the great noble lines of the realm, both with potential claims to the throne, and the two families enjoyed close relations from the time of the marriage. Presumably this was exactly what Wolsey had hoped to avoid: now he had been slighted.

Independently or otherwise, suspicion began to fall on the Poles.[3] From March 1521 until Buckingham's execution, the countess of Salisbury, Reginald's mother, was temporarily replaced as Mary Tudor's governess; Henry Lord Montagu and Geoffrey, Reginald's brothers, were imprisoned in the Tower under suspicion of treason; and another brother, Arthur, was ejected from court.[4] As Buckingham's most recent biographer writes, 'When the Duke was arrested in 1521, no family came in for a greater share of the king's displeasure than the Poles.'[5]

There has been some difficulty over the precise dating of Pole's first departure for, and arrival in, Padua, but it is clear that these took place in March and April 1521 respectively.[6] His decision to go to Padua has never been linked to his family circumstances in that year, but the particular timing of his journey is suggestive. His certainly genuine intention to study at one of Europe's most renowned universities may have been supplemented by a desire to escape a difficult situation at home or may have been prompted by the king himself. After all, he was being sent there by the king as part of the continuing royal patronage of his education.[7] There is no evidence that aspersions were cast on Pole's loyalty personally, but his family situation certainly affected Henry's view of him; in a letter from the Venetian ambassador in London, Antonio Surian, to the Venetian government, which must have arrived in Venice very soon after Pole's arrival, he is named in connection with the arrest of his brother. Surian recounts that when Henry VIII learned how much was being done in Padua for his cousin, the king said that too much ought not to be done for him, in case he proved disloyal 'like the others.'[8]

The 'refugee' element in Pole's early experience of Padua can be multiplied for other students throughout the century; the presence of a number of opponents of Henry VIII's religious policies gathered around Pole at Padua and Venice in the early 1530s has already been discussed. Religion also explains the departure of Hugh Turnbull from England in 1547; he gained a Paduan doctorate in theology in 1550, along with George Dudgeon. On the other hand, the Welshman William Thomas's journey to Italy at about the same time had been undertaken in order to escape creditors in England. Having taken with him letters of exchange belonging to his patron Sir Anthony Browne, he was arrested on his arrival in Venice in 1546 on the instructions of the English ambassador, Edmund Harvel. But the Protestant Thomas must then have benefited from the relaxed religious attitudes in the Venetian Republic about which he remarks in *The History of Italy*.[9] This may indeed explain his later journey out of the Papal State and back to the Veneto in 1547, where he stayed until the following year.

Due to fortuitous documentary survival, notably of the diary of Thomas Hoby, the largest single cluster of Englishmen in Padua before the 1590s can be identified during the reign of Mary. The evidence is lacking to describe each of those encountered by Hoby in 1554 as a 'Marian exile'; a number of them had been travelling abroad in the late 1540s, like Hoby himself.[10] But the contemporary observation of the law student Basilius Amerbach, that a number of Englishmen had arrived in the city from France in around July 1554, does suggest that a large and socially cohesive group of Englishmen were to be found in Padua in that year.[11] And for those, identified by Christina Garrett, who went on to join Protestant congregations in Switzerland or Germany, their presence in Padua is easily explained;[12] from this period to the beginning of the seventeenth century, Padua was famous in England for the liberties – religious and otherwise – allowed to its students.[13] Nevertheless, we do not know what John Ashley, John Cutts, Henry Neville, Richard Bertie, Roger Carew, Henry Cornwallis, Henry Kingsmill, Thomas Wyndham, Thomas Fitzwilliams, and John Brooke, all of them encountered by Hoby in 1554, were doing in Padua, though we may guess that Hoby's more intimate companions, his brother Sir Philip, Thomas Wrothe, and Anthony Cooke (as well as John Cheke) joined him in the study of Italian, and, like him, attended some lectures at the *studium*. Hoby encountered two known students of the law university, John Orphinstrange and Henry Denny, and it would not be surprising if Denny's brothers Charles and Anthony, also encountered by Hoby, were formal students as well. We know that Hoby's acquaintances Francis Southwell, John Tamworth, John Schiere, Matthew Carew (the brother of Roger), and William Drury also studied in the city. John Pelham and his tutor John Everard, and John Jewel were also students at Padua in this period, though Hoby does not record encounters with them.

In the later Marian period, a larger number of formal students of the law university are identifiable. These included William Morley, John Hambey, Sebastian Bryskett, George Acworth, and Francis Alford; the electoral figures for the English nation show a corresponding increase in numbers from 1556. In the mid-1550s, Edward Courtenay, earl of Devon, seems also to have been a student at the law university, and it is probable that his acquaintance there, Thomas Wilson, attended lectures in law in 1555 and 1556. After advancing an Englishman's divorce suit at Rome and imprisonment by the Roman Inquisition,

Wilson took a doctorate in civil law at Ferrara in 1559. He had been in Padua at the same time as Francis Walsingham, whose epitaph was to contrast his travels as an 'adolescent' for the sake of education with his travels in early manhood as an exile.[14]

Padua was also a refuge for a significant number of Catholics in the 1560s and 1570s, a fact which has gone entirely unnoticed in the voluminous literature on the English diaspora in the reign of Elizabeth. This literature has concentrated on more assertively political and religious centres of opposition to the Elizabethan regime. English institutions existed to train Catholic missionaries, and politically subversive plots were hatched, and Catholic literature printed, in Spain, the Low Countries, and Rome. Dozens of English students fled to these centres, especially from an Oxford which had remained persistently Catholic, but which was beginning to demand stringent oaths of religious obedience from its students.[15] Due to the religious schism, there was a decline in diplomatic relations between England and Venice in the Elizabethan period, with fewer Venetian ambassadors visiting England and no fully accredited resident English ambassador in Venice between Peter Vannes, who was recalled in 1556, and Sir Anthony Standen, who was installed in 1603.[16] Despite the Elizabethan intelligence network, little information on English residents in Padua seems to have reached the English government in this period. Rawdon Brown's *Venetian Calendar* indicates a corresponding decline in intelligence reaching the Venetian government about the Englishmen resident in its territories. Therefore much information on some Englishmen in Padua for this period is available only in unpublished and hitherto unexplored material in Padua's notarial archive.

By its very nature, this material is limited in what it can tell us about religion, but the fact that so many of these students came from Oxford, and several from Oxford's most Catholic institution, New College, is itself a strong indication of where their sympathies lay. Four of the Englishmen who emerge from these records had pursued BCLs in Oxford: Anthony Fortescue, George Gattacre, John Le Rous, and Jerome Sapcot. These were students of law at Padua, and, as suggested above, the rising association in the minds of later Elizabethans of the civil law with popish tyranny suggests in itself that some of them were also exiles for religion. For some of these law students there is more solid evidence of religious inclination. Sapcot's father probably remained a Catholic under Elizabeth.[17] Robert Poyntz and Richard White, both from New College, Oxford, were the authors of Catholic religious works. The declarations of Catholic faith in the doctoral examinations in law of John Le Rous and John Hart may suggest that they too were Catholics. This is confirmed in the case of Le Rous by the fact that he names Henry Fitzalan – who was implicated in the Northern Rising of 1569 and in the Norfolk conspiracy of 1571 – and John Lumley, Fitzalan's son-in-law, as his guarantors in a *procura* at Padua of 1571,[18] and by the fact that he associated there with Richard Shelley in the same year.[19] In the words of his cousin Philip Sidney, Richard Shelley, *consiliarius* of the English nation in 1567, was 'sadly addicted to popery';[20] the Grand Prior of the Knights of St John, Shelley later moved to Rome, where he was involved in the affairs of the English hospice. John Hart may be identical with the Catholic missionary who later supplied information on recusants to Francis Walsingham and entered the Society of Jesus. Nicholas Wendon, a witness to Hart's doctorate in 1574, was ordained as a priest in Rome in 1578. Robert Peckham, a friend of Jerome Sapcot and Richard White, also gravitated to Rome.

In the 1580s and 1590s, only occasional students from Oxford and Cambridge seem to have migrated to Padua for religious reasons. English Jesuits and seminary priests from the English College in Rome occasionally spent some time in the city, and no doubt the larger number of tourists to the Veneto in this period included some Englishmen with Catholic sympathies. All of these would have been in contact in Padua with Richard Willoughby. A friend of Galileo's, Willoughby, later described by the English ambassador in Venice as 'an infectious papist,' was, as Anthony Fortescue had also become, a permanent resident in Padua, involved in the law university and a friend to most of the other English visitors in the city.[21]

But for other Englishmen, exile was more politically than religiously motivated. Like Reginald Pole decades before, Henry Fitzalan, earl of Arundel, found Padua a convenient place of respite from the wrath of his monarch in 1566; on the pretext of his gout he sought out the baths around Padua.[22] Although Fitzalan had no official dealings with the university there, it may be that he took the opportunity to improve himself through the purchase of books. For example, a copy of Johannes Paduanus's *Viridarium mathematicorum* published in Venice in 1563 has his name – and that of Lord Lumley, to whom he bequeathed his library – inscribed on the frontispiece.[23] Fitzalan's amanuensis, the Welsh antiquarian Humphrey Llwyd, purchased two books in Venice during this visit,[24] and possibly more, and took the opportunity, while in Padua, of discussing Welsh orthography with Richard White.[25] Llwyd also owned a copy of Leandro Alberti's *Descrittione di tutta l'Italia*, which may even have inspired the visit – Alberti recommends the baths at Abano near Padua.[26] Although Fitzalan's anonymous biographer claimed that 'he returned home again within fourteen months, perfectly restored to his former strength of limb and perfect health,'[27] in a later work Llwyd denigrates the efficacy of the baths in Italy. Having been kicked by a horse in Milan on the way to Padua, he was in pain for twelve months until, returning to England, the waters at Bath cured him within six days.[28]

If this stream of exiles suggests continuity in the English uses of Padua, it should not be allowed to disguise the fact that from the late 1540s, a different type of traveller came to visit the city. Having usually spent some years in Oxford and Cambridge and at the Inns of Court, he was drawn by a new vogue for secular, educational travel, characterized by a self-conscious interest in the contemporary state of foreign societies, their histories, peoples, cultures, and their political and social organizations – a kind of anthropology of the foreign by way of travel, by which the self, and England, were to be known better. Thus Ralph Winwood's licence to go abroad in the 1590s says that the aim of his travels is 'that by the increase of his experience in the world, and learning of languages, he may return the more able to do service in his own country.'[29] 'He therefore that intends to travel out of his own country,' wrote Robert Dallington in his *Method for travell* of circa 1605, 'must likewise resolve to travel out of his country fashion, and indeed out of himself … He must determine that the end of his travel is his ripening in knowledge and the end of his knowledge is the service of his country.'[30]

As an historical phenomenon, later Tudor travel is difficult to pin down, because of its lack of structure and scattered sources. But the sheer numbers frequenting the Paduan *studium* before or after spells in Germany, Switzerland, other places in Italy, and France, suggest that foreign travel was becoming an educational institution no less real than the places of learning in England where most travellers had spent some time immediately prior to their departure. Travel was also a rite of passage for the young and self-consciously English gentleman, and the literature which it generated was another 'form of nationhood.'[31] And consequently travel to Padua became politicized, with a closer relationship between students there and the English government emerging particularly in the 1590s, when the survival of the law university's matriculation register enables us to see its real extent.

Earlier in the century, the English students Richard Morison and Thomas Starkey both represent a transitional moment in these respects in their combining a humanistic education with an interest in the contemporary organization of Italian societies. For Morison there is explicit evidence in his writings that he studied ancient Greek authors and Scripture as well as moderns such as Machiavelli, while his letters reveal him as a fluent speaker of the Italian vernacular.[32] The heavily humanistic atmosphere more fully imbibed by Starkey – the friend of Niccolò Leonico Tomeo – may also help to explain why it has proved so difficult to trace in his intellectual biography an explicit interest in the contemporary politics of the Venetian Republic, yet such an interest is suggested by his *Dialogue between Pole and Lupset*. Starkey's discretion, as it were, is to be contrasted with the open interest in contemporary Italian political forms displayed about two decades later in the writings of William Thomas, who stayed in Padua in 1548.

Thomas was a member of the gentry circles encountered by Thomas Hoby in the Veneto in this period. Indeed the two had already met in Strasbourg, and later travelled together to France. Although it is unlikely that Thomas was a formal student at Padua, the city seems to have functioned for him, as for Hoby, as a place of study – he remarks in his *History of Italy* on the university[33] – and, implicitly, as a respite from more energetic travels. There Thomas wrote his ground-breaking *Principal Rules of the Italian Grammar* at the request of John Tamworth.[34] Thomas's interest in foreign places is underscored by a fierce patriotism and an anxiety about the contemporary state of England. In the dedicatory letter to his English translation of Josaphat Barbaro's Italian account of his travels in Persia, for example, Thomas explains that the purpose of the work is to show how barbarously other peoples live compared to the civilized English.[35] His *Il pellegrino inglese*, a dramatic dialogue set in Bologna in 1546, in which the author defends the schismatic policy of Henry VIII against a group of Italian detractors, functions towards similar ends.[36] Remarkable for its impartiality, seriousness, and comprehensiveness, given it was written in 1549, Thomas's *History of Italy* is nevertheless intended to instruct the reader in the benefits of prudent and honourable rule on the one hand, and the shame of 'tyranny and ill governance' on the other. Thomas's dedicatory letter to the earl of Warwick catalogues such moral antitheses; as in Elizabethan drama, Italy for Thomas is already a theatre in which to observe the consequences of extreme human vice and virtue.[37] In the same letter Thomas demonstrates a Machiavellian preoccupation with the workings of fortune in history and the problems involved in making alterations in political and legal institutions. In Thomas's 'Disquisitions on affairs of state,' these preoccupations are mobilized more directly for the service of English government: the 'Disquisitions' were written for the young King Edward, and contain Thomas's thoughts on subjects such as 'Whether it be expedient to vary with the time' and 'Whether it be better for a common wealth that the power be in the nobilitie or in the commonaltie'; Machiavelli's *Discourses* are quoted directly.[38]

This is entirely in keeping with Thomas's interest in contemporary forms of political organization and vernacular tongues. In the dedicatory letter to his English translation of Johannes Sacrobosco's *De sphaera*, written some time before 1552, Thomas rebels against the humanist elevation of a Latin education which had informed the Paduan sojourns of so many of his predecessors. Why, he asks rhetorically, are there so few good authors in the vernacular, answering that it is because children learn Latin more thoroughly than English.[39] The purpose of his work is to inspire Englishmen to knowledge of science in their own tongue, a key feature, in Thomas's eyes, of the glory and achievements of so many other nations: 'Wherefore if our nation desier to triumphe in Civile knoledge, as other nations do, the meane must be that eche man first covett to florishe in his owne naturall tongue, withoute the whiche he shal have much ado to be excellent in any other tongue.' Aware of the difficulties of this endeavour, Thomas provides the reader with a glossary of scientific terms appearing in *De sphaera*, which he has anglicized from the Latin.[40]

The resources of the English vernacular in education had already been advanced and promoted in England in the writings of Sir Thomas Elyot in the 1530s. But Thomas's sojourn in Padua took place during the first decade of the Paduan academic movement, when the Accademia degli Infiammati sought to systematize and promote scientific learning in the Italian vernacular. Indeed this period marked an important stage in the fragmentation of education in the city: the Accademia defined itself in opposition to subjects available for study in the universities;[41] it also established its own elaborate constitution and ceremonial. No English attendees at Infiammati lectures are known, but the demise of the *volgare* ideals of the academy was said to have resulted from the enormous popularity of the lectures among foreign students, which forced speakers to address their audiences in Latin rather than Italian.[42] This new type of extramural, vernacular activity at Padua coincided with the arrival of informal English gentlemen-students like Thomas and Hoby. In the English context, the rise of a genuine Italian literary and scientific culture in the 1540s can again be contrasted with the way in which vernacular issues were treated earlier. Although Pietro Bembo came to be the hero and champion of the Infiammati, Niccolò Leonico Tomeo's account to Reginald Pole of the discussion about the vernacular at Bembo's villa in 1522, discussed above, is a humanistic, set-piece dialogue written in Latin.[43] In the 1530s, Richard Morison, as fierce a patriot as Thomas, also eschewed the vernacular, recommending legal rejuvenation through a Latin systematization of the English common law. In his unequivocal advocacy of vernacular writing, Thomas thus represents an important stage in concurrent and interconnected English and Italian cultural processes. His informal and vernacular-based 'civic' ethic anticipates by a few years the rising numbers of English students of 'civil science' in the more structured and Latinate atmosphere of Padua's law university.[44] And in choosing to translate Johannes Sacrobosco, a British writer of the thirteenth century, Thomas also presages the partial rehabilitation of medieval scientific writers which was to take place in England and elsewhere from the second half of the sixteenth century.[45] It is a telling indication of new priorities that the only previous work on astronomy by a Paduan alumnus was on the ancient *Sphaera* of pseudo-Proclus, translated from Greek into Latin by Thomas Linacre.

William Barker, in Italy and Padua at the same time and after William Thomas, is a similar case. He expanded the corpus of English translations from the Italian,[46] and he also published a collection of ancient and near-contemporary inscriptions which he had seen in the many Italian cities he visited.[47] And more famous is Thomas Hoby, who translated Castiglione's *Cortegiano* into English (published in 1561 and prefaced by a rousing defence of the vernacular written by John Cheke). His diary is full of descriptions of the history, topography, and political and social life of Italian cities, though much of this material was copied out of Leandro Alberti's *Descrittione di tutta l'Italia*.[48]

These basically positive English experiences of Italy were to be challenged during the confessional 'cold war' of the 1570s and 1580s. Some indication of a changed atmosphere comes already from the 1563 diary of Richard Smith, the travelling companion of Edward Unton; he criticizes Thomas's *History of Italy* for exaggerating the virtues of the city of Venice.[49] The mid-Elizabethan fulminations against educational travel – and especially travel to Italy – are well known and have recently been discussed elsewhere.[50] Roger Ascham in *The Schoolmaster* famously warned against the 'enchantments of Circe' abroad, and this was repeated by countless later commentators such as William Harrison.[51] In the 1570s he observed that the sons of noblemen and gentlemen bring home from Italy 'nothing but mere atheism, infidelity, vicious conversation, and ambitious and proud behaviour.' The 'earnest Protestant,' according to Harrison, returns asserting that 'faith and truth is to be kept where no loss or hindrance of a future purpose is sustained by holding of the same; and forgiveness only to be shewed when full revenge is made.'[52]

But to some extent these warnings were a function of the institution of travel itself. After all, English identity implicitly constituted itself from dialectical encounters with cultures which, on the one hand, were 'un-English,' but on the other, partook of a shared European identity made up of the classical and Christian heritages. Travel would have been purposeless had it not involved some risk, some voyage into the unknown. While there is no doubt that during this period the threat of the Inquisition and the Elizabethan government's anxieties about its political and religious relations with Catholic Europe served to limit the extent of English visits to Italy, this should not be exaggerated. A large number of impeccably loyal Englishmen still made the journey, even if not all of them visited Rome. In fact in some senses the Veneto benefited from these restrictions because it was usually considered a safe place to be from a religious point of view, and it was sometimes the southernmost point of a traveller's tour in this period. In March 1581 Nicholas Faunt had reported from Paris to his friend Anthony Bacon that the 'humbling of our nation in Italy is daily worse,' that the Inquisition was operating in Venice, and that at Rome 'all ... English of the least suspicion can be gathered up.' But from Padua in July of the same year, urging Bacon to join him, he wrote 'I can promise you the state of Venice is more secure for all strangers than any place of France'; that he had heard it to be the same about his next destination (Tuscany); and he praised the Italians for not enquiring about foreigners' religious views, even if they suspected them of not being Catholics. 'I speak of the best sort,' he adds, 'and with the other there is no conversation.' He names eight Englishmen he has met in Padua, 'with others.'[53] Venice, said to be the home of the ideal constitution and of religious liberty, and a crossroads between east and west, was an important place to visit from an educational point of view.[54] It was also well known for its courtesans; travel necessarily retained the thrill of moral danger, and no doubt more English travellers enjoyed this feature of Venice than appears from the contents of their letters to friends, patrons, and family at home, which form the bulk of the evidence for their activities in this period.

Philip Sidney is a good example of a tourist to Padua, because his Protestant credentials are above suspicion, though his 'Grand Tour' took place soon after the Northern Rising, the queen's excommunication by the pope, and the Ridolfi Plot. Due to the combination of the enormous promise which contemporaries invested in him and his early death, a great deal of documentary evidence for his travels in 1573–4 has survived, and his itinerary and correspondence have been exhaustively reconstructed by James Osborn in *Young Philip Sidney*.

Sidney vacillated between Venice and Padua a total of seven times over a nine-month period, with a one-month tour of northern Italy in the middle.[55] Much of his time was spent in the expensive entertainment of other eminent noblemen, mainly from Germany and eastern Europe, and including Wolfgang Zündelin, who later became a friend in Venice of Henry and Thomas Savile.

Sidney was specifically advised by his mentor Hubert Languet not to study harder than befitted a man of his high station.[56] In this period he practised a little astronomy, geometry, and music, worked on his Latin and French, using Cicero's letters as his raw material, and contemplated applying himself to German and Greek; Languet encouraged the former and, as mentioned above, discouraged the latter.[57] Sidney was also interested in contemporary Venetian history, recommending to Languet Donato Giannotti's *Libro della repubblica de'Viniziani* and Contarini's *De magistratibus et republica Venetorum*, as well as Tarcagnota's *Delle historie del mondo* and the *Imprese* of Girolamo Ruscelli.[58] Presumably he himself bought copies of these books in Padua or Venice: his copy of Francesco Guicciardini's *La historia d'Italia* (Venice, 1569), now in the Houghton Library of Harvard University, is marked 'Philippo Sidneio. Patavii 20 Junii 1574.' His only participation in university life at Padua emerges in a document unknown to Osborn, his witnessing of the doctoral examination in law of John Hart on 7 June, 1574, together with his companion Griffin Maddox, and Nicholas Wendon, Rudolph Hopton, Jacobus Randolph, Richard Valiseso(?), and Vito Vassel(?).[59]

Sidney's impressions of Italy were not always positive.[60] The eclecticism of his interests and activities there, however, came to be typical: it is repeated in the quite large circle of English visitors to Padua in 1581 whose movements can be reconstructed from the detailed diary of one of them, Arthur Throckmorton.[61] He and a group of travellers which intermittently included Henry Neville, Robert Sidney, his cousin George Carew, and Henry Savile travelled through the

Netherlands, Germany, and Austria. Throckmorton arrived in Padua in June 1581 and hired for himself 'a chamber with a stable and a garderobe in Borgo Socco in John Bassan's house.'[62] In August he was joined by Carew, Neville, and Savile, and the whole group moved on to Ferrara, Florence, and Bologna in September. In Padua Throckmorton hired men to teach him Italian (at a rate of seven *lire* per month) and the lute (at a rate of eight *lire* per month);[63] he noted in his diary encounters with other Englishmen in the city, such as two Jesuit fathers on their way to Poland,[64] and Nicholas Faunt. Faunt stayed in Padua for about two months, but at the end of the academic year ('when the intermission beginneth') he moved on to Tuscany 'where the best language is,' and he carried a letter from Throckmorton out of Padua.[65] In Venice Throckmorton purchased a looking-glass and copies of Livy and Josephus in Italian;[66] in Padua he bought the *Della filosofia naturale* of the (formerly Paduan) philosopher Alessandro Piccolomini (Venice, 1565); and in Florence, immediately after departing from Padua, he bought G.B. Pigna's *Historia dei principi di Este* (Ferrara, 1570) and B. Scardeone's great celebration of Padua's cultural history, *De antiquitate urbis Patavii* (Basle, 1560).[67] He also notes in his journal that on 1 August 'the rector was chosen by the twenty-three nations' counsellors' at Padua.[68]

Throckmorton's travelling companion, Henry Savile, was a more serious scholar, and some of his activities in this respect have been mentioned above. But typically for this period, Savile was also interested in contemporary customs and politics during his Italian sojourn, noting in his commonplace book information about government, religion, trade, revenue, methods of warfare, foreign relations, and customs of various countries. Much of this material was written in Italian and was drawn from ancient histories as well as from contemporary Venetian diplomats and travellers such as Marc'Antonio Barbaro, Josaphat Barbaro, Giacomo Soranzo, and Bernardo Navagero.[69] Samuel Foxe, in Padua for a year and a half during 1584–6, did something similar in his commonplace book, noting down the major political events, English, Italian, and European, that took place during his stay. In his notes there are also Latin poems and epigrams, extracts from ancient Latin writers such as Livy and Valerius Maximus, and in Italian extracts from Castiglione's *Cortegiano*.

After his tour Foxe served as an MP and became a servant of Sir Thomas Heneage, vice-chamberlain to the queen. Throckmorton became a courtier and MP, as did Neville, and Carew became a lawyer. A striking number of visitors like these, during this period and later, became government agents abroad, diplomats, and ambassadors: they include Foxe, Neville, and Carew, and also Henry Wotton, John Finet, Henry Unton, Richard Spencer, Ralph Winwood, Ralph Eure, Edward Zouche, and Christopher Parkins. And several travellers of this period also produced relations of foreign countries or analyses of the political and religious situation in Europe, which came to be published. These include George Carew's *A relation of the state of France*, Edwin Sandys' extraordinary *A relation of the state of religion used in the west parts of the world* (first printed in 1605),[70] *The state of Christendom*, possibly authored by Henry Wotton,[71] and Fynes Moryson's monumental *Itinerary*, and his other European analysis, published only in this century, which also contains the most detailed description of the *studium* of Padua by any English traveller in this period.[72] Increasingly, travel was seen as both a useful preparation for service to the state and especially diplomatic service, and a means by which the government could gather information on the disposition of foreign governments, and on the activities of enemies to England abroad.[73] This institutionalization of travel was furthered in particular by two Elizabethan statesmen in the 1590s and early 1600s, first the earl of Essex, and then Sir Robert Cecil.[74]

In 1595 a long letter was written to the young Roger Manners, earl of Rutland (who appears in Padua later that year) advising him about his European tour.[75] The letter was a 'set piece' disquisition on the subject which circulated widely in manuscript, and was eventually printed in 1633. It has been ascribed to Francis Bacon or Henry Savile, but most commonly to the earl of Essex.[76] Even if Bacon or Savile or for that matter Henry Cuffe had a hand in it, all three were closely connected to Essex in this period, and it is clear that Rutland's travels were promoted by Essex and, from internal evidence, that the letter was intended to have been understood as written by him.[77]

The letter shows how completely the vogue for educational travel had been rehabilitated by the 1590s. Essex argues that the purpose of travel is the cultivation of the mind. Encounters with 'new delights,' as well as dangers such as war, are both to be encouraged – a striking change from the prudishness and paranoia of two decades earlier. Dangers will stir terrors and delights will stir passions in the young traveller, by which means he will learn something about himself, what desires in himself he will have to beware of in the future, what fears he will have to confront: 'In discovering your passions and meeting with them, give not way to yourself nor dispense with yourself in little, though resolving to conquer yourself in great.' Cultivation of the mind also includes acquiring 'civil knowledge' by 'study, by conference, and by observation.' He advises that private study means staying in the best places for some time, rather than frequently moving from place to place, that after a grounding in the liberal arts 'be conversant in the Histories, for they will best instruct you in matter moral, military, and politic.' Manners should take a tutor with him, 'or make some abode in the universities abroad, where you may hear the professors in every art,' and he should 'choose to confer with expert men.' In a further two letters, sent while Manners was already abroad, Essex advises him on what exactly to observe and note down, a wide range of information about topography, customs, arts, trade, government, the nobility, religion, and foreign affairs.[78]

No doubt Essex wanted some of this information for himself. Part of his bid to dominate the Elizabethan privy council and to encourage an active English foreign policy involved creating an extensive foreign intelligence network, and fostering the travels of many young Englishmen.[79] Even before this period, many of Essex's servants or allies, Anthony and Francis Bacon, for example, had had extensive foreign experience, and this had sometimes included periods in Venice and Padua, as in the cases of John Cecil (alias Snowden), Philip Sidney, Henry Wotton, Henry Scrope, Henry Unton, Henry Savile, Anthony Myly, Henry Neville, and Ralph Winwood.[80] At the beginning of his first letter to Manners, Essex notes that 'I hold it for a principle in the course of intelligence of state not to discourage men of mean sufficiency from writing to me,' and this very broad description of his intelligence activity is the only one that matches the other evidence, for this work ranged from the encouragement of gentleman tourists like Manners, to the establishment of semi-official diplomatic and intelligence missions in Venice and Florence.[81] At one end of the scale, it had simply become the thing to do for a traveller abroad to send his patron the occasional newsletter. At the other end, there was Essex's paid agent in Venice, the civil lawyer Dr Henry Hawkins, who as early as 1593 had been receiving intelligence reports at Doctors' Commons in London from the Paduan resident Richard Willoughby.[82] Moving to Venice in 1595, Hawkins sent intelligence reports on a weekly basis to Essex's friend Anthony Bacon, and these were digested, excerpted and then read to the queen until Hawkins's return to England in 1598.[83] The reports were to include, instructed Essex, 'an account by every post of the affairs not only of that state, and the state of Italy, but of Turkey and all places which are anywhere near to Venice.' Essex wanted up-to-date political news, especially concerning foreign relations, diplomacy, war, and armies, but also broader information about political organization, justice, revenues, and commodities.[84] Hawkins was ordered to make contacts with intelligencers in Europe to supply him with information, and in Venice he also played host to other of Essex's friends. These included Manners, whom he described to Anthony Bacon as 'an affectionate dependent of my most honourable good lord'[85] (Manners went on to marry Essex's stepdaughter in around 1599); Peregrine Bertie, Lord Willoughby d'Eresby, who was in Padua in 1596;[86] Thomas Sackville; and Thomas Lord Gray.[87] Hawkins was also in contact with a long-term Paduan resident, the astronomer Edmund Bruce, who was employed as an agent for Essex and reported to Anthony Bacon. Francis Davison was another Essex client, and was in Padua in 1597. Essex procured his licence to travel for three years in 1595[88] and gave him money to cover his expenses. Davison's task was to draw up relations of the places he visited, possibly on the plan which his father had set out for him.[89] (Davison's description of Saxony was sent to Essex but subsequently went missing, and his planned relations of Italian states remained unwritten.)[90] Henry Archer, who matriculated at Padua at the end of 1596, was known to Davison while in Italy and, on Anthony Bacon's instructions, made himself known to Hawkins and to Edmund Bruce, writing to Bacon about their affairs.[91] In 1597 he delivered to Essex the letter of one of his Italian intelligencers, Lorenzo Guicciardini.[92] Essex also sent his secretary Henry Cuffe abroad, where he visited the Grand Duke of Tuscany at Florence, matriculated at Padua in 1597, and from France supplied intelligence to another Essex client, Cuffe's former tutor Henry Savile.[93]

Essex invested a vast amount of money in this activity (it was probably Anthony Bacon's financial ruin as well), but with the appointment of his rival Sir Robert Cecil as principal secretary of state in 1596, his intelligence network faced serious competition. In this new position of undisputed power, Cecil naturally inherited the responsibilities for intelligence which had earlier been the work of Francis Walsingham, Thomas Heneage, and of his father Lord Burghley, and he revived and extended their work to an extent which would eventually outshine Essex's.[94]

In fact he had already used English intelligencers on the continent before this period. John Cecil (alias Snowden) acted as an agent for him in the early 1590s.[95] Seth Cocks had reported to him from Padua and elsewhere in 1593–4.[96] But from about 1597 to the early 1600s a larger number of English travellers in Italy began to send him news reports, or at least tried to. In the summer of 1597, for example, George Cranmer wrote to him from Padua: 'To write any of the ordinary and weekly advices which are current, and perhaps also coined here, were, as I conceive, nothing else but a tedious repetition of things long before known; neither can the knowledge of a poor stranger easily arise to any higher pitch of intelligence in regard of the private and retired nature of the Italian, on whom it is a matter difficult to fasten any acquaintance, but more difficult in that kind.'[97] Cranmer was not born for intelligence work, if this letter is anything to go by; evidently Italian discretion, which Nicholas Faunt had praised, had its disadvantages. But it is also true that Padua, unlike Venice, was probably not the best place from which to gather information on current affairs. Cranmer's presence there is an important reminder that he was not abroad merely to supply intelligence: in 1598 from Orleans – another university city – he wrote to Cecil with apologies and a request to reenter his service.[98] Better sources proved to be John Daniels, Aurelian Townshend, and Simeon Foxe. Foxe was a medical student in Padua whose studies were financed by Cecil on condition of regular news reports. About two dozen of these survive, sent from Padua and Venice to Cecil and to Cecil's secretary for intelligence matters, Thomas Wilson (who himself had also sent reports from Padua and Venice a year or so earlier).[99] Some of Cecil's intelligence came to him indirectly. Thomas Sackville, Lord Buckhurst, passed on to him his son Thomas's news from the continent in 1602.[100] John Payton's father, who had received newsletters from his son during his foreign tour of 1598–1601 (including Padua in 1599), promptly passed on the material he received to Cecil,[101] although we do not know whether Cecil was sent Payton's quite substantial political analyses of Germany and Bohemia, which he wrote up at Basle in 1599 and addressed to his father.[102] In the early 1600s Cecil also received regular newsletters from his agent in Venice, Giorgio Limauer.

Cecil, whose father had long recognized the value of educational travel,[103] also promoted or financed the tours of gentlemen whose intelligence reports are not extant and may not even have existed. Such men include Robert Bertie, *consiliarius* of the English nation at Padua in 1603–4,[104] and Edward Silliard, present in the city in 1602; Cecil also relied on the information sent by his friend Lord Gray.[105]

Since the 1530s English travellers abroad had been informing the government about foreign opinion and activity, and this included many reports from Italy. The foreign intelligence network of Sir Francis

Walsingham in the 1570s and 1580s was extensive, and had included some informers from the Veneto, such as the Paduan students Sebastian Bryskett and John Wroth.[106] However, at least in terms of Italy, the activities of Essex and Cecil were on an altogether different scale.

Nevertheless, although this material may explain how an Englishman could afford a visit to Padua, in few cases does it explain why he was there. The survival of dozens of letters to government secretaries should not distort the fact that most visitors remained tourists and students primarily, albeit with an interest in the contemporary state of foreign societies which the government – which, after all, issued the passports – was in a position to exploit. What this intelligence material does reveal is that, three-quarters of a century after Henry VIII had financed Reginald Pole's studies in Padua, Englishmen in significant numbers were again acquiring official or semi-official support for their journeys there, due to the burgeoning diplomatic ambitions of the late Tudor government. By these means the English grand tour came of age at the end of the Tudor period.

Conclusion

The university and city of Padua had a remarkable impact on England's culture in the Tudor period. Padua influenced a range of extraordinary English cultural, intellectual, and institutional developments, some of them more sustained than others, some of them fairly self-evident in sources such as letters, and others only visible through the collective biographies of a particular group of individuals, or through the teasing out of meaning from particular texts. Any study of something as intangible as the cultural and intellectual relations between two countries must manage several complex issues: how to detect and describe the sometimes unknown ways in which different cultures draw on each other to produce something which may seem both completely new to each of them and at the same time all too characteristically a part of themselves; given this, how at the same time to allow for the rich diversity within single cultural contexts, such as England and Padua; how to take account of simultaneous but different processes of cultural transformation in the different countries; and how, in encountering the past, to negotiate the inescapable framework of today's cultural and national categories, themselves partly the product of the historical processes which must be described. In attempting to remain aware of these issues, this study of the Tudor experience in Italy has tried to show that Padua's extraordinary impact on sixteenth-century England was culturally wide-ranging, manifested itself in different ways, and can be accessed as a whole only through a variety of approaches.

In part, Padua did what Italy as a whole is always supposed to have done for Renaissance England. It played a fundamental role in fostering humanistic studies in the period from the 1490s to the 1530s when these studies were still relatively new in England, particularly in the fields of the Greek language and the study of humanistic Aristotelianism, and, after Erasmus began to reorient the intellectual agenda, the study of the church fathers. Far from making Italy irrelevant, the humanism of Erasmus and his north European *familia* reinvigorated Padua's place as a centre for these studies, a development guaranteed by the crucial role of mentor and friend played by Niccolò Leonico Tomeo. If these intellectual interests seem more intermittent after Leonico's death in 1531, it is no coincidence that the 1530s also witnessed England's first Reformation, which served to transform the English uses of Padua. Though he could not have known the Paduan philosopher, John Caius's lectures at Padua in the early 1540s on the Greek texts of Aristotle were Leonico's particular legacy to the university, since he had been the first to undertake such lectures over four decades earlier. And this vivid Aristotelian tradition also animated the studies of William Harvey and his contemporaries towards the end of the period. But Caius and Harvey were students of medicine, and they were as much the inheritors of that illustrious Paduan tradition as of any other broader movement. Equally I have sought to demonstrate that the social credo of a political thinker like Thomas Starkey was heavily indebted to the Paduan medical tradition. The English medical Renaissance, itself a variegated phenomenon – the work of philology of Linacre, Caius, and John Clement, the College of Physicians which these and other Paduan alumni sustained and nurtured, the naturalistic studies of Wotton, the discoveries of Harvey – is scarcely conceivable without Padua.

In other humanistic and 'arts' fields, there are few individuals in the second half of the sixteenth century for whom Padua offered the opportunity of real scholarly discovery, textual, scientific, or otherwise, though Henry Cuffe and the Saviles are probably among the exceptions. For by this period, the resources which Padua offered to a changed and changing England were rather different. The fact that the English nation existed in Padua's university of jurists rather than in that of arts and medicine is a reminder that in the past and up to the fifteenth century Englishmen had come to Padua to study civil and canon law. If these numbers were dwindling in the early Tudor period, the Reformation, ironically, came to ensure that Padua again became a centre for legal studies, most intensively from the late 1540s to the 1570s; but English law students in an earlier period who went on to influential careers in England – for example, Cuthbert Tunstall and Henry Coles – ensured the continuity of this medieval tradition, while students of law of the 1550s, like Matthew Carew and Laurence Huse, were extremely active as equity lawyers until the end of the Tudor period. It was not, perhaps, in the nature of the study of traditional, Bartolist law that many law students should have left us letters which conjure up a particular legal ambience like those of Leonico do for students of humanistic subjects. We have only the law university itself: the records of that political playground reveal – much more than they help us to understand – a lost world of ambition, cooperation, and conflict, all taking place within the structure of national organizations. But the prosopographical and institutional evidence deriving from both Padua and England is incontrovertible in its indication that the 'law of Padua' – the Roman law of the Bartolists – had an important role to play in the development of English law and political consciousness.

However, the history of English legal study at Padua is also the history of religious and political exile, and law students like Richard White and Anthony Fortescue, who awaited the return of a Catholic regime in England in vain, were joined in the Elizabethan period by other exiles, all of whom had had their counterparts among Protestants at Padua in the reign of Mary. It is sometimes suggested that the English Reformation had a disastrous impact on the development of enlightened, educational travel in England, but this was not always the case. Thomas Hoby's extraordinary travel diary spans the period from Edwardian Protestantism to Marian reaction, and Hoby's tourist successors, whether they were devoutly attached to old or new religions or were largely indifferent, continued to visit Venice and Padua throughout the Elizabethan period, reaching unprecedented numbers by the 1590s. Many of these served as intelligence agents for the English government, a fact which accelerated the process by which Padua became institutionalized as a destination on the English grand tour. At the time when Shakespeare chose to change the Ferrarese setting of George Gascoigne's *Supposes* to 'Fair Padua, nursery of arts' for his *Taming of the Shrew* (c. 1592),[1] and to have his Lucentio arrive there to 'haply institute a course of learning and ingenious studies,' the city had become a cultural symbol, a place to be seen and to be seen in, and a school for gentlemanly and political attributes like Italian, the lute, and, to an extent which has previously been underestimated, the observation of foreign societies for political purposes.

In numerical terms, and excluding some outstanding exceptions, English study in Padua in the Tudor period thus transformed itself from the classicizing to the contemporary, from the Latinate to the vernacular, from the scholarly to the gentlemanly, and from the pursuit of the relatively few to that of a large number. That process begins, perhaps, with Richard Morison and Thomas Starkey, it includes Hoby and William Thomas, and it culminates in Fynes Morison, Roger Manners, and the other gentle and noble tourists of the Elizabethan *fin de siècle*. This set the pattern for the seventeenth century. In around 1612 the English ambassador in Venice, Sir Dudley Carleton, claimed to the doge that there were about seventy English gentlemen in Venice and Padua.[2] And from 1618 a separate English matriculation register records the signatures and payments to an English bedel of every English visitor to Padua, and continues to do so well into the eighteenth century.[3] Constantly in the background are the attempts of successive English monarchs, governments, polemicists, writers, and artists to prescribe, define and describe the nature of their country and polity.

It is the flavour of this endeavour and its intimate relationship to the large-scale cultural phenomenon of travel to Padua which is evoked by the memorial picture for Sir Henry Unton, reproduced as a frontispiece in this volume, now in the National Portrait Gallery in London.[4] Painted in or after 1596 and celebrating the public events of Unton's life and death, it is a potent testimony to Padua's reputation and resonance. In this episodic and idiosyncratic work the young Unton, a visitor to Padua in the late 1570s or early 1580s, is first shown installed in a room in an Oxford college. In the next 'scene,' across the Channel, the city of Padua is represented set against the Alps, adjacent to a tiny depiction of Venice. Unton on horseback rides in front of Padua to the next 'scene,' which represents his military service in the Netherlands. Unton's visit was evidently a prestigious event which helped to define him publicly and was as worthy of commemoration as his other accomplishments as a gentleman – study at Oxford, and military and diplomatic service. But the fact that Unton is shown travelling *past* Padua, rather than dwelling in it, is suggestive more of an enlightened tourism than of scholarly immersion. The picture testifies to the resilience of Padua's English uses in the Tudor period, but it also hints at the ways in which these uses had been transformed by the end of the sixteenth century.

Notes

Introduction

1 General studies of the English in Padua include A. Andrich, *De natione Anglica et Scota iuristarum Universitatis Patavinae ab a. 1222 p. Ch. n. usque ad a. 1738* (Padua, 1892); H.F. Brown, 'Inglesi e Scozzesi all'Università di Padova dall'anno 1618 sino al 1765,' in *Monografie storiche sullo Studio di Padova* (Venice, 1922), 137–213; and R.J. Mitchell, 'English Students at Padua, 1460–75,' *Transactions of the Royal Historical Society* 19 (1936), 101–17. For a call for further research on the subject, see A.C. Krey, 'Padua in the English Renaissance,' *Huntington Library Quarterly* 2 (1947), 129–34, fulfilled in part for the period dealt with here by K.R. Bartlett, 'English Students at Padua, 1521–58,' *Proceedings of the PMR Conference* 4 (1979), 88–107, and K.R. Bartlett, 'Worshipful Gentlemen of England: The *Studio* of Padua and the Education of the English Gentry in the Sixteenth Century,' *Renaissance and Reformation* 6 (1982), 235–48.

2 The English College in Rome, which trained Catholic priests for missionary activity in England in the Elizabethan period, is a special case and is not included in this statement. See *The English Hospice in Rome, The Venerabile*, Sexcentenary Issue 21 (1962); M.E. Williams, *The Venerabile English College, Rome: A History, 1579–1979* (London, 1979); and *The Liber Ruber of the English College, Rome*, ed. W. Kelly (London, 1940), I. For English students in Italy generally see G.B. Parks, *The English Traveller in Italy* (Rome, 1954), esp. 621–40; E.J. Baskerville, 'The English Traveller to Italy, 1547–60,' (PhD dissertation, University of Columbia, 1967); K.R. Bartlett, *The English in Italy, 1525–1558* (Geneva, 1991); R. McCain, 'English Travellers in Italy during the Renaissance,' *Bulletin of Bibliography* 19 (1947–8), 68–9, 93–5, 117–19; and C. Howard, *English Travellers of the Renaissance* (London, 1914).

3 See Parks, *English Traveller*, 621–8.

4 I have been able to identify only a handful of English students at the university of Bologna in the period immediately after that dealt with by Parks, from 1526 to 1603: John Pelham and Laurence Huse, for whom see Appendix; Laurence Bush (Bologna, Archivio di Stato, Studio 140, fols 34–5 records his doctoral examination in civil law in 1543); John Forrest (ibid., Studio 379, no fol. no., May 1566, records him as *consiliarius* of the English nation at Bologna); Andrew 'Silius' (ibid., May 1567, records him as *consiliarius* of the English nation at Bologna); and the medical students John Symyngs, Alban Hill (a Welshman), Martin Corembeck, and Peter Daquet, on whom see W. Munk, *The Roll of the Royal College of Physicians of London* (London, 1878), I, 51, 55–6. Also note the presence of the English Dominican, John Hopton, in the late 1520s (see *DNB*). The 'matricola Belvisi' of the *studium* of Bologna records the matriculation of fourteen Englishmen into the law university between 1553 and 1603: one in each of the years 1554–6, 1575–6, 1582, and 1603, two in 1557 (perhaps including John Pelham), and five in 1580. See G.P. Brizzi, 'Matricole ed effettivi. Aspetti della presenza studentesca a Bologna fra Cinque e Seicento,' *Studi e memorie per la storia dell'Università di Bologna* 7 (1988), table 1 and 239–58.

5 For English attendance at Louvain see P. Vandermeersch, 'Some Aspects of the Intellectual Relationships between the Southern Netherlands and England, Sixteenth and Seventeenth Centuries,' in *Academic Relations between the Low Countries and the British Isles, 1450–1700*, ed. H. de Ridder-Symoens and J.M. Fletcher (Ghent, 1989), 5–23, esp. 23. For Leiden see O.P. Grell, 'The Attraction of Leiden University for English Students of Medicine and Theology, 1590–1642,' in *The Great Emporium: The Low Countries as a Cultural Crossroads in the Renaissance and the Eighteenth Century*, ed. C.C. Barfoot and R. Todd (Amsterdam and Atlanta, GA, 1992), 83–104. For English students abroad generally see M. Dowling, *Humanism in England in the Reign of Henry VIII* (London, 1986), 140–75 and C.H. Garrett, *The Marian Exiles* (Cambridge, 1938).

6 For examples see Sir Thomas Hoby, 'A Booke of the Travaile and Life of Me Thomas Hoby,' *Camden Society 10* (London, 1902), 9–10; 'The Grand Tour of an Elizabethan,' ed. A.H.S. Yeames, *Papers of the British School at Rome 7* (1914), 106; F. Moryson, *An Itinerary* (Glasgow, 1907), I, 150, 155; T. Wilson, *Arte of Rhetorique*, ed. J. Derrick (New York and London, 1982), xxxi, cxxix.

7 Richard Guylforde, Robert Langton, and Richard Torkington.

8 For example, Henry Fitzalan, the Welshman Humphrey Llwyd, and

Arthur Throckmorton. (For the latter see Canterbury, Canterbury Cathedral Archives, MS U. 85, Box 38, I, fol. 67v.)

9 See *Relazioni dei rettori veneti in terraferma*, IV: *Podestaria e capitanato di Padova* (Milan, 1975), 17, 25.

10 See his letter to Hugo Blotius from Padua in 1591 in Vienna, Österreichische Nationalbibliothek, MS 9737z[17], fol. 172.

11 See T. Coryat, *Coryat's Crudities* (Glasgow, 1905), I, 297.

12 See especially the works of Vivian Nutton cited in the bibliography.

13 See A.G. Brotto and G. Zonta, *La facolta teologica dell'Università di Padova* (Padua, 1922), and L. Gargan, *Lo Studio teologico e la biblioteca dei domenicani a Padova nel Tre e Quattrocento* (Padua, 1971). But note that the status and extent of theology teaching is the subject of current controversy. See J. Monfasani, 'Aristotelians, Platonists, and the Missing Ockhamists: Philosophical Liberty in Pre-Reformation Italy,' *Renaissance Quarterly* 46 (1993), 247–76; A. Poppi, 'Il dibattito sull'esclusione della teologia dal ruolo universitario nello Studio di Padova (1363–1806), un aggiornamento,' *Atti e memorie dell'Accademia Patavina di Scienze, Lettere ed Arti* 103 (1990–1), 41–56.

14 See *DNB*.

15 Hugh Turnbull and George Dudgeon.

16 John Cecil, Christopher Bagshaw, and George Gifford.

17 For example see *The Cambridge Companion to Renaissance Humanism*, ed. J. Kraye (Cambridge, 1996).

Chapter 1: The English Nation at Padua

1 BL, MS Harley 288, fol. 284v.

2 Before 1534 it was the 'English with Scottish' nation, a composite like most of the other nations.

3 This discussion draws on the following studies: F. Dupuigrenet Desroussilles, 'L'Università di Padova dal 1405 al Concilio di Trento,' in *Storia della cultura veneta*, ed. G. Arnaldi and M. Pastore Stocchi (Vicenza, 1980), III, pt 2, 607–47; N.G. Siraisi, *Arts and Sciences at Padua* (Toronto, 1973); P.F. Grendler, 'The University of Padua, 1405–1600: A Success Story,' *History of Higher Education Annual* 10 (1990), 7–17; L. Rossetti, *The University of Padua: An Outline of Its History* (Milan, 1972); R.E. Ohl, 'The University of Padua, 1405–1509: An International Community of Students and Professors' (PhD dissertation, University of Pennsylvania, 1980); P. Kibre, *The Nations in the Medieval Universities* (Cambridge, MA, 1948); P. Kibre, *Scholarly Privileges in the Middle Ages* (London, 1961); *A History*

of the University in Europe, ed. H. de Ridder-Symoens (Cambridge, 1992), I; H. Rashdall, *The Universities of Europe in the Middle Ages*, ed. F.M. Powicke and A.B. Emden (Oxford, 1936), I and II; and A.B. Cobban, 'Medieval Student Power,' *Past and Present* 53 (1971), 28–66. For the general institutional history of the nations see Kibre, *Nations*; Rashdall, *Universities*, II, esp. 299–320; G. Fedalto, 'Stranieri a Venezia e a Padova,' in *Storia della cultura veneta*, ed. G. Arnaldi and M. Pastore Stocchi (Vicenza, 1980), III, pt 1, 526–34; A. Sorbelli, 'La nazione nelle antiche università italiane e straniere,' *Studi e memorie per la storia dell'Università di Bologna* 16 (1943), 93–232; M. Bellomo, *Saggio sull'università nell'età del diritto comune* (Catania, 1979).

4 Sorbelli, 'La nazione,' 122–8, 133–4. The abortive community at Vicenza, colonized from Bologna in 1204, had four national universities: English, German, Provençale, and Italian.

5 For Paduan recognition of student rights in this period see *Statuti del Comune di Padova*, ed. A. Gloria (Padua, 1873), 375–9.

6 See H. Denifle, 'Die Statuten der Juristen-Universität Padua vom Jahre 1331,' *Archiv für Literatur- und Kirchengeschichte des Mittelalters* 6 (1892), 378, and R. Cessi, 'Lo Studio bolognese e lo Studio padovano,' in R. Cessi, *Padova medioevale*, ed. D. Gallo (Padua, 1985), II, 553–62.

7 See Denifle, 'Statuten,' 521–2.

8 Ibid., 399. See Kibre, *Nations*, 29–30, and *Statuta spectabilis et almae Universitatis Iuristarum Patavini Gymnasii* (Venice, 1551), fols 37v, 44.

9 See Denifle, 'Statuten,' 401. The *massarius* was the treasurer and purchasing agent of the university.

10 On the relationship between universities and guilds, see Rashdall, *Universities*, I, 148–50; Ridder-Symoens, *History*, I, passim; and Cobban, 'Medieval Student Power,' 35. For an example of a nation's functions at Bologna see *Acta nationis Germanicae Universitatis Bononiensis*, ed. E. Friedlaender and C. Malagola (Bologna, 1887), 4–15.

11 See Denifle, 'Statuten,' 483.

12 For the colleges in Italian universities generally, see P. Denley, 'The Collegiate Movement in Italian Universities in the Later Middle Ages,' *History of Universities* 10 (1991), 29–91, and specifically for Padua, 41–3, 82–6; and Rashdall, *Universities*, II, 19.

13 See Denifle, 'Statuten,' 410; Rashdall, *Universities*, I, 158–9, 162–4, 184–6, II, 14–15; and Kibre, *Nations*, 117–21.

14 See Denifle, 'Statuten,' 401–2, 410, 420–3. Cf. G. De Sandre, 'Dottori, università, comune a Padova nel Quattrocento,' *QSUP* 1 (1968), 21.

15 Cf. Rashdall, *Universities*, I, 186; Kibre, *Scholarly Privileges*, 74; and Ohl,

'University of Padua,' 158. A similar change had occurred in Bologna. See Cobban, 'Medieval Student Power,' 42–3.

16 This was still the case in the sixteenth and seventeenth centuries. See *Statuta* (1551), fol. 3 ('Patavinorum una nullam habens vocem ...') and *Statuta artistarum Patavini Gymnasii* (Padua, 1607), fol. 2.

17 See Ohl, 'University of Padua,' 15, note 47.

18 The 1331 statutes of the law university name nine ultramontane nations – the German, Bohemian, Hungarian, Polish, Provençale, Burgundian, Spanish, English, and Ultramarine (eastern Mediterranean) – and nine cismontane nations – Rome, Sicily, March of Ancona, Apulia, Lombardy, Venetia, Tuscany, March of Treviso, and Aquila. See Denifle, 'Statuten,' 399. By the sixteenth century Apulia and Aquila had been absorbed into other nations, Lombardy and Milan had been separated, a Friulian nation had come into being, Piedmontese and Scottish nations were created in 1534, and a Genoese nation was carved out of the Milanese in 1562. The Venetian nation had a vote but did not elect its own representative. A Paduan nation had no vote and no representative. See *Statuta* (1551), esp. fol. 2v; Kibre, *Nations*, 117.

19 For a mid-sixteenth-century perception of the arts university as subordinate to the law university see the comments of Giovan Francesco Trincavello in R. Gallo, 'Due informazioni sullo Studio di Padova della metà del Cinquecento,' *Nuovo Archivio Veneto* 72 (1963), 41.

20 For their papal privileges, see L. Rossetti, 'I collegi per i dottorati *auctoritate veneta*,' in *Viridarium floridum: Studi di storia veneta offerti dagli allievi di Paolo Sambin*, ed. M.C. Billanovich, G. Cracco, and A. Rigon (Padua, 1984), 365.

21 On the issue generally see De Sandre, 'Dottori, università, comune,' 15–47.

22 In the middle of the century, Giovan Francesco Trincavello listed eleven posts named by the Venetian Senate (comprising the first and second chairs from which Paduans were banned), eleven less prestigious and lower paid positions named by the students, and four reserved for Paduans. See Gallo, 'Due informazioni,' 26–7, 49–50, 62–3, 67–9. Also see A. Riccoboni, *De Gymnasio Patavino* (Padua, 1598), fols 8v, 10v–11. For an unusual primary source reflecting on student elections of professors at Padua in the fifteenth century, see Hartmann Schedel's Latin comedy of the 1460s, printed in Johannes Bolte, 'Zwei Humanistenkomödien aus Italien,' *Zeitschrift für vergleichende Litteraturgeschichte und Renaissance-Litteratur* 1 (1887–8), 77–84. Cf. A. Stäuble, *La commedia umanistica del Quattrocento* (Florence, 1968), 96–8.

23 See AAU 652, fols 27, 35v. Guidonus and Gulielmus were possibly the same person, as implicitly suggested by Facciolati, an early historian of the university, who conflated the names into 'Guido Gulielmus.' See J. Facciolati, *Fasti Gymnasii Patavini* (Padua, 1757), pt 2, 188–9.

24 Hence the nation does not appear in the table on pages 26–7.

25 For examples see Dupuigrenet Desroussilles, 'L'Università di Padova,' 630, 646; *Relazioni dei rettori veneti in terraferma*, IV, xxx–xxxi, 53, 81–2. These features of contemporary student life may have contributed to the demise of the student-dominated universities generally. See Cobban, 'Medieval Student Power,' 57–60.

26 The project of publication commenced in 1550, the year which appears on the frontispiece, but the year of printing is 1551, as on the final page.

27 *Statuta* (1551), fols 4v–5: 'Omnia fieri debent per nationes, non per voces. Ne ob hanc universitatis unionem ultramontani laesi reperiantur, cum pauciores communiter sint in illa universitate quam citramontanorum, statuimus quod omnia agenda, & constituenda per universitatem fiant per nationes, non per voces ... Ultramontanorum propter eorum praerogativas & numerum minorem nationes constent quatuor scholaribus, citramontanorum vero sex compleantur ... Bellorum turbines, qui multas civitates perdidere, illud etiam malum invexere, ut transalpini homines non valde frequentes ad Patavinum Gymnasium se conferant. Ex quo saepe evenit, ut defectu scholarium numerus nationum expleri non possit, ideo antiqua constitutio, per quam cautum erat, ut quattuor, & eo amplius scholares nationem facerent, corrigatur, ita ut tres scholares transalpini in albo descriptae, & scholas frequentantes satis sit ad explendam nationem.' As previously, Venetians and Paduans are denied political rights. Ibid., fols 3, 5v–6, 7v, 38v–9, 41v, 43. Note that Trincavello describes the law university as more of an aristocracy than a democracy because representation is through nations rather than individuals. See Gallo, 'Due informazioni,' 41.

28 Cf. Dupuigrenet Desroussilles, 'L'Università di Padova,' 617, and the printed edition of the statutes of the law university in 1645, which has as its title *Instituta et privilegia ab excellentissimo Senatu Veneto Almae Universitatis D. D. Iuristarum Patavini Archigymnasii concessa.*

29 See A. Stella, 'Tentativi controriformistici nell'Università di Padova e il rettorato di Andrea Gostynski,' in *Relazioni tra Padova e la Polonia: Studi in onore dell'Università di Cracovia nel VI centenario della sua fondazione* (Padua, 1964), 75–9; A. Stella, 'Giurisdizionalismo veneziano e tolleranza religiosa,' in G. Cozzi et al., *Venezia e la Germania* (Milan, 1986), 141–58; B. Brugi, 'Gli studenti tedeschi e la S. Inquisizione a Padova nella sec-

onda metà del secolo XVI,' in B. Brugi, *Gli scolari dello Studio di Padova nel Cinquecento* (Padua, 1905), 80.

30 Native Paduan dissatisfaction is particularly evident in connection with the war of the League of Cambrai, during which the universities were effectively closed, 1509–17. See A. Bonardi, *I padovani ribelli alla Repubblica di Venezia (a. 1500–30): Studio storico con appendici di documenti inediti* (Venice, 1902). For other examples see G. Dalla Santa, 'Un maestro di umanità a Padova nel 1531 e le idee ribelli al governo di alcuni suoi scolari,' *Nuovo Archivio Veneto* 24 (1917), 167–8; Fedalto, 'Stranieri,' 527–8; and A. Simioni, *Storia di Padova* (Padua, 1968), 770–5.

31 For contemporary testimony see Gallo, 'Due informazioni,' 39.

32 These were also sometimes organized by (cismontane) nationality.

33 Cf. F. Heal and C. Holmes, *The Gentry in England and Wales, 1500–1700* (London, 1994), 263–4. For discussion of the social composition of the English universities in this period and relevant bibliography see L. Stone, 'The Educational Revolution in England, 1560–1640,' *Past and Present* 28 (1964), 41–80; J.K. McConica, 'The Prosopography of the Tudor University,' *Journal of Interdisciplinary History* 3 (1973), 543–54; J.K. McConica, 'The Social Relations of Tudor Oxford,' *Transactions of the Royal Historical Society* 27 (1977), 115–34; J.K. McConica, 'The Collegiate Society,' in *The History of the University of Oxford, III: The Collegiate University*, ed. J.K. McConica (Oxford, 1986), 666–93; and E. Russell, 'The Influx of Commoners into the University of Oxford before 1581: An Optical Illusion?' *English Historical Review* 92 (1977), 721–45.

34 E.g., Francis Alford, John Boxall, Henry Denny, William Morley, Francis Walsingham, John Pelham, Robert Poyntz, Henry Scrope, Edward Cecil.

35 See *Atti della nazione germanica dei legisti nello Studio di Padova*, ed. B. Brugi (Venice, 1912), 51. In August 1556 there were nine Englishmen present at the election of Edmund Wyndham as English *electionarius* and John Pelham as English *consiliarius*, so Courtenay may have been among them.

36 See K.R. Bartlett, ' "The misfortune that is wished for him": The Exile and Death of Edward Courtenay, Earl of Devon,' *Canadian Journal of History* 14 (1979), 1–28.

37 AAU 30, fols 93–4.

38 Ibid: they are Nicholas Calwoodley (1594), John Frear (1595), William Clement and Joseph Lister (1597), and James Gomund (1598).

39 From August 1591 to July 1592 there were eight English matriculations and one Englishman mentioned in the acts, compared to four Englishmen present at the election in August 1592; from August 1592 to July 1593 there were ten matriculations and two Englishmen mentioned in the

acts, compared to eight Englishmen at the August 1593 election; from August 1593 to July 1594 there were six matriculations and two mentioned in the acts, compared to four at the August 1594 election; from August 1595 to July 1596 there were six matriculations and one mentioned in the acts, compared to five at the August 1596 election; from August 1596 to July 1597 there were fifteen matriculations and two mentioned in the acts, compared to six at the August 1597 election.

40 It is also possible that John Froso, who was involved in an electoral dispute in the law university in 1586, was a medical student.

41 From 1551 the number of students necessary to render an ultramontane nation quorate was reduced from four to three. Otherwise the 'ius supplendum' was applied. See *Statuta* (1551), fols 4v–5.

42 See Brugi, *Atti*, 23, but see also 49, 50.

43 See AAU 2, fols 181, 168v, 188; AAU 3, fols 46v, 53v, 65v, 71v,126v, 261, 263v; AAU 4, fol. 322; AAU 5, fols 1v, 2v, 4, 8, 45v, 70v; AAU 6, fols 169v, 249, 252, 355v; AAU 7, fols 94v, 164v, 195, 221v, 290. Cf. Andrich, *De natione*, 20–9 and G. Toso Rodonis, *Scolari francesi a Padova agli albori della Controriforma* (Padua, 1970), 163–74.

44 They were Christophorus Iulius, Egidius Bellinger, Andreas Ortensius, and Wolfgangus 'alemannus.' See AAU 6, fols 3v, 22, 82v, 92v. Cf. Andrich, *De natione*, 30–1.

45 These features might in fact date from earlier. See *Matricula Nationis Germanicae Artistarum in Gymnasio Patavino, 1553–1721*, ed. L. Rossetti (Padua, 1986), esp. ix–x; *Atti della natione germanica artista nello Studio di Padova*, ed. A. Favaro (Venice, 1911), esp. xix–xxiii; and Brugi, *Atti*, esp. ix. Also see E. Martellozzo Forin and E. Veronese, 'Studenti e dottori tedeschi a Padova nei secoli XV e XVI,' *QSUP* 4 (1971), 49–102; L. Rossetti, 'Nuovi manoscritti nell'Archivio Antico dell'Università di Padova: Lettere della *natio germanica*,' *QSUP* 2 (1969), 93–8; and Brugi, 'Gli studenti tedeschi.' For late-fifteenth-century German cohesion, see L. Rossetti, 'Un documento del 1493 degli scolari tedeschi nello Studio di Padova,' *Atti e memorie dell'Accademia Patavina di Scienze, Lettere ed Arti* 70 (1959–60), 65–72.

46 See Favaro, *Atti*, xx–xxii.

47 For Starkey see *Somerset Medieval Wills, 1531–58*, ed. F.W. Weaver, Somerset Record Society 21 (London, 1905), 47; for Harvey see G. Whitteridge, *William Harvey and the Circulation of the Blood* (London, 1971), 11.

48 See PRO, SP1 70, fol. 168.

49 Cf. BL, MS Cotton, Nero B vi, fol. 150; *LP*, X, no. 321.

50 See Pace, *De fructu qui ex doctrina percipitur*, ed. F. Manley and R.S. Sylvester (New York, 1967), 38–9.

51 See BL, MS Cotton, Nero B vi, fol. 147; *LP*, X, no. 321.

52 See Oxford, Bodleian Library, MS Rawlinson D 400, fols 171v–2.

53 LPL, MS 647, fol. 65.

54 PRO, SP98 1, fol. 55.

55 For Clement see BL, MS Egerton 2604, fol. 6v; for Mason see Dowling, *Humanism in England*, 159–60.

56 For Wotton see *Letters of Richard Fox*, ed. P.S. Allen and H.M. Allen (Oxford, 1929), 126–7; for Chamber see *Registrum Annalium Collegii Mertonensis, 1483–1521*, ed. H.E. Salter (Oxford, 1923), 274. And for the Saviles see R.B. Todd, 'Henry and Thomas Savile in Italy,' *Bibliothèque d'Humanisme et Renaissance* 58 (1996), 440, 443.

57 F. Davison, *The Poetical Rapsody*, ed. N.H. Nicolas (London, 1826), xxiii–iv.

58 See PRO, SP1 103, fols 120–1; SP1 102, fols 144–6; SP1 86, fol. 98; SP1 81, fols 52–3; SP1 95, fols 85–8; and BL, MS Cotton, Nero B vi, fols 117, 135, 151, 160–1.

59 For his radically altered financial circumstances by 1537, see PRO, SP1 127, fols 158–9.

60 See B. Brugi, 'Una descrizione dello Studio di Padova in un ms del secolo XVI nel Museo Britannico,' *Nuovo Archivio Veneto* 15 (1907), 6. For the fifteenth-century price see Ohl, 'University of Padua,' 64–5.

61 For degrees awarded by counts palatine, see below. We know that others acquired degrees in Padua, but the records of their degree examinations or doctoral diplomas are not extant. Michael Van der Stigen is described as 'anglus' in the record of his payment to the law university's bedel on taking his degree in 1594. Given his Dutch-sounding name, I expect this is an error. See AAU 54, fol. 331.

62 The four doctors who each assigned a topic from the legal texts on which he was to be examined.

63 See AAU 144, fol. 103.

64 ASP, AN 1811, fols 328–9v. Beysell was a canon of the church of St Saviour in Utrecht. See Martellozzo Forin and Veronese, 'Studenti e dottori,' 62.

65 Cf. J.M. Fletcher, 'University Migrations in the Late Middle Ages, with Particular Reference to the Stamford Secession,' in *Rebirth, Reform and Resilience: Universities in Transition, 1300–1700*, ed. J.M. Kittelson and P.J. Tramsue (Columbus, 1984), 163–89.

66 For Clement see Erasmus, *Opus epistolarum*, ed. P.S. Allen (Oxford, 1906–58), IV, xxiv. (References below to the letters of Erasmus are to the Latin edition by P.S. Allen, cited by letter number, and to *CWE*, the English edition, cited by page number. Where *CWE* is not cited, it is

because the relevant volume has not yet been published, or because my reference is to Allen's notes, as here.) For Fisher, Walter, and Pelham see Bologna, Archivio di Stato, Studio 140, fol. 46 and Studio 129, fol. 45v, and Parks, *English Traveller*, 627–8. For Huse see G.D. Squibb, *Doctors' Commons: A History of the College of Advocates and Doctors of Law* (Oxford, 1977), 153. For White see his *Orationes* (Arras, 1596),126–44, 158, 203. For Wilson see HMC, *Fifth Report* (London, 1876), 304.

67 *AGA, 1501–50*, no. 1053.

68 Ibid., nos 1725, 1730, 1736, 1940.

69 See AAU 143, fol. 327.

70 Cf. L. Rossetti, 'Nel quarto centenario della nascita di William Harvey,' *QSUP* 9–10 (1977), 239–43 and Toso Rodonis, *Scolari francesi*, 8–9, 16.

71 See AAU 143, fol. 327 and ACV, Diversorum 56, fol. 53.

72 *AGA, 1601–5*, no. 782.

73 Cf. J.K. McConica, 'The Catholic Experience in Tudor Oxford,' in *The Reckoned Expense: Edmund Campion and the Early English Jesuits*, ed. T.M. McCoog (Woodbridge, 1996), 50–1, 57–8.

74 See Stella, 'Tentativi,' 76–9.

75 Ibid., 75–84; Brugi, 'Gli studenti tedeschi,' passim; Dupuigrenet Desroussilles, 'L'Università di Padova,' 645–6; and Rossetti, 'I collegi.'

76 Rossetti, 'I collegi,' 368. Cf. late-fifteenth-century objections to degrees by count palatine in Ohl, 'University of Padua,' 210.

77 Many degrees by count palatine for the period 1501–50 appear in *AGA*. Publication of Paduan degrees for the period 1551–65 is forthcoming.

78 See entries on John Cecil, Christopher Bagshaw, and George Gifford in the Appendix and, for the papal decree, M.A. Tierney, *Dodd's Church History of England* (London, 1840), III, cii–civ.

79 For the protest in 1566 see Stella, 'Tentativi,' 76 and *Relazioni dei rettori veneti in terraferma*, IV, xxxii, 60; for the protest in 1610 see *Cal. Ven. 1607–10*, XI, no. 437, which records James I's request to the Venetian ambassador that English students should not have to make the profession. See also *Life and Letters of Sir Henry Wotton*, ed. L.P. Smith (Oxford, 1907), II, 214. For Hawkins see P. Hammer, 'Essex and Europe: Evidence from Confidential Instructions by the Earl of Essex, 1595–6,' *English Historical Review* 111 (1996), 361.

80 ASP, AN 5007, fols 26–7v.

81 ASP, AN 2342, fols 411v, 473.

82 See ASP, AN 4104, fols 548–550v.

83 See A. Maladorno Hargraves, 'I diplomi dottorali di John Frear (1610) e di Samuel Turner (1611) al British Museum,' *QSUP* 13 (1980), 169–77.

84 Their awarding count palatine was Sigismondo Capodilista. See Rossetti, 'Nel quarto centenario,' 241.

85 Ibid., 242.

86 See E. Veronese Ceseracciu, 'Ebrei laureati a Padova nel Cinquecento,' *QSUP* 13 (1980) 151–6, esp. 154.

87 See ASP, AN 5026, fol. 314 and *AGA, 1501–50*, nos 3881, 3888. The degrees were promoted by Sebastiano di Castello and Iacobo Antonio Marano di Gisono. It may be significant that Capodilista was one of the counts who awarded degrees to Jews. See Veronese Ceseracciu, 'Ebrei,' 153.

88 See *Calendar of State Papers, Foreign, of the Reign of Edward VI, 1547–53*, ed. W.B. Turnbull (London, 1861), 148. Besides those already mentioned, there is only one other known record of a degree by count palatine awarded to an Englishman in this period, that of Edward Maners in canon law in 1505, awarded by Taddeo Porcelini. See *AGA, 1501–50*, no. 377.

89 See A. Maladorno Hargraves, 'Un dottore di Padova alla berlina: John Bastwick,' *QSUP* 3 (1970), 101–2.

90 Nations are listed in the table in the order in which they are generally listed in the acts of the law university. The material, hitherto unpublished, is drawn from the following volumes of those acts. The corresponding year and the name of the *consiliarius* elected and, where this is different, the name of the *electionarius* elected, are given in brackets: AAU 2, fols 41–2 (1500 – William Walter); AAU 3, fols 28v–30v (January 1508 – Robert Wingfield); AAU 3, fol. 36v (July 1508 – Robert Spencer); AAU 4, fols 228–9 (1533 – Cosimus Passerius); AAU 4, fols 302–3 (1534 – Richard Morison); AAU 5, fol. 1v (1538 – Peter Bigod); AAU 8, fols 162–3v (1551 – William Huse); AAU 8, fols 227–8v (1552 – John Orphinstrange); AAU 9, fols 141–2 (1555 – John Bromus); AAU 9, fols 201–3 (1556 – John Pelham and Edmund Wyndham); AAU 9, fols 287–8v (1557 – John Hambey); AAU 10, fols 3–4v (1558 – Henry Denny and Francis Alford); AAU 10, fols 60–2 (1559 – John Voley); AAU 10, fols 116–17 (1560 – Richard Petiero); AAU 10, fols 148–9 (1561 – Anthony Fortescue); AAU 10, fols 187v–8v (1562 – George Gattacre); AAU 10, fols 220–1v (1563 – George Vastopolis: see p. 35 for discussion of this case); AAU 11, fols 3–4 (1564 – Richard White); AAU 11, fols 64–5 (1565 – Jerome Sapcot); AAU 11, fols 120–1v (1566 – John Gardiner and Jerome Sapcot); AAU 11, fols 169–70v (1567 – Edward Bichier); AAU 11, fols 224v–6 (1568 – Hercules Meride); AAU 12, fols 155–7 (1576 – Jacobus Randolph); AAU 12, fols 177–8 (1577 – Jacobus Randolph); AAU 13, fols 2–4 (1580 – Tertullian

Pyne); AAU 13, fols 61–2v (1581 – Richard Spencer); AAU 13, fols 101–2v (1582 – Paulus Tolius); AAU 13, fols 159–160v (1583 – Richard Willough- by); AAU 13, fols 179–180v (1584 – Richard Willoughby); AAU 14, fols 1–2v (1592 – Edmund Bruce); AAU 14, fols 1v–2v (1593 – Henry Scrope); AAU 14, fols 40v–2 (1594 – Thomas Trillus); AAU 15, fols 1–2 (1596 – Peter Barnes); AAU 15, fols 1–2 (1597 – Henry Gray). In the table, the letter 'S' signifies that the election was by 'ius supplendum'; 'n/a' ('not applicable') signifies that the nation did not yet exist. A blank space signifies that no indication of size was recorded.

91 For the 1538 case see the discussion at 29–30.

92 AAU 13, fol. 101. The man elected was Paulus Tolius.

93 Dominicus Cini. See AAU 2, fol. 107.

94 John Marbury. See AAU 8, fol. 3v.

95 AAU 13, fols 112v–3; cf. Andrich, *De natione*, 42. On the same day Froso stood for election as Spanish *consiliarius* by 'ius supplendum,' but did not win this either: AAU 13, fol. 113v.

96 These are AAU 459.

97 The nations of the arts university were Ultramontane, Ultramarine, Tuscan, Lombard, Trevisan, and Roman. See Rossetti, *University of Padua*, 37–8. By the seventeenth century there was also an Anconitan nation. See *Statuta* (1607), fol. 1.

98 The acts are AAU 675–6, covering only the years 1530–1, 1541–5, 1554–7, and 1568–76. For officials of the arts university also see *Album, sive elenchus nominum magnificorum rectorum atque pro-rectorum necnon illustris- simorum & generosissimorum syndicorum almae Patavinae Accademiae D. D. theologorum, philosophorum atque medicorum* ... (Padua, 1706).

99 BL, MS Harley 3829, fol. 27, printed in Brugi, 'Una descrizione,' 9. Cf. Gallo, 'Due informazioni,' 55.

100 See the discussion at p. 48.

101 See AAU 15, fols 84–5v and Rossetti, 'Nel quarto centenario,' 239–43. Cf. L. Rossetti, 'Membri del "Royal College of Physicians" di Londra laureati nell'Università di Padova,' *Atti e memorie dell'Accademia Patavina di Scienze, Lettere ed Arti* 75 (1963), 177.

102 AAU 4, fol. 298v: 'In opposuit contra d. Henricum Callum anglicum quod non est scholaris & nescit aliquid respondere in iure & quod non solvit collectana bidello generali. Fuit assignatus terminus ipsi d. Hen- ricio ad cras domane ad probandum solvisse collectam.'

103 See AAU 7, fol. 195 and *Statuta* (1551), fol. 44v.

104 AAU 5 fols 20–20v. Cf. Andrich, *De natione*, 24 and Toso Rodonis, *Scolari francesi*, 49–50.

105 See AAU 5, fol. 4 and Toso Rodonis, *Scolari francesi*, 105–11.

106 See the letter of Doge Andreas Gritti, dated 13 March 1534, in *Statuta* (1551), fols 3–4. Also see fols 37v–8 quoted in note 112 below. The account of Piedmontese status given in the statutes is confirmed by Trincavello, writing about the same time, in Gallo, 'Due informazioni,' 44–5, 47.

107 That the Venetian Senate had attemped to intervene in the conflict was noted by Marin Sanudo in 1531. See M. Sanuto, *I diarii* (Venice, 1893), LIV, col. 322.

108 See AAU 4, fols 299, 319.

109 See A. De Lazzari Bumbaca, 'Schede per scolari francesi a Padova, 1532–6,' *QSUP* 3 (1970), 138–9, and E. Picot, 'Les Français à l'Université de Ferrare au XVe et au XVIe siècle,' *Journal des Savants*, Cahiers de février et mars (1902), 21. Claudius was the son of the late Andreas Brocard, the seigneur of Chaudenet and La Grange and a member of the *parlement* of Bourgogne. Also see Toso Rodonis, *Scolari francesi*, 52, 165.

110 AAU 15, fol. 8v.

111 See J. Barton, 'The Faculty of Law,' in McConica, *History*, 257–62; and J.K. McConica, 'The Social Relations of Tudor Oxford,' 118.

112 *Statuta* (1551), fols 37v–8: 'Pedemontanos vero, de quibus pluries contro-versia fuit cum provincialibus multis de causis, et certa sententia, ut removeatur omnis difficultas, de speciali privilegio ascribendum duxi-mus in universitate ultramontanorum. Ideo eis assignamus nationem anglicam iam complures annos vacantem, in qua debeant, & possint describi una cum angliis, etiam si quo tempore affuerunt, quibuscumque incontrarium non obstantibus, etiam si de eis individuo mentio facienda esset.' This text must predate August 1551 when there were six voters present at the election of the English *consiliarius* William Huse, all of whom must have been English, for the Piedmontese nation is listed separately as having ten voters. On the other hand, the English *consiliar-ius* of 1549, John Marbury, was elected by 'ius supplendum,' as may have been the English *consiliarius* of 1550, John Boxall. See AAU 8, fols 3v, 65, 162v. We know the statutes were being written in 1550.

113 See *Gli stemmi dello Studio di Padova*, ed. L. Rossetti (Trieste, 1983).

114 Ibid., 241, no. 1181. The next English arms are those of John Payton, dating to 1598.

115 The nation's library was not started until 1626. See *Matricula et Acta Hungarorum in universitate Patavina studentium, 1264–1864*, ed. A. Varess (Budapest, 1915), x, xiv.

116 See W. McCuaig, 'Andreas Patricius, Carlo Sigonio, Onofrio Panvinio

and the Polish Nation at the University of Padua,' *History of Universities* 3 (1983), 87–100.

117 See *Metryka Nacji Polskiej w Uniwersytecie Padewskim,1592–1645*, ed. H. Barycz, (Warsaw, 1971). Also see S. Windakiewicz et al., *Omaggio dell' Accademia Polacca di Scienze e Lettere all'Università di Padova* (Cracow, 1922), and *Relazioni tra Padova e la Polonia*, esp. Stella, 'Tentativi,' 75–87. Also see Brugi, 'Gli studenti tedeschi,' 74.

118 The matriculation list is Padua, Biblioteca del Seminario, MS 634, printed in Brown, 'Inglesi e Scozzesi,' 137–213. On the library see J.P. Tomasini, *Gymnasium Patavinum* (Udine, 1654), 46–53, and L. Rossetti, 'Le biblioteche delle *nationes* nello Studio di Padova,' *QSUP* 2 (1969), 54.

119 The following account draws on and supplements research into the acts of the law university published in Toso Rodonis's *Scolari francesi*, 15, 22–6, 59, 86–7, and Table 1. On French students at Padua generally, see also B. Brugi, 'Gli antichi scolari di Francia nello Studio di Padova,' in *Mélanges offerts à M. Emile Picot*, I (Paris, 1913), 535–55, and De Lazzari Bumbaca, 'Schede.'

120 These are described in the letter of Trincavello. See Gallo, 'Due informazioni,' 45–6.

121 See N. Zemon Davis, *The Return of Martin Guerre* (Harmondsworth, 1985), 95–100, 114–15.

122 See Toso Rodonis, *Scolari francesi*, 15.

123 See De Lazzari Bumbaca, 'Schede,' 140.

124 See Toso Rodonis, *Scolari francesi*, 23–4.

125 Ibid., 24–5.

126 It was not proved (ibid., 25). For information regarding Malamort, Podio, and Rabot see De Lazzari Bumbaca, 'Schede,' 141–2.

127 See Toso Rodonis, *Scolari francesi*, 47 and Table 1. It was proved.

128 Ibid., Table 1.

129 Only the latter charge was proved (ibid., 25).

130 Ibid., 26. The case was not proved. Gymnasius was appointed a lecturer in the law university a few months later. See Facciolati, *Fasti*, pt 2, 114.

131 See Toso Rodonis, *Scolari francesi*, 59.

132 Ibid., 23.

133 See AAU 4, fols 296, 299.

134 Ibid., fol. 298v.

135 Ibid., fol. 299.

136 Ibid., fol. 301.

137 Ibid., fol. 302.

138 Ibid., fol. 311: 'Dominus Francescus Gymnasio opposuit contra Dominum

Ricardum Marisonum quod fuit electionarius in conventicula scisma asserte creationis rectoris galli in ecclesia San Firmi et ideo privari voce quia contra statuta fecit. Qui D. Ricardus negavit, presentum fuisse illi conventicule. Ideo fuit locatus terminus ipsi Domino Francesco ad probandum et tandem qui idem D. Ricardus noluit iurare non interfuisse dicte conventicule. Ideo fuit cassus privatus voce iuxta forma statutorum.'

139 Ibid., fol. 319.

140 Ibid., fol. 322.

141 AAU 10, fol. 223. Cf. Andrich, *De natione*, 35–6.

142 See AAU 10, fol. 3v; Garrett, *The Marian Exiles*, 144; and Hoby, 'Travaile and Life,' 116.

143 His father had died in 1549, his mother in 1553, while his two brothers survived well beyond this period. See *DNB* and P. Morant, *The History and Antiquities of the County of Essex* (London, 1768), I, 43.

144 AAU 10, fols 16v–17v. In the new election for English *consiliarius* by 'ius supplendum,' Acworth lost to Johannes Matthias from Bohemia. Ibid., fols 17v–18.

145 AAU 10, fol. 18v.

146 Andrich, *De natione*, 38.

147 See AAU 10, fol. 171. William McCuaig has reconstructed the episode from other sources in his *Carlo Sigonio: The Changing World of the Late Renaissance* (Princeton, 1989), 45. An earlier account is in Tomasini, *Gymnasium Patavinum*, 411–12. For the wider conflict between the two humanists see McCuaig, *Carlo Sigonio*, 43–9, and L. Thorndike, *University Records and Life in the Middle Ages* (NewYork, 1971), 378–9.

148 The syndic's duties are described in *Statuta* (1551), fols 29v–31.

149 For Voley see AAU 10, fol. 62v. For Fortescue, see AAU 10, fol. 175. Facciolati discussed this revision of the statutes in *Fasti*, pt 2, 16. Also see Tomasini, *Gymnasium Patavinum*, 412.

150 See AAU 11, fol. 182. Cf. Andrich, *De Natione*, 37.

151 See AAU 12, fol. 153. Cf. Andrich, *De Natione*, 40.

Chapter 2: Students of Law

1 'Facts and Fallacies: Interpreting English Humanism' and 'English Humanism and the Body Politic,' in A. Fox and J. Guy, *Reassessing the Henrician Age: Humanism, Politics and Reform, 1500–1550* (Oxford, 1986), 9–51.

2 Ibid., 11.

3 Ibid., 16.

4 See G.R. Elton, 'Humanism in England,' in *The Impact of Humanism on Western Europe*, ed. A. Goodman and A. MacKay (London and New York, 1990), 260.

5 See J.B. Trapp, *Erasmus, Colet and More: The Early Tudor Humanists and Their Books* (London, 1991), 4.

6 BL, MS Harley 283, fol. 129v. (*LP*, VIII, no. 214). See pp. 97–8 for a fuller quotation and discussion of this document.

7 For this letter sent from Padua and one from Venice to Elizabeth I, both of 1558, see PRO, SP1 70, fols 42–5v, 65–6v. Translations are in L.G.H. Horton-Smith, *George Acworth* (n.p., 1953), 15–26.

8 See White, *Orationes*, 126–44, and Hammer, 'Essex and Europe,' 361–2.

9 See B.P. Levack, 'The English Civilians, 1500–1750,' in *Lawyers in Early Modern Europe and America*, ed. W. Prest (London, 1981), 108–28. For the later medieval background see C.T. Allmand, 'The Civil Lawyers,' in *Profession, Vocation and Culture in Later Medieval England*, ed. C.H. Clough (Liverpool, 1982), 155–80.

10 In the following discussion I am in debt to the thinking of Donald Kelley about the place of law in Renaissance intellectual history.

11 On the college generally see M. Roberti, 'Il collegio padovano dei dottori giuristi,' *Rivista italiana per le scienze giuridiche* 35 (1903), 171–249.

12 See B. Brugi, *La scuola padovana di diritto romano nel secolo XVI* (Padua, 1888), 11.

13 See Roberti, 'Il collegio padovano,' 191–3.

14 The answer was negative. Ibid., 196–7 and *Responsum Juris per Jurisconsultos Patavinos editum* (Augsburg, 1551).

15 The answer was positive, but Cosimo I, duke of Florence, organized the case to be revoked to Rome, where the pope ruled in his favour. See Roberti, 'Il collegio padovano,' 236–7.

16 Ibid., 203–5.

17 See, for example, J.J. Scarisbrick, *Henry VIII* (London, 1981), 256, and G. de C. Parmiter, *The King's Great Matter: A Study of Anglo-Papal Relations, 1527–34* (London, 1967), 124. Henry's manipulation of Oxford and Cambridge, where more was at stake, is particularly open to this charge. See G. Bedouelle and P. Le Gal, *Le Divorce du roi Henry VIII* (Geneva, 1987), 59–75, and C. Cross, 'Oxford and the Tudor State, 1509–58,' in McConica, *History*, 124–5.

18 See Roberti, 'Il collegio padovano,' 186.

19 See BL, MS Cotton, Vitellius B xiii, fol. 133, and E. Surtz, *Henry VIII's Great Matter in Italy: An Introduction to Representative Italians in the King's Divorce, Mainly 1527–35* (Ann Arbor, 1975), 50. No manuscript record of a

corporate judgment by the lawyers survives among the other sixteenth-
century *consulti* of the college of jurists. See Roberti, 'Il collegio padovano,' 185.

20 Their positive opinion was printed in Henry VIII's propagandistic tracts
of 1531, *Gravissimae, atque exactissimae illustrissimarum totius Italiae, et
Galliae Academiarium censurae* (London, printed date 1530), and *The
Determinations of the moste famous and mooste excellent universities of Italy
and Fraunce* (London, 1531).

21 See Surtz, *Henry VIII's Great Matter,* 266.

22 See D. Kelley, 'Law,' in *The Cambridge History of Political Thought, 1450–
1700,* ed. J.H. Burns (Cambridge, 1991), 81.

23 The *Collectanea satis copiosa* is BL, MS Cotton, Cleopatra E vi, fols 16–135,
to be distinguished from a body of manuscript materials whose compilation began two or three years earlier, and which are described in V.
Murphy, 'The Debate over Henry VIII's First Divorce,' (PhD thesis,
University of Cambridge, 1984). On the *Collectanea*, see G.D. Nicholson,
'The Act of Appeals and the English Reformation,' in *Law and Government under the Tudors,* ed. C. Cross, D. Loades, and J.J. Scarisbrick (Cambridge 1988), 19–30; and for a longer treatment G.D. Nicholson, 'The
Nature and Function of Historical Argument in the Henrician Reformation,' (PhD thesis, University of Cambridge, 1977). Also see J. Guy,
'Thomas Cromwell and the Intellectual Origins of the Henrician Revolution,' in Fox and Guy, *Reassessing the Henrician Age,* 151–78. Virginia
Murphy's recent study suggests that papal authority was under attack
from even earlier. See her 'The Literature and Propaganda of Henry
VIII's First Divorce,' in *The Reign of Henry VIII: Politics, Policy and Piety,*
ed. D. MacCullogh (London, 1995), 135–58.

24 See Bedouelle and Le Gal, *Le Divorce,* 57, 63–4. For other recent accounts
see D. Katz, *The Jews in the History of England, 1485–1850* (Oxford, 1994),
15–48; G. Bedouelle, 'The Consultation of the Universities and Scholars
Concerning the "Great Matter" of Henry VIII,' in *The Bible in the Sixteenth Century,* ed. D.C. Steinmatz (Durham, 1990), 21–36; D. MacCulloch,
Thomas Cranmer: A Life (New Haven and London, 1996), 41–78.

25 See Nicholson, 'Historical Argument in the Henrician Reformation,' 77,
175.

26 See Guy, 'Thomas Cromwell,' in Fox and Guy, *Reassessing the Henrician
Age,* 160, and H. Chadwick, 'Royal Ecclesiastical Supremacy,' in *Human-
ism, Reform and Reformation: the Career of Bishop John Fisher,* ed. B.
Bradshaw and E. Duffy (Cambridge, 1991), 177.

27 See Fox and Guy, *Reassessing the Henrician Age,* 171.

28 Contained in BL, MS Cotton, Faustina C ii, fols 27–8.
29 See Surtz, *Henry VIII's Great Matter*, pt 2, esp. chapters on Pietro Paolo Parisio, Mariano Sozzini, Franceschino Curzio, and Marco Mantova Benavides. Also see Scarisbrick, *Henry VIII*, 255–8; Parmiter, *The King's Great Matter*, 120–43; and *The Divorce Tracts of Henry VIII*, ed. V. Murphy and E. Surtz (Angers, 1988).
30 The following brief survey of traditional and humanistic law relies on P. Stein, *The Character and Influence of the Roman Civil Law: Historical Essays* (London, 1988); R.C. Van Caenegem, *Judges, Legislators and Professors: Chapters in European Legal History* (Cambridge, 1987); D. Kelley, 'Vera Philosophia: The Philosophical Significance of Renaissance Jurisprudence,' *Journal of the History of Philosophy* 14 (1976), 267–79; D. Kelley, 'Civil Science in the Renaissance: Jurisprudence Italian Style,' *The Historical Journal* 22 (1979), 777–94; Kelley, 'Law,' 66–94; and I. Maclean, *Interpretation and Meaning in the Renaissance: The Case of Law* (Cambridge, 1992).
31 Maclean, *Interpretation*, 16.
32 See Brugi, *La scuola padovana*, 8, 10.
33 On Amerbach see the correspondence between him and his son Basilius, a student of law at Padua in the 1550s, in M. Gribaldi Mofa, *Epistolae Patavinae* (Basle, 1922).
34 See Erasmus, *Opus epistolarum*, IX, no. 2594, and T.F. Mayer, 'Marco Mantova and the Paduan Religious Crisis of the Early Sixteenth Century,' *Cristianesimo nella storia* 7 (1986), 43. Viglius went on to teach briefly at Padua. Also see Brugi, *La scuola padovana*, 27.
35 See B. Brugi, 'L'Università dei giuristi in Padova nel Cinquecento,' *Archivio Veneto-Tridentino* 1 (1922), 27.
36 For his relations with Padua, see Brugi, *La scuola padovana*, 66–71.
37 For the following discussion I am indebted to the works of Mayer, 'Marco Mantova and the Paduan Religious Crisis,' and T.F. Mayer, 'Marco Mantova, a Bronze Age Conciliarist,' *Annuarium historiae conciliorum* 14 (1984), 385–408.
38 For Orphinstrange see AAU 144, fols 102v–3v; for Le Rous see AAU 143, fol. 327, and ACV, Diversorum 56, fol. 53; for White see his *Orationes*, 126–44, 158, 203. Mantova was also the count palatine who awarded the doctoral degree in both laws to the Englishman John Hart in 1574 and to the Scotsman John Russell in the same year. Mantova also knew Reginald Pole at Padua. See his letter to Pole of 1555 recalling their friendship of the early 1520s: Venice, Biblioteca Nazionale Marciana, MS Ital. X 91 (6606), fol. 34 (cf. M. Mantova, *Di lettere famigliari diverse* (Padua, 1578), fols 32–3.)

39 See Mayer, 'Marco Mantova and the Paduan Religious Crisis,' 44–6.

40 *Aelia Laelia Crispis, epitaphium antiquum quod in agro Bononiensi adhuc videtur, a diversis hactenus interpretatum varie: novissime autem a Ricardo Vito Basinstochio amicorum precibus explicatum* (Padua, 1568), fol. 9. For the inscription generally, see N. Muschitiello, *Aelia Laelia Crispis: La Pietra di Bologna* (Bologna, 1989).

41 Mantova, *Epitoma* (Venice, 1559), fols 10–11, 14–18.

42 See White, *Orationes*, 126–44, 158, 203, and Hammer, 'Essex and Europe,' 361.

43 See Venice, Marciana, MS Ital. X 24 (6527), fols 157v–8. For a bio-bibliographical account of Panciroli, see I. Ferrari, *Memoria storica della vita e degli scritti di Guido Panciroli* (Reggio Emilia, 1896).

44 Pancirollus, 'De magistratibus municipalibus,' 'De corporis artificum,' 'Urbis Romae descriptio,' 'De quattuor urbis regionibus commentariis,' in Joannes Georgius Graevius, *Thesaurus Antiquitatum Romanorum* (Lyons, 1694–9), III, cols [47]–12, 17–22, 317–92. 'De magistratibus municipalibus' was also printed with Alciati's 'De magistratibus civilisque & militaribus officiis' in Panciroli's *Notitia utraque Dignitatum cum Orientis tum Occidentis ultra Arcadii Honoriique tempora ...* (Lyons, 1608); G. Pancirolo, *De quattuordecim regionibus urbis Romae* (Venice, 1602); *Notitia dignitatum utriusque Imperii cum commentariis* (Venice, 1593).

45 In L.A. Mutarius, *Anecdota ex Ambrosianae Bibliothecae codicibus* (Padua, 1713), I, 1–56.

46 Venice, 1611.

47 The title is of the English translation of 1715 printed in London, preceded by *Rerum memorabilium iam olim deperditarum & contra recensatque ingeniose inventarum libri duo a Guidone Pancirollo* (Hamburg, 1599), translated into Latin from the Italian by Henricus Salmuth.

48 Venice, 1637.

49 For Deciani and Le Rous, see AAU 143, fol. 327; ACV, Diversorum 56, fol. 53. For Deciani and White, see White, *Orationes*, 126–44, 158, 203.

50 For Le Rous, Menochio, and Cieffalo, see AAU 143, fol. 327 and ACV, Diversorum 56, fol. 53. For Vettori, Menochio, and Cieffalo, see BL, MS Additional 10268, fols 357–60v. For Menochio generally see V. Pisano, *Nel quarto centenario della nascita di Jacopo Menochio* (Pavia, 1932), and L. Franchi, *Memorie biografiche di Giacomo Menochio* (Pavia, 1925).

51 For claims that he was a student of law see C. Sturge, *Cuthbert Tunstall, Churchman, Scholar, Statesman and Administrator* (London, 1938), 13, the entry on Tunstall in *CE*, III, 349–54, and Squibb, *Doctors' Commons*, 125. He had acquired a doctorate in both laws by 1505 and became an ecclesi-

astical lawyer. He was a friend of the law students Jerome Busleyden, Antonio Surian, and Robert Fisher at Padua. (For Surian, see Venice, Archivio di Stato, Consiglio di X, Lettere ai Capi, 14, no. 49. For Fisher see Venice, Biblioteca Correr, MS Correr 1349, fol. 16.) His copy of Budé's *Annotationes in Pandectas* is in Durham Cathedral Library: Sturge, *Cuthbert Tunstall*, 394.

52 See *LP*, IX, no. 103.

53 See *LP*, VIII, no. 581, IX, no. 1034, X, no. 320. Cf. the later comment of Paolo Giovio: 'Georgius Lilius in Italia elegantioribus studiis excultus ...' in his *Descriptiones* (Basle, 1578), 13.

54 For Coles's library see *BRUO*, 717–18.

55 Thomas Wilson was definitely present. See T. Wilson, *The Three Orations of Demosthenes* (London, 1570), dedicatory letter, no page no., and T. Wilson, *Arte of Rhetorique*, xxx–xxxi, cxxix–cxxx.

56 See AAU 9, fols 157, 163v, and 201v, and ASP, AN 1828, fols 239–40.

57 This eclecticism is a common pattern among students of law at Padua. See Brugi, *La scuola padovana*, 41–3.

58 See Kelley, 'Civil Science,' 784.

59 See Stein, 'Elegance in Law,' in his *The Character and Influence of the Roman Civil Law*, 3–17.

60 Cf. legists' defence of the Donation of Constantine even after it had been exposed as a fraud. See Kelley, 'Law,' 74.

61 For further details see Stein, 'Safety in Numbers: Sharing of Responsibility for Judicial Decision in Early Modern Europe,' and 'Civil Law Reports and the Case of San Marino,' in his *The Character and Influence of the Roman Civil Law*, 101–25; and Kelley, 'Law,' 71.

62 On the phenomenon generally see especially G. Gorla and L. Moccia, 'A "Revisiting" of the Comparison between "Continental Law" and "English Law" (16th–19th Century),' *Journal of Legal History* 2 (1981), 143–56; L. Moccia, 'English Law Attitudes to the "Civil law,"' ibid., 157–68; and J.H. Baker, 'English Law and the Renaissance,' *Cambridge Law Journal* 44 (1985), 46–61.

63 Cf. Maclean, *Interpretation*, 85: 'What was the effect of the input of humanist material in the course of the fifteenth and sixteenth centuries? I would venture to reply: not very great.'

64 His oration was printed at Venice, 1574. Also see Facciolati, *Fasti*, pt 2, 314.

65 Cf. L. Martines, *Lawyers and Statecraft in Renaissance Florence* (Princeton, 1986), 80–1.

66 An important exception is Mattheo Gribaldi Mofa's *De methodo ac ratione studendi libri tres* (Venice, 1559).

67 E.g., Jean Coras, author of *Tractatus de iuris arte*, written 1560; Giulio Pacio, author of *De iuris civilis difficultate ac docendi methodo*; Ulrich Zasius; and the Englishman Jerome Sapcot.

68 See V. Piano Mortari, 'Dialettica e giurisprudenza: Studio sui trattati di dialettica legale del sec. XVI,' *Annali di Storia del Diritto* 1 (1957), 293–401.

69 See Brugi, 'L'Università dei giuristi,' esp. 12–14. The program is described in the statutes of the law university, where lecturers are required to follow their explanation of a passage from the *Corpus iuris* with an explanation of its related glosses. See Brugi, *La scuola padovana*, 14–19, and A. Belloni, *Professori giuristi a Padova nel secolo XV* (Frankfurt, 1986), 71. Also see Gallo, 'Due informazioni,' 87–9. For an English description of the curriculum see F. Moryson, *Shakespeare's Europe: Unpublished Chapters of Fynes Moryson's Itinerary* (London, 1903), 431. For the medieval background see A. Belloni, *Le questioni civilistiche del secolo XII* (Frankfurt, 1989).

70 See, for examples, the details of John Le Rous's examination in AAU 143, fol. 327, and John Orphinstrange's examination in AAU 144, fol. 103, the latter printed in Bartlett, 'English Students,' 106. Richard White describes the same experience for his examination at Pavia in his *Orationes*, 145–7. For further discussion see Brugi, *La scuola padovana*, 17–18.

71 Brugi, *La scuola padovana*, 17–18.

72 Brugi, 'L'Università dei giuristi,' 69.

73 See Maclean, *Interpretation*, 50–9, and V. Piano Mortari, 'Il problema dell'*interpretatio iuris* nei commentatori,' *Annali di Storia del Diritto* 2 (1958), 29–109.

74 In his *Opera* (Basle, 1582), IV, 283–582. This last book was first published posthumously in 1551, but earlier books of the *Parergon* had been appearing since 1536.

75 Tiberio Deciani, 'Apologia pro iurisprudentibus,' *Responsa* (Venice, 1579), III, fols 1–36.

76 See Maclean, *Interpretation*, 17. The result of this appointment was Deciani's important *Tractatus criminalis* (Frankfurt, 1571).

77 Deciani, 'Apologia,' fol. 6. This is derived from the *Digest*. See R.W. Lee, *The Elements of Roman Law* (London, 1956), 9.

78 Deciani, 'Apologia,' fol. 14.

79 Ibid., fol. 22. On Deciani generally see *Dizionario biografico degli italiani*, XXXIII, 538–41; A. Marongiu, 'Tiberio Deciani (1509–82): lettore di diritto, consulente, criminalista,' *Rivista di storia del diritto italiano* 7 (1934), 135–202, and specifically for the 'Apologia,' ibid., 162–202; and F. Todescan, *Giurisprudenza veneta nell'età umanistica* (Milan, 1984), 33.

80 For White see White, *Orationes*, 126–44, 158, 203; for Hart see ASP, AN 5007, fols 26–7v; for Maners see *AGA, 1501–50*, no. 377.

81 See Levack, 'English Civilians.'

82 But any educational input in Doctors' Commons was very informal. For a complete account of the organization, see Squibb, *Doctors' Commons*.

83 For the general issue of the impact of Henry VIII's ban on the canon law at Oxford, see Barton, 'The Faculty of Law,' in McConica, *History*, 257–62.

84 Among recent works Van Caenegem's *Judges, Legislators and Professors* is unusual in its insistence on the difference. Cf. primarily D. Kelley, 'History, English Law and the Renaissance,' *Past and Present* 65 (1974), 24–51, and the response to Kelley by Christopher Brooks and Kevin Sharpe, and Kelley's rejoinder to them, in *Past and Present* 72 (1976), 133–46.

85 Baker, 'English Law,' and J.H. Baker, *The Reports of John Spelman* (London, 1978), II. Cf. R. Helgerson, *Forms of Nationhood* (Chicago, 1992), 63–104 and Maclean, *Interpretation*, 186–202.

86 P. Brand, *The Origins of the English Legal Profession* (Oxford, 1992), 154–7; J.L. Barton, 'Roman Law in England,' *Ius Romanum Medii Aevi* 5 (1971), 8–24; Baker, *Reports*, 33.

87 R.H. Helmholz, *Roman Canon Law in Reformation England* (Cambridge, 1990), 121–57. See also D.M. Owen, *The Medieval Canon Law: Teaching, Literature and Transmission* (Cambridge, 1990).

88 A. Wijffels, 'Law Books in Cambridge Libraries, 1500–1640,' *Transactions of the Cambridge Bibliographical Society* 10 (1993), 359–412. See also similar findings in A. Wijffels, *Late Sixteenth-Century Lists of Law Books at Merton College* (Cambridge, 1992), xix–xxiv.

89 L. Jardine and W. Sherman, 'Pragmatic Readers: Knowledge Transactions and Scholarly Services in Late Elizabethan England,' in *Religion, Culture and Society in Early Modern Britain: Essays in Honour of Patrick Collinson*, ed. A. Fletcher and P. Roberts (Cambridge, 1994), 113–24.

90 See J.D.M. Derrett, *Henry Swinburne (?1551–1624): Civil Lawyer of York* (York, 1973), esp. 29–50.

91 A. Wall, 'For Love, Money or Politics? A Clandestine Marriage and the Elizabethan Court of Arches,' *The Historical Journal* 38 (1995), 511–33, esp. 528–30.

92 Cf. L.A. Knafla, *Law and Politics in Jacobean England: The Tracts of Lord Chancellor Ellesmere* (Cambridge, 1977), 69–70.

93 This is not to imply that other ecclesiastical courts did not suffer severely during the Tudor period as a result of the Reformation, but this is a disputed matter. Some types of increased business, for example tithe disputes, may not reflect the popularity of ecclesiastical courts as much as a

growing disrespect for ecclesiastical power. On the issue generally see R. Houlbrooke, 'The Decline of Ecclesiastical Jurisdiction under the Tudors,' in *Continuity and Change: Personnel and Administration of the Church of England, 1500–1642*, ed. F. Heal and R. O'Day (Leicester, 1976), 239–57; R. Houlbrooke, *Church Courts and the People during the English Reformation, 1520–70* (Oxford, 1979); R.A. Marchant, *The Church under the Law: Justice, Administration and Discipline in the Diocese of York, 1560–1640* (Cambridge, 1969); R.M. Wunderli, *London Church Courts and Society on the Eve of the Reformation* (Cambridge, MA, 1981); M. Ingram, *The Church Courts, Sex and Marriage in England, 1570–1640* (Cambridge, 1987); and Helmholz, *Roman Canon Law*, esp. 42–54. The recent research of Helmolz suggests that the ecclesiastical courts underwent prolonged attacks over their jurisdiction from common lawyers in the early Tudor period, but that by 1529 they had in fact adapted to changed circumstances, survived the decades of uncertainty with few substantive changes to their activities, and were in a position to rise again from the 1570s.

94 See Levack, 'English Civilians,' 109.

95 See Squibb, *Doctors' Commons*, 38–9.

96 In fact the process started before the Reformation. Advocates in minor orders took to living as laymen in the 1520s. See Squibb, *Doctors' Commons*, 26–9.

97 I.J. Churchill, *Canterbury Administration* (London, 1933), II, 236, 245.

98 See Squibb, *Doctors' Commons*, 128, 140 and 143. Most of the court's sixteenth-century records were destroyed in the 1666 fire of London, so information about the court comes almost exclusively from the records of Doctors' Commons and from the records of commissions to advocates in the archbishops' registers.

99 Technically 'Dean of the Peculiars.' The 'Peculiars' were those districts outside the diocese of Canterbury which came within the archbishop of Canterbury's immediate jurisdiction and were exempt from the jurisdiction of the diocese in which they belonged. Cases from these districts were heard in the Arches, but the Dean of the Peculiars was the effective head of the whole court.

100 For Huse see PRO, SP12 109, fol. 88 and LPL, Register of Archbishop Pole, fol. 22. Huse's father had been a clerk in the early Faculty Office. See D. S. Chambers, *Faculty Office Registers* (Oxford, 1966), xxvii.

101 See Squibb, *Doctors' Commons*, 154–6, 160, and 164, and LPL, Register of Archbishop Whitgift, fol. 113. Three other Paduan alumni, William Walter, Robert Spencer, and Richard White were members of Doctors' Commons who, as far as we know, did not practise in the Arches.

102 For the Faculty Office, see Chambers, *Faculty Office Registers*, xi–lxv. For the Prerogative Court of Canterbury, see C. Kitching, 'The Prerogative Court of Canterbury from Warham to Whitgift,' in Heal and O'Day, *Continuity and Change*, 191–213. For the courts of the archbishop of Canterbury generally, see Churchill, *Canterbury Administration*, I, 380–519.

103 Barton, 'The Faculty of Law,' in McConica, *History*, 271–2; and McConica, 'The Social Relations of Tudor Oxford,' 116–19.

104 On Chancery generally see Baker, *Reports*, 74–83; G.R. Elton, *The Tudor Constitution* (Cambridge, 1982), 148–62; J.A. Guy, *The Public Career of Thomas More* (Brighton, 1980); and W.R. Jones, *The Elizabethan Court of Chancery* (Oxford, 1967).

105 See Maclean, *Interpretation*, 175–8 and 185–6, and a contemporary account in Christopher St German's *Doctor and Student*, ed. T.F. Plucknett and J.L. Barton (London, 1974), 94–9.

106 On Star Chamber see J.A. Guy, *The Cardinal's Court: The Impact of Wolsey in Star Chamber* (Hassocks, 1977). On all these courts see Elton, *The Tudor Constitution*, 163–217; J.H. Baker, *An Introduction to English Legal History* (London, 1979), 135–45; Baker, *Reports*, 51–83; and the contemporary observations in Thomas Smith, *De republica Anglorum*, ed. M. Dewar (Cambridge, 1982, first published 1582), second and third books. For the council in the north, see R.R. Reid, *The King's Council in the North* (London, 1921). For this council's equity jurisdiction, ibid., 261–79. For Requests see J. Caesar, *The Ancient State of the Court of Requests, 1597* (Amsterdam and Norwood NJ, 1976, repr.): 'The forme of the proceeding in this court, was altogether according to the processe of summary causes in the civill law' (no page no.).

107 See Elton, *The Tudor Constitution*, 149.

108 Cf. S.F.C. Milsom, *Historical Foundations of the Common Law* (London, 1981), 88–91; Baker, *Introduction*, 119.

109 See E. Heward, *Masters in Ordinary* (Chichester, 1990).

110 For the fifteenth century see N. Pronay, 'The Chancellor, the Chancery and the Council at the End of the Fifteenth Century,' in *British Government and Administration*, ed. H. Hearder and H.R. Loyn (Cardiff, 1974), 87–103, esp. 91. The following findings result from a collation of material in Heward, *Masters in Ordinary*, Squibb, *Doctors' Commons*, R.G. Usher, *The Rise and Fall of the High Commission* (Oxford 1913), 345–61, and I.S. Leadam, *Select Cases in the Court of Requests, 1497–1569* (London, 1898), cii–cxxiv. The figures are provisional as these sources are not without their problems. I intend to follow up this research.

111 Dozens of Carew's and Huse's reports are in PRO, C 38 1–3.

112 See Guy, *The Public Career*, 40.

113 See Cambridge, Cambridge University Library, MS Baker 37 (Mm I 48), fols 202–20v.

114 For Wriothesley see A.J. Slavin, 'The Fall of Lord Chancellor Wriothesley: A Study in the Politics of Conspiracy,' *Albion* 7 (1975), 265–86. For Somerset's patronage of neoclassical architecture see B. Ford, *The Cambridge Guide to the Arts in Britain: Renaissance and Reformation* (Cambridge, 1989), 66–7. Somerset financed the visit to Italy of John Shute, author of the classicizing *The First and Chief Grounds of Architecture*.

115 J.R. Dasent, ed., *Acts of the Privy Council of England* (London, 1890), II, 49.

116 Stowe quoted in Elton, *The Tudor Constitution*, 156. R. Robinson, *A brief collection of the queenes majesties most high and most honourable courtes of record*, ed. R.L. Rickard (London, 1953), 11–12. See the lists of Elizabethan masters in Heward, *Masters in Ordinary*, 79–91.

117 See J. Conway Davies, *Catalogue of Manuscripts in the Library of the Honourable Society of the Inner Temple* (Oxford, 1972), II, 726.

118 See *Accounts and Papers* VIII, 1830–1 (Parliamentary Papers), II (London, 1830–1), 1–2. Also see Jones, *The Elizabethan Court of Chancery*, 106–7.

119 Printed in *A Collection of Tracts Relative to the Law of England*, ed. F. Hargrave (London, 1787), I, 293–319. See W.J. Jones, 'The Treatise of the Masters in Chancery,' *The National Library of Wales Journal* 10 (1957–8), 403–8.

120 Carew, 'A Treatise,' 309.

121 Ibid., 313. Note also Carew's citation of Guido Panciroli, 'A Treatise,' 296. Carew was also the author of *Reports or causes in Chancery collected by Sir George Cary, one of the masters of the Chancery in anno 1601* (London, 1650).

122 Robinson, *A brief collection*, 14.

123 Sir Thomas Smith, *De republica Anglorum*, 94. The book gives an account of the whole English legal system, especially useful for its civilian perspective.

124 See Baker, *Reports*, 95–100.

125 For Chaloner see Reid, *The King's Council*, 490–1. For Savage see Leadam, *Select Cases*, cx. For Savage at Bologna and Padua see Parks, *English Traveller*, 626, Facciolati, *Fasti*, pt 1, 15, and Andrich, *De natione*, 11–12.

126 Smith mentions it as an opportunity for civilians in his inaugural oration at Cambridge. See Cambridge, Cambridge University Library, MS Baker 37 (Mm I 48), fol. 206v. George Carew's 'A Treatise of the Maisters in Chauncerie' also argues for a connection between Chancery masters and diplomatic and mercantile matters. See Carew, 'A Treatise,' 303.

127 For Tudor diplomacy generally see D. Potter, 'Foreign Policy,' in Mac-Cullogh, *The Reign of Henry VIII*, 102–6; and G.M. Bell, 'Elizabethan Diplomacy: The Subtle Revolution,' in *Politics, Religion and Diplomacy in Early Modern Europe: Essays in Honour of De Lamar Jensen*, ed. M.R. Thorp and A.J. Slavin (Kirksville, MO, 1994), 267–87.

128 Quoted in E.R. Adair, *The Exterritoriality of Ambassadors in the Sixteenth and Seventeenth Centuries* (New York, 1929), 10.

129 For an account of the embassy by Morison's secretary, see R. Ascham, *English Works*, ed. W.A. Wright (Cambridge, 1904), 121–69.

130 Both treatises should be compared with Sir Thomas Elyot's comments on law in *The Boke named the Governour*, first printed in 1531, ed. H.S. Croft (New York, 1967), I, 144–62.

131 Thomas Starkey, *A Dialogue between Pole and Lupset*, ed. T.F. Mayer (London, 1989), 79. Spelling has been modernized in this quotation and in those following.

132 Ibid., 128.

133 Ibid., 82.

134 Ibid., 129.

135 See above, p. 40.

136 Starkey, *Dialogue*, 11.

137 Ibid.

138 See Lee, *The Elements*, 35.

139 See T.F. Mayer, *Thomas Starkey and the Common Weal: Humanist Politics and Religion in the Reign of Henry VIII* (Cambridge, 1989), esp. 1 and 156.

140 Starkey, *Dialogue*, 121–2 and 128–9.

141 For links between the Poles and the Staffords, see chapter 5 below.

142 See G.D. Squibb, *The High Court of Chivalry* (Oxford, 1959).

143 See Starkey, *Dialogue*, 132. Mayer suggests a Paduan jurist source for Starkey's conciliarism in Marco Mantova Benavides. See Mayer, *Thomas Starkey*, 184–7.

144 An extract from the draft copy entitled 'A discourse touching the reformation of the lawes of England,' BL, MS Cotton, Faustina C ii, fols 5–22, was published with comments by Sidney Anglo, 'An Early Tudor Programme for Plays and Other Demonstrations against the Pope,' *Journal of the Warburg and Courtauld Institutes* 20 (1957), 176–9. This corresponds to fols 15v–19 of the fair copy presented to the king, which is BL, MS Royal, 18 A. i. Discussions of the work appear in J.K. McConica, *English Humanists and Reformation Politics* (Oxford, 1965), 185–8; Baker, *Reports*, 29–31; G.R. Elton, *Studies in Tudor and Stuart Politics and Government* (Cambridge, 1974), II, 247–9; S.E. Thorne, 'English Law and the Renaissance,'

La storia del diritto nel quadro delle scienze storiche (Florence, 1966), 440–2.
Also see L.A. Knafla, 'The Influence of Continental Humanists and
Jurists on English Common Law in the Renaissance,' *Acta Conventus Neo-
Latini Bononiensis* (Binghamton, 1985), 60–71. Morison also presented the
king with a Latin systematization of English land law as an example of
what could be done: BL, MS Royal, 11 A. xvi.

145 BL, MS Royal, 18 A. i, fol. 7.
146 Ibid., fol. 7v.
147 Ibid., fol. 8.
148 Ibid., fol. 8v.
149 Ibid., fols 8v–9.
150 Ibid., fol. 9.
151 Ibid., fols 22–3v, his translation of *De oratore*, I, 185–8.
152 BL, MS Royal, 18 A. i, fols 9v–10. Spelling has been modernized in this
    quotation and in those following.
153 Ibid., fol. 20.
154 Ibid., fol. 2v.
155 For the association between Henry and Moses in the Reformation see
    J.N. King, *Tudor Royal Iconography* (Princeton NJ, 1989), 74–5, 251–2.
156 BL, MS Royal 18 A. i, fol. 13.
157 Ibid., fol. 21v.
158 See Helgerson, *Forms of Nationhood*, esp. chapters 1 and 2.
159 BL, MS Royal 18 A. i, fol. 24. Cf. the brief comparison of England and
    Italy in Morison's tract of 1536, 'A Remedy for Sedition,' in *Humanist
    Scholarship and Public Order*, ed. D.S. Berkowitz (Washington DC, 1984),
    137.
160 It should be remembered that Morison had spent a brief spell in an Inn
    of Court around 1532.
161 In *LP*, XVII, Appendix 2, 707, it is calendared in 1542 but this is obvious-
    ly much too late; the putting out of the bishop of Rome was hardly news
    by then. On the other hand, the internal evidence noted in the calendar
    would seem to place it after the dissolution of the monasteries. Morison
    returned to England from Padua in 1536 and entered Cromwell's service
    immediately, writing important propaganda tracts for the government.
    Elton, *Studies*, II, 248, suggested 1535 or 1536, but this may not allow for
    the leisure hours which Morison writes that he had just had (BL, MS
    Royal 18 A. i, fol. 3v), unless Elton is suggesting that the tract was
    written before Morison's return to England, in which case it would not
    make sense to show the king what he has been doing in his leisure time,
    for they would not be acquainted. Moreover, if it was written soon after

the Pilgrimage of Grace, one would have expected a mention of the uprising in Morison's discussion of propaganda. Yet Anglo notes in 'Early Tudor Programme,' 177, that many of the tract's propagandistic proposals were already being deployed by the late 1530s. All of this dates the treatise to around 1538.

162 BL, MS Royal 18 A. i, fol. 11.

163 On Gardiner see G. Redworth, *In Defence of the Church Catholic: The Life of Stephen Gardiner* (Oxford, 1970), esp. 10–11, 66–7. For Morison's tracts see Berkowitz, *Humanist Scholarship*, 85–165.

164 For an illustration of this, see PRO, SP1 92, fols 45–6.

165 See St German, *Doctor and Student*, xliv–li.

166 See D.S. Bland, 'Henry VIII's Royal Commission on the Inns of Courts,' *Society of Public Teachers of Law* 10 (1969), 178–94.

167 This is the suggestion of Guy, *The Public Career*, 85.

168 See Kelley, 'History,' 25.

169 Vespasiano da Bisticci, *Vite di uomini illustri del secolo XV*, ed. P. D'Ancona and E. Aeschlimann (Milan, 1951), 227.

170 See generally B. Levack, *The Civil Lawyers in England, 1603–40* (Oxford, 1973), and now J. Guy, 'The Elizabethan Establishment and the Ecclesiastical Polity,' in *The Reign of Elizabeth I: Court and Culture in the Last Decade*, ed. J. Guy (Cambridge, 1995), 126–49.

171 They were both accused of harbouring Catholic sympathies.

172 See Kelley, 'History,' and Helgerson, *Forms of Nationhood*, 78–104.

173 Kelley speaks of a 'guild mentality, with the compulsive utilitarianism accompanying it' among English civilians and common lawyers alike. See Kelley, 'History,' 46. The thesis of D.R. Coquilette, *The Civilian Writers of Doctors' Commons, London* (Berlin, 1988), that English civilians established a continuous and coherent intellectual tradition, is unconvincing for many reasons.

174 See *Civitates Orbis Terrarum*, ed. R.A. Skelton (New York, 1966), II, i.

175 For English canonical thought in the last quarter of the sixteenth century and the first third of the seventeenth, see Helmholz, *Roman Canon Law*, 121–57.

Chapter 3: Students of Medicine and Natural Philosophy

1 Salter, *Registrum*, 274.

2 See generally and for relevant bibliography J. Bylebyl, 'The School of Padua: Humanistic Medicine in the Sixteenth Century,' in *Health, Medicine and Mortality in the Sixteenth Century*, ed. C. Webster (Cambridge,

1979), 335–70; also useful is G. Ongaro, 'La medicina nello Studio di Padova e nel Veneto,' in *Storia della cultura veneta*, ed. G. Arnaldi and M. Pastore Stocchi (Vicenza, 1981), III, pt. 3, 75–134.

3 For a useful brief summary of the movement's main aims and achievements see V. Nutton, 'John Caius and the Linacre Tradition,' *Medical History* 23 (1979), 374–7. For academic medicine before medical humanism see N.G. Siraisi, *Medieval and Early Renaissance Medicine* (Chicago and London, 1990).

4 In Galen, *Exhortatio ad bonas arteis, praesertim medicinam* (Paris, 1526).

5 Pace, *De fructu*, 36.

6 For the relationship between theory and practice in medical humanism see V. Nutton, 'Humanist Surgery,' in *The Medical Renaissance of the Sixteenth Century*, ed. A. Wear, R.K. French, and I.M. Lonie (Cambridge, 1985), 75–99, and his '*Prisci dissectionum professores*: Greek Texts and Renaissance Anatomists,' in *The Uses of Greek and Latin, Historical Essays*, ed. C. Dionisotti et al. (London, 1988), 111–26. Charles Schmitt investigated the relationship between medicine and natural philosophy in the Renaissance in 'Aristotle among the Physicians,' in Wear, *Medical Renaissance*, 1–15, and Per-Gunnar Ottosson does the same for the medieval period in his *Scholastic Medicine and Philosophy* (Naples, 1984), esp. 68–87. For this issue in medieval Padua see Siraisi, *Arts and Sciences at Padua*. For Renaissance Galenism generally, see O. Temkin, *Galenism* (Ithaca and London, 1973); and R.J. Durling, 'A Chronological Census of Renaissance Editions and Translations of Galen,' *Journal of the Warburg and Courtauld Institutes* 24 (1961) 230–305.

7 See Schmitt, 'Aristotle,' in Wear, *Medical Renaissance*, 5.

8 Bylebyl, 'The School of Padua,' in Webster, *Health*, 364.

9 There is some evidence of a general drift towards medical study and practice amongst clergymen during the religious crises of the 1530s. See G. Lewis, 'The Faculty of Medicine,' in McConica, *History*, 224–5.

10 Although note that the first *fen* of Avicenna's *Canon* remained a basic text for the teaching of medical theory, together with Hippocrates' *Aphorisms* and Galen's *Ars medica*, throughout the sixteenth century and beyond. See N. Siraisi, *Avicenna in Renaissance Italy: The* Canon *and Medical Teaching in Italian Universities after 1500* (Princeton, 1987), and, for contemporary testimony, Thorndike, *University Records*, 374. Also see P. Dilg, 'The Antarabism in the Medicine of Humanism,' in *La diffusione delle scienze islamiche nel Medio Evo europeo* (Rome, 1987), 269–90.

11 In the next few paragraphs I have relied on the following studies:

Madison et al., *Linacre Studies*; G. Lewis, 'The Faculty of Medicine,' in McConica, *History*; M. Davidson, *Medicine in Oxford* (Oxford, 1953); V.L. Bullough, 'Medical Study at Mediaeval Oxford,' *Speculum* 36 (1961), 600–12; A. Chaplin, 'History of Medical Education in the Universities of Oxford and Cambridge,' *Proceedings of the Royal Society of Medicine* 13 (1920), 83–106; A.H.T. Robb-Smith, 'Medical Education in Cambridge before 1600,' in *Cambridge and its Contribution to Medicine*, ed. A. Rook (London, 1971), 1–25; D.R. Leader, *A History of the University of Cambridge* (Cambridge, 1988), I, esp. 202–10; and Bylebyl, 'The School of Padua,' in Webster, *Health*, 335–70.

12 See J. Fletcher in 'Linacre's Lands and Lectureships,' in Madison et al., *Linacre Studies*, 119. C.A. Mallett identified less than fifty medical degrees of all kinds in the records for the period 1571 to 1600, and only thirty-five licences to practise. See Mallett, *A History of the University of Oxford* (New York and London, 1924), II, 133. For Cambridge, cf. H.D. Rolleston, *The Cambridge Medical School* (Cambridge, 1932), 4, and A. Rook and M. Newbold, 'David Edwardes: His Activities at Cambridge,' *Medical History* 19 (1975), 389–92.

13 See Fletcher, 'Linacre's Lands and Lectureships,' in Madison et al., *Linacre Studies*, 118.

14 See Leader, *A History of the University of Cambridge*, 205; R. Hunt, The Medieval Library,' in *New College, Oxford*, ed. J. Buxton and P. Williams (Oxford, 1979), 332–3; Lewis, 'Faculty of Medicine,' in McConica, *History*, passim; W.M. Palmer, 'Cambridgeshire Doctors in the Olden Time,' *Proceedings of the Cambridge Antiquarian Society* (April 1911), 272–9.

15 See Fletcher, 'Linacre's Lands and Lectureships,' in Madison et al., *Linacre Studies*, 118.

16 See F. Madan, 'The Daily Ledger of John Dorne, 1520,' in *Collectanea*, First Series, ed. C.R.L. Fletcher, Oxford Historical Society (Oxford, 1885), 73–177, 454–78.

17 'Duces ceci.' See H.E. Salter, *Munimenta civitatis Oxonie*, Oxford Historical Society 71 (Oxford, 1917), 249.

18 This is obviously true not only for Englishmen amongst Padua's student population. One of the earliest transmitters of Greek learning to the north was the German Hartmann Schedel, a physician by profession, who had been a medical student in Padua in the 1460s and studied under Chalcondylas there. See O. Meyer, 'Hartmann Schedel,' *Medizin historisches Journal* 4 (1969), 55–68.

19 See Fletcher, 'Linacre's Lands and Lectureships,' in Madison et al., *Linacre Studies*, 118.

20 For Poliziano see A. Persosa, 'Codici di Galeno postillati dal Poliziano,' in *Umanesimo e Rinascimento: Studi offerti a Paul Oskar Kristeller*, ed. V. Branca et al. (Florence, 1980), 75–95.

21 See Madison et al., *Linacre Studies*, 38.

22 For this and relations between Poliziano and Leoniceno in general see A. Politianus, *Opera* (Basle, 1553), 17–22. Leoniceno had visited England in the late 1450s or early 1460s on the invitation of some English colleagues at Padua, was to instruct Richard Pace in 1508, and owned two of Linacre's translations of Galen. See D. Mugnai Carrara, 'Profilo di Niccolò Leoniceno,' *Interpres* 2 (1978), 175, and D. Mugnai Carrara, *La biblioteca di Niccolò Leoniceno tra Aristotele e Galeno: cultura e libri di un medico umanista* (Florence, 1991), 159.

23 See D.J. Geanakoplos, *Interaction of the 'Sibling' Byzantine and Western Cultures* (New Haven and London, 1976), 231–64. (Cf. Munich, Bayerische Staatsbibliothek, MS Lat. 28128, esp. fol. 5.)

24 See Schmitt in Madison et al., *Linacre Studies*, 62–3, and B. Bertolaso, 'Ricerche d'archivio su alcuni aspetti dell'insegnamento medico presso l'Università di Padova nel Cinque e Seicento,' *Acta medicae historiae patavina* 6 (1959–60), 23.

25 See Madison et al., *Linacre Studies*, 51–2.

26 Ibid., 60, note 6. He also promoted John Chamber.

27 Ibid., note 4.

28 Ibid., 67, note 4. He was also a promoter of Chamber.

29 Linacre's witnesses were Maurice O'Fihely, Calphurnius Brixiensis, Joannes Weppe, and Giovan Battista Novello. The text of his doctoral examination is printed in R.J. Mitchell, 'Thomas Linacre in Italy,' *English Historical Review* 50 (1935), 696–8. For O'Fihely, the Irish professor of Scotist theology, see Brotto and Zonta, *La facolta teologica*, 183–5.

30 See Munk, *The Roll of the Royal College of Physicians*, I, 2.

31 See G. Whitteridge, 'Some Italian Precursors of the Royal College of Physicians,' *Journal of the Royal College of Physicians of London* 12 (1977), 67–80.

32 See Fletcher in Madison et al., *Linacre Studies*, 107–97.

33 On Corpus Christi College generally see J.K. McConica, 'The Rise of the Undergraduate College,' in McConica, *History*, 17–29, and his 'The Collegiate Society,' ibid., 666–93. For Claymond, Linacre, and Corpus see J.M. Woolfson, 'John Claymond, Pliny the Elder, and the Early History of Corpus Christi College, Oxford,' *English Historical Review* 112 (1997), 882–903.

34 Only one of Wolsey's medical lecturers ever performed – Thomas Mos-

groffe in 1522. See Anthony Wood, *Athenae oxonienses* (London, 1641), col. 664.

35 See *Orationes Richardi Croci duae, altera a cura, qua utilitatem laudemque Graecae linguae tractat, altera a tempore, qua hortatus est Cantabrigiensis, ne desertores essent eiusdem*, n.p., 1520, no page no. My translation draws on J.T. Sheppard's in his *Richard Croke, a Sixteenth-Century Don* (Cambridge, 1919), 18.

36 See R.S. Gottfried, 'English Medical Practitioners, 1340–1530,' *Bulletin of the History of Medicine* 58 (1984), 175.

37 BL, MS Sloane 1047.

38 See *AGA, 1501–50*, no. 1053.

39 J. Leland, *Principum ac illustrium aliquot et eruditorum in Anglia virorum encomia* (London, 1589), 63.

40 'Sed quando tu unus, velut imperator, bellum hoc patrare tam difficile et arduum non poteras, et grati est animi fateri cui debeas, agent etiam gratias Graeci Latinique restituti Galeni, Clementi et Odoardo et Roseo Britannis, qui te veluti centuriones acerrimi in victoria hac consequenda plurimum adjuvere; sed nec Lupsetum in hoc munere contempseris, qui omnibus elaboravit nervis ut, quatenus fieri posset, laboranti tibi veluti Atlanti, dum axem humero torques, tanquam alter Hercules successerit: sed nec Georgius Agricola non parvam laudem est meritus, nam et ipse in emendando Galeno nihil sibi ad industriam et laborem reliqui fecit, ut honestissima tandem provincia et optimo imperatore, et strenuis maxime militibus dextro, quod aiunt, Hercule sit confecta.' See B. Botfield, *Prefaces to the First Editions of the Greek and Roman Classics and the Sacred Scriptures* (London, 1861), 352–65. Giovan Battista Opizo was professor of medicine at the *studium* of Pavia.

41 See N. Mani, 'Die griechische Editio princeps des Galenos (1525), ihre Entstehung und ihre Wirkung,' *Gesnerus* 13 (1956), 29–52; N. Mani, 'Die Editio princeps des Galen und die anatomisch-physiologische Forschung im 16. Jahrhundert,' in *Das Verhältnis der Humanisten zum Buch*, ed. F. Krafft and D. Wuttke (Boppard, 1977), 209–26; and V. Nutton, *John Caius and the Manuscripts of Galen* (Cambridge, 1987), 38–42. The project is described from the English point of view by G.W. Zeeveld, *Foundations of Tudor Policy* (Cambridge, MA, 1948), 54–6. See also C.F. Bühler, 'Some Documents Concerning the Torresani and the Aldine Press,' *Transactions of the Bibliographical Society* 25 (1944–5), 115.

42 Letter of More, in Erasmus, *Opus epistolarum*, II, no. 468 (*CWE*, IV, 80).

43 More to Erasmus, ibid., IV, no. 1087 (*CWE*, VII, 254).

44 *The Correspondence of Sir Thomas More*, ed. E.F. Rogers (Princeton, 1947), 136.

45 On the date of Clement's arrival in Italy, see Erasmus, *Opus epistolarum*, V, nos 1256 and 1271 (*CWE*, IX, 17 and 56).

46 See BL, MS Egerton 2604, fol. 6v. But note that Clement was already in Italy at this date, having arrived in spring, 1522. Cf. Nutton, *John Caius and the Manuscripts of Galen*, 72, note 58.

47 Italians comprised by far the largest group of foreign medical practitioners in England; see Gottfried, 'English Medical Practitioners,' 175. On Agostini, see E.A. Hammond, 'Doctor Augustine, Physician to Cardinal Wolsey and King Henry VIII,' *Medical History* 19 (1975), 215–49. Both Agostini and Guercie became active in the College of Physicians.

48 Others were John Mason (to Paris) and Reginald Pole.

49 Erasmus, *Opus epistolarum*, IV, xxiv.

50 See BAV, MS Rossiano 997, fols 37v–8.

51 See C. Longolius, *Opera* (Forence, 1524), fol. 143.

52 Information on Clement's library derives from a catalogue dating from the 1550s, for which reason it is not clear which books were acquired by him in Italy. But noteworthy are the editions of Aristotle, Galen, Hippocrates, Johannes Grammaticus, and Michael Ephesius, all in Greek, and in Latin Avicenna, Averroes, Celsus, Galen, Georg Agricola, Hippocrates, Niccolò Leoniceno, Giovanni Manardi, Michele Savonarola, and Aristotle. See A.W. Reed, 'John Clement and His Books,' *The Library* 6 (1925–6), 329–39. For further information see G. Mercati, 'Sopra Giovanni Clemente e i suoi manoscritti,' in G. Mercati, *Opere minori* (Vatican City, 1937–84), IV, 292–315; R.W. Hunt, 'The Need for a Guide to the Editors of Patristic Texts in the Sixteenth Century,' in *Studia Patristica* 17, ed. E.A. Livingstone (Kalamazoo, MI, 1982), 365–71; A. Cameron, 'Sir Thomas More and the Greek Anthology,' in *Florilegium Columbianum: Essays in Honor of Paul Oskar Kristeller*, ed. K-L. Selig and R. Somerville (New York, 1987), 187–98; Nutton, 'John Caius and the Linacre Tradition,' 379.

53 He also treated Reginald Pole. See BL, MS Cotton, Nero B vi, fol. 145 (*LP*, VII, no. 1016).

54 He later recommended the work to young men to maintain their health, in his 'Exhortation.' See J.A. Gee, *The Life and Works of Thomas Lupset* (New Haven, 1928), 246.

55 For Clement's work see Nutton, 'John Caius and the Linacre Tradition,' 379, and Nutton, *John Caius and the Manuscripts of Galen*, 41.

56 See Allen and Allen, *Letters of Richard Fox*, 126–7.

57 See letter of Wotton to Pole: Venice, Biblioteca Nazionale Marciana, MS Ital. VII 1934 (9013), fol. 1.

58 On this work see C.E. Raven, *English Naturalists from Neckham to Ray*

(Cambridge, 1947), 40–2; V. Nutton, 'Conrad Gesner and the English Naturalists,' *Medical History* 29 (1985), 93–7; and now Ä. Bäumer, 'Das erste zoologische Kompendium in der Zeit der Renaissance: Edward Wottons Schrift "Über die Differenzen der Tiere,"' *Berichte zur Wissenschaftsgeschichte* Bd. 13, Heft 1 (1990) 13–29.

59 In the dedication to his *De differentiis animalium*, sig. a.iiv. Cf. Nutton, *John Caius and the Manuscripts of Galen*, 40. Also, Leland, *Encomia*, 65, calls him 'Cultor denique maximus Galeni.' See Thomas Vicary, *The Anatomie of the Bodie of Man* (London, 1888), 99, for records of royal payments to Clement and Wotton.

60 See Nutton, *John Caius and the Manuscripts of Galen*, 39.

61 J. Constable, *Epigrammata* (London, 1520), sig. d 3.

62 See Nutton, *John Caius and the Manuscripts of Galen*, 38–9 and *BRUO*, 492.

63 For a discussion of the identity of More's 'Rosseus' see *The Complete Works of Thomas More* (New Haven, 1981), VI, pt. 2, 798–802.

64 (London, 1950), 64. Note that the inventory of Clement's library contains a copy of 'Rosseus contra Lutherum': see Reed, 'John Clement and His Books,' 339.

65 Parts of Claymond's manuscript, now Basle, Universitätsbibliotek, MS KI4, later came into the hands of John Caius. See Woolfson, 'John Claymond,' 894.

66 Noted in a letter of Lupset to Erasmus, in Erasmus, *Opus epistolarum*, VI, no. 1595 (*CWE*, XI, 233).

67 I cannot trace the tradition that he did so back beyond Thomas Phillips, *The History of the Life of Reginald Pole* (Oxford, 1765), I, 5, and Philip Bliss's additions in his London, 1813 edition of Anthony Wood, *Athenae oxonienses*, 279.

68 T. Fowler, *The History of Corpus Christi College* (Oxford, 1893), 58.

69 Longolius, *Opera*, 275–6.

70 See *Collectanea*, Second Series, ed. M. Burrows, Oxford Historical Society (Oxford, 1890), 326.

71 See Erasmus, *Opus epistolarum*, III, no. 907 (*CWE*, VI, 215).

72 See Sanuto, *I diarii*, XXXVI, col. 382.

73 For Linacre and Aldo, see M. Lowry, *The World of Aldus Manutius* (Oxford, 1979), 259–63. Note that Linacre's copy of the Aldine Aristotle is now in New College, Oxford. Lowry, 261, suggests that other Aldine works in New College may have come to England with Linacre.

74 See Botfield, ed., *Prefaces*, 199. Cf. the preface to the Aldine *editio princeps* of Aristophanes, 1498, in Botfield, 218.

75 'Quanquam (ut spero) eosque et alios in philosophia medicinaque perutiles libros aliquando dabit, ut ex eadem Britannia, unde olim

barbarae, et indoctae literae ad nos profectae, Italiam occuparunt, et adhuc arces tenent, Latine et docte loquentes bonas artes accipiamus, ac Britannis adiutoribus fugata barbarie, arces nostras recipiamus, ut eadem hasta sanetur a qua illatum est vulnus.' Botfield, ed., *Prefaces*, 240. The translation is Lowry's in *The World of Aldus Manutius*, 259.

76 See Schmitt in Madison et al., *Linacre Studies*, 73.

77 Letter to Baptista Egnatius, in Erasmus, *Opus epistolarum*, VI, no. 1707, to James Tusanus, no. 1713, and to Joachim Martinius, VII, no. 2049. But note that Erasmus had an old bone to pick with Torresani, for which see M.J.C. Lowry's entry on Torresani in *CE*, III, 332–3.

78 J. Manardus, *Epistolae medicinales* (Basle, 1540), 462.

79 See Erasmus, *Opus epistolarum*, VIII, no. 2216.

80 Georg Agricola, *Bermannus: Un dialogue sur les mines*, ed. R. Halleux and A. Yans (Paris, 1990), 59.

81 See Erasmus, *Opus epistolarum*, II, no. 520 (*CWE*, VI, 198–202).

82 See Rogers, *Correspondence*, no. 19.

83 See Croke, *Orationes*.

84 See E. Tilley, 'Greek Studies in England in the Early Sixteenth Century,' *English Historical Review* 53 (1938), 221–39, 438–56, and J.W. Binns, 'Latin Translations from the Greek in the English Renaissance,' *Humanistica Lovaniensia* 27 (1978), 128–59.

85 'Sunt optimae spei iuvenes, qui hoc praestare poterunt, inter quos primas tribuerim Ioanni Clementi Anglo, quem nescias an Graecia an Latium rectius sibi vindicet, ita est utriusque linguae et medicinae peritus, prudens praeterea et integer.' Agricola, *Bermannus*, 57. Agricola's contact with English humanism dated back to his being taught by Richard Croke at Leipzig University in the mid-1510s. See O. Hannaway, 'Georgius Agricola as Humanist,' *Journal of the History of Ideas* 53 (1992), 554–6.

86 Nutton, *John Caius and the Manuscripts of Galen*, 42.

87 As recounted by John Caius, *De libris propriis*, 18, in J. Caius, *Works*, ed. E.S. Roberts (Cambridge, 1912).

88 *AGA, 1501–50*, no. 1736.

89 He was the brother of William Bill, Linacre Lecturer in Physic at Cambridge. See J. Venn and J.A. Venn, *Alumni Cantabrigienses* (Cambridge, 1922), pt 1, I, 151.

90 See *AGA, 1501–50*, nos. 2216 and 2220. He was a witness to Bill's degree.

91 See, for example, tributes in George Edrych, *In libros aliquot Pauli Aeginetae* (London, 1558), sig. Aiv, and Nicholas Carr, *De scriptorum Britannicorum paucitate* (London, 1576), 'Praefatione' of Walter Barker.

92 *Hippocratis Coi Aphorismi versibus scripti* (London, 1567). Further of his

Latin verse translations from the Greek are in Demosthenes, *Olythiacae orationes tres, & Philippicae quattuor* (London, 1571), sig. Ciiv and 67.

93 See *AGA, 1501–50*, no. 2793.

94 See Caius, *De libris propriis*, 58, in his *Works*.

95 See Bylebyl, 'The School of Padua,' in Webster, *Health*, 346–9.

96 He also had dealings with Lazzaro Bonamico, a witness to his doctorate, and, in Venice, with Giovan Battista Egnazio. At Pisa he knew the Galenic polemicist who had previously taught at Padua, Mattheo Curzio. See his *De libris propriis*, 76–7, 87, and 102 in his *Works*. On his relations with Vesalius note also the comments of C. D. O'Malley in his 'The Vesalian Influence in England,' *Acta medicae historiae patavina* 10 (1963–4), 12–13.

97 He supplies evidence that, like himself, Clement had taken the opportunity of his time in Italy to acquire copies of Galen, which Caius later used. See Caius, *De libris propriis*, 83, in his *Works*: 'Quocirca conquisitis undique exemplaribus manuscriptis non solum Italicis, sed & Anglicis quoque cum reverteram (ex quibus duo porrexerunt Ioannes Clemens & Georgius Owenus clariss. medici) studuimus emendare, quoad eius fieri potuit, diligenter omnia.' I have not taken this statement to mean that George Owen had been to Padua. Cf. Nutton, 'John Caius and the Eton Galen: Medical Philology in the Renaissance,' *Medizinhistorisches Journal* 20 (1985), 238. *De libris propriis* does supply evidence for the presence in Padua at the same time as Caius of Henry Knolles, later a diplomat and MP and a brother of the more famous Francis. But it may be doubted that he was a medical student. Although 'familiarissimus' with Caius, he bought a Galen manuscript for him only 'pro amicitia' (*De libris propriis*, 83).

98 See Whitteridge, *William Harvey*, 9.

99 See *DNB*.

100 See AAU 333, fol. 61. In addition, an anonymous despatch from Venice dated 1576 describing the plague situation in Padua reports that a young English quack was promising to cure the local inhabitants. See BAV, Urb. Lat. 1044, fol. 523.

101 Six of the fifteen medical students mentioned in what follows came to Padua from Cambridge, four from Oxford. William Harvey benefited from Caius's medical fellowship at Gonville and Caius College, which permitted study abroad (see Whitteridge, *William Harvey*, 9). As is the case with some other English students at Padua, knowledge of Jordan's Paduan doctorate comes from the record of his admission to the College of Physicians, where he had to present his doctoral diploma. We know from its annals that the college was rigorous on this matter. See for example London, Royal College of Physicians, Annals of the College of

Physicians of London 3, fols 14 and 62v. The absence of known medical degrees probably means that they were awarded by counts palatine and the record of them has either been lost or remains undiscovered in Padua's Archivio Notarile.

102 See Bertolaso, 'Ricerche,' 23, 26.

103 The tradition of English medical study at Padua continued well beyond 1603. For examples see Maladorno Hargraves, 'Diplomi dottorali' 169–78; Maladorno Hargraves, 'John Bastwick,' 101–2; and for testimony from 1605, *Memorials of Father Augustine Baker*, ed. J. McCann and H. Connolly (London, 1933), 83.

104 The most useful comprehensive works on Harvey are Whitteridge, *William Harvey and the Circulation of the Blood*, W. Pagel, *William Harvey's Biological Ideas* (Basle and New York, 1967), and G. Keynes, *The Life of William Harvey* (Oxford, 1966).

105 On this point see Pagel, *William Harvey's Biological Ideas*, 19. On Fabricius generally there is a large amount of secondary literature, but see most recently *Dizionario biografico degli italiani*, 43, 768–74, and for bibliography L. Premuda, 'Girolamo Fabrizio d'Acquapendente nella storiografica medico-scientifica,' *Acta medicae historiae patavina* 34 (1987–8), 101–17.

106 See for example, K. Plochmann, 'William Harvey and his Methods,' *Studies in the Renaissance* 10 (1963), 192–210; and W. Pagel, 'The Philosophy of Circles – Cesalpino – Harvey: A Penultimate Assessment,' *Journal of the History of Medicine and Allied Sciences* 12 (1957), 140–57.

107 See Plochmann, 'William Harvey,' Whitteridge, *William Harvey*, passim, and C. Schmitt, 'William Harvey and Renaissance Aristotelianism,' in *Humanismus und Medizin*, ed. G. Keil and R. Schmitz (Weinheim, 1984), 117–38.

108 Schmitt, 'William Harvey,' and R. French, *William Harvey's Natural Philosophy* (Cambridge, 1994), esp. 64–8. Cf. A.R. Cunningham, 'Fabricius and the "Aristotle Project" in Anatomical Teaching and Research in Padua,' in Wear, *Medical Renaissance*, 195–222.

109 J. Bylebyl, 'Harvey, William,' in *Dictionary of Scientific Biography*, ed. C.C. Gillispie (New York, 1972), VII, 150–62. Cf. Joseph Lister's basically Aristotelian thesis on the human soul, printed for the defence of his master's degree at Basle in July 1597, immediately prior to his arrival in Padua: J. Lister, *De anima humana* (Basle, 1597: Basle, Universitätsbibliothek, Diss. 442, N. 18). For Harvey on the soul see in addition G. Gorham, 'Mind-body Dualism and the Harvey-Descartes Controversy,' *Journal of the History of Ideas* 55 (1994), 211–34; and W. Pagel, 'Harvey Revisited (Part I),' *History of Science* 8 (1969), 8–11.

110 For the first, see for examples V. Nutton, 'Harvey, Goulston and Galen,' *Koroth* 8 (1985), 112–22; M.H. Shank, 'From Galen's Ureters to Harvey's Veins,' *Journal of the History of Biology* 18 (1985), 331–55, and his 'The Growth of Harvey's *De motu cordis*,' *Bulletin of the History of Medicine* 47 (1973), 427–90. For the second, see for example Pagel, *William Harvey's Biological Ideas*, 132–6.

111 On this see especially C. Webster, 'William Harvey's Conception of the Heart as a Pump,' *Bulletin of the History of Medicine* 37 (1965), 508–17, and also W. Pagel, 'Harvey Revisited (Part II),' *History of Science* 9 (1970), 1–21.

112 C. Schmitt, 'William Harvey,' 132.

113 For Zabarella, see ibid., 128–31. It may be added that there are some striking similarities between their conceptions of the soul. On Zabarella on the soul see E. Kessler, 'The Intellective Soul,' in *The Cambridge History of Renaissance Philosophy*, ed. C.B. Schmitt, Q. Skinner, E. Kessler, and J. Kraye (Cambridge, 1988), 530–4, and E. Michael, 'The Nature and Influence of Late Renaissance Paduan Psychology,' *History of Universities* 12 (1993), 65–94.

114 See Pagel, 'Harvey Revisted (Part I),' 14–15.

115 See Pagel, *William Harvey's Biological Ideas*, 169–209; and J. Bylebyl, 'Cesalpino and Harvey on the Portal Circulation,' in *Science, Medicine and Society in the Renaissance: Essays to Honour Walter Pagel*, ed. A.G. Debus (New York,1972), II, 39–52.

116 See French, *William Harvey's Natural Philosophy*, 61–3.

117 See Schmitt, 'William Harvey,' 135–6; Pagel, 'Harvey Revisited (Part II),' 33–4, and Whitteridge, *William Harvey*, 33. Cremonini was also the teacher of Father Augustine Baker at the Benedictine monastery of S. Giustina in Padua in 1605. See McCann, *Memorials*, 86.

118 On Minadous and Casserius see Whitteridge, *William Harvey*, 15, 28–9, 32–3. The other promoters of his doctorate were Fabricius and Georgius Raguseus (ibid., 14).

119 See Keynes, *Life of William Harvey*, 431. The other teachers mentioned by Aubrey were Minadous and Fabricius. Rudio was one of the promoter's of John Frear's doctorate in 1610; see Maladorno Hargraves, 'Diplomi dottorali,' 170. From 1599 to 1608 Rudio held the second ordinary chair in medical practice, from 1608 to 1614 the first ordinary chair; see Bertolaso, 'Ricerche,' 24; cf. Facciolati, *Fasti*, pt. 2, 332–3.

120 See *AGA, 1601–5*, no. 787.

121 See the entry on Pace in *CE*, III, 37–9. For Pace and Linacre see Pace's *De fructu*, 62–3, 96–7. Note also his acquaintance in Rome with the physician

Francesco Vittorio. See Pace's *Plutarchi Cheronaei Opuscula* (Venice, 1523), prefatory letter.

122 Pace, *De fructu*, 36–9.

123 See D. De Bellis, 'La vita e l'ambiente di Niccolò Leonico Tomeo,' *QSUP* 18 (1980), 69–72.

124 The first edition is Aristotle, *Parva quae vocant Naturalia, omnia in latinum conversa et explicata a Nicolao Leonico Thomaeo* (Venice, 1523).

125 First published posthumously by his nephew Magnus Leonicus as *Conversio in Latinum atque explanatio primi libri Aristotelis de partibus animalium* (Venice, 1540), with a dedicatory letter from Magnus Leonicus to Reginald Pole.

126 In Niccolò Leonico Tomeo, *Opuscula* (Venice, 1525), apparently taken from Leonico's university lectures.

127 Ibid. For a contemporary manuscript version of the *Quaestiones naturales*, see BL, MS Sloane 3280. The *Opuscula* also includes the pseudo-Aristotelian *Quaestiones mechanica*, Leonico's translation of Proclus's commentary on Plato's *Timaeus*, and his own *Quaestiones amatoria* on the ethics and physiology of love.

128 See especially D. De Bellis, 'Niccolò Leonico Tomeo interprete di Aristotele naturalista,' *Physis* 17 (1975), 71–93; D. De Bellis, '*Autokineton* e *entelechia*. Niccolò Leonico Tomeo: l'anima nei dialoghi intitolati al Bembo,' *Annali dell'Istituto di Filosofia dell'Università di Firenze* 1 (1979), 47–68; D. De Bellis, 'I veicoli dell'anima nell'analisi di Niccolò Leonico Tomeo,' ibid., 3 (1981), 1–21; and G. Saitta, *Il pensiero italiano nell'Umanesimo e nel Rinascimento* (Florence, 1961), I, 436–51. On the *Quaestiones naturales* see B. Lawn, *I quesiti salernitani* (Naples, 1969), 159.

129 In Galen, *Opuscula aliquot* (Parıs, 1546), and other editions of Galen's collected works dating from the 1540s to the 1580s. A small doubt concerning his authorship arises from the fact that sixteenth-century editors and subsequent writers have sometimes confused him with the translator of Galen, Niccolò Leoniceno.

130 See Venice, Biblioteca Nazionale Marciana, MS Lat. VI 272 (2883), fol. 380. Leonico, Bembo, and Navagero are also mentioned together in an anonymous letter of 1530: Venice, Biblioteca Nazionale Marciana, MS Lat. XIV 61 (4241) fol. 245. Montesdoch wrote a prefatory letter dated 1522 for Leonico's commentary on the *Parva naturalia*, published in the Paris edition of 1530.

131 BAV, MS Rossiano 997, fol. 24.

132 BL, MS Cotton, Vitellius B xiii, fol. 85v.

133 See BAV, MS Rossiano 997, fol. 26v. Leonico told Latimer that his com-

mentaries had been published and sent him a copy (ibid., fol. 37). In a third letter he thanks Latimer for praise of the commentaries (ibid., fol. 24).

134 P.S. Allen, 'Linacre and Latimer in Italy,' *English Historical Review* 18 (1903), 514–17. For text of the letter to Aldo, see *Les Correspondants d'Alde Manuce*, ed. P. De Nolhac (Rome, 1888), 96. For further evidence of Latimer's relations with Aldo see Erasmus, *Opus epistolarum*, I, no. 207 (*CWE*, II, 132). At Padua Latimer knew the Aldine academician Girolamo Aleandro (see Erasmus, *Opus epistolarum*, I, no. 256; *CWE*, II, 223).

135 See Paulo Giovio, *Opera* (Rome, 1984), IX, 100. Cf. Giovio's *Gli elogi degli uomini illustri* (Rome, 1972), 89.

136 See *I due primi registri di prestito della Biblioteca Apostolica Vaticana*, ed. M. Bertòla (Vatican City, 1942), 72 and pl. 52*. The entry is dated 1510 (not 1519 as in Erasmus, *Opus epistolarum*, XI, xxiii). Latimer was admitted to the English hospice at Rome in 1511. See *EH*, 192.

137 Leland, *Encomia*, 18.

138 BAV, MS Rossiano 997, fol. 37. The letter is dated 1 July 1524. See Leonico, *Dialogi*, fol. 80: 'Dominicus Bonominus brixianus, qui nuper Tarvisi est defunctus, vir fuit (ut nosti) Latymere doctissime cum grecis & latinis literis liberaliter eruditius ...' For Bonomino see G. Mazzuchelli, *Gli scrittori d'Italia* (Brescia, 1762), II, pt 3, 1684–5.

139 Definitely belonging to him were the works he donated to Cambridge University Library in 1529, which included some volumes of the Aldine Aristotle, and Ammonius and Simplicius commentaries. The possiblity that the inventory of books in BL, MS Additional 40676 represents Tunstall's library in the 1550s would expand Tunstall's ownership of medical and natural philosophical works. Of particular interest in this inventory are the works of Niccolò Leoniceno, the complete Aldine Aristotle, the complete Aldine Galen and, catalogued separately, another copy of the fifth volume of the Aldine Galen, the volume in which the participation of the English editors is mentioned. For further discussion and references, see chapter 4, p. 107. Tunstall is linked to Aldo in Erasmus, *Opus epistolarum*, I, no. 207 (*CWE*, II, 132).

140 See the letter of Robert Fisher from Bologna to Mantova at Padua, delivered by Tunstall and dated 1504, which found its way into the letter collection of Marco Mantova: Venice, Biblioteca Correr, MS Correr 1349, fol. 16.

141 BAV, MS Rossiano 997, fol. 50.

142 Ibid., fols 30v–1: 'Totum Galenum perlegi, atque in eo pleraque, maxime que ad philosophiam pertinere videbantur ...'

143 See V. Nutton, '*De placitis Hippocratis et Platonis* in the Renaissance,' in *Le opere psicologiche di Galeno*, ed. P. Manuli and M. Vegetti (Pavia, 1988), 295–6. Note that Leonico and Leoniceno may have met in Venice in 1522. See G. Rustico, 'Due umanisti veneti: Urbano Bolzanio e Piero Valeriano,' *Civiltà moderna* 4 (1932), 368 (cf. Mugnai Carrara, 'Profilo,' 185).

144 Venice, Biblioteca Nazionale Marciana, MS Gr. Z. 225 (307). See Lowry, *The World of Aldus Manutius*, 23; L. Labowsky, 'Manuscripts from Bessarion's Library Found in Milan,' *Medieval and Renaissance Studies* 5 (1961), 125, and Biblioteca Nazionale Marciana, *Manoscritti e stampe venete dell'aristotelismo e averroismo* (Venice, 1958), 26. Leonico's copy of the Aldine Galen is in the Yale Medical Library.

145 BAV, MS Rossiano 997, fol. 34. By 1525 he had read all of Plato and Aristotle; see Erasmus, *Opus epistolarum*, VI, no. 1595 (*CWE*, XI, 233).

146 On this issue see G. B. Parks, 'Did Pole Write the "Vita Longolii?"' *Renaissance Quarterly* 26 (1973), 274–85, and A. Vos, 'The "Vita Longolii": Additional Considerations about Reginald Pole's Authorship,' ibid., 30 (1977), 324–33.

147 Longolius, *Opera*, fol. 4.

148 Erasmus, *Opus epistolarum*, XI, 381–3; Longolius, *Opera*, fol. 153.

149 For further discussion see chapter 4.

150 See Mayer, *Thomas Starkey*, esp. 43–76. The *Dialogue* remained unpublished until the nineteenth century and exists only in one rough draft, PRO, SP1 90. The authoritative edition is Thomas Starkey, *A Dialogue between Pole and Lupset*, ed. T.F. Mayer (London, 1989). All references in this discussion to the *Dialogue* refer to this edition, but I have modernized the spelling where possible.

151 Mayer, *Thomas Starkey*, 3.

152 There are some exceptions – for example Longueil, who knew John Clement; Bembo, who knew Marmaduke Waldby; and Leonico, who knew several members of Pole's circle.

153 See Erasmus, *Opus epistolarum*, VI, no. 1627 (*CWE*, XI, 314–17); Pole, *Epistolarum collectio*, ed. A.M. Quirinus (Farnborough, 1967, repr.), I, 383–93; *LP*, IV, pt 1, no. 79; and Sanuto, *I diarii*, XXXIX, col. 63. See also BL, MS Cotton, Vespasian F xiii, fols 283–5.

154 *LP*, IV, nos 4405, 4756, and 5224 are BL, MS Egerton 1998, fols 2–5. Mayer, *Thomas Starkey*, 77–8.

155 On the movements of Pace and Amaseo, see, respectively, *CE*, III, 37–9, and *Dizionario biografico degli italiani*, II, 660–6.

156 See Erasmus, *Opus epistolarum*, VI, no. 1761 and VII, no. 1817; and Bembo, *Lettere*, ed. E. Travi (Bologna, 1987–93), II, 376. In a letter of

Leonico's to Pole from Padua, dated May 1527, he writes, 'Nescio quid
cause sit procum iampridem e gallia discesseris, britaniamque petieris ...'
(BAV, MS Rossiano 997, fol. 22v).

157 See PRO, SP1 55, fol. 152.
158 BAV, MS Rossiano 997, fol. 22v.
159 S.J. Herrtage, *England in the Reign of King Henry the Eighth* (London,
1878), vi (cf. *LP*, IV, pt 1, 873).
160 W.T. Mitchell, *Epistolae academicae, 1508–96* (Oxford, 1980), 128.
161 *BRUO*, 23.
162 *A Register of the Members of St Mary Magdalen College, Oxford*, ed. W.D.
Macray (London, 1894), I, 156.
163 Mitchell, *Epistolae academicae*, 381; Erasmus, *Opus epistolarum*, V, no. 1360
(*CWE*, X, 9–10); BAV, MS Rossiano 997, fol. 38v. Gee, *Life and Works*, 106,
followed by Zeeveld, *Foundations*, 51, took this Thomas to be Wolsey's
illegitimate son Thomas Winter, but Mayer, *Thomas Starkey*, 46–8, argues
the case for it being Starkey.
164 See *AGA, 1501–50*, no. 1059. Starkey's will suggests that his father
supported his education. See Weaver, *Somerset Medieval Wills*, 47.
165 For Wotton's MD, see *AGA, 1501–50*, no. 1059. Wotton and Starkey remained friends, Wotton eventually becoming the chief executor of Starkey's will and the inheritor of his books; see Weaver, *Somerset Medieval
Wills*, 47–8. For Pole, Lupset, and Leonico, see the *Dialogue*, and the letter of
Leonico to Starkey of 1529, BAV, MS Rossiano 997, fols 29v–30v.
166 See BL, MS Cotton, Nero B vi, fol. 169 (*LP*, V, no. 301). This is Harvel's
earliest documented contact with Starkey, but their friendship must have
been forged in Padua and Venice.
167 BL, MS Cotton, Nero B vi, fol. 145 (*LP*, VII, no. 1016).
168 Also present were the English law students Bartholomew Bainham and
Michael Throckmorton. *AGA, 1501–50*, no. 1943, transcribes Starkey's
name as 'Acceren,' but I am confident of my identification after consult-
ing the original, ACV, Diversorum 54, fol. 97.
169 BL, MS Cotton, Nero B vi, fol. 147 (*LP*, IX, no. 648). For further relations
between Friar and Starkey see PRO, SP1 99, fol. 124 and *LP*, IX, no. 1011.
170 BL, MS Harley 6989, fol. 43 (*LP*, VII, i, no. 900, dated by the editors
1534): '... de illius valetudine vellem me effecisses certiorem qualis nunc
esset, an melior quam hic, et quam (si ita est) eius eventus putares
causam non nihil quoquam de istius aeris qualitatibus. non enim erant
hec impertinentia summo philosopho scribenti ad medicum sui amantis-
simum.' Starkey's reply is BL, MS Harley 6989, fols 43–4.
171 For example, Pole's friend Henry Coles, whose 1559 bequest of books to

St John's College, Oxford, includes Venetian 1535 editions of Aristotle's *Physica* and *De anima* in Greek and a 1534 edition of Alexander of Aphrodisias's commentary on *De anima*. See *BRUO*, 717–18.

172 This quotation expands on the one given above, p. 40.

173 BL, MS Harley 283, fol. 129v (*LP*, VIII, no. 214).

174 PRO, SP1 90, fol. 1 (*LP*, VIII, no. 217; printed in full in Herrtage, *England in the Reign of King Henry the Eighth*, lxxiii–lxxv).

175 Starkey, *Dialogue*, 3.

176 Ibid., 17.

177 Starkey's use of the metaphor is briefly discussed in D.G. Hale, *The Body Politic: A Political Metaphor in Renaissance English Literature* (The Hague, 1971), 61–8, and P. Archambault, 'The Analogy of the "Body" in Renaissance Political Literature,' *Bibliothèque d'Humanisme et Renaissance* 29 (1967), 39–43. On the subject generally see also I. Kajanto, 'The Body Politic: On the History of a Famous Simile,' *Arctos* 29 (1995), 49–80.

178 Starkey, *Dialogue*, 22–3.

179 Ibid., 31.

180 Ibid., 33.

181 Ibid.

182 Ibid., 39.

183 Ibid., 46–7.

184 Ibid., 48. Cf. Sir Thomas Elyot's English definition of 'tabes' in his *Dictionary* of 1538: 'corruption in the body. Also extreme leannesse, by a large consumynge sycknesse. It is also matter and corrupte blode myxte togither. Also the impostume of the lunges, procedynge of humoure, descendynge frome the heed into the stomake, and so woundynge and corruptyng the lounges.' For 'tabes' in Galen, see Galen, *Opera omnia*, ed. C.G. Kühn (Hildesheim, 1965), XX, 586.

185 PRO, SP1 90, fol. 50. Not 'πλεθοριθον,' as in *Dialogue*, 52. For uses in Galen, cf. R. J. Durling, *A Dictionary of Medical Terms in Galen* (Leiden, New York, Köln, 1993), 270.

186 Starkey, *Dialogue*, 54–5.

187 Ibid., 55–6

188 Ibid., 57–8.

189 Ibid., 58–9.

190 Ibid., 95.

191 Ibid., 96.

192 Ibid., 96–100.

193 Ibid., 101–7.

194 See Starkey's *Exhortation to Unitie and Obedience* (London, 1540), passim,

for an analogous extended metaphor of blindness. The discussion of the transition from classicizing to contemporary interests among English students in Padua, described here in chapter 5, also sheds light on the historical context of Starkey's endeavour.

195 See Plato, *Laws*, ed. R.G. Bury, (London, 1926), II, 552–6.
196 See John of Salisbury, *Policraticus*, books 2 and 3, passim. But see A. Momigliano, 'Notes on Petrarch, John of Salisbury and the *Institutio Trajani*,' *Journal of the Warburg and Courtauld Institutes* 12 (1949), 1–2.
197 See G. Rosen, 'The Historical Significance of Some Medical References in the *Defensor pacis* of Marsilius of Padua,' *Archiv für Geschichte der Medizin* 37 (1953), 350–6. For Starkey and Marsilius, see F.L. Baumer, 'Thomas Starkey and Marsilius of Padua,' *Politica* 2 (1936), 188–205, and H.S. Stout, 'Marsilius of Padua and the Henrician Reformation,' *Church History* 43 (1974), 308–18. Mayer argues against any direct influence from Marsilius to Starkey in his *Thomas Starkey*, esp. 139–47, 215–18, 226–7, and, for Marsilius's use of Aristotle's naturalistic conception of the state, ibid., 152–3. For a more certain case of Marsilian influence in the 1530s, see S. Lockwood, 'Marsilius of Padua and the Case for the Royal Ecclesiastical Supremacy,' *Transactions of the Royal Historical Society* 1 (1991), 89–120.
198 See A.J. Parel, *The Machiavellian Cosmos* (New Haven and London, 1992), 101–12, and D. Giannotti, *Della repubblica Fiorentina*, in his *Opere politiche* (Florence, 1850), I, 72–7.
199 See W.R.D. Jones, *William Turner: Tudor Naturalist, Physician and Divine* (London, 1988), 129–34.
200 T. Elyot, *Castel of helth* (London, 1541), sig. Aiiv. The work was first published in 1534. For Elyot's friendship with Agostino de'Agostini, the royal physician from Venice, see ibid., sigs Iv, X3, and O2. For his possible study of medicine with Thomas Linacre, ibid., sigs Aii–Avv; and P. Hogrefe, *The Life and Times of Sir Thomas Elyot, Englishman* (Iowa, 1967), 244–62. On the *Castel* generally see ibid., 244–62; and S.E. Lehmberg, *Sir Thomas Elyot, Tudor Humanist* (Texas, 1960), 132–47.
201 PRO, SP1 18, fol. 281 (*LP*, III, 1, no. 411).
202 Rogers, *Correspondence*, 136.

Chapter 4: Humanists

1 Colet was in Rome and Florence between 1492 and 1495. See J. Gleason, *John Colet* (Berkeley and Los Angeles, 1989), 45–52. Grocyn was in Florence and Venice between 1488 and 1491 and Lily was in Italy around

the same time. Neither of them have left documentary traces to demonstrate a sojourn in Padua. See *CE*, II, 135–6, 329–30.

2 One of these, at fols 5–6 does not carry Tunstall's name, but he can be identified as the addressee from the fact that the recipient is described as a 'praesul' from whom Leonico had received letters dated at London, of which Tunstall was then bishop. The year of the letter, 1528, was two years before Leonico's association with Tunstall's successor as bishop of London, John Stokesley, and with the bishop of Worcester, Girolamo Ghinucci. See Sturge, *Cuthbert Tunstall*, 351. The undated letter to Tunstall at fol. 6 was printed as the dedicatory letter in Niccolò Leonico Tomeo, *De varia historia libri tres* (Basle, 1531), sig. aa2, and dated there 1 February 1531.

3 One of these, at fol. 57, is a variant of the letter at fol. 52. The letter at fols 57v–8 does not carry Pace's name, but he can be identified as the addressee from the fact that the recipient is described as being present in Rome at the time of the election of Clement VII and as an intimate of Reginald Pole and Thomas Lupset.

4 The two letters at fols 13v–14v do not carry Pole's name, but he can be identified as the addressee from the fact that the letters concern the health of Pace, whom Pole was with in Italy in 1525.

5 BAV, MS Rossiano 997, fols 4v–5 includes a letter probably directed to Croke; fol. 7 probably to Stokesley. For other information about their relationships see Surtz, *Henry VIII's Great Matter*, 225–33. In the same connection Leonico corresponded with Girolamo Ghinucci; see MS Rossiano 997, fols 6v–7.

6 Ibid., fol. 46 is a letter to Poyntz. In a letter to Pole at fol. 46v Leonico discusses Poyntz.

7 See Labowsky, 'Manuscripts from Bessarion's Library,' 123, and P.L. Rose and S. Drake, 'The Pseudo-Aristotelian *Questions of Mechanics* in Renaissance Culture,' *Studies in the Renaissance* 18 (1971), 79, note 36.

8 See De Bellis, 'La vita.' For Leonico generally see in addition to works already cited A. Serena, *Appunti letterari* (Rome, 1903), 5–32; D.J. Geanakoplos, 'The Career of the Little-known Renaissance Greek Scholar Nicholas Leonicus Tomaeus and the Ascendancy of Greco-Byzantine Aristotelianism at Padua University (1497),' *Byzantina* 13 (1985), 357–71; I. Favaretto, 'Appunti sulla collezione rinascimentale di Niccolò Leonico Tomeo,' *Bollettino del Museo Civico di Padova* 68 (1979), 15–29; I. Favaretto, *Arte antica e cultura antiquaria nelle collezioni venete al tempo della Serenissima* (Rome, 1990), 100–3; M. King, *Venetian Humanism in an Age of Patrician Dominance* (Princeton, 1986), 432–4; A. Gregory and J. Woolfson,

'Aspects of Collecting in Renaissance Padua: A Bust of Socrates for Niccolò Leonico Tomeo,' *Journal of the Warburg and Courtauld Institutes* 58 (1995), 252–65.

9 His 'promotores' were Pietro Roccabonella, Paolo dal Fiume, Gerolamo Polcastro, Gerolamo della Torre, and Nicoletta Vernia. The witnesses included Alessandro Zeno, Giovanni Calfurnio, and Raffaele Regio. See AAU 316, fols 55–7, and ACV, Diversorum 42, fol. 91. Calfurnio and Regio were later incumbents of the chair of Latin grammar and rhetoric at Padua. With Giovanni Calfurnio (as well as Lorenzo Cretico, Alvise Mocenigo, Pandolfo Collenuccio, Benedetto Brugnoli, and Giorgio Valla), Leonico is recorded as having frequented the house of Filippo Bonaccorsi (Callimaco Esperiente), the Polish ambassador in Venice, in 1486. A close relationship with Calfurnio is suggested in a letter from Casandra Fedele to Leonico. Regio and Leonico feature together as interlocutors in Pomponio Guarico's *De sculptura* (1504). For some further information on these see De Bellis, 'La vita,' 39–40.

10 On Leonico and Cretico see BL, MS Additional 19061, fol. 15, a Latin poem of Leonico's addressed to Cretico. Aldo published Leonico's translation of the astronomy of Ptolemy in 1516, and Leonico seems to have lent manuscripts to the Aldine press. For a 1502 letter from Leonico to Marin Sanudo see Venice, Biblioteca Nazionale Marciana, MS Ital. IX 364 (7167), fols 176v–7. (Sanudo's brother, Marco, also mentioned in this letter, was an interlocutor in two of Leonico's *Dialogi*.)

11 This is according to his elegy by Lazzaro Bonamico; see De Bellis, 'La vita,' 45.

12 The possibility of their meeting is suggested by Erasmus's remark that Leonico was the first to describe to him the good qualities of Giacomo Sadoleto; see De Bellis, 'La vita,' 45–6, and Surtz, *Henry VIII's Great Matter*, 225–6 and 231.

13 Quoted by De Bellis, 'Niccolò Leonico Tomeo interprete di Aristotele naturalista,' 78.

14 See BAV, MS Rossiano 997, fols 5–6. Pole himself sent money to Leonico, an unidentified sum in 1524 and thirty Venetian ducats in 1529. Ibid., fols 27–9v, 30v–1.

15 See Venice, Archivio di Stato, Consiglio di X, Misti 45, fol. 70 (cf. fol. 125v).

16 BAV, MS Regin. Lat. 1291, fol. 33.

17 See Padua, Biblioteca del Seminario, MS 71, fols 139v–42v.

18 BAV, MS Rossiano 997, fols 10–11; cf. fol. 58. Leonico's theological

orientation drew the praise of Erasmus; see Surtz, *Henry VIII's Great Matter*, 226.

19 Leonico was a vernacular poet; see De Bellis, 'La vita,' 66.

20 B. Castiglione, *Il libro del cortegiano*, ed. V. Cian (Florence, 1947), 251, and D. Giannotti, *Libro della repubblica de'Viniziani*, in his *Opere* (Pisa, 1819), I, 8–10.

21 See BAV, MS Rossiano 997, fol 43. Cf. Mayer, *Thomas Starkey*, 50 and 72–6, where a more political orientation is suggested.

22 The character Hythlodaeus in More's *Utopia* not only advocates withdrawal from the political life, but is also 'thoroughly learned in Greek' and 'wholly given over to the study of philosophy'; see More, *Utopia* (New Haven and London, 1965), 49–52.

23 See Ptolemy, *Opera omnia* (Basle, 1551). The *Mechanica* first appeared in Leonico's 1525 *Opuscula*; it was reprinted many times and became the standard sixteenth-century translation; see Rose and Drake, 'The Pseudo-Aristotelian *Questions of Mechanics* in Renaissance culture,' 76–80.

24 The Proclus commentary is in Leonico's 1525 *Opuscula*. The *Dialogi* were published in Venice in 1524.

25 Marcantonio Michiel noted 'infinite medaglie' among Leonico's collections. See *Der Anonimo Morelliano*, ed. T. Frimmel (Vienna, 1888), 18. Other friends of Tunstall were coin collectors and numismatists: Budé for example, whose *De asse* was used by Tunstall for his *De arte supputandi*, and Jerome Busleyden, whom Tunstall knew at Padua in the early 1500s. See Erasmus, *Opus epistolarum*, II, no. 584 (*CWE*, IV, 369) and H. De Vocht, *Jerome de Busleyden* (Turnhout, 1950), 33–4.

26 See Frimmel, *Der Anonimo Morelliano*, 30. Leone was, with Leonico, Pole's teacher in the early 1520s.

27 The observations in Michiel's *Notizie* were built up over several decades, especially the 1520s to the 1540s, making the dating of particular observations extremely difficult. But as a visitor to the collections of Bembo and Leonico, and as a correspondent of Longueil, he is surely likely to have known the identity of Pole. See Longolius, *Opera*, fols 94–5, 151, 154.

28 For further discussion and relevant bibliography see *The Genius of Venice, 1500–1600*, ed. J. Martineau and C. Hope (London, 1983), 369–70. In this work, B. Boucher and A. Radcliffe agree with the identification of Pole with the 'English bishop' and suggest that the Judgment of Solomon was commissioned, made, and given to Pole during his first Italian period, between 1521 and 1526. The later provenance of the work supplies no further clues, since it does not surface again until about 1800, in Paris.

29 Latimer took a BTh at Oxford before 1531 and was said by Erasmus in
1528 to prefer theology to Ciceronian eloquence; see *CE*, II, 302–3, and
Erasmus, *Ciceronianus* (*CWE*, XXVIII), 424. Also note that in an anonymous list of English friends of Johannes Reuchlin of 1516, he is described
as a 'theologus'; see Erasmus, *Opus epistolarum*, II, 350.

30 See, as examples, the letters of Erasmus and Budé, praising Tunstall's
Latin and Greek, in Erasmus, *Opus epistolarum*, II, nos 480 and 493. Cf.
Sturge, *Cuthbert Tunstall*, 387. Tunstall did, however, own a Hebrew and
Chaldaic dictionary, which was bound with the Complutensian Bible,
published in 1522, and he was friendly with Johannes Reuchlin by *c.*
1516, both long after Tunstall's return from Italy. See Erasmus, *Opus
epistolarum*, II, 350, and J.C.T. Oates and H.L. Pink, 'Three Sixteenth-
century Catalogues of the University Library,' *Transactions of the Cambridge Bibliographical Society* 1 (1949–53), 325. If the library inventoried in
BL, MS Additional 40676, belonged to Tunstall it indicates more reassur-
ing evidence of a knowledge of Hebrew. See W.H. Herendeen and K.
Bartlett, 'The Library of Cuthbert Tunstall, Bishop of Durham,' *Papers of
the Bibliographical Society of America* 85 (1989), nos 12, 13, 29, 401. Tunstall
is praised as a scholar of Hebrew in Francis Godwin's *A Catalogue of the
Bishops of England* (London, 1601), 532.

31 Containing a dedicatory letter to More, the work became a standard
mathematical textbook in the sixteenth century. Leonico's mathematical
interests emerge particularly from his *Quaestiones mechanica* and he is
recorded as having complained about a poor knowledge of mathematics
among his contemporaries. See De Bellis, 'Niccolò Leonico Tomeo
interprete di Aristotele naturalista,' 78.

32 See Oates and Pink, 'Three Sixteenth-century Catalogues,' 325–7, and
J.C.T. Oates, *Cambridge University Library, a History* (Cambridge, 1986),
60–9.

33 See Herendeen and Bartlett, 'The Library of Cuthbert Tunstall,' 235–96.
The authors draw attention to some editions which have a particular link
to Tunstall, including the Greek Aldine Galen and Aristotle in this
collection, discussed above. There are eighty-three Greek items, catalogued separately, in all. Also note the works of Pace (nos 74 and 244),
Thomas Linacre (nos 224 and 308–9), Longueil (no. 226), Leonico (no.
263), Niccolò Leoniceno (no. 257), Peter Gillis (no. 100), Jacques Lefèvre
d'Etaples (no. 80), Budé (nos 77, 213, 335, and 416), and Erasmus (over
fifty items) as well as Tunstall's own *De arte supputandi* (no. 390). There is
a strong interest in mathematics, philosophy, medicine, and civil and
canon law.

34 On Pace generally see *CE*, III, 37–9, and J. Wegg, *Richard Pace, a Tudor Diplomatist* (New York, 1971).
35 See Wegg, *Richard Pace*, 11–12.
36 See C. Calcagnini, *Opera aliquot* (Basle, 1544), 155. On Calcagnini and Henry VIII generally, see Surtz, *Henry VIII's Great Matter*, 568–87. An Italian acquaintance of Pace who is mentioned in the prefatory material to Pace's translation of Plutarch (*Plutarchi Cheronaei Opuscula*, Venice, 1523), the poet Francesco Maria Molza, wrote a poem in defence of Catharine of Aragon to which Calcagnini replied. See A. Roncaglia, 'La questione matrimoniale di Enrico VIII e due umanisti italiani contemporanei,' *Giornale Storico della Letteratura Italiana* 110 (1937), 106–19.
37 Lowry, *The World of Aldus Manutius*, 260–1, suggests the oration may have been connected to a campaign to promote Greek studies launched by friends of Aldo.
38 See Pace, *De fructu*, 124, and Pace's dedicatory letter to Tunstall in his *Plutarchi Cheronaei Opuscula* (Venice, 1523), where he recalls Leonico as their teacher together. This, and the strong affection between Pace and Tunstall on the one hand and Leonico on the other, revived in the 1520s in the wake of Pole's arrival in Padua, make it unlikely that Leonico was the 'ignorant' or 'idle' teacher whom Latimer suggested in a letter to Erasmus had held up the progress in Greek studies of Tunstall and Pace. See Erasmus, *Opus epistolarum*, II, no. 520 (*CWE*, IV, 202). P.S. Allen, in Erasmus, *Opus epistolarum*, II, no. 520, suggested Marcus Musurus, professor of Greek in Padua in the 1500s.
39 Lupset and Pace were friends at least from 1517 or 1518, when Lupset wrote to him from Paris; see BL, MS Additional, 29549, fol. 7. Of the three surviving extant letters of Latimer, one is to Pace, BL, MS Additional 29549, fol. 8. Sent from Oxford to Pace, 'Secretary unto the king's grace,' it asks Pace to speak to Cardinal Wolsey about the suit of 'Doctor Bissus,' public lecturer in canon law at Oxford, whom Pace had known in Rome and who was 'most studious in good letters.' Robert Bysse had his Oxford DCL incorporated at the Roman curia in 1513, and was DCnL at Oxford in 1518. See A.B. Emden, *A Biographical Register of the University of Oxford to A.D. 1500* (Oxford, 1965–9), I, 336. The letter probably dates from the late 1510s.
40 E.g., Leonico's letter to Pace of 1 November, 1522: BAV, MS Rossiano 997, fol. 52.
41 Ibid., fols 13v–14v, 17–18, 21v–2v, 40–3v, 45, 50–2, 56–7. The three Englishmen apparently witnessed the siege of Pavia but were back in Venice just before the Battle of Pavia. This is suggested by Leonico's

letter to Pole of 23 February 1525 (ibid., fols 42–3), which requests Pole to send Leonico the newly printed Aldine edition of Cicero's *Letters to Atticus*, a work which was also a point of discussion between Pole and Bembo (Pole, *Epistolarum collectio*, I, 390).

42 BAV, MS Rossiano 997, fols 56v–7.

43 See Venice, Archivio di Stato, Senato Terra 23, p. 21, in which Leonico is granted a privilege to publish his commentary on the *Parva naturalia* in June 1523, at the request of Pace, and Consiglio di X, Misti 46, fol. 12, in which Pole is permitted to carry arms in Padua in March of the same year, again through the mediation of Pace. For the intimacy between Pace on the one hand, and Pole, Longueil, and Leonico on the other, see Longolius, *Opera*, fols 152–3, and *Cal. Ven.* 1520–6, III, no. 924. For Pace and Bembo, see Pole, *Epistolarum collectio*, I, 390.

44 Latimer's letter to Erasmus of 1517 recommending that Bishop Fisher should send for an Italian if he wished to learn Greek is obviously significant here; see Erasmus, *Opus epistolarum*, II, no. 520 (*CWE*, IV, 202).

45 See Surtz, *Henry VIII's Great Matter*, 227.

46 For Pole's life in the 1510s and 1520s, see W. Schenk, *Reginald Pole, Cardinal of England* (London, 1950); Zeeveld, *Foundations*; Parks, *English Traveller*, 475–82; D. Fenlon, *Heresy and Obedience in Tridentine Italy: Cardinal Pole and the Counter-Reformation* (Cambridge, 1972), 24–36; and Mayer, *Thomas Starkey*. Also see P.S. Donaldson, *Machiavelli and Mystery of State* (Cambridge, 1988), 1–35. The account here pays attention to some significant features mainly drawn from primary sources. I have not dealt in any depth with Pole's second period in the Veneto after Leonico's death, from 1532–6, because he seems to have been more in Venice than in Padua during this time and because this period has received more treatment from Pole's biographers.

47 See Fowler, *History*, 58.

48 See *BRUO*, 600.

49 BAV, MS Rossiano 997, fols 50–1.

50 See Erasmus, *Opus epistolarum*, VI, no. 1595 (*CWE*, XI, 233), and L. Beccadelli, *Monumenti di varia letteratura* (Bologna, 1797), I, pt 2, 277–333.

51 Lupset arrived in Padua with a commendatory letter from Tunstall to Leonico; see BAV, MS Rossiano 997, fol. 53. Lupset knew both Pace and Tunstall from 1517 at the latest; see Gee, *Life and Works*, 66.

52 Note the patent made out to Pole to export plate and clothes from the Veneto in 1521 in Sanuto, *I diarii*, V, col. 30. Also note his attendance at official ceremonies in Venice, cols 38–9 and *Cal. Ven.* 1520–6, III, no. 1343.

53 See BAV, MS Rossiano 997, fol. 29, and Venice, Biblioteca Nazionale Marciana, MS Ital. X 91 (6606), fol. 34.

54 See Bembo, *Lettere*, II, 230.

55 See BL, MS Egerton, 1998, fols 2–5.

56 See Venice, Biblioteca Nazionale Marciana, MS Ital. X 91 (6606), fol. 34.

57 See Pole, *Epistolarum collectio*, I, 385, 387; *LP*, IV, no. 4405.

58 See Bembo, *Lettere*, II, 367.

59 See ibid., and BAV, MS Rossiano 997, fol. 10.

60 See P. MacNair, *Peter Martyr in Italy* (Oxford, 1967), 98.

61 See Pole, *Epistolarum collectio*, I, 385, 388.

62 Ibid., 382, and Longolius, *Opera*, fol. 152.

63 Longolius, *Opera*, fol. 152.

64 See Bembo, *Lettere*, II, 340.

65 See *LP*, IV, no. 1685.

66 See *Cal. Ven.* 1520–6, III, no. 1405. For Pole's attendance in 1525 at a comedy in Padua performed for the 'Valorosi,' see Sanuto, *I diarii*, V, col. 37. It seems unlikely to me that Pole knew Lazzaro Bonamico in this period, despite the case made in Mayer, *Thomas Starkey*, 51–2, against Avesani in *Dizionario biografico degli italiani*, XI, 535. Bonamico was not in Padua or Venice until 1527 at the very earliest, after Pole had left Italy.

67 For Pole, Bembo, and Longueil see Bembo, *Lettere*, II, no. 419. Venice, Biblioteca Nazionale Marciana, MS Lat. XIV 171 (4665), fol. 228 is an epigram by Bembo addressed to Longueil. For Longueil and Navagero see Longolius, *Opera*, fols 89–90, 143, 154. For Longueil and Sadoleto, ibid., fols 91–2, 113–16, 146–9, 151–2, 158–63; Padua, Biblioteca del Seminario, MS 71, fol. 139v. For Longueil and Pace, see Longolius, *Opera*, fol. 152, where Longueil praises Pace's hospitality during Longueil's visit to England. They had a common friend in the poet Francesco Maria Molza; see F. Baiocchi, 'Sulle poesie latine di Francesco M. Molza,' *Annali della R. Scuola Normale Superiore di Pisa* 13 (1905), 38. For Longueil and Leonico, see Longolius, *Opera*, fols 83, 108–9, 119, 152–3, 156. Longueil was also acquainted with John Clement; ibid., fol. 143. For Longueil generally, see T. Simar, *Christophe de Longueil* (Louvain, 1911).

68 See Longolius, *Opera*, fol. 119. For an English translation of the letter, see Parks, *English Traveller*, 565–6.

69 Longolius, *Opera*, fol. 153. It is likely that Pole and Longueil had met in England. For another letter from Longueil to Pole, see ibid., fol. 152.

70 See Parks, 'Did Pole Write the "Vita Longolii?"' and Vos, 'The "Vita Longolii."'

71 See BAV, MS Rossiano 997, fols 34–5v.

72 Ibid., fols 4–4v and 38–9v. Pole seems also to have been used by Leonico as a go-between in his dealings with printers. See ibid., fols 39v–40.

73 This is according to B. Scardeone, *De antiquitate urbis Patavii* (Basle, 1560), 218.

74 Leone was an interlocutor in 'Alverotus,' one of Leonico's *Dialogi*. His library included works of Aristotle, Plato, Lucian, Galen, Ptolemy, and Proclus. He was a friend of Giovan Battista della Torre, Pietro Bembo, Ermolao Barbaro, and Giovan Battista Ramusio, and one of the promoters of Edward Wotton's doctoral degree in 1525. See F. Saxl, 'Pagan Sacrifice in the Italian Renaissance,' *Journal of the Warburg Institute* 2 (1938–9), 353–5.

75 See Pole, *Epistolarum collectio*, I, 388.

76 Twenty-seven separate works are now extant. See the list in Erasmus, *Opus epistolarum*, XI, 379–83.

77 Ibid. Pole's reading of Bembo's *De imitatione* is obviously significant here, as is the *Vita Longolii*. Longueil was the object of Erasmus's attack in his *Ciceronianus* for his obsessive Ciceronian imitation, whereas Erasmus found Bembo's style more satisfactory. In a letter to Pole of 1526, Erasmus suggested that Pole publish Longueil's annotations on Cicero; see Erasmus, *Opus epistolarum*, VI, no. 1675. In the *Ciceronianus* Pole is described as a competent Ciceronian; see Erasmus, *Ciceronianus* (*CWE*, XXVIII), 424, 430ff.

78 See Erasmus, *Opus epistolarum*, VI, 186, and nos 1675, 1720; and VII, no. 1817. Also note Leonico's description of Pole's library as 'omnis antiquitatis refertissima' in the dedicatory letter to Leonico's 1524 *Dialogi*.

79 Oxford, New College, MS 143 contains works by Philo Judaeus and was copied in 1533.

80 They were originally copied in 1497 by Joannes Serbopoulos, a Greek refugee scribe, at Reading for Thomas Linacre; they are marked for the printer and were used for the Aldine edition of 1536.

81 Also copied by Serbopoulos, in 1497.

82 See I. Hutter, 'Cardinal Pole's Greek Manuscripts in Oxford,' in *Manuscripts at Oxford: An Exhibition in Memory of R.W. Hunt* (Oxford, 1980), 108–14. Note that Hutter suggests a *terminus ad quem* for the purchase by Pole of one of the Chrysostom texts, Oxford, New College, MS 74, of 1530, and the same date for the purchase of another Pole manuscript containing homilies of Gregory Nazianzus, Oxford, Trinity College, MS 44; see Hutter, ibid., 110–11. For further discussion of Pole's books, see R. Hunt in Buxton and Williams, *New College*, 336–7; A. Pastore, 'Due biblioteche umanistiche del Cinquecento (I libri del cardinal Pole e di

Marcantonio Flaminio),' *Rinascimento* 19 (1979), 269–90; E. Lobel, 'Cardinal Pole's Manuscripts,' *Proceedings of the British Academy* 17 (1931), 3–7; and *BRUO*, 733–4. I intend to follow up this research.

83 In his *Opera*. His library contained the works of Basil.

84 See, for example, the texts of Chrysostom belonging to Clement in the 1550s in Reed, 'John Clement and His Books,' 337–8. Clement wrote translations of the letters of Gregory Nazianzus and of Pope Celestine I, and of the homilies of Nicephorus Calixtus. See *CE*, III, 311–12.

85 Leonico was also a reader of Chrysostom in this period.

86 Beccadelli, *Monumenti*, I, pt. 2, 287.

87 See Fenlon, *Heresy and Obedience*, 36.

88 See, for example, ibid., and Schenk, *Reginald Pole*, passim.

89 See Donaldson, *Machiavelli*, 1–35.

90 See *LP*, XI, no. 93.

91 See Pole, *Epistolarum collectio*, I, 385–8.

92 See Bembo's comment that Pole was one of the most learned young men in all of Italy, in Bembo, *Opere* (Milan, 1809), V, 89. For other tributes see Erasmus, *Opus epistolarum*, VI, nos 1595 and 1627 (*CWE*, XI, 314–17, 232–3); Leonico, *Dialogi*, dedicatory letter to Pole; Pole, *Epistolarum collectio*, I, 383–93; and *LP*, IV, pt 1, no. 79

93 See, for example, BAV, MS Rossiano 997, fols 10, 22v–4, two letters to Pole reprimanding him for breaking his promise to write regularly (probably in 1527), and ibid., fol. 18, a letter to Tunstall of 1530 or 1531 (cf. Sturge, *Cuthbert Tunstall*, 351, who dates it 1526 or earlier, mistakenly taking Leonico to be claiming that Lupset and Pole are with him in Padua; since Tunstall is addressed as bishop of Durham, 1530 must be the earliest year).

94 BAV, MS Rossiano 997, fols 29v–30.

95 See for discussion J. Rice Henderson, 'Erasmus on the Art of Letter-writing,' in *Renaissance Eloquence: Studies in the Theory and Practice of Renaissance Rhetoric*, ed. J.J. Murphy (Berkeley, Los Angeles, and London, 1983), 336–7, 340–1; C. Clough, 'The Cult of Antiquity: Letters and Letter Collections,' in *Cultural Aspects of the Italian Renaissance*, ed. C. Clough (Manchester, 1976), 33–67; and cf. J. Matthews, 'The Letters of Symmachus,' in *Latin Literature in the Fourth Century*, ed. J.W. Binns (London, 1974), 64.

96 For classical gift giving, see G. Herman, *Ritualised Friendship and the Greek City* (Cambridge, 1987).

97 For example, BAV, MS Rossiano 997, fol. 29.

98 Ibid., fols 34–5v, where the clock is described; Erasmus, *Colloquia*, ed. L.-

E. Halkin, F. Bierlaire, and R. Hoven, in Erasmus, *Opera omnia*, 1–3 (Amsterdam, 1972), 262–3. Another gift which appears in Leonico's correspondence is a basket of fruit, sent by Severino in 1525; see BAV, MS Rossiano 997, fols 31v–2.

99   For books as gifts see N. Zemon Davis, 'Beyond the Market: Books as Gifts in Sixteenth-Century France,' *Transactions of the Royal Historical Society* 33 (1982), 69–88.

100   For the letter to More, BAV, MS Rossiano 997, fols 25v–6, see Rogers, *Correspondence*, no. 131. The letter to Linacre is BAV, MS Rossiano 997, fol. 24.

101   *The Table of Cebes the Philosopher* (STC 4891), no date but *c.* 1530 and written between 1523 and 1527. See McConica, *English Humanists*, 116, and H.B. Lathrop, *Translations from the Classics into English from Caxton to Chapman, 1477–1620* (New York, 1967), 46–7. Poyntz translated from the Latin of Lascaris.

102   See Madison et al., *Linacre Studies*, xxx–xxxi. On cramp rings generally, see R. Crawford, 'The Blessing of Cramp-Rings: A Chapter in the History of the Treatment of Epilepsy,' in *Studies in the History and Method of Science*, ed. C. Singer (Oxford, 1917), I, 165–87.

103   Longolius, *Opera*, fols 109–10.

104   BAV, MS Rossiano 997, fol 46. For Leonico's relations with Poyntz, also see ibid., fols 46v and 50.

105   Ibid., fol. 37v–8.

106   See L. Jardine, *Erasmus, Man of Letters* (Princeton, 1993), 174–80. Note that in 1556 Pole recommended Clement's son Thomas to Marc Antonio Genoa and Guido Panciroli, recalling his dear friendship with John Clement. See Venice, Biblioteca Nazionale Marciana, MS Ital X 24 (6527), fols 157v–8.

107   On this subject see L. Firpo, 'Thomas More e la sua fortuna in Italia,' *Il Pensiero Politico* 9 (1976), 209–36. Despite the 1519 Florentine edition of *Utopia*, which must have ensured some early transmission of the work in Italy, Firpo's first documentary response to the work is Paolo Giovio's, dating to 1549.

108   BAV, MS Rossiano 997, fol. 38.

109   On this subject generally, see Jardine, *Erasmus, Man of Letters*. On *Utopia* specifically, Jardine notes that a central theme of the work is that 'the Utopians are temperamentally and intellectually allied to Greek culture. Greek culture is the source of the kind of humaneness which Raphael Hythlodaeus presents as the most appropriate model,' an observation which is as relevant here as it is to Jardine's discussion of the Yale

University Library first edition volume (177). Later on, Pole's *Pro ecclesi-asticae unitatis defensione*, written in 1535–6 and printed probably in 1539 would contain a fundamental and influential defence and panegyric of More.

110 In this he echoes precisely the earlier comment of Budé. See Rogers, *Correspondence*, 90–2.

111 BAV, MS Rossiano 997, fols 12–13v, a discussion of forms in the natural world.

112 Ibid., fol. 26v.

113 Ibid., fols 14v–17.

114 See G. Pollard, *Medals of the Renaissance* (London, 1978), 93.

115 Aulus Gellius, *Noctes Atticae*, ed. P.K. Marshall (Oxford, 1968), II, 399–400.

116 BAV, MS Rossiano 997, fol. 47v.

117 See the letter to Tunstall, ibid., fol. 18. Leonico also took an opposite side to Pietro Bembo on the king's 'great matter.'

118 See Surtz, *Henry VIII's Great Matter*, 328–30.

119 See McConica, *English Humanists*, 134.

120 The evidence for their studies is fragmentary. Greek studies by Coles are suggested by the books in his library in the 1550s – see *BRUO*, 717–18 – and by one of Leland's *encomia*, 79–80. Greek studies by Goldwell are suggested by his father's letter to him in Padua, probably of 1532, urging him to write to his patron the archbishop of Canterbury in good Greek; see PRO, SP1 70, fol. 149 (*LP*, V, no. 1155).

121 Caius drew on his wide Italian experience for his *De pronunciatione Graecae et Latinae linguae* (London, 1574), and may be identified with the Englishman encountered by Thomas Smith, who had been in Venice and Padua for a long time and who had known there a famous Greek called 'Janus,' whose opinions on Greek pronunciation accorded with Smith's. See Smith, *De recta et emendata linguae Graecae pronuntiatione*, 34, in his *Literary and Linguistic Works* (Stockholm, 1963), I. Caius's knowledge of Paduan art and artistic symbolism may have inspired the architecture of Gonville and Caius College. See A. Radcliffe, 'John Caius and Paduan Humanist Symbolism,' *The Caian* (1987), 121–6.

122 For further details see Todd, 'Henry and Thomas Savile in Italy,' 439–44; M. Feingold, *The Mathematicians' Apprenticeship: Science, Universities and Society in England, 1560–1640* (Cambridge, 1984), 128; M. Grendler, 'A Greek Collection in Padua: The Library of Gian Vincenzo Pinelli (1535–1601),' *Renaissance Quarterly* 33 (1988), 404; A. Rivolta, *Catalogo dei codici pinelliani dell'Ambrosiana* (Milan 1933), 64; and D. Rhodes, 'Some English,

Welsh, Scottish and Irish Book-Collectors in Italy, 1467–1850,' *Bookbindings and Other Bibliophily* (1994), 25–6.

123 See Moryson, *Shakespeare's Europe*, 434: 'Besydes no place is better then Padoa for the Studye of the Mathematicks, wherof, besydes the publike, many private teachers may here be founde ...'

124 Our chief source for the disquisitions is Thomas Wilson's dedicatory letter in Wilson's *Three Orations*: 'And thinking of my being with him in Italy in that famous university of Padua, I did call to mind his care that he had over all the Englishmen there to go to their books, and how gladly he did read to me and others certain Orations of Demosthenes in Greek, the interpretation whereof I and they had then from his mouth.'

125 Besides Wilson, the audience definitely included William Temple and probably Edward Courtenay and Francis Walsingham. A large number of other Marian exiles may have been present.

Chapter 5: Exiles, Tourists, and Intelligencers

1 See PRO, SP1 16, fols 208–11; BL, MS Additional 1938, fol. 44 (*LP*, II, nos 4057, 4124; and III, no. 1).

2 *LP*, II, pt.1, nos 1893, 1970.

3 See, for example, PRO, SP1 16, fols 208–11.

4 See BL, MS Cotton, Vitellius B iv, fol. 84v; and Sanuto, *I diarii*, XXX, col. 298.

5 B.J. Harris, *Edward Stafford, Third Duke of Buckingham* (Stanford, 1986), 61.

6 See especially BL, MS Additional 28035, fol. 90. Cf. BL, MS Cotton, Vespasian F xiii, fols 283–4 (letter of Pole to Wolsey).

7 See BL, MS Cotton, Nero B vi, fol. 122, and BL, MS Harley 6989, fols 42–3, letter of Pole to Henry VIII on arrival in Padua in 1521: 'Nam cum urbs patavina, quo a tua maiestate literarum causa sum missus ...' Also see PRO, E36 216, fol. 248.

8 Quoted in Sanuto, *I diarii*, XXX, col. 298.

9 William Thomas, *The History of Italy*, ed. G.B. Parks (London, 1963), 83.

10 For example, John Schiere, Thomas Fitzwilliams, John Tamworth, and possibly John Orphinstrange.

11 See Gribaldi Mofa, *Epistolae Patavinae*, 18.

12 For example, Richard Bertie, John Bromus, John Cheke, Anthony Cooke, the Denny brothers, Thomas Wrothe, John Jewel, William Morley, and John Pelham; see Garrett, *The Marian Exiles*, passim.

13 See, for examples, Hoby, 'Travaile and Life,' 8–10; Thomas, *History of Italy*, 10–11; Samuel Lewkenor, *A Discourse* (London, 1600), fol. 32; and Moryson, *An Itinerary*, I, 156.

14 'Adolescens, peregrinatus in exteras Regiones, carum Instituta, Linguas, Politiam, ad civilem scientam Reiq; publicae usum didicit. Iuvenis, exilium, Maria regnante, subiit voluntarium, Religionis ergo.' See C. Read, *Mr Secretary Walsingham and the Policy of Queen Elizabeth* (Oxford, 1925), I, 17–27. On the Marion exiles generally see K.R. Bartlett, 'The Role of the Marion Exiles,' in *The House of Commons, 1558–1603*, ed. P.W. Hasler (London, 1981), I, 102–10.

15 For details see McConica, 'The Catholic Experience in Tudor Oxford,' 39–63.

16 Cf. G. Bell, *A Handlist of British Diplomatic Representatives* (London, 1990), 289.

17 Hasler, *The House of Commons*, III, 344.

18 See ASP, AN 831, fol. 366.

19 See ASP, AN 4856, fol. 297 for a contract at Padua involving Le Rous and Shelley.

20 See E. Chaney, '*Quo vadis?* Travel as Education and the Impact of Italy in the Sixteenth Century,' in *International Currents in Educational Ideas and Practices*, ed. P. Cunningham and C. Brock (London, 1988), 15.

21 See for example Coryat, *Coryat's Crudities*, I, 299.

22 See the anonymous biography of Fitzalan, BL, MS Royal, 17 A ix, fol. 30: 'He fell to the extreme disease of the gout, whereby he was forced for remedy to seek the baths about Padua.' Evidence of Fitzalan's residence in Padua in the district of S. Croce is supplied by the notarial attestation of John Barker, witnessed by Richard Appleby and Thomas Cooke; Barker was staying with Fitzalan for a month in June 1566: ASP, AN 4852, fol. 398.

23 BL, Pressmark 531. h. 1 (3).

24 C. Bartoli, *Del modo di misurare le distantie* (Venice, 1564: BL, Pressmark 531. g. 5), and G. Fallopio, *Secreti diversi et miracolosi* (Venice, 1565: BL, Pressmark 1038. d. 8) have 'Io sono del humfredo Lhoyd, 1566, 23 May, Venetiis' and 'Io sono del humfredo Lhoyd, 1566, Venetiis' inscribed on their frontispieces respectively. Cf. Rhodes, 'Some English, Welsh, Scottish and Irish Book-Collectors in Italy, 1476–1850,' 255.

25 See White's *Historiarum Britanniae insulae libri novem* (Douai, 1597–1607), I, 64.

26 Venice, 1553, 426. Llwyd's copy is BL, Pressmark 573. i. 19.

27 BL, MS Royal, 17 A ix, fol. 30v.

28 See Llwyd's *Commentarioli Britanniae descriptionis fragmentum* (Cologne, 1572), fol. 16. Llwyd's Welsh antiquarianism later made him the butt of an extended joke carried on between Philip Sydney in Padua and Venice and his mentor Hubert Languet in Vienna; see J. Osborn, *Young Philip Sydney* (London, 1972), 140–50.

29 HMC, *Report on the MSS of the Duke of Buccleuch and Queensberry preserved at Montagu House, Whitehall* (London, 1899), I, 26.

30 Robert Dallington, *A method for Travell. Showed by taking the view of France* (London, ?1605), sig. B. For some further relevant comments see Chaney, '*Quo vadis?*' and L. Stone, *The Crisis of the Aristocracy, 1558–1641* (Oxford, 1965), 692–702.

31 Cf. Helgerson, *Forms of Nationhood*. For an interesting discussion see also J. Haynes, *The Humanist as Traveler* (Cranbury, NJ, 1986), 27–39. On this kind of travel generally Chaney, '*Quo vadis?*' is the best short introduction.

32 See, for example, PRO, SP1 95, fol. 86. On his use of Machiavelli see Berkowitz, *Humanist Scholarship*, 70–80.

33 See Thomas, *History of Italy*, 10–11.

34 Printed as *Principal Rules of the Italian Grammar* (London, 1562). For the connection with Tamworth see verso of title page.

35 See J. Barbaro and A. Contarini, *Travels to Tana and Persia* (London, 1873), 1–2, transcribed from BL, MS Royal, 17. C. x.

36 The Italian edition is dated 1552, with no place given. An English edition entitled *The Pilgrim* was edited by J.A. Froude (London, 1861).

37 Thomas, *History of Italy*, 3–5.

38 BL, MS Cotton, Vespasian D xviii, fols 1–48, printed in *The Works of William Thomas*, ed. A. D'Aubant (London, 1774), 131–94.

39 BL, MS Egerton 837, fols 2v–3.

40 Ibid., fols 4v–10. Quotation on fol. 3.

41 At least this was true from the presidency of Sperone Speroni in 1542. He insisted that law, theology, and medicine were the preserve of the universities and that the Infiammati should distinguish themselves by promoting other fields of learning in the vernacular. See Bernardino Tomitano's *Ragionamenti della lingua toxcana* (Venice, 1546), 17–18.

42 See R. Samuels, 'Benedetto Varchi, the Accademia degli Infiammati, and the Origins of the Italian Academic Movement,' *Renaissance Quarterly* 39 (1976), 623.

43 See above, pp. 115–16.

44 On Thomas generally see E.R. Adair, 'William Thomas: A Forgotten Clerk of the Privy Council,' in *Tudor Studies*, ed. R. Seton-Watson (London, 1924), 133–60; S. Rossi, 'Un "italianista" nel Cinquecento inglese: William Thomas,' *Aevum* 3–4 (1966), 281–314; S. Anglo, ' "Our extremist shift is to work by policy." William Thomas and Early Tudor Machiavellism,' *Transactions of the Honourable Society of Cymmrodorion* (1984), 31–50. The most comprehensive account of Thomas remains P.J.

Laven's MA dissertation, 'The Life and Writings of William Thomas'
(University of London, 1954).

45 For English examples and further bibliography see J. McConica, 'Humanism and Aristotle in Tudor Oxford,' *English Historical Review* 94 (1979),
291–317.

46 See *The Fearful Fansies of the Florentine Couper, written in Toscane by John
Battista Gelli, one of the free Studie of Florence, & for recreation translated into
English by William Barker* (London, 1568), a translation of Giovanbattista
Gelli's *I capricci del bottaio; The Nobility of Women by William Barker, 1559*,
ed. R.W. Bond (London, 1904), which is a translation of Ludovico Dome-
nichini's *La nobiltà delle donne* (Venice, 1549). His English translation of
Xenophon's *Cyropaedia*, printed at London as *The Bookes of Xenophon
contayning the discipline, schole and education of Cyrus*, was probably also
translated from an Italian edition.

47 *Epitaphia et inscriptiones lugubres a Gulielmo Berchero, cum in Italia, animi
causa, peregrinaretur, collectur* (London, 1566). From Padua he records
incriptions on Livy's supposed tomb, an epitaph for Christophe de
Longueil written by Pietro Bembo, and an inscription accompanying a
bust of Bembo himself, erected at about the time of Barker's visit. The
Epitaphia mistakenly records that Bembo died in 1558 rather than 1547,
the year before the creation of the bust.

48 See Chaney, *'Quo vadis?'* 5–6.

49 'Their manners, laws and customs you shall in the book of William
Thomas, although as it seemeth unto me as well as to others that hath
been there that he speaketh more in the praise of it than it doth deserve.'
See Yeames, 'The Grand Tour of an Elizabethan,' 106; spelling has been
modernized.

50 Chaney, *'Quo vadis?'* 12–16, and S. Warneke, *Images of the Educational
Traveller in Early Modern England* (Leiden, 1995).

51 See Ascham, *The Schoolmaster (1570)*, ed. L.V. Ryan (Ithaca, NY, 1967), 63,
and in general 61–8.

52 See William Harrison, 'A description of Elizabethan England,' in *Chron-
icle and Romance*, ed. C.V. Eliot (New York, 1965), 223 (first printed in
Holinshead's *Chronicles* of 1577). For its writing and relationship to Sir
Thomas Smith's *De republica Anglorum*, see D.M. Palliser, *The Age of
Elizabeth: England under the Later Tudors, 1547–1603* (London, 1983), 390–1.

53 See LPL, MS 647, fol. 110.

54 For English interest in the Venetian polity in this period, see R. Chavasse, 'The Reception of Humanist Historiography in Northern Europe:
M.A. Sabellico and John Jewel,' *Renaissance Studies* 2 (1988), 327–38; I.

Ross, 'The English Renaissance Image of Paolo Sarpi,' in *Italy and the English Renaissance*, ed. S. Rossi and D. Savoia (Milan, 1989), 213–31; and now M. Peltonen, *Classical Humanism and Republicanism in English Political Thought, 1570–1640* (Cambridge, 1996), 102–18.

55 For this period of Sidney's tour see Osborn, *Young Philip Sidney*, 105–201.

56 Ibid., 139–40, 143.

57 Ibid., 121–2, 126–7, 135–7, 145, 147–8, 155.

58 Ibid., 121.

59 ASP, AN 5007, fols. 26–7v.

60 See Osborn, *Young Philip Sidney*, 105, 117, 200–1.

61 The diary was drawn on extensively by A.L. Rowse in his *Ralegh and the Throckmortons* (London, 1962) though curiously he does not cite its whereabouts: Canterbury, Canterbury Cathedral Archives, MS U. 85, Box 38, I–III.

62 Rowse, *Ralegh and the Throckmortons*, 89. This is probably Borgo Zucho, a popular residence for students; see O. Ronchi, 'Alloggi di scolari a Padova nei secoli xiii–xviii,' *Bollettino del Museo Civico di Padova* 56 (1967), 293–319.

63 Canterbury, Canterbury Cathedral Archives, MS U. 85, Box 38, I, fol. 64. Cf. the comment of Fynes Moryson, that Padua was 'an excelent place to learn and practise the Art of Musicke and playing upon any Instrument' (Moryson, *Shakespeare's Europe*, 434).

64 Canterbury, Canterbury Cathedral Archives, MS U. 85, Box 38, I, fol. 65.

65 Ibid., fol. 67v.

66 Ibid., fol. 65.

67 For his books cf. Rhodes, 'Book-Collectors,' 257.

68 Canterbury, Canterbury Cathedral Archives, MS U. 85, Box 38, I, fol. 66.

69 See J.R.L. Highfield, 'An Autograph Manuscript Commonplace Book of Sir Henry Savile,' *Bodleian Library Record* 7 (1963), 73–83.

70 Sandys matriculated at Padua in 1597. He notes religious practices which he saw at Padua at sigs B2v and B3. He knew Paolo Sarpi, who translated the work into Italian. His English version was later reprinted as *Europae Speculum*.

71 On the question of his authorship see Smith, *Henry Wotton*, II, 455–9; G. Ungerer, *A Spaniard in Elizabethan England: The Correspondence of Antonio Pérez's Exile* (London, 1976) II, 80–323; P. Hammer, 'The Uses of Scholarship: The Secretariat of Robert Devereux, Second Earl of Essex, c. 1585–1601,' *English Historical Review* 109 (1994), 46.

72 See *Shakespeare's Europe*, 430–4.

73 See also some relevant comments in Jardine and Sherman, 'Pragmatic

Readers'; W. Boutcher, 'Vernacular Humanism in the Sixteenth Century,' in Kraye, ed., *The Cambridge Companion to Renaissance Humanism*, 189–202. On the development of diplomacy in the Elizabethan period see Bell, 'Elizabethan Diplomacy: The Subtle Revolution,' 267–87.

74 On Essex see especially P. Hammer, ' "This bright Shininge Spark": The Political Career of Robert Devereux, Second Earl of Essex, c. 1585–c.1597,' (PhD thesis, University of Cambridge, 1991); P. Hammer, 'Patronage at the Court: Faction and the Earl of Essex,' in Guy, *The Reign of Elizabeth*, 65–86. Hammer, 'Uses of Scholarship,' 26–51; Hammer, 'Essex and Europe,' 357–81; and also Ungerer, *A Spaniard in Elizabethan England*, esp. II, 168–217.

75 See Hammer, ' "This bright Shininge Spark," ' 94–5.

76 Manuscript copies which I have seen are London, British Library, MS Harley 6265, fols 115–19v (ascribing it to Essex) and MS Egerton 2262, fol. 1–4v (an incomplete copy which ascribes it to Henry Savile). Versions of the letter are printed in *Profitable Instructions* (n.p., 1633, ascribing it to Essex); W.B. Devereux, *Lives and Letters of the Devereux, Earls of Essex* (London 1853), I, 322–32 (from BL, MS Harley 4888); and, probably more reliably, in J. Spedding, *Letters and Life of Francis Bacon* (London, 1861–74), II, 6–15. For discussion of the authorship see ibid., 4–6. Bacon was the author, much later, of an essay on travel.

77 No manuscript source ascribes it to Henry Cuffe, though there is a similarity between the style and content of the letter and Cuffe's *The differences in the ages of man's life*. Cuffe seems to have been involved in Manners's education abroad (see note 93 below).

78 Printed in Spedding with discussion of authorship, in *Letters and Life*, II, 15–20.

79 See generally A. Haynes, *Invisible Power: The Elizabethan Secret Services, 1570–1603* (Stroud, 1992).

80 For John Cecil's intelligence work for Essex see Hammer, ' "This bright Shininge Spark," ' 116, and for Wotton's ibid., 124, 128, and HMC, *Calendar of the MSS of the Most Honourable the Marquis of Salisbury preserved at Hatfield House* (London, 1883–1967), XIII, 555–6, 571.

81 For Florence see Hammer, ' "This bright Shininge Spark," ' 129.

82 BL, MSS Harley 288, fol. 242, and Harley 296, fol. 54; and HMC, *Hatfield* V, 45–6, 189–91.

83 On Hawkins's activities see esp. Ungerer, *A Spaniard in Elizabethan England*, II, 185–6, 170–3, 185–92, 205–6; Hammer, ' "This bright Shininge Spark," ' 129–32; Hammer, 'Uses of Scholarship,' 36–7. Some of Hawkins's correspondence is also printed in T. Birch, *Memoirs of the Reign of*

Queen Elizabeth (London, 1754), passim. Note that Essex's original choice as the agent in Venice was Peter Wroth, the brother of John Wroth, who died on his way there in 1595.

84 London, University of London Library, MS 187, fols 9v–11 (cf. Hammer, 'Essex and Europe,' 357–81). Besides his regular intelligence reports, Hawkins also wrote a relation of Ferrara; see Birch, *Memoirs*, II, 195.

85 LPL, MS 659, fol. 410.

86 Hammer, ' "This bright Shininge Spark," ' 227. See especially LPL, MS 659, fol. 227; Birch, *Memoirs*, I, 428.

87 Ungerer, *A Spaniard in Elizabethan England*, II, 173; Birch, *Memoirs*, I, 428.

88 PRO SO3 1, fol. 528.

89 This is printed in *Profitable Instructions*, sigs B1–C4v.

90 See Ungerer, *A Spaniard in Elizabethan England*, I, 256–7; LPL, MS 654, fol. 104. See also BL, MS Hargrave 225, fols 39–40v; Davison, *Poetical Rapsody*, xi–xiii, xix, xxvi.

91 LPL, MS 655, fol. 9; see also MS 654, fols 37, 82.

92 HMC, *Hatfield*, VII, 235–6. See also 547.

93 Ibid., 234–5, 524–5; Ungerer, *A Spaniard in Elizabethan England*, I, 257–9. On Cuffe's activities see also Hammer, ' "This bright Shininge Spark," ' 198–9, 248. On Essex and Savile ibid., 146, 244. See also the note of Sir Thomas Arundel quoted by A. Grafton and L. Jardine in 'Studied for Action: How Gabriel Harvey Read his Livy,' *Past and Present* 129 (1990), 33, which suggests that Cuffe was sent abroad by Essex and that he may have tutored Manners on the continent.

94 On Cecil's intelligence activities see P. M. Handover, *The Second Cecil,* (London 1959), 262–73.

95 Ibid., 108–9.

96 See for example HMC, *Hatfield*, IV, 492.

97 Ibid., VII, 217.

98 Ibid., VIII, 270. Cranmer was dead by November 1600. See ibid., X, 393.

99 PRO, SP99 2 passim; SP98 1, fols 181–2; HMC, *Hatfield*, XVI, 356–7. The record of his payment is PRO, SP98 1, fol. 55. See J.M. Woolfson, 'The Paduan Sojourns of Samuel and Simeon Foxe,' *QSUP* 30 (1997), 123. Note also Samuel Foxe's letter to Cecil of 1597: HMC, *Hatfield* VII, 491.

100 HMC, *Hatfield*, XII, 461.

101 See, for example, Payton's letter from Cracow in 1598, ibid., VIII, 166–8, and his father's report of a letter from Padua in 1599, ibid., IX, 237. See also ibid., X, 434.

102 Now Cambridge, Cambridge University Library, MS Kk. v. 2 (see esp. fol. 2).

103 See *Advice to a Son: Precepts of Lord Burghley, Sir Walter Ralegh and Francis Osborne*, ed. L.B. Wright (Ithaca, NY, 1962), esp. xiii–xix. Thomas Friar had sent Burghley intelligence reports from Padua in the late 1560s.
104 See HMC, *Hatfield*, XI, 292, and XII, 219.
105 See Handover, *The Second Cecil*, 265.
106 See *Cal. SP For. Eliz.*, 1586–8, XXI, 475–6; *Lists and Analyses of State Papers, Foreign Series, Elizabeth I*, ed. R.B. Wernham (London, 1964–93), III (1591–2), 435; PRO, SP99 1, passim.

Conclusion

1 *Taming of the Shrew*, I.i.2.
2 HMC, *Buccleuch and Queensberry*, I, 120–1.
3 Padua, Biblioteca del Seminario, MS 634.
4 On this work see R. Strong, 'Sir Henry Unton and his Portrait: An Elizabethan Memorial Picture and Its History,' *Archaeologia* 99 (1965), 53–76.

Appendix

Biographical Register of English Visitors to Padua, 1485–1603

This register is intended to serve as a biographical orientation to the subject, as an aid and supplement to the main chapters of this book, and as a starting point for further research. With its 350 entries, the register is wide-ranging: for reasons explained in the Introduction, I have attempted to include all Englishmen whose presence in Padua is documented. It is almost certainly incomplete, however, for I am increasingly aware of the vast range of sources which might yield information on this subject but which I have been unable to examine systematically. Some of the material which does appear here is dependent on secondary sources, especially other biographical registers and dictionaries, and so the margin of factual error must partly depend on the diligence of those who have gone before me. The emphasis, however, is on information which I have excavated from archival sources, and on those individuals who are important to arguments in this book and who spent significant periods in Padua. I have not attempted to supply complete biographies: for the more obscure individuals this would be practically impossible, and for major personalities in Tudor history it is unecessary. Usually I have restricted the material to the nature of an individual's experience in Padua, his former and subsequent education, relevant aspects of his career and writings, and suggestive family relationships and friendships. I have attempted to keep to a minimum repetition of information and references which can be found elsewhere in this book, and readers are therefore referred to the index for further material.

I have included Welshmen, foreigners denizened in England, and officers of the English nation in Padua who may have been English. I have not included officers of the English nation who definitely were not English; Englishmen whose presence is documented only in nearby Venice; those whose presence in Padua has been claimed in the secondary literature where there is a clear lack of positive primary evidence to confirm this; or those for whom only their intention of travelling to Padua is documented.

Individuals appearing with asterisks against their names are subjects of separate entries. References to 'History of Parliament draft biography' indicate that some of the material was drawn from draft biographies of MPs which I was kindly permitted to consult by the History of Parliament Trust. Several modern abbreviations of university degrees are anachronistic for the sixteenth century. Since they are used in this register only for the sake of convenience, I have also adopted English abbreviations for degrees from non-English universities. In addition to the abbreviations listed on pp. xi–xii, the following abbreviations are used here:

adm.   admitted
apptd   appointed
BA   bachelor of arts
BCL   bachelor of civil law
BMus   bachelor of music
BTh   bachelor of theology
DCL   doctorate in civil law
DCnCL   doctorate in canon and civil law
DCnL   doctorate in canon law
DTh   doctorate in theology
incorp.   incorporated
JP   justice of the peace
kt   knighted
MA   master of arts
matr.   matriculated
MD   doctorate in medicine
MP   member of parliament
vac.   vacated

ACWORTH, George. 1534–c.1592.

Advocate and divine. Son of Thomas. Matr. Peterhouse, Cambridge 1548, BA 1552, MA 1555, fellow 1553–62. Subscribed to Roman Catholic articles Cambridge 1555. Louvain and Paris during latter part of Mary's reign, Italy from 1557, when war broke out between England and France. *Consiliarius* of English nation Padua 1558–9 (AAU 10, fols 17–18). His *procura* at Padua witnessed by Thomas Geniston* 1558 (ASP, AN 4849, fols 643v–5). Orator of university of Cambridge 1559. Delivered oration in memory of Martin Bucer and Paul Fagius (printed in John Foxe's *Acts and Monuments*, ed. S.R. Cattley, London, 1839, VIII, 287–91). Cambridge DCL 1561 (incorp. Oxford c. 1566: cf. *DNB*). Adm. Doctors' Commons as advocate 1561. Chancellor and vicar general of bishop of Winchester by 1563. Visitor to various Oxford colleges in this capacity. Adm. advocate of the Arches 1562. Possibly MP for Hindon 1563–7. Member of household of Archbishop Parker c. 1570. Master of the Faculties and judge of the Prerogative Court in Ireland 1576–9. Various benefices. Married Elizabeth, daughter of Bishop Horne of Winchester, 1564. Wrote *De visibili Romanarchia* (London, 1573), a Protestant reply to Nicholas Sanders's *De visibili Monarchia Ecclesiae*; preface to second book of Bucer's *Works* (1577); and helped in compilation of Archbishop Parker's *De antiquitate Britanniae ecclesiae* (1572), having written the opening *Life* of St Augustine.

   Andrich, 32–3. Squibb, 155. W.H. Frere, ed., *Registrum Matthei Parker Diocensis Cantuariensis A.D. 1559–75* (Oxford, 1928), 399. Baskerville, 113–16. Horton-Smith, passim. Hasler, I, 327–8.

ALEN, Christopher. See Thomas Hoby.*

ALENUS, Nicolaus.
Son of 'Guaremus.' Witness to DTh of Hugh Turnbull* Padua 1550. *Consiliarius* of English nation Padua 1551.
   AGA, 1501–50, nos 3881, 3888. *Statuta* (1551), fol. 2v.

ALFORD, ALPHORD, Francis. 1530–92.
MP. Son of Robert. Adm. Trinity College, Cambridge 1548, BA 1549. Christ Church, Oxford 1550, resigned 1555. Proctor in vice-chancellor's court and clerk of the market in Oxford between 1550 and 1555. Marian exile (claimed defensively in 1578 to have left England in his youth on account of his hatred of Catholicism), probably going first to France. Italy from 1557. *Consiliarius* and *electionarius* of English nation Padua 1558, 1559 (AAU 10, fols 3v, 19–23). Returned to England 1560, when unsuccessfully supplicated for Oxford DCL. His cousin Thomas Sackville,* Lord Buckhurst, seems to have supported him through a series of financial difficulties and property litigation. MP in six parliaments 1563–89, active on various parliamentary committees. Married Agnes, Catholic widow of Cardinal Wolsey's Italian physician, Agostino de'Agostini. (She was protected from heresy prosecution by the intervention of Francis Walsingham* in 1582.) Associated with Mary, Queen of Scots, during a later visit to France, and defended her subsequently. This and accusations of Catholic sympathies curtailed royal favour and support in parliament and prevented realization of early promise. Failed to be appointed to many offices for which he petitioned, including, in 1586, official historian of the reign of Elizabeth. Wrote on a proposed reorganization of London courts which would reduce legal fees (1585: BL, MS Lansdowne 44, no. 1). Strongly

civilian interests emerge from his collection of political letters and petitions dating mainly to the late 1580s.

Andrich, 32–3. Baskerville, 116–18. Hasler, I, 335–8. Conway Davies, II, 712. C. Russell, *The Causes of the English Civil War* (Oxford, 1990), 92–3. BL, MS Lansdowne 43, no. 19.

AMBERTO, Johannes.

Consiliarius and *electionarius* of English nation Padua 1575–6. Possibly not English as elected by 'ius supplendum.'

Andrich, 39, assumed that he was English.

ANDRIZONO, ANDERTONUS, ANDERTON? ANDERSON? Roger. B. c. 1570.

Law student. Possibly a son of judge Sir Edmund Anderson. Matr. Basle 1597 ('Roger Andertonus, iurium baccalaureus'). Matr. Padua same year (AAU 30, fol. 95); *consiliarius* of English nation 1598 (AAU 15, fol. 8v). Probably the Roger Anderton of county Lancaster who matr. Brasenose College, Oxford 1584–5 age 15 and who was adm. Gray's Inn 1593.

H.G. Wackernagel, ed., *Die Matrikel der Universität Basle* (Basle, 1951–80), III, 448. J. Foster, ed., *The Register of Admissions to Gray's Inn, 1521–1889* (London, 1889), 82. Andrich, 45, 136. *AO*, I, 22.

ANGALL, John.

Matr. Padua 1594 (AAU 30, fol. 94).

Andrich, 134.

ANGELUS, ANGEL? Hyeronimus, John?

Electionarius of English nation Padua 1566–7 (AAU 11, fol. 120v, where elected by three English voters). Possibly the John Angel of Corpus Christi College, Oxford who was BA 1557 and BTh 1572, or the John Angel who was chaplain to King Philip and Queen Mary, and published *The Agreement of the Holy Fathers* in 1555, arguing for the Real Presence.

Andrich, 37. *DNB*. *AO*, I, 26.

ANSELM, Robert. See Robert Beech, Anselm.*

APPLEBY, Richard. See Henry Fitzalan.*

ARCHER, Henry. D. 1615.

Of London. Probably brother of the Edward Archer who petitioned Sir Robert Cecil for licence to travel to Padua to study medicine between 1596 and 1603

(HMC, *Hatfield*, XIV, 280). Matr. fellow commoner Corpus Christi College, Cambridge 1586. Adm. Gray's Inn same year. Abroad 1596–7, Vienna late 1596, and known on travels to Francis Davison,* who wrote in November 1596 to his father William that he was expecting Archer to arrive in Italy but had not yet heard of his arrival (Davison, xxiv). Matr. Padua December 1596 (AAU 30, fol. 94v). Wrote to Anthony Bacon from Padua January 1597 concerning the affairs of Henry Hawkins* in Venice and of Edmund Bruce* in Padua (LPL, MS 655, fol. 9; see also MS 654, fol. 37, and Bacon's reply, ibid., fol. 82).

    Venn, I, 37.

ARUNDLE, John. See Thomas Hoby.*

ASHLEY, ASTLEY, John. 1507–95.
Marian exile and writer on horsemanship. Son of Thomas of Norfolk. Married Catherine Champernown, aunt of the Denny* brothers. Servant of Prince Edward and Princess Elizabeth in 1540s. Friend of Roger Ascham. MP 1547, 1553. Encountered by Thomas Hoby* Padua 1554. Remained on continent until accession of Elizabeth. Master of the Jewel House. Various local government offices under Elizabeth. Wrote *The Art of Riding* (London, 1584, based on Xenophon).

    Bartlett, *English in Italy*, 189–90. Hoby, 116. *DNB*. A. Stewart, *Close Readers: Humanism and Sodomy in Early Modern England* (Princeton, NJ, 1997), 156–60.

ASTLOW, Luke. D. 1575.
Law student. Travelled with Robert Persons* and George Lewkenor* through Antwerp and Frankfurt to Padua 1574, where a student of law. Acquainted with Edward de Vere* in the Veneto, who reported his conversion to Catholicism. Intended to follow Persons* to Rome following year but died before leaving Padua.

    J.H. Pollen, ed., *Memoirs of Father Robert Persons* (London, 1906), 23–5. B.M. Ward, *The Seventeenth Earl of Oxford, 1550–1604* (London, 1928), 108.

BAGSHAW, Christopher. c. 1552–c. 1625.
Priest. MA Balliol College, Oxford, principal of Gloucester Hall 1579–81. Rheims 1582, ordained 1583. Rome where expelled from English College 1585. Padua same year with George Gifford* where acquired doctorate in theology. Rheims, where sent immediately on mission to England, and arrested there May 1585. Wisbech Prison 1588 where involved in disputes with other Catholic prisoners. Left England 1601, involved in Archpriest controversy. Schemed against Jesuits in England from Paris. Wrote works opposing the Jesuit role in the Catholic mission to England.

P. Renold, ed., *The Wisbech Stirs* (London, 1958), xiii, 19, 294–5, 301–2. J. Gillow, *Bibliographical Dictionary of the English Catholics* (London and New York, no date), I, 100–1. P. Renold, ed., *Letters of William Allen and Richard Barrett, 1572–1598* (London 1967), 54–5, 57–8, 66, 68, 70, 144–7, 159, 163. See also Edmund Wyndham.*

BAINHAM, BAYNHAM, Bartholomew.
Son of Robert. Possibly expelled from Inner Temple 1522 and readmitted at Henry VIII's request (*A Calendar of the Inner Temple Records*, ed. F.A. Inderwick, London, 1806, 45, 68). Witness to Paduan MD of Thomas Bill* 1533. Possibly related to heretic lawyer James Baynham burned at the stake in 1532. In service of Thomas Cromwell by 1538. Apptd keeper of the Staple Inn at Calais 1542.
    AGA, 1501–50, no. 1943. M.L. Robertson, 'Thomas Cromwell's Servants: The Ministerial Household in Early Tudor Government and Society' (PhD dissertation, University of California, 1975), pt. 2, 445. *Cal. Ven.* 1527–33, IV, no. 765.

BAKER, Richard. c. 1572–1645.
Religious and historical writer. Son of John. Nephew by marriage of Thomas Sackville,* Lord Buckhurst. Matr. Hart Hall, Oxford as commoner 1584, studied at Inn of Court, MA Oxford 1594. Foreign tour including Poland. Matr. Padua 1596 (AAU 30, fol. 94v). A friend of Henry Wotton.* MP 1593, 1597. Kt 1603, died in Fleet 1645. His *Discourses upon Cornelius Tacitus* (London, 1642) were translated from the Italian of Virgilio Malvezzi. Wrote devotional works and *Chronicle of the Kings of England* (1643).
    AO, I, 58. Andrich, 135. Smith, *Henry Wotton*, I, 5, II, 369–70, 461. Hasler, I, 387. *DNB*. See also Henry Leonard.*

BALL, BAUL, BAULE, Robert.
New College, Oxford 1569, BA 1573, MA 1577. Matr. Padua 1594 (AAU 30, fol. 94). Possibly MP 1593.
    Andrich, 134. *AO*, I, 63. Hasler, I, 406.

BAOSONY? BARSONY? Robert.
Matr. Padua 1595 (AAU 30, fol. 94, same day as John Stackvoaellus,* Robert Shirley,* John Gibson,* and John Frear*).
    Andrich, 135.

BARKER, BERKER, John. See Henry Fitzalan.*

BARKER, BERKER, William. c. 1522–c. 1576.
Translator. BA, St John's College, Cambridge 1536, MA 1540. Padua c. 1550. In Rome with Thomas Hoby,* Peter Whytehorne, and Henry Parker same year. MP 1557–9, 1571, 1562–3. Secretary of duke of Norfolk, implicated in his plot and imprisoned 1571.

DNB. Bindoff, I, 380. Hasler, I, 396. G.B. Parks, 'William Barker, Tudor Translator,' *Papers of the Bibliographical Society of America* 51 (1957), 126–40.

BARNES, Peter.
Matr. fellow commoner Queens' College, Cambridge 1587. Matr. Padua 1595 (AAU 30, fol. 94v), *consiliarius* of English nation 1596–7 (AAU 15, fols 1v, 7). Probably the Peter Barnes, the son of Sir George of London, who was adm. Middle Temple 1591.

Andrich, 44, 135. Venn, I, 93.

BEDREMS? BULEINIS? BEDEIS? BEDEUS? Edward.
Matr. Padua 1594 (AAU 30, fol. 93v).

Andrich, 134.

BEECH, ANSELM, Robert. D. c. 1633.
Benedictine priest. Of Manchester. Adm. English College Rome 1590. Became novice at Benedictine house of S. Giustina, Padua 1595, professed 1596. England 1603. Rome 1607. Chief organizer of Benedictine mission to England.

McCann, 163.

BEEST, Thomas. See Roger Manners.*

BENEDICT, Edward.
Medical student. MD Padua 1601 witnessed by John Finet,* Richard Willoughby,* Francis Josselyn,* Richard Millieis,* Samuel Smalman,* John and Joseph Webb,* and William Harvey* (ASP, AN 4105, fols 262–3).

BERTIE, Peregrine. 1555–1601.
Lord Willoughby d'Eresby, soldier and statesman. Son of Richard.* Father of Robert.* Ambassador to Denmark 1582, 1585. Military campaigns in Netherlands and France between 1586 and 1590. Abroad from 1594 for recovery of his health: Spa 1594–5, Venice same year, where reported by Henry Hawkins* to be with Lord Thomas Gray* (Birch, I, 377; cf. LPL, MS 659, fol. 227) and knew Francis Davison* (Davison, ix, x, xii). Matr. Padua 1596 (AAU 30, fol.

94v), and taken ill there same year (Birch, I, 428). Vienna and England same year. Governor of Berwick upon Tweed 1597–8.

DNB. Lady Georgina Bertie, *Five Generations of a Loyal House* (London, 1845). Andrich, 135. A. Maladorno Hargraves, 'From Padua to the Field of Edgehill: An Outline of the Career of Robert Bertie, Thirteenth Baron Willoughby d'Eresby,' *Atti e memorie dell'Accademia Patavina di Scienze, Lettere ed Arti* 87 (1974–5), 109–29. See also John Payton* and Richard Willoughby.*

BERTIE, Richard. 1517–82.
Marian exile. Son of Thomas, master mason employed by Bishop Richard Fox. Father of Peregrine.* Corpus Christi College, Oxford, adm. 1534, BA and fellow Magdalen College 1537. Servant of Lord Chancellor Wriothesely, then steward to the Protestant Katherine Brandon, dowager duchess of Suffolk. Married her c. 1553. Licensed to go abroad to collect debts owing to his wife. Encountered by Thomas Hoby* Padua 1554, Venice same year where permitted to view treasury of St Marks. Returned to England same year, illegally escaped the country in disguise with his wife same year, staying in Wesel where again encountered by Thomas Hoby* 1555. Departed for Frankfurt same year, Strasbourg, Poland by 1558. Various attempts to arrest them and have their goods confiscated by English government. England by 1559. MP 1563 and served on various parliamentary committees. JP 1564. Denmark c. 1580. Wrote an answer to John Knox's *Monstrous Regiment of Women.*

Bartlett, *English in Italy,* 190–1. *BRUO,* 45–6. Hasler, I, 434–5. Garrett, 87–9. Account of his second period of travel in Foxe, VIII, 569–76. Hoby, 116, 124. See also Philip Hoby.*

BERTIE, Robert. 1582–1642.
Baron Willoughby d'Eresby. MP, statesman, and soldier. Eldest son of Peregrine.* Grandson of Richard.* Godson of Queen Elizabeth. Nephew of Edward de Vere.* Corpus Christi College, Oxford adm. 1594. Inherited barony 1601. France from 1598. Florence November 1602, from where wrote a newsletter to Sir Robert Cecil thanking him for his many kindnesses (PRO, SP98 2, fol. 51). Padua by July 1603 when wrote to King James I congratulating him on his accession. *Consiliarius* of English nation Padua August 1603 and for a year (AAU 15, fols 8, 9v). One of the *consiliarii* chosen to preside over the usual discussions about setting up the coats of arms of the rectors and other office holders July 1604. England same year. Commander-in-chief of royalist forces 1642, died at Battle of Edgehill same year.

Andrich, 46. Maladorno Hargraves, 'From Padua to the Field of Edgehill,' 109–29. *DNB.* 408–9. See also Henry Cuffe.*

BICHIER, BOURCHER? BURCHAR? BURCHETT? Edward.
Consiliarius and *electionarius* of English nation Padua 1567–8 (AAU 11, fol. 169v), and of Scottish nation 1568. Probably the scholar of Eton who matr. King's College, Cambridge age 16 1562, BA 1566–7, MA 1570, fellow 1565–73.
   Andrich, 37, 94. Venn, I, 187, 255. Cf. Garrett, 100–1.

BIGOD, Nicholas.
Consiliarius of English nation Padua 1538 (AAU 5, fols 4, 20). Brother of Peter.* Born in England but had lived in France since childhood.
   Toso Rodonis, 49–50, 105–11.

BIGOD, Peter.
Consiliarius of English nation Padua 1538 (AAU 5, fols 4, 20). Brother of Nicholas.* Born in England but had lived in France since a child.
   Toso Rodonis, 49–50, 105–11.

BILL, Thomas.
Physician. MA Pembroke College, Cambridge, leave to travel abroad for three years 1530. MD Padua 1533 witnessed by John Friar,* Thomas Starkey,* Michael Throckmorton,* and Bartholomew Bainham* (ACV, Diversorum 54, fol. 97. Cf. *AGA, 1501–50,* no. 1943). MD incorp. Cambridge 1534. Censor and *consiliarius* of College of Physicians of London 1543. Physician to Henry VIII and Edward VI, attending Princess Elizabeth in 1549.
   AGA, 1501–50, nos 1940–3. Venn, I, 151. Munk, I, 35.

BIRCH, BYRCHE, Robert. D. by 1535.
Advocate. Supplicated for BCL Oxford 1513. Witness to MD of Edward Wotton* Padua 1525, where described as scholar of law. DCnCL by 1527, when adm. to Doctors' Commons as advocate. Rector of Wyddial, Herts from 1530.
   BRUO, 93–4. *AGA, 1501–50,* no. 1059. Squibb, 143.

BOXALL, John. 1525–71.
Principal secretary of state of Queen Mary and equity lawyer. Scholar of Winchester College, adm. 1538. Scholar of New College, Oxford, adm. 1540, fellow 1542. Took orders but as a Catholic did not exercise ministry during reign of Edward VI. *Consiliarius* of English nation Padua 1550 (AAU 6, fol. 65). MA incorp. Oxford 1554, BTh Oxford same year. Held various canonries and deaneries and the archdeaconry of Ely. Elected warden of Winchester College 1554, vac. 1556. Privy councillor, master and councillor of the Court

of Requests, apptd 1556 (cf. Leadam, civ). Probably a master in Star Chamber in reign of Mary (Leadam, cvii). Principal secretary of state 1557, vac. on death of Mary I. DTh by 1558. Registrar of the Order of the Garter, apptd 1558. One of the overseers of Reginald Pole's* will. Encouraged continental studies in law of fellow Wykehamist Richard White.* Committed to the Tower on refusal to take Oath of Supremacy 1560, then held in 'free custody' by archbishop of Canterbury. Wrote oration in praise of king of Spain.

Andrich, 29. *DNB. BRUO*, 65. *Statuta* (1551), sig. Aiii. J. Le Neve, *Fasti ecclesiae Anglicanae* (Oxford, 1854), I, 257, 352, II, 476. J.M. Horne, ed., *Fasti ecclesiae Anglicanae, 1541–1857* (London, 1969–), VII, 13.

BROMUS, BROME, BROWNE? John.

Consiliarius and *electionarius* of English nation Padua 1555 (AAU 9, fol. 141v). Possibly the John Brome or Browne who was MA at Christ Church, Oxford 1566, who may or may not be identical with the John Browne present in Strasbourg 1557 and Frankfurt 1559, and with the 'Mr Brome' who was Archbishop Parker's Commissary 1571. A further possibility is John Browne, son of Robert, adm. Middle Temple 1552 and MP in 1558.

Andrich, 31. Bartlett, *English in Italy*, 191–2. Bindoff, I, 522–3. Garrett, 98.

BROOKE, BROKE, COBHAM, John. 1535–94.

Marian exile, Elizabethan seaman, and MP. Son of Lord Cobham of Hawley. Brother of George and William Brooke.* Encountered by Thomas Hoby* Padua 1554. Venice by 1555 where licensed to bear arms and associated with entourage of Francis Russell.* Inner Temple, adm. 1556. Captain of the *Foresight* under Elizabeth, occasional intelligencer, and administrator for the English government on the continent, including dealings with Thomas Wilson.* MP in four parliaments, gentleman pensioner of the queen. JP by 1564.

Bartlett, *English in Italy*, 192. Garrett, 97–8. Hasler, I, 996. Hoby, 117.

BROOKE, BROKE, COBHAM, William, Lord. 1527–97.

Son of Lord Cobham of Hawley. Brother of George and John Brooke.* Licensed to go abroad 'for his further increase of virtue and learning' 1541 (after initial government refusal previous year: *LP*, XV, no. 217) and urged by father to study civil law, rhetoric, and Greek. Padua and Venice 1543, where licensed to carry arms same year together with his tutor John Schiere* (Venice, Archivio di Stato, Consiglio di X, Lettere ai Capi, filza n. 45, 11 October 1543, fols 204, 214, 217). By 1545 his inclination was 'rather to war than letters,' and he was permitted to view Venetian munitions same year (Venice, Archivio di Stato, Consiglio di X, Parti Communi, Reg. 17, fol. 37).

Also visited Netherlands. Succeeded to family title 1555. Various government offices under Edward and Mary, some of them military and diplomatic, but implicated in Thomas Wyatt's* rebellion. MP 1547, 1555. Privy council adm. 1586, lord chamberlain 1596.

LP, XX, pt. 2, no. 518. Bindoff, I, 512–13. Stone, 693.

BROOKES, __.
Jesuit priest. Encountered by Arthur Throckmorton* in Padua 1581 with Father Lawrence Fant,* on way from Rome to Poland.

Canterbury, Canterbury Cathedral Archives, MS U. 85, Box 38, I, fol. 65.

BRUCE, Edmund.
Astronomer. Encountered by Samuel Foxe* Padua c. 1585. *Consiliarius* of English nation intermittently 1588–94 (AAU 14, fols 1v, 5, 7, 16v, 23–6). Friend of Paduan *eruditi* Giovan Vicenzo Pinelli and Lorenzo Pignoria, and the astronomers Giovan Antonio Magini and Galileo, about whom he gossipped to Johannes Kepler. Recruited into Elizabethan intelligence service, reporting from Padua during the late 1590s to Anthony Bacon, and knew in Padua Henry Archer* and Roger Manners* in this connection, and in Venice Henry Hawkins.*

Andrich, 42–3, 134. P. Gualdo, *Vita Joannis Vincentii Pinelli*, in *Vitae selectorum aliquot virorum*, ed. W. Bates (London, 1681), 342. Rivolta, lx, 93–4. C. Bellinati, 'Galileo e il sodalizio con ecclesiastici padovani,' in *Galileo e la cultura padovana*, ed. G. Santinello (Padua, 1992), 341. W. Von Dyck and M. Caspar, eds, *Johannes Kepler gesammelte Werke* (Munich, 1938–), XIV, 7–16, 256, 441, 450. E. Rosen, ed., *Kepler's Conversation with Galileo's Sidereal Messenger* (New York and London, 1965), 11, 38, 67. S. Drake, *Galileo Studies* (Ann Arbor, 1970), 126–32, 134, 137–8. S. Drake, *Galileo at Work* (Chicago and London, 1978), 46, 48, 63, 65, 442. LPL, MS 654, fols 34–7; MS 655, fols 9, 24, 82; MS 658, fol. 169; MS 659, fols 51, 264; MS 660, fols 23, 155, 156.

BRUNING, Richard.
Encountered by Nicholas Faunt* Padua 1581. *Consiliarius* of English nation Padua 1582–3 (AAU 13, fols 90, 116v, 159v). Probably the Richard Browning who was BCL Oxford 1575.

Andrich, 40–1. *AO*, I, 199.

BRYSKETT, Sebastian. 1536–91.
Intelligencer. Son of Antonio Bryskett, Italian Protestant merchant denizened in England. Elder brother of Sir Philip Sidney's* travelling companion Ludovic. Trinity Hall, Cambridge matr. 1552. Scholar of English nation Padua

1556–7 (Andrich, 131). Student of philosophy Rome late 1550s. Intelligencer in Rome for William Cecil and Francis Walsingham* until 1564 when returned to England and entered service of Robert Dudley (cf. PRO SP85 1, fol. 22). Resident Venice early 1570s, met Philip Sidney,* but then returned to England where married.

K.R. Bartlett, 'Papal Policy and the English Crown, 1563–1565: The Bertano Correspondence,' *Sixteenth Century Journal* 23 (1992), 643–59. Frere, 1067. Bartlett, *English in Italy*, 193–4.

BUCKLER, Walter. D. 1553.
Diplomat. Merton College, Oxford, adm. 1521, fellow 1522. BA 1521, BTh 1534. Student at Paris 1530, 1536, 1539. Padua same year. Secretary to Catharine Parr. Diplomat in Germany.

Bartlett, *English in Italy*, 55. *BRUO*, 81.

BUCLAM, BUCKLOND? BUKLOND? Thomas.
Consiliarius of English nation Padua 1508 (AAU 6, fol. 35). Possibly the Bucklond, BCL, elected a fellow of All Souls College, Oxford 1501, still present there 1504–5; and the Thomas Buklond mentioned as a member of Oxford University in 1517 in a letter from the university to Cardinal Wolsey in that year.

Andrich, 21. *LP*, II, no. 3770. Emden, I, 299.

BYNG, Robert.
Matr. Padua 1597 (AAU 30, fol. 95). Probably the Robert Byng, son of Regius Professor of Law at Cambridge Thomas Byng, who matr. as pensioner Clare College, Cambridge, c. 1593, BA 1596–7, MA 1600, DTh 1630, died c. 1658–9.

Venn, I, 152. Andrich, 136.

CAIUS, John. 1510–73.
Humanist and physician. Son of Robert. Gonville Hall, Cambridge, adm. 1529, BA 1533, fellow same year, MA 1535. Italy 1539, residing at Padua with Andreas Vesalius, taught by G.B. da Monte. MD Padua 1541, and apptd as lecturer same year, together with Realdus Columbus. Toured Italy 1543 collecting manuscripts mainly of Galen. Fellow of College of Physicians, adm. 1547, *consiliarius* 1550–3, censor same year, president 1555–60, 1562–3, 1571–2. Wrote college's *Annals* 1555–72. Assiduous defender of the college against unlicensed practitioners and professional incursions of surgeons. Suspected of Catholicism 1568. Rebuilt and refounded Gonville Hall in late 1550s and early 1560s. MD incorp. Cambridge 1558, master of Gonville and Caius College 1559.

Again suspected of maintaining Catholic practices Cambridge 1572. Friend of Conrad Gesner and John Clement,* and an admirer of Thomas Linacre.*

Nutton, 'John Caius and the Linacre Tradition.' Nutton, *John Caius and the Manuscripts of Galen*. See also Henry Knolles,* John Mason,* and Edward Wotton.*

CALWOODLEY, Nicholas. D. between 1621 and 1623.
Medical student. Son of John. Matr. Padua 1595 (AAU 30, fol. 94, same day as Edward Cecil*). Doctorate in philosophy and medicine at Padua July 1597 by count palatine (Sigismondo Capodilista: ASP, AN 4104, fol. 283) witnessed by Anthony Fortescue.* Kt beyond the seas.

Andrich, 135. J.L. Vivian, ed., *The Visitations of the County of Devon* (Exeter, 1895), 132. J. Maclean, *The Parochial and Family History of the Deanery of Trigg Minor in the County of Cornwall* (London and Bodmin, 1876), II, 39–40.

CAREW, George. D. 1612.
Lawyer and diplomat. Son of Thomas. Nephew of Matthew.* Married Thomasine, sister of Sir Francis Godolphin.* Younger brother of Richard Carew, author of the *Survey of Cornwall*, who wrote that 'in his younger years [George Carew] gathered such fruit as the university, the Inns of Court and foreign travel could yield him.' Probably educated at Oxford; Middle Temple 1577. Travelled on continent 1580–1 with Henry Savile* and Henry Neville,* and encountered with them his cousin Arthur Throckmorton* in Nuremburg 1580 and Prague and Padua 1581. Wrote from Padua to Hugo Blotius, the imperial librarian in Vienna, thanking him for his hospitality (Vienna, Österreichische Nationalbibliothek, MS 9737z[14-18], fol. 294). Also knew on the continent Joseph Scaliger, Jacques-Auguste de Thou and Isaac Casaubon. Assisted Henry Savile* in work on astronomical MSS in Vienna 1581. MP 1584, 1586, 1589, 1593, 1597, 1601, 1604. Kt 1603. JP from 1580. Prothonotary in Chancery from 1593 (mainly concerned with enrolling of treaties); master in Chancery from 1599, master of Requests from 1602, master of Wards 1612. Embassies to Poland, Sweden, Brunswick, Denmark 1598, ambassador to France 1605–9. Author of *A treatise of the maisters in chancery; A relation of the state of France* (dedicated to James I, first printed with Thomas Birch's *An historical view of the negociations between the courts of England, France and Brussels for the years 1592–1617*, London, 1749). Carew also supplied material on Poland included in de Thou's *Historia sui tempori* (Geneva, 1621). Compiled *Cary's Reports* (of causes in Chancery) mainly from notes left by William Lambarde, first printed 1650.

Jones, 106–8, 112–17, 427, 436–7. *DNB*. Feingold, 127–8. Hasler, I, 538–9.

CAREW, Matthew. 1531–1618.
Archdeacon and advocate. Son of Sir Wymond. Brother of Roger.* Uncle of
George Carew* and the Denny* brothers. Westminster School. Trinity College, Cambridge, scholar, adm. 1548, BA and fellow 1551. Archdeacon of
Norfolk 1552. Marian exile, encountered by Thomas Hoby* Padua 1554 with
his brother Roger.* DCL Louvain. Travelled to Italy again 1565–6 as interpreter of Henry Fitzalan,* earl of Arundel. Doctors' Commons, adm. contributor 1559, as advocate of the Arches 1573. Master in Chancery 1577–1618. Kt
1603.
   Squibb, 154, 160. Levack, *The Civil Lawyers*, 217. Garrett, 104. Hoby, 117.
Bartlett, *English in Italy*, 194. *DNB*. Heward, 81, 91. Frere, 1067. Le Neve, II,
485. Horne, VII, 46.

CAREW, Roger. c. 1528–90.
Son of Sir Wymond. Brother of Matthew.* Uncle of Denny* brothers. BA
Oxford 1546. Fellow of Trinity College, Cambridge same year. Adm. Gray's
Inn 1551. Encountered by Thomas Hoby* Padua 1554. England by 1559, when
apptd receiver for Bedfordshire and Buckinghamshire. MP 1563–7. Various
government duties.
   Hoby, 117. Garrett, 108. Bartlett, *English in Italy*, 196. Hasler, I, 544.

CAVENDISH, Charles. 1553–1617.
MP. Son of Sir William. Brother of Henry.* Brother-in-law of Gilbert Talbot.*
Adm. Cambridge 1567, MA 1575. Witness to DCnCL of John Le Rous* Padua
1571. Kt 1582. MP 1593, 1601. Suspected of harbouring Catholic sympathies.
   Hasler, I, 565–6.

CAVENDISH, Henry. 1550–1616.
MP. Son of Sir William. Brother of Charles.* Brother-in-law of Gilbert Talbot,*
and travelled with him to Padua 1570. Eton, adm. 1560. Gray's Inn, adm.
1567. Witness to DCnCL of John Le Rous* Padua 1571. MP 1572, 1584, 1586,
1589, 1593. Soldier in Netherlands. Passed through Venice on journey to
Constantinople in 1589, and found it 'a most foul stinking sink.'
   Hasler, I, 566–7.

CECIL, Edward. 1572–1638.
Military commander and MP. Son of Thomas, earl of Exeter. Godson of
Francis Manners.* Grandson of Lord Burghley. Brother of William.* Gray's
Inn 1591. Licence to travel abroad for three years 1594, together with his
brother Richard (PRO E157 26). Matr. Padua 1595 (AAU 30, fol. 94, same day

as Nicholas Calwoodley*). *Consiliarius* of English nation 1595–6 (AAU 15, fol. 1v). Received by the grand duke of Tuscany Ferdinando de'Medici August 1596. Wrote from Florence to his uncle Sir Robert Cecil in Italian November 1596. Stayed with duke of Bracciano (head of Orsini family) near Rome. Possibly corresponded from Italy 1596 with Sir Francis Bacon (Spedding, 37–8). London 1598, where obtained new passport to go and serve under Sir Francis Vere in Holland, and commenced a military carreer. MP 1601, 1604, 1621, 1624. Kt 1601. Married daughter of Sir William Drury* 1617. Created Viscount Wimbledon 1625. JP. Gentleman of privy chamber 1603–4. Member council of war 1621–38. Member High Commission 1629–39. Director Virginia Company 1609–24. Associated with John Coke* by 1625.

Andrich, 44, 135. *DNB*. C. Dalton, *A Life of Edward Cecil Viscount Wimbledon* (London 1885), 8–14. Hasler, I, 570–1. A. Maladorno Hargraves, 'I Cecil e lo Studio Patavino,' *QSUP* 16 (1983), 119–26. History of Parliament draft biography.

CECIL (*alias* SNOWDEN), John. B. 1558.
Seminary priest and spy. Trinity College, Oxford matr. 1572, scholar 1573, BA 1576, fellow 1576, MA 1580. Rheims 1583. English College Rome adm. same year, ordained 1584, expelled 1585. Stayed in Dominican house of S. Agostino Padua same year, intending to acquire doctorate in theology, where encountered by Samuel Foxe.* Rome same year, then Sicily and the English College Valladolid. England 1590. Recruited by English government as an intelligencer following year to c. 1597, and also informed Catholics of the English government's activities. Member of the second Appellant Embassy to Rome 1602. England 1603, but from then on seems to have been abroad.

Renold, *Wisbech Stirs*, 67, 69–71, 80–3, 158–9, 207. HMC, *Hatfield*, IV, 115, 473–4, 478–90. *Calendar of State Papers relating to Scotland and Mary, Queen of Scots, 1547–1603*, XII, ed. M.S. Giuseppi (Edinburgh, 1952), 267. Birch, I, 263, 407, II, 32, 306–7. Handover, 107–9. P. Hammer, 'An Elizabethan Spy Who Came in from the Cold: The Return of Anthony Standen to England in 1593,' *Historical Research* 65 (1992), 288. M.A.S. Hume, *Treason and Plot* (London 1908), 41–9, 69–74, 201–3, 210–15. C. Devlin, *The Life of Robert Southwell* (London, 1956), 227–8. A.J. Loomie, *The Spanish Elizabethans* (New York, 1963), 73–4. Kelly, 49. *AO*, I, 253. Renold, *Letters*, 58, 67, 69, 70–1, 80–3, 158–9, 163.

CECIL, William. 1566–1640.
Son of Thomas, earl of Exeter. Brother of Edward.* Married Elizabeth, daughter of Edward Manners. Trinity College, Cambridge, 1578. Paris 1583.

Rome 1585, where fell under suspicion of heresy, protected by Christopher Parkins.* Encountered by Samuel Foxe* Padua 1585 (and travelled with him through France 1586). Wrote to his grandfather Lord Burghley from Padua 1585 (*Cal. SP Dom. Eliz.*, 1581–90, 254) and to Francis Walsingham* same year (ibid., 287 = PRO, SP12 184, fol. 113) requesting him to intercede with his father for having been to Rome contrary to his commandment. MP 1586, 1589, 1597. Gray's Inn 1589. Italy 1599–1600. Kt 1603. Second earl of Exeter from 1623.

Hasler, I, 581–2. Dalton, 6–8. *Cal. SP For. Eliz.*, 1585–6, 449. See also John Finet.*

CEULE, Robert.
Consiliarius of English nation 1596 (AAU 15, fol. 6v).
Andrich, 44.

CHALONER, Robert. c. 1491–1541.
Advocate and king's councillor in the north. Winchester College, scholar, adm. 1502. New College, Oxford, scholar, adm. 1507, fellow 1509, vac. by 1510 on transferring to study of civil law. BCL adm. 1521. Witness to MD of Edward Wotton* Padua 1525, where described as scholar of law. DCL by 1526, probably of Padua or another Italian university. Adm. Doctors' Commons as advocate 1526. Member of king's council in the north 1526–37. Bequeathed a book to Winchester College. Not to be confused with the Gray's Inn lawyer of the same name, the cousin of Robert Nowell, who died in 1555 (cf. *The Pension Book of Gray's Inn, 1569–1669*, ed. R. J. Fletcher, London, 1901, I, xxi).
AGA, 1501–50, no. 1059. Squibb, 142. *BRUO*, 109.

CHAMBER, John. 1470–1549.
Royal physician. Merton College, Oxford, bachelor 1492, bachelor fellow adm. 1493, fellow 1495, vac. 1508, bursar 1499–1500, 1501–2, king of the beans 1506, warden 1525–44, MA 1495. Studied medicine Padua from 1503. Witness to loan of money by John Lupus* to Nicholas Beysell of Liège Padua 1505, to doctorate of Edward Maners* same year, and to another contract at Padua same year (ASP, AN 1811, fols 355–6). MD at Padua same year witnessed by Robert Spencer* (ACV, Diversorum 47, fol. 334), incorp. Oxford 1531. English hospice Rome 1506. England same year. Royal physician 1506–46. One of the 'chief advisers' of Lady Margaret Beaufort, mother of Henry VII. One of the founders of the College of Physicians of London in 1518 with Thomas Linacre,* censor 1523. Commanded to pass on to Linacre* king's request to be

dedicatee of Linacre's* *De sanitate tuenda* 1522. President of the Barber-Surgeons' Guild of London at its incorporation 1541 (and is represented in Holbein's group portrait of the granting of the Guild's charter by Henry VIII, now in London, Barber-Surgeons' Hall; another Holbein portrait of him is in Vienna, Kunsthistorisches Museum). Contributor to pharmacopoeia of plasters, lotions, and unguents compiled by royal physicians (BL, MS Sloane 1047). Various benefices and was dean of St Stephen's Chapel, Westminster, where spent 11,000 marks on rebuilding the cloisters. Left money to Merton College in his will.

BRUO, 385. *LP*, III, nos 601, 2373. *DNB*. M.K. Jones and M.G. Underwood, *The King's Mother: Lady Margaret Beaufort, Countess of Richmond and Derby* (Cambridge, 1992), 270. *AGA, 1501–50*, no. 418.

CHARD, Thomas.
Matr. Padua 1596 (AAU 30, fol. 94v, same day as Henry Gray*).
Andrich, 136.

CHEKE, John. 1514–57.
Cambridge humanist and Marian exile. Son of Peter. St John's College, Cambridge, fellow 1529, BA 1530, MA 1533, King's Scholar 1534. Apparently studying abroad late 1530s. Regius Professor of Greek Cambridge 1540–51, where pupils included Thomas Wilson.* Public Orator of the university 1544, tutor to Prince Edward same year. Gentleman of the privy chamber 1547. MP same year and 1553. Provost of King's College, Cambridge 1548. A friend of the Italian physician Girolamo Cardano in England in 1540s. Present at conferences on the sacrament in home of Richard Morison* 1551. Kt next year. Clerk of the council and secretary of state 1553. Imprisoned on accession of Mary, then licensed to travel abroad 1554 with Richard Morison* and Anthony Cooke.* Basle and Strasbourg, then Padua with Sir Thomas Wrothe* same year where intended to study Italian and civil law. Shared house there with Wrothe,* Thomas and Philip Hoby,* and Cooke.* This group travelled to Mantua same year. Tutor to Englishmen at Padua, held readings of Demosthenes' *Three Orations* in Greek with his interpretations. The audience definitely included Thomas Wilson* and William Temple* and possibly also Edward Courtenay* and Francis Walsingham* (Wilson, *Three Orations*, dedicatory letter, no page no.; Wilson, *Arte of Rhetorique*, xxx–xxxi, cxxix–cxxx). Left Padua 1554 with Wrothe,* Cooke,* and the Hobys,* travelling around northern Italy. Joined the Hobys* at Caldiero following year, probably for the baths due to illness and to avoid the plague at Padua. Medal commemorating him in Italy made by Ludovico Leoni. Verona, Venice, and Padua with

Hobys* same year, then Strasbourg until 1556. Kidnapped en route to Brussels 1556, committed to the Tower same year on charge of authoring seditious books. Recanted heresy. Writings include *The Hurt of Sedition* (London, 1549), *De pronuntiatione Graecae* (Basle, 1555), and various religious works.

Bindoff, I, 626–30. Hoby, 116–21. *DNB*. Pollard, 94. G. Cardano, *Della mia vita* (Milan, 1982), 71. See also John Friar* and John Mason.*

CINI, CYNY, Dominicus.
Consiliarius of English nation Padua 1502–3, 1507–8 (AAU 2, fols 107, 21v, 23v–4). Witness to *procura* of Gamaliel Clifton* Padua 1508. Probably a member of the Venetian Cini family resident in London in 1470s. His payment to the Crown for the fine of Bonsham on being made denizen recorded 1513.

Andrich, 20–1. *Cal. Ven.* 1509–19, II, Appendix, nos 1328–9. *LP*, II, 1486. For alternative identification see Parks, *English Traveller*, 634–5.

CLEMENT, John. D. 1572.
Humanist, physician and associate of Thomas More. Son of Robert (Erasmus, *Opus epistolarum*, V, xxiv). Father of Thomas.* Pupil at St Paul's School 1510s. Servant–pupil, then tutor to children, in household of Thomas More from c. 1514, and accompanied More to Bruges and Antwerp 1515. Taught Greek to John Colet following year. Cardinal Wolsey's first reader in rhetoric and humanity at Oxford 1518 (to be succeeded by Thomas Lupset*), residing in Corpus Christi College until 1520, by which time he was devoted to the study of medicine. Knew Reginald Pole* from 1518 at latest. Studied Louvain 1521 where knew Juan Luis Vives. Padua 1522, probably funded by the king, as certainly was by 1525 (BL, MS Egerton 2604, fol. 6v), but possibly had returned to England between these two dates. MD Siena 1525. Collaborator on Aldine edition of complete works of Galen in Greek at Venice same year, together with Thomas Lupset,* Edward Wotton,* and Anthony Rose. Almost certainly knew Thomas Starkey* at this time (BL, MS Cotton, Nero B vi, fol. 145). Bought books and manuscripts in Italy. Fellow of College of Physicians of London 1528, *consiliarius* 1529–31, 1547, 1556–8, president 1544, censor 1555, exempted from attendance requirement 1555 on account of age and infirmity. Royal physician from 1528, and treated Pole* and the dying Wolsey following year. Lectured in Oxford c. 1530 and married More's ward Margaret Giggs around same time. Catholic exile in Louvain from 1547, returning to England 1554 when commenced litigation to recover his property, but settled in Mechelen on accession of Elizabeth, where died. Owned

MS of Galen later used by his friend John Caius.* Talents for Greek and Latin scholarship praised by More and Georg Agricola, and for medicine by G.B. Opizo and John Caius.*

Munk, I, 25–7. *CE*, I, 311–12. Erasmus, *Opus epistolarum*, II, no. 468 (*CWE*, IV, 80); IV, no. 1087 (*CWE*, VII, 254); V, nos 1256 and 1271 (*CWE*, IX, 17, 56). Rogers, 136. Caius, *De libris propriis*, 77, 83 in Caius. Agricola, 57. J.B. Trapp and H. Schulte Herbrüggen, eds, *'The King's Good Servant': Sir Thomas More, 1477/8–1535* (London, 1978), nos 51, 78.

CLEMENT, Thomas. D. 1595.
Law student. Son of John.* Law student Padua 1555 and possibly 1556, whom Reginald Pole* commended to the Paduan law professor Guido Panciroli via Marcantonio Genova as the son of his friend (Venice, Biblioteca Nazionale Marciana, MS Ital. X 24 (6527), fols 157v–8). Lived in parish of San Daniele in Padua. (His *procura* is ASP, AN 4848, fol. 701.) English hospice Rome 1578. Resident in Louvain at time of death.

Cal. Ven. 1555–7, VI, no. 442. *EH*, 236, 238. Trapp and Schulte Herbrüggen, no. 78.

CLEMENT, William. c. 1569–1636.
Physician. Son of William of Hampton, Mddx. BA Trinity College, Cambridge 1590–1, MA 1594, incorp. Oxford 1594. Matr. Leiden 1596 as a medical student, same day as Joseph Lister,* matr. Basle 1596, probably same day as Joseph Lister.* Matr. Padua 1597 (AAU 30, fol. 95, same day as Joseph Lister*). Paduan MD 1599 awarded by count palatine Sigismondo Capodilista (ASP, AN 4104, fols 547v–50v) witnessed by John Payton* and Anthony Fortescue,* promoted by Prospero Alpino, Fabricius ab Acquapendente, and Thomas Minadous. Asked for licence to practise from College of Physicians of London 1600; decision postponed (London, Royal College of Physicians, Annals of the College of Physicians of London 2, fol. 147), licentiate permitted to practise 1605 (ibid., fol. 184), fellow 1607 (ibid., fols 193v–4), censor 1612 (ibid., 3, fol. 11), censor and elect 1628 (ibid., fol. 83v), registrar 1629 (ibid., fol. 93). Physician to Christ's Hospital. Author of a small book regarding precautions against and treatment of the plague (ibid., fol. 98).

Andrich, 136. Venn, I, 353. Rossetti, 'Membri,' 182. Munk I, 146. H.J. Cooke, *The Decline of the Old Medical Regime in Stuart London* (Ithaca and London, 1986), 266, 269. R.W. Innes Smith, *English-Speaking Students of Medicine at the University of Leyden* (Edinburgh and London, 1932), 47–8. See also William Harvey.*

CLEREGATUS, Simeon.
Consiliarius of English nation Padua May 1574, substituting for Jerome Sapcot.* Possibly not English, as Sapcot* had been elected by 'ius supplendum' the previous August (AAU 12, fols 47v, 65).
   Andrich, 39.

CLERK, James.
Matr. Padua 1597 (AAU 30, fol. 95).
   For possible identifications see *AO*, I, 280; Venn, I, 342; Hasler, I, 610.

CLIFFORD, Simon. B. c. 1569.
Matr. Brasenose College, Oxford 1586, BA Broadgates Hall 1590. Middle Temple 1594. Matr. Padua 1597 (AAU 30, fol. 95). *Consiliarius* of English nation 1598–9 (AAU 15, fols 11v, 12v).
   AO, I, 291. Andrich, 45, 136.

CLIFTON, CLYFFTON, Gamaliel. D. by 1541.
Royal chaplain and prebendary of York. Son of Sir Gervase. BCL Cambridge 1504. Named Robert Spencer* as his guarantor in his *procura* Padua 1506, witnessed by Dominicus Cini* (ASP, AN 1812, fol. 334). Turin University, DCnL 1508, incorp. Oxford 1521. Doctors' Commons adm. as contributor same year. A proctor by 1515 when described as such and as being in Paris in a letter to Wolsey of that year. King's chaplain by 1522. Dean of Hereford apptd 1529. As a respected canonist he advised Convocation on Henry VIII's first divorce, and was a signatory to the decree invalidating Henry's marriage with Anne of Cleves 1540.
   LP, II, no. 299, III, no. 2482 (item 8). Parks, *English Traveller*, 640. Squibb, 128. Le Neve, I, 477. Horne, II, 5.

CLODIUS, Joannes.
Consiliarius of English nation Padua, August to November 1594. Possibly not English as elected 'substitutus' (AAU 14, fol. 48).
   Andrich, 44.

COCKS, Seth.
Intelligencer. Magdalen College, Oxford, matr. 1579. Sent newsletters to Sir Robert Cecil from Padua 1593–4.
   Wernham, IV (1593–4), 462, 477–8, 508, 516–17. PRO, SP85 1, fol. 163, SP85 2, fols 30, 34. HMC, *Hatfield*, IV, 492. *AO*, I, 297.

COKE, John. 1563–1644.
Secretary of state. Son of Christopher. A relative of William Godolphin.* Trinity College, Cambridge 1580, fellow 1583. Entered service of Lord Burghley. Deputy treasurer of the navy 1591. Abroad 1593–6: Germany, Italy, Switzerland, France. Matr. Padua 1593 (AAU 30, fol. 93v). Siena 1595, where Thomas Gray* wrote to him from Florence concerning a Greek and Italian copy of Euclid (HMC, *12th Report*, Appendix Part I: *MSS of the Earl Cowper preserved at Melbourne Hall, Derbyshire*, London, 1888, 18). Eleazar Hickman in Venice wrote to him same year in Siena, and Isaac Casaubon in Geneva wrote to him in Orleans July 1596, asking him to send his regards to [Thomas] Savile* (ibid.). In service of Fulke Greville 1597. A client of the duke of Buckingham from 1618, commissioner for the navy same year. MP 1621, 1624, 1625, 1626, 1628. Kt 1624. Master of Requests 1622–5. Principal secretary of state 1625.

Hasler, I, 645–6. M.B. Young, *Servility and Service: The Life and Work of Sir John Coke* (London, 1986). *DNB*. Hammer, 'Uses of Scholarship,' 46. Andrich, 134.

COKK, __.
Encountered by Samuel Foxe* Padua c. 1585.
BL, MS Lansdowne 679, fols 44–5.

COLES, COLE, Henry. c. 1505–80.
Canon lawyer and Catholic divine. Winchester College scholar adm. 1519. New College, Oxford scholar adm. 1521, fellow 1523, BCL adm. 1530. Padua by same year. (BL, MS Cotton, Nero B vi, fols 150, 175). Member of the English nation and student of law Padua 1533–4 (AAU 4, fols 296v, 298v; Leland, 79–80). Apparently in Padua and Venice with Reginald Pole* during Pole's writing of *Pro ecclesiasticae unitatis defensione*, at least until September 1536 when sent Richard Morison* a remedy for catarrh devised by Paduan physicians for Coles's patron Dr William Knight, although claimed to be the only Englishman in Padua in March 1536, after the departure of John Friar* (BL, MS Cotton, Nero B vi, fol. 150; PRO, SP1 102, fol. 141, which also supplies evidence for his connection with Thomas Starkey* in this period). Paris 1537. DCL incorp. Oxford 1540, probably from French or Italian university. Adm. Doctors' Commons as advocate same year. Warden of New College 1542, Provost of Eton 1554, and a disputant in the trial of Cranmer, Ridley, and Latimer, and preached at Cranmer's execution same year. Archdeacon of Ely 1553. Dean of St Paul's 1556. Vicar general in spirituals under

Cardinal Pole,* offical and dean of the Court of Arches, judge of the Archi-
piscopal Court of Audience in 1557, commissary of Prerogative Court of
Canterbury 1558–9. Member of High Commission. DTh incorp. Cambridge
1557 (M. Parker, 'Catalogus Cancellariorum,' in *De antiquitate Britanniae
ecclesiae*, London, 1572, 13). Overseer of Pole's* will. Catholic divine in 1559
Westminster Abbey disputation, sent to Tower following year. Donated sixty-
three books to St John's College, Oxford. Acquainted with Michael Throckmorton* and Edward Wotton.* Author of various theological works, probably
including an anonymous MS treatise on the General Council of the Church.

   DNB. *BRUO*, 128–9. Squibb, 47, 148. Andrich, 130. R. Ascham, *Epistolarum
libri* (Oxford, 1703), 261. *LP*, XI, nos 402, 513, XII, pt 2, nos 40, 45. P.A.
Sawada, 'Two Anonymous Tudor Treatises on the General Council,' *Journal of
Ecclesiastical History* 12 (1961), 197–214. Le Neve, I, 352, II, 314, III, 555. Usher,
348. C. Kitching, 'The Prerogative Court of Canterbury,' in Heal and O'Day,
200–1. See also George Lily.*

CONINGSBY, Humphrey. c. 1566–1601.
MP. Son of John. Christ Church, Oxford, matr. 1581. Matr. Padua 1594 (AAU
30, fol. 93v). *Consiliarius* of English nation 1597–8 (AAU 15, fol. 4). Probably
still in Padua 1599 when the servant of one 'Mr Conysbie' delivered letters
from Padua to Francis Manners* (HMC, *The MSS of his Grace the Duke of
Rutland, preserved at Belvoir Castle*, London, 1905, IV, 424). MP 1584, 1586,
1589, 1593, 1607. JP. St Alban's corporation official and steward 1584–8.
Served on parliamentary committees.
   Andrich, 45, 134. *AO*, I, 316. Hasler, I, 636–7.

COO, Arthur. See Robert Fisher.*

COOKE, Anthony. c. 1505–76.
Marian exile and humanist. Son of John. Educated privately and possibly at
Cambridge. Inner Temple adm. 1523. MP 1547, 1549, 1563. Present at the
conference on the sacrament at the house of Richard Morison* 1551. Gentleman of the privy chamber 1546–53. JP for Essex 1537–54. Tutor to Prince
Edward with John Cheke.* Sent to Tower for support of Queen Jane 1553,
pardoned and licensed to go abroad. Strasbourg 1554, where attended
lectures of Peter Martyr. Padua 1554, where associated with Cheke,* the
Hobys,* and Sir Thomas Wrothe.* Left for Germany 1555, where associated
with English exiles in Strasbourg until 1558. Wrote Latin translation of
Gregory Nazianzus's *Theophania*; a contribution to the memorial volume for

Martin Bucer; and a translation of St Cyprian's sermon on prayer dedicated
to Henry VIII.

  Bartlett, *English in Italy*, 199–200. Bindoff, I, 689–9. Hoby, 117. M.K. McIn-
tosh, 'Sir Anthony Cooke, Tudor Humanist, Educator and Religious
Reformer,' *Proceedings of the American Philosophical Society* 119 (1975), 233–50.
See also John Friar* and Henry Killigrew.*

COOKE, Thomas. See Henry Fitzalan.*

CORNWALLIS, Henry. After 1519–before 1599.
Catholic traveller and Elizabethan JP. Son of John. Encountered by Thomas
Hoby* Padua 1554. England following year. JP in Norfolk under Elizabeth.

  Bartlett, *English in Italy*, 200. Hoby, 116.

COTTON, John. See Thomas Hoby.*

COTTON, Thomas.
Intelligencer. Antwerp 1566, Padua next year, where reported to William
Cecil that Edward Courtenay's* tomb had been removed and the coffin
'thrown into an old cloister.' Arranged with Venetian government for it to be
set up again. Greece 1567. English hospice Rome early 1570s.

  Cal. SP For. Eliz., 1566–8, nos 665, 1050, 1122, 2261. *EH*, 225. On Courtenay's tomb cf. Coryat, I, 287.

COURTENAY, Edward. c. 1526–56.
Earl of Devon. Suitor to Queen Mary, political prisoner, and exile. Cousin of
Reginald Pole.* Imprisoned in Tower from 1538 after accusations of treason
made against his father, Henry Courtenay, who was executed 1539. Tutored
in Tower by Nicholas Udall, and made MS translation of *Il Beneficio di Cristo*
promoted in Pole's* Viterbo circle, entitled *The Benefit of Christ's Death*, in
1548. Released from the Tower on accession of Mary and congratulated on
this by Pole* (Venice, Biblioteca Nazionale Marciana, MS Ital. X 24 (6527), fol.
806). Rejected suitor of Mary I, exiled for alleged involvement in Wyatt's*
rebellion 1554. Visited emperor at Brussels same year, already the subject of
controversy and intrigue, Venice 1556, Padua same year. Apparently a
student of law at the university, as university officially attended his funeral
in St Anthony's, Padua September 1556 (Brugi, *Atti*, 51). Thomas Wilson*
composed and read his funeral oration, which attributes his death in this
severe plague year to tertian fever (text in J. Strype, *Ecclesiastical Memorials*,
Oxford, 1822, III, Appendix, 191–5). The *podestà* of Padua wrote a Latin elegy

on his death (Scardeone, 398). Possibly assassinated by poison by English or imperial agents.

C. Babington, ed., *The Benefit of Christ's Death* (London, 1855). Baskerville, 145–218. Bartlett, 'Edward Courtenay, Earl of Devon.' See also Thomas Cotton,* John Cheke,* Philip Hoby,* Henry Killigrew,* Humphrey Michell,* Henry Neville,* and Michael Throckmorton.*

COVERTE, Alexander. B. c. 1562.
St Mary's Hall, Oxford, matr. 1580, BA 1582. Gray's Inn 1585. Matr. Padua 1591 (AAU 30, fol. 93).

AO, I, 338. Andrich, 133.

CRANMER, George. 1563–1600.
Tourist and intelligencer. Son of Thomas. Corpus Christi College, Oxford c. 1577, fellow 1583, taught by Richard Hooker. In service of William Davison, then Sir Henry Killigrew.* Abroad with Edwin Sandys* 1596–7. Vienna, Siena, and Florence 1596, encountered Francis Davison* (Davison, xxxii, xxiv). Summer 1597 Padua, from where sent newsletter to Sir Robert Cecil (HMC, *Hatfield*, VII, 217; cf. PRO, SP98 1, fol. 116, his letter of November 1596 to Cecil from Siena, in which he says, in connection with supplying intelligence, that the university of Siena is not overly full of knowledge in those things which scholars usually know, let alone those which they usually do not know).

DNB.

CROKE, Richard. c. 1489–1558.
Humanist and diplomat. Eton. King's College, Cambridge, adm. 1506, BA 1510. Oxford where studied Greek. Paris c. 1513 where knew Guillaume Budé. Louvain, Cologne 1510s. Greek lecturer Leipzig 1516. England following year, MA Cambridge, public lecturer in Greek 1518, public orator 1522, fellow of St John's College 1523, DTh following year. Italy with John Stokesley* 1530 to seek opinion on Henry VIII's divorce: Venice, Padua, Vicenza, Bologna, Milan, Ferrara. Oxford from early 1530s to death. Knew Erasmus, Johannes Reuchlin, Ulrich von Hutten.

DNB. Surtz, passim. Katz, 15–48.

CUFFE, Henry. 1563–1601.
Greek professor and servant of the earl of Essex. Son of Robert. Trinity College, Oxford, adm. 1578, Greek scholar aided in his studies by Henry Savile,* BA 1580, fellow 1583, expelled, tutor at Merton College 1586 under

patronage of Savile,* MA 1589, lecturer at Queen's College 1590, Regius Professor of Greek same year, junior proctor. Secretary to earl of Essex. Apparently sent to Paris to read to the earl of Southampton and as an intelligencer in Italy 1597–8; dealings with grand duke of Tuscany in Florence. Assisted on *editio princeps* of Longus's *Pastoral Story of Daphnis and Chloe* (Florence, 1598). Matr. Padua July 1597 (AAU 30, fol. 95). Studied Greek manuscript of Photius with Giovan Vicenzo Pinelli Padua same year (Milan, Biblioteca Ambrosiana, MS Q. 122 sup., fol. 244). Accompanied Essex on Cadiz expedition and to Ireland 1599. Urged him to be bold against his opponents and communicated his plan to Sir Henry Neville,* who had just been recalled from French embassy. Imprisoned in Tower with Essex and executed 1601. In 1607 an editor signing himself R.M. (Roger Manners*?) dedicated to Robert Bertie* Cuffe's *The differences of the ages of man's life* (written 1600, printed London, 1607).

   Andrich, 136. BL, MS Harley 1327, fols 58–9. McConica, *History*, 355–6. Hammer, ' "This bright Shininge Spark," ' 136, 199, 243. Hammer, 'Uses of Scholarship,' passim. *DNB*.

CUTTS, John. D. 1555.

Sheriff of Cambridgeshire and Huntingdonshire 1551. Part of marquis of Northampton's embassy to France same year. Encountered by Thomas Hoby* Padua 1554, probably fleeing privy council charges against him connected with his opposition to Queen Mary. Venice next year, where died of pleurisy.

   Bartlett, *English in Italy*, 202. Hoby, 66, 116, 120.

DANIELS, John.

Intelligencer. Matr. Padua 1597 (AAU 30, fol. 94v). Named c. 1597 as an intelligencer abroad for Sir Robert Cecil (PRO, SP12 265, fol. 207). Possibly brother of poet Samuel Daniel, who was BMus Christ Church, Oxford 1604 and wrote in 1604 *Songs for the Lute, Viol and Voice*. In 1618 he was appointed inspector of the children of the queen's revels, succeeding his brother Samuel, who had been in Italy and had published sonetts about his visit.

   Andrich, 136. *DNB*. *AO*, I, 370. J. Rees, *Samuel Daniel* (Liverpool, 1964), 8. A.B. Grossart, ed., *The Complete Works in Verse and Prose of Samuel Daniel* (London, 1885), I, 71–2.

DARCEY, DARCY? Robert.

Witness to Paduan MDs of Thomas Hearne* and William Harvey* 1602. Probably Sir Robert Darcy of Kent, matr. Magdalen College, Oxford 1597 age 15.

   Rossetti, 'Nel quarto centenario.' *AO*, I, 372. Cf. Venn, I, 10.

DAVISON, Francis. c. 1575–before 1619.
Poet and intelligencer. Son of William. Matr. fellow commoner Emmanuel College, Cambridge 1586. Adm. Gray's Inn 1593, and composed a Gray's Inn masque (the *Masque of Proteus*) performed following year. A client of the earl of Essex. 1595 sent by father to travel, loaned money for the journey by Anthony Bacon. Henry Wotton* advised his father on expenses. Licence to travel from the queen for him and Edward Smyth his tutor (PRO, SO3 1, fol. 528). Germany, Venice, Lucca, Florence 1595–6. Smith considered Italy a place 'where God is dishonoured, true religion abolished, piety contemned, and all horrible and monstrous sins publicly maintained' (Davison, xi). Davison acted as intelligencer in Europe for the earl of Essex, corresponding with Anthony Bacon in this connection (ibid., xii–xiii, xix). In letter to his father from Lucca of November 1596 he describes the 'diverse matters I have to attend to' as 'writing, speaking and reading Italian; desire to frame an indifferent style in English; especially having so often occasion of undergoing so great and curious eyes; reading story, and policy; observing what I hear and see; and, which is the greatest labour, to dispose all of it so as other men may understand of my knowledge, and find that perhaps in half an hour that cost me half a week' (ibid., xxvi). Matr. Padua 1597 (AAU 30, fol. 94v). Also knew in Italy Henry Archer,* Henry Hawkins,* and Peregrine Bertie.* England same year, bringing back with him a large number of political writings. Published *Poetical Rapsody* 1602, much of it written abroad, including 'Ode, being by his absense in Italy deprived of her looks, words and gestures, he desireth her to write unto him' (Davison, 128–30). Between 1605 and 1612 seems to have been preparing a relation of England never written (ibid., xlix–li). Also wrote 'A censure upon Machiavel's Florentine history' (ibid., 384–6).

LPL, MS 654, fols 29, 97, 104, 243; MS 653, fol. 167; MS 658, fols 287, 366–7; MS 660, fols 235–6. BL, MS Hargrave 225, fols 39–40v. Andrich, 136. Venn, II, 17. *DNB*. Hammer, '"This bright Shininge Spark,"' 131. Hammer, 'Essex and Europe,' 364. R. McCoy, 'Lord of Liberty: Francis Davison and the Cult of Elizabeth,' in Guy, *The Reign of Elizabeth I*, 212–28.

DEE, John. 1527–1608.
Mathematician and astrologer. Son of Roland. St John's College, Cambridge, BA 1545, MA 1548. Louvain and Paris 1548–51. Antwerp 1562. Padua same year, where purchased copy of pseudo-Aristotle, *Secretum secretorum*. Venice and Hungary 1563. Further travels 1570s and 1580s. Writer on navigation and geometry. Occult, astrological, and alchemical interests.

J. Roberts and A.G. Watson, *John Dee's Library Catalogue* (London, 1990), 9, 155. *DNB*. P.J. French, *John Dee: The World of an Elizabethan Magus* (London,

1972). W.H. Sherman, *John Dee: The Politics of Reading and Writing in the English Renaissance* (Amherst, MA, 1995).

DENNY, Anthony. D. 1572.
Lawyer. Second son of Sir Anthony Denny (Henry VIII's groom of the stole who had sent his nephew John Denny to study in Venice in 1543 under the care of Edmund Harvel*). Brother of Charles and Henry Denny.* Nephew of Roger and Matthew Carew.* Related to John Ashley.* Pembroke College, Cambridge, matr. 1551. Marian exile encountered Padua 1554 by Thomas Hoby* with his two brothers in the charge of John Tamworth.* Basle following year. Middle Temple 1557.
  Hoby, 116. H.A.C. Sturgess, ed., *Register of Admissions to the Honourable Society of the Middle Temple* (London, 1949), I, 23. Bartlett, *English in Italy*, 260–1. Garrett, 143. See also Francis Walsingham.*

DENNY, Charles.
Youngest son of Sir Anthony Denny. Brother of Anthony* and Henry.* Nephew of Roger and Matthew Carew.* Related to John Ashley.* Encountered by Thomas Hoby* Padua 1554. Basle next year. Possibly a student at Merton College, Oxford late 1550s.
  Bartlett, *English in Italy*, 204. Hoby, 116. See also Francis Walsingham.*

DENNY, Henry. B. 1540.
Lawyer. Eldest son of Sir Anthony Denny. Brother of Anthony* and Henry.* Nephew of Roger and Matthew Carew.* Related to John Ashley.* Pembroke College, Cambridge, matr. 1551. Marian exile encountered Padua 1554 by Thomas Hoby* with his two brothers in the charge of John Tamworth.* A student at Basle from 1555, where met Heinrich Bullinger. *Consiliarius* of English nation Padua 1558. England late 1558 or early 1559 (AAU 10, fols 3v, 17–18). Inner Temple 1562. Joined Francis Walsingham* in France 1572.
  Andrich, 32. Garrett, 144. Hoby, 116. Bartlett, *English in Italy*, 204. W.H. Cooke, ed., *Students admitted to Inner Temple, 1547–1660* (London, 1877), 48. See also Francis Walsingham.*

DRURY, William. D. by 1590.
Jurist. Son of John. Trinity Hall, Cambridge BCL 1553. Encountered by Thomas Hoby* Padua 1554. Regius Professor of Civil Law at Cambridge 1559–61, DCL 1560. Adm. Doctors' Commons as advocate 1561 and advocate of the Arches same year. Secretary to Archbishop Parker same year, Commissary for the Faculties following year. Sympathetic to Catholicism, committed

to Tower in 1570 for religious disobedience. Master of Prerogative Court of Canterbury and vicar-general for Archbishop Grindal 1577. Master Extraordinary in Chancery 1580–4, master in Ordinary 1585–9. Converted to Catholicism on deathbed.

Squibb, 154. Bartlett, *English in Italy*, 204–5. *DNB*. Hoby, 116. Frere, 370. Heward, 81.

DUDGEON, George. D. c. 1552.
Son of William. Precentor of Bath and Wells diocese 1541. Paduan DTh 1550 promoted by Sebastiano di Castello and Iacobo Antonio Marano di Gisono, witnessed by Hugh Turnbull,* Laurence and William Huse,* Nicolaus Alenus,* and Clement Sentlo* (ASP, AN 5026, fol. 314). Doctorate of Dudgeon (and of Turnbull*) reported to royal council in England by Peter Vannes, English agent in Venice, and presence of Sentlo* and of one Herbert (George Herbert*?) noted.

AGA, 1501–50, no. 3888. Turnbull, 148. Horne, VIII, 7.

DUOHOMS? Thomas.
Matr. Padua 1598 (AAU 30, fol. 95).

Andrich, 137.

ENGLEFIELD, Francis. D. c. 1596.
Catholic exile. Son of Thomas. Resisted Protestant injunctions under Edward VI and was imprisoned. Privy councillor and MP under Mary and friend of Cardinal Pole.* Abroad 1559, passing through Louvain, then Padua, where met Parry* brothers. Valladolid 1560s, granted pension by Philip II, attainted 1565. Resident in Spain and Spanish Netherlands.

DNB. Loomie, 14–51.

EURE, Ralph. 1558–1617.
Politician. Son of William, second Lord Eure. St John's College, Cambridge 1568. Gray's Inn 1575. France and Italy 1582–3. Sent an account from Paris of his travels in Italy to Francis Walsingham* in 1583, including Padua (*Cal. SP Dom. Eliz.*, 1580–1625, Addenda, no. 98). MP 1584. Inherited peerage 1604. Member of council in the north 1594–1617, vice president in 1600. Ambassador extraordinary to the king of Denmark and the emperor 1602. President of council in the Marches of Wales 1607–17.

Hasler, II, 92–3.

EVEN, Thomas. See Richard White.*

EVERARD, John. See John Pelham.*

FABER, John. See Edward Maners.*

FANT, Lawrence. c. 1553–91.
Jesuit priest. Son of William. Merton College, Oxford c. 1568. Louvain 1570, Munich 1572. English hospice Rome 1575 where teacher of divinity. Pope sent him to be rector of Jesuit College in Posna in Poland 1581. Encountered with Father Brookes* in Padua 1581 by Arthur Throckmorton,* on journey from Rome to Poland (Canterbury, Canterbury Cathedral Archives, MS U. 85, Box 38, I, fol. 65). Professor of Greek and theology in Poland.
    Gillow, II, 226–7. T.M. McCoog, *Monumenta Angliae* (Rome, 1992), II, 303.

FARR, Henry.
Matr. Padua 1596 (AAU 30, fol. 94v). Probably the Henry Farr, BA 1569 Pembroke Hall, Cambridge, fellow 1570, MA 1573, proctor 1586, a benefactor to the college. His verses on Sir Philip Sidney's* death are in *Academiae Cantabrigiensis lachrymae tumulo nobilissimi equitis D. Philippi Sidneii sacratae per Alexandrum Nevillum* (London, 1587), 16. May also be the Henry Farr who was a servant of Roger Manners.*
    HMC, *Rutland*, IV, 425–7. Andrich, 135. Venn, II, 122.

FAULERIUS, Richard.
Matr. Padua 1596 (AAU 30, fol. 94v).
    Andrich, 136. For possible identifications see *AO*, II, 525.

FAUNT, Nicholas. 1554–1608.
MP and government official. Son of John. Gonville and Caius College, Cambridge, scholar 1572, BA Corpus Christi College, Cambridge 1576. Foreign agent for Francis Walsingham* c. 1578 when sent on a mission to William Davison, ambassador in the Netherlands. Foreign tour 1580–2. 1580–1 Paris where met his lifelong friend Anthony Bacon, who had lent him money for his travels. 1581 Germany and travelled from there with Richard Knightley* to Padua same year, where encountered Arthur Throckmorton* (Canterbury, Canterbury Cathedral Archives, MS U. 85, Box 38, I, fol. 67v), [Richard] Spencer,* 'Tooly' [Paulus Tolius*?], Middleton [Christopher Middleton*?], Richard Brunning,* Randall [Jacobus Randolph*?], Edward Unton,* Kirton* 'with others' (LPL, MS 647, fol. 110), as well as [Edward?] Ratcliffe.*

Venice, Pisa, Geneva, Paris same year. England 1582. MP 1584, probably under Walsingham's* patronage. Paris 1588. Clerk of the signet office 1595. Apparently entered Burghley's service by 1595.

LPL, MS 647, fols 65, 100, 102, 104 , 106, 108–10 , 113–14 , 116 , 119–23. *DNB*. Hasler, II, 109–10. C. Hughes, ed., 'Nicholas Faunt's Discourse Touching the Office of Principal Secretary of Estate etc, 1592,' *English Historical Review* 20 (1905), 499–508.

FINET, John. 1571–1641.
Stuart master of ceremonies. Son of Robert. Grandson of Sienese John Finet. Witness to Edward Benedict's* MD Padua 1601. With William Cecil, Viscount Cranbourne, in Padua again 1610. Diplomatic work for James I, and master of ceremonies for him and Charles I, entertaining foreign envoys and working out diplomatic precedence. Kt 1615. Wrote verses for James I's court and published *The beginning, continuance and decay of estates, written in French by R. de. Lusing, L. of Alymes* (London, 1606); and *Finetti Philoxenis, some choice observations of Sir John Finett, knight, and master of the ceremonies to the two last kings, touching the reception and precedente, the treatment and audience, the puntillios and contests of foreign ambassadors in England* (London, 1656).

A.G.R. Smith, 'The Secretaries of the Cecils, circa 1580–1612,' *English Historical Review* 83 (1968), 481–504. A.J. Loomie, ed., *Ceremonies of Charles I: The Notebooks of John Finet, 1628–41* (New York, 1987). Maladorno Hargraves, 'I Cecil,' 121. *AO*, II, 498. *DNB*.

FISHER, Robert. D. after 1516.
Royal chaplain and friend of Erasmus. Kinsman of Bishop John Fisher. Studied Paris 1497–8 where taught by Erasmus and had various dealings with him subsequently. Italy same year to study law (Erasmus, *Opus epistolarum*, I, no. 118; *CWE*, I, 235–6). Apparently *consiliarius* of English nation Padua 1499 (ASP, AN 1809, fol. 301v). Witness to doctorate of William Rott Ferrara 1500. His *procura* at Padua, drawn up with that of Arthur Coo* and dated 1503, notes his place of residence in the district of Eremitani and describes him and Coo* as scholars of law (ASP, AN 1810, fols 354–5v, 347). Witness to doctoral examination of Jerome Busleyden at Padua same year (and had been witness with him to doctoral examination at Padua of Antonius Bernagian of Breda in 1501). DCnL Bologna 1503 (supplicated for incorporation Oxford 1507). Wrote from Bologna to his friend at Padua Giovanni Pietro da Mantova, a doctor of medicine and the father of Marco Mantova Benavides, 1504; Cuthbert Tunstall* delivered the letter (Venice, Biblioteca Correr, MS Correr 1349, fol. 16). English hospice Rome 1505. Chaplain to Henry VII and present at his funeral, then in service of Henry VIII.

CE, I, 39–40. *AGA, 1501–50*, nos 27, 199. Parks, *English Traveller*, 627, 629. *LP*, II, pt 1, 876.

FITZALAN, Henry. 1511–80.

Son of William. Became twelfth earl of Arundel 1544. In service of Henry VIII 1520s, 1530s. MP 1533. Deputy of Calais 1540–3. Led forces against France 1544. Lord chamberlain same year. Associated with faction of duke of Somerset under Edward VI, imprisoned in Tower on Somerset's fall. Favoured under Mary and Elizabeth. Potential suitor to the latter, alienating her, leading to visit to Padua 1566 with Humphrey Llwyd.* (John Barker* recorded in June 1566 as residing for one month in the Paduan home of Fitzalan* in the district of S. Croce, in an attestation witnessed by Richard Appleby* and Thomas Cooke*: ASP, AN 4852, fol. 398.) Implicated in Northern Rebellion 1569 and Ridolfi plot 1571. Named as a guarantor of John Le Rous* same year. Father-in-law of Lord Lumley and owner of Nonsuch Palace.

DNB.

FITZWILLIAM, FITZWILLIAMS, Roger.

Consiliarius of English nation Padua February 1559 (AAU 10, fol. 20v). Probably the Fitzwilliam who had been a student in Italy who arrived in Paris in August 1559 in the company of Elias Heywood. Possibly the Mr Fitzwilliams listed as a fugitive living abroad, together with Nicholas Wendon* and John Hart* 1575 (PRO, SP12 105, fol. 105).

Andrich, 33. Baskerville, 304.

FITZWILLIAMS, Thomas.

Encountered by Thomas Hoby* at Edmund Harvel's* house Venice 1548 and visited Padua with Thomas Hoby* same year. Encountered by Thomas Hoby* Padua 1554. Permitted to carry arms in Venice 1555 (Venice, Archivio di Stato, Consiglio di X, Parti Communi, Reg. 22, July 1555).

Hoby, 8, 117. Bartlett, *English in Italy*, 205. See also Francis Russell.*

FORTESCUE, Anthony.

BCL, Oxford 1559. *Consiliarius* and *electionarius* of English nation Padua 1561–2, and elected for *ad hoc* duties for the university (AAU 10, fols 148v, 150, 171, 175). Represented English nation to rector 1563 (ibid., fol. 223). *Consiliarius* again for a month 1564 (ibid., fol. 223v). Witness with George Gattacre* to the *procura* of Thomas Parry* 1562. Encountered by Ralph Lacy* at Padua same year or 1561. His own *procura* at Padua, describing him as holding the benefice of Symonsbury in the county of Dorsetshire, witnessed by George Gattacre,* Robert Poyntz,* and Richard White* 1563 (ASP, AN 4851, fol. 53). Witness to the doctoral examination of Claudius Rorarius 1564 (ASP, AN 2333, fol. 72), of John Le Rous* 1571, of Blasius Dalbiar 1576 (ASP, AN 2337, fols 472–4v), of Nicholas Calwoodley* 1597, of William Clement* 1599, and of Thomas Hearne* and William Harvey* 1602.

Andrich, 34–6. Rossetti, 'Nel quarto centenario,' 240–1. *AO*, II, 518.

FOXE, Samuel. 1560–1630.
Son of John. Brother of Simeon.* Magdalen College, Oxford 1575, fellow 1581. Germany, Switzerland, Italy, France 1583–6. Leipzig for one year 1583, six months at Basle 1584, eighteen months in Padua to 1586, where resided in Borgo di Piove and 'by ye Bo in Ca di Madonna Magdalena Tedesca.' Encountered at Padua Mr Griffin [Griffith*? or William Grisinus*?], Richard Willoughby,* Edmund Bruce,* [Christopher?] Middleton,* John Wroth,* William Cecil,* John Cecil (*alias* Snowden),* George Talbot,* Maneringe,* Herson,* Cokk,* Loke,* Martin,* Vere,* William Tedder,* Dr Walker.* England 1586 and tried unsuccessfully to gain the 'lawyer's place' at Magdalen; gained instead the 'physician's place' 1587 (Ralph Winwood* apptd to lawyer's place). Became servant and manorial official of Sir Thomas Heneage. Government agent in Hamburg 1588. MP 1589, 1593.

DNB. AO, II, 527. Hasler, II, 155–6. R. O'Day, *Education and Society, 1500–1800: The Social Foundations of Education in Early Modern Britain* (London, 1982), 91. HMC, *Buccleuch and Queensberry*, I, 25. J.K. McConica, 'Scholars and Commoners in Renaissance Oxford,' in *The University in Society*, ed. L. Stone (Princeton NJ, 1975), I, 175.

FOXE, Simeon. 1568–1642.
Physician. Son of John. Brother of Samuel.* Eton. King's College, Cambridge BA 1587, MA 1591. *Consiliarius* of Scottish nation Padua 1603 (AAU 15, fols 8v–9v, 11). Witness to MDs at Padua of Thomas Hearne* and William Harvey* 1602. Padua and Venice to 1604, when operating as an intelligencer for English goverment. MD Padua c. 1604. College of Physicians of London, examined and approved as a doctor of Padua June and July 1605, adm. candidate 1605, fellow 1608, censor 1614, registrar 1629, treasurer 1629. Ministered to countess of Rutland 1612. Probably author of a biography of his father.

DNB. Andrich, 102. Rossetti, 'Membri,' 182. Munk, I, 147–8. London, Royal College of Physicians, MS 307 (Baldwin Hamey's *Bustorum aliquot reliquiae*), no. 40. HMC, *Hatfield*, XVI, 356–7. PRO SP98 1, fol. 55, SP99 2, passim. J. Ward, *The Lives of the Professors of Gresham College* (London 1740), 266. See also Thomas Wilson.*

FREAR, FRIAR, John. B. c. 1574.
Physician. Son of Thomas Friar.* Matr. Padua 1595 (AAU 30, fol. 94, same day as John Stackvoaellus,* John Gibson,* Robert Shirley,* and Robert Baosony*). *Consiliarius* of Scottish nation 1604. Paduan MD 1610 (had studied philosophy and medicine at Padua continuously for five years), promoted by Fabricius ab Acquapendente, Eustachio Rudio, Alessandro Vigonza, Cesare Cremonini, Nicolò Trevisan, Antonio Negro, Annibale Bimbiolo, Benedetto Selvatico, Tarquinio Carpeneto, and Prospero Alpino, witnessed by Thomas Turner, John Hawkins, Richard Willoughby,* and Francis Willoughby. Physician of Venetian ambassador in England Antonio Foscarini c. 1612–14. Examined, approved and adm. candidate of College of Physicians of London 1613 (London, Royal College of Physicians, Annals of the College of Physicians of London 2, fols 9–10).
   Andrich, 135. Rossetti, *Stemmi*, 203, no. 956. Cf. HMC, *Hatfield*, XXIV, 147. Maladorno Hargraves, 'Diplomi dottorali,' 169–77.

FRIAR, John. D. 1561.
Humanist and physician. Father of Thomas.* Eton. King's College, Cambridge, adm. 1517, BA 1521, MA 1525. Poached by Wolsey for his Oxford foundation same year, where accused of heresy. Client of Edward Foxe. Padua by 1533 when witness to MD of Thomas Bill* and described as scholar of arts and medicine. A friend of Thomas Starkey* and knew Henry Coles,* Reginald Pole,* and Richard Morison.* MD Padua 1536, promoted by Benedicto Faventino, Ludovico Carensio, Hieronymo de Urbino, Hieronymo Tolentino, Odo de Odis, Francesco Frigimelica, and Hieronimo Coradino. Physician of Sir Thomas Wriothesley 1545 and MP same year. Adm. fellow of College of Physicians of London 1536, held various offices, president 1549–50. Part of a humanistic circle at Cambridge in 1550 which included John Cheke,* Thomas Wilson,* Anthony Cooke,* and William Malim.* Imprisoned for religion under Elizabeth and died of plague shortly after his release. Wrote *Hippocratis Coi Aphorismi versibus scripti* (London, 1567).
   AGA, 1501–50, nos 2216, 2220. S. Brigden, 'Henry Howard, Earl of Surrey, and the "Conjured League,"' *The Historical Journal* 37 (1994), 535–6. J.W. Binns, *Intellectual Culture in Elizabethan and Jacobean England* (Leeds, 1990), 719. Munk, I, 31–2. PRO, SP1 47, fol. 52; SP1 102, fol. 141. *LP*, IX, nos 917, 1011.

FRIAR, Thomas. D. 1623.
Physician. Son of John.* Possibly a relative of John Froso.* BA, MA Cambridge, and also studied in Oxford. Granted prebendary of Erthamme in 1557 by Archbishop Pole* (LPL, Register of Archbishop Pole, fols 12v–13). Granted

licence by Lord Burghley to study medicine in Padua, and wrote him news reports from there (HMC, *Hatfield*, XVIII, 400–1). MD Padua 1570, promoted by Aloysius Bellacato, Paulo Crasso, Bernadino Trevisano, Bernardino Tomitano, Bernardino Paterno, Hieronymo Merculiale, Hieronymo Capodivacce, Angelo Balasio, and Alberto Bottono (AAU 333, fol. 61). Returned to England via Spain. Member of College of Physicians 1572, elect 1603 (London, Royal College of Physicians, Annals of the College of Physicians of London 2, fol. 173v), *consiliarius* 1608 (ibid., fol. 202). A Catholic recusant protected by the Cecils.

Rossetti, 'Membri,' 181. Hutter, 'Cardinal Pole's Greek MSS in Oxford,' 111.

FROSO, FREAR? FRYER? John.

Failed candidate for disputed election for English *consiliarius* at Padua August 1586 (AAU 13, fols 112v–13). Possibly the John Frear or Fryer, native of Godmanchester, Huntingdon, who acquired MD Cambridge 1555 and stayed in Padua after 1564 for religious reasons. Possibly a relative of Thomas Friar.*

Andrich, 42. Maladorno Hargraves, 'I Diplomi dottorali,' 170. Venn, II, 183.

FYNEUX, William. D. 1557.

Marian exile. Son of Sir John. Named in John Brett's commission to recall those refugees on the continent absent without licence, where said to have left Padua for England in 1556.

Bartlett, *English in Italy*, 206. Garrett, 159.

GALE, John.

Traveller. Reported in 1592 to have been in Padua briefly in 1591. Possibly the John Gale matr. pensioner Christ's College, Cambridge 1582.

Cal. SP Dom. Eliz., 1591, 224, no. 29. Venn, II, 188.

GARDINER, John? D. by 1594.

Advocate. *Consiliarius* of English nation Padua 1566–7 (AAU, 11, fol. 120v, where 'Gardenerius' is followed by a series of dots). Probably the Dr John Gardiner, DCL, of Trinity Hall, Cambridge, adm. advocate of the Arches 1585 and Doctors' Commons same year.

LPL, Register of Archbishop Whitgift, fol. 113. Andrich, 37. Squibb, 164.

GATTACRE, George. D. c. 1619.

Law student. Son of William. Probably brother of Thomas Gataker, chaplain to earl of Leicester. Fellow of New College, Oxford 1548–64, BCL 1556. *Consiliarius* of English nation Padua 1562 (AAU 10, fols 187v–8v). Witness to *procura* of

Thomas Parry* and Anthony Fortescue* Padua same year. Tutor with Robert
Poyntz* of Anthony Mason* and also knew Jerome Sapcot* and Robert Peck-
ham* there, as well as Richard White,* who described him as 'jurisperitus.'
  White, 109, 127. Venn, II, 199. *AO*, II, 552.

GENISTON, Thomas.
Witness to *procura* of George Acworth* Padua 1558.
  ASP, AN 4849, fols 643v–5.

GIBSON, John. 1576–1639.
MP and lawyer. Son of civilian Sir John, who bequeathed his law books to
him 1613. Gray's Inn 1594. Matr. Padua 1595 (AAU 30, fol. 94, same day as
John Stackvoaellus,* Robert Shirley,* Robert Baosony,* and John Frear*). JP
Yorks 1605–39. Member of council in the north 1616–39. Kt 1607. MP 1621.
Travelled abroad again 1616, 1624.
  Andrich, 135. Levack, *The Civil Lawyers*, 232–3. History of Parliament draft
biography.

GIFFORD, George. B. c. 1561.
Seminary priest. Younger brother of Gilbert. Pont-à-Mousson and Rheims
early 1580s. Adm. English College Rome as a student of theology 1584,
entered minor orders, but left 1585 due to ill health. Noted as with
Christopher Bagshaw* in Padua same year, then returned to Rheims.
  Kelly, 52. Renold, *Letters*, 144–7.

GODOLPHIN, William. c. 1565–1613.
MP. Son of Sir Francis. Brother-in-law of George Carew.* Relative of John
Coke.* Matr. fellow commoner Emmanuel College, Cambridge 1585. Lincoln's
Inn 1587. Abroad from 1591. Germany, Italy, Padua 1593. Matr. Padua June
1593 (AAU 30, fol. 93v, same day as Henry Scrope*). Lieutenant-governor
Scilly Isles 1597 and governor 1608–13. Kt 1599, MP 1605.
  Venn, II, 228. Andrich, 133. Wernham, IV (1593–4), 461, no. 628.

GOLDWELL, Thomas. c. 1500–85.
Bishop of St Asaph and chaplain of Reginald Pole.* Oxford BA 1528, MA
1531, BTh 1534. Possibly the Goldwell of Canterbury College, Oxford, ques-
tioned in early 1530s concerning books written in defence of Catherine of
Aragon. Padua 1532. Matr. at Louvain 1536, Heidelberg and Ingoldstadt
following year, Padua 1538 with Pole,* joined his household same year and
was attainted with him 1539. Rome 1538. England with Pole* on accession of

Mary. Apptd bishop of St Asaph 1555. Active in the reintroduction of Catholicism and in the examination of heretics. Returned to Rome on accession of Elizabeth. *Custos* of English hospice Rome from 1560. Participated in Council of Trent 1561. Apptd master of English College Rome. Attainted in England for participation in Catholic plots.

Dowling, 161. PRO, SP1 131, fols 171–2. *EH*, passim. *BRUO*, 239–40. See also Arthur Hall.*

GOMUND, James.

Medical student. Of Kenchester, Hertfordshire. Matr. Padua 1598 (AAU 30, fol. 95, and appears in matriculation register of German artists' nation 1599, where described as a lover of the art of medicine). Probably the James Gomund, the son of John, who appears in a list of suspected Catholics of 1574.

Andrich, 137. Whitteridge, 39. Rossetti, *Matricula*, 115, no. 966. J. Bannerman Wainwright, ed., 'Two Lists of Supposed Adherents of Mary Queen of Scots, 1574 and 1582,' Catholic Record Society Publications, *Miscellanea* VIII (London, 1913), 115.

GRATTEY, GRATEY? Edward?

One Grattey was reported to be held by Inquisition in Padua 1588. Probably the Edward Gratey adm. to English College Rome 1579.

R. Lemon, ed., *Calendar of State Papers, Domestic Series, of the Reigns of Edward VI, Mary, Elizabeth, 1547–80* (London, 1856), vol. ccxiv, no. 35 (August 5, 1588). Kelly, 9.

GRAY, Henry.

Matr. Padua 1596 (AAU 30, fol. 94v, same day as Thomas Chard*). *Consiliarius* of English nation 1597 (AAU 15, fol. 1v). Probably brother of John Gray.*

Andrich, 45, 136. Cf. Hasler, II, 222.

GRAY, John. c. 1570–1611.

MP. Son of Sir Henry, Baron Gray of Groby. Probably brother of Henry.* Lincoln's Inn 1589, Gray's Inn 1593. Matr. Padua 1593 (AAU 30, fol. 93v). Kt 1596. MP 1601, 1610. Sat on parliamentary committees. Gentleman of privy chamber 1603. Embassy to Brussels 1605.

Andrich, 134. Hasler, II, 223–4. History of Parliament draft biography.

GRAY, GREY, Thomas. D. 1614.

Son of Arthur, Baron Gray of Wilton. Inherited barony 1593. Matr. Padua 1594 (AAU 30, fol. 94). Mentioned in letter of Edward Smith to William Davison of February 1596 from Venice as agreeing with him about the immorality and impiety of Italy (Davison, xii). Also knew in Italy John Coke.* Vienna same year (Birch, I, 428). Military activities c. 1597–8. Accompanied Essex to Ireland 1599. Service in Flanders 1600. Associated with Sir Robert Cecil, helped suppress Essex rebellion in 1601, and sat on commission which tried Essex and Southampton. 1602 Low Countries. Implicated in Bye plot 1603.

Oxford, Bodleian Library, MS Carte 205, fols 67–83. Cf. M. Nicholls, 'Sir Walter Ralegh's Treason: A Prosecution Document,' *English Historical Review* 110 (1995), 902–24, and 'Two Winchester Trials: The Prosecution of Henry Brooke, Lord Cobham, and Thomas Lord Grey of Wilton, 1603,' *Historical Research* 63 (1995), 26–48. Andrich, 135. *DNB*.

GREEN, William.
Letter from William Green at Padua was sent to 'Mr Atey' and dated September 23 1580 (Lemon, 677, no. 26). Probably the William Green who was adm. fellow commoner Gonville and Caius College, Cambridge 1564, who belonged to a circle of Catholic students there, and who was named as a recusant in 1578.

Venn, II, 258. J. Venn and J.A. Venn, *Admissions to Gonville and Caius College, Cambridge* (London, 1887), under Nicholas Cobbe, 1564. O'Day, 94. Cf. Hasler, II, 213–14.

GRIFFITH, __.
A Mr Griffith was reported as being at Padua 1579 (Lemon, 633, no. 10). Possibly Hugh Griffin or his brother, whose name is not known, both of whom were involved in the affairs of English Catholic exiles in Rome in the late 1570s and elsewhere in Europe in the early 1580s. Possibly the 'Mr Griffin' encountered by Samuel Foxe* in Padua c. 1585.

Renold, *Letters*, 15, 17, 20–1. Cf. Hasler, II, 226–8.

GRISINUS, William.
Consiliarius of English nation 1589–90 (AAU 14, fol. 1v). Possibly the 'Mr Griffin' encountered by Samuel Foxe* in Padua c. 1585 (cf. Griffith*).

Andrich, 42. For possible identifications see Venn, II, 266; *AO*, II, 613; Hasler, II, 228.

GUIARD, Marinus.
Matr. Padua April 1593 (AAU 30, fol. 93) where described as 'Anglus.' Andrich, 133.

GUIDONUS ANGLICUS.
Lecturer in law university of Padua, 1519 (AAU 652, fol. 27v).

GULIELMUS ANGLICUS.
Lecturer in law university of Padua, 1520 (AAU 652, fol. 35v).

GUYLFORDE, Richard. c. 1455–1506.
Master of the Ordinance. Padua 1506, on pilgrimage to Jerusalem, where died.
Bartlett, *English in Italy*, 8. *DNB.*

HALL, Arthur. 1539–1605.
Translator and MP. Son of Francis. Ward of Sir William Cecil. St John's College, Cambridge. Possibly Gray's Inn adm. 1556. Travels in France, Italy, Spain, Germany, Constantinople 1567–9. Italy 1568: Venice, Ferrara, Pesaro, Rome (where treated kindly by Thomas Goldwell* at the English hospice, but denounced by other English residents), Naples, Rome, Siena, Florence, Bologna, Ferrara, Padua (where noted the tomb of Antenor), Venice (from where detailed his travels in a letter to Sir William Cecil printed in H.G. Wright, *The Life and Works of Arthur Hall of Grantham*, Manchester, 1919, 180–4). MP 1571, 1572, 1584. Translated Homer's *Iliad* into English (London, 1581). Author of *A letter sent by F. A.* (London, c. 1579); *A Hungaryous History* (c. 1586, no longer extant); and unpublished treatises on commercial and economic matters.
DNB. Hasler, II, 240–2.

HAMBEY, John.
Consiliarius and *electionarius* of English nation Padua 1557–8. England before November 1560, when licensed to go abroad 'for the increase of his study in the civil lawes and knowledge in languages.'
Garrett, 174. *Calendar of the Patent Rolls Preserved in the Public Record Office: Elizabeth, I, 1558–60* (London, 1939), 415.

HANDFORD, John. See Thomas Hoby.*

HARINGTON, Perceval?
Student. Brother of Robert.* Said by Thomas Randolph to have been in Padua 1558 with his brother where their tutor was a 'Mr Noel,'* who had taught them in France and 'professed the mathematicalls.' The Haringtons were signatories of the 'new discipline' in Frankfurt in 1557.
Garrett, 177. *Cal. SP For. Eliz.*, 1558–9, no. 68.

HARINGTON, Robert? See Perceval Harington.*

HART, John.
Law student. Son of William. Paduan DCnCL 1574, witnessed by Philip Sidney,* Nicolas Wendon,* Vito(?) Vasell(?),* Rudolph Hopton,* Richard Valiseso(?),* Griffin Maddox,* and Jacobus Randolph,* promoted by Georgio Gregelio (ASP, AN 5007, fols 26–7v). Listed as a fugitive living abroad in 1575, together with Nicholas Wendon* and [Roger?] Fitzwilliams* (PRO, SP12 105, fol. 105). Possibly the London proctor whose daughter Sarah married Richard Zouche, advocate, and whose son Richard entered Doctors' Commons in 1629, or the Catholic missionary active in Douai in the 1570s, who was arrested in England in 1581 and supplied evidence on Catholic recusants to Francis Walsingham.* This John Hart remained in prison in England until 1585, becoming a Jesuit there 1583. Verdun and Rome 1585, died Poland 1586.

Squibb, 171, 174. Read, II, 321. Gillow, III, 153–5. For other possibilities see Venn, II, 319.

HARVEL, Edmund. D. 1550.
Merchant resident in Venice and English ambassador to Venice. First documented in Venice 1524 when corresponded with Niccolò Leonico Tomeo as a friend of Reginald Pole* and Thomas Lupset* (BAV, MS Rossiano 997, fols 46–7). Subsequently visited Leonico Padua 1529 (ibid., fol. 27). Acted as agent for Richard Croke* Venice 1530 (LP, IV, nos 6192, 6491, 6540, 6595, 6607, 6694, 6696, 6670, 6786). Also a friend of Richard Morison,* Thomas Theobald,* and Thomas Starkey,* with whom he continued a correspondence after Starkey's* departure from Italy (LP, V, no. 301; VIII, nos 511, 535, 579, 874; IX, nos 1025, 1029; X, nos 223, 803, 970); and Thomas Winter,* who helped him advance into Thomas Cromwell's service c. 1535 (LP, VIII, nos 373, 511). Host to Pole's* household in Venice same year (LP, IX, no. 512), and host to a number of other Englishmen resident in Venice including Thomas Fitzwilliams* 1548. Permitted to carry arms in Venice with thirteen members of his household (including four Englishmen) 1542 (Venice, Archivio di Stato, Consiglio di X, Parti Communi, Reg. 15). Protestant sympathies. Married daughter of German merchant Venice 1537. Apptd English accredited agent to Venice, then English ambassador to Venice from late 1530s (cf. Venice, Archivio di Stato, Senato Terra 34, p. 62). Involved in the arrest of William Thomas* Venice 1546.

LP, IV, nos 2244, 6620; X, no. 945; XIII, no. 507; XIV, pt 2, no. 768; XV, Appendix, no. 2; XVII, nos 840–1. Cal. Ven., V, nos 282, 354. BAV, MS Rossiano 997, fol. 54. Bell, Handlist, 289. H.F. Brown, 'The Marriage Contract, Inventory and Funeral Expenses of Edmund Harvel,' English Historical Review 20

(1905), 70–7. Mayer, *Thomas Starkey*, passim. See also Anthony Denny* and
Thomas Hoby.*

HARVEY, William. 1578–1657.
Physician and discoverer of the circulation of the blood. Son of Thomas.
King's College, Canterbury 1588. Adm. pensioner Gonville and Caius College,
Cambridge 1593, BA 1597. *Consiliarius* of English nation Padua intermittently
1600–3 (AAU 15, passim). Witness to MD of Edward Benedict* Padua 1601,
and of Thomas Hearne* 1602. Doctorate in philosophy and medicine April
1602, witnessed by Anthony Fortescue,* Richard Willoughby,* Matthew
Lister,* Peter Mounsel,* Simeon Foxe,* and Robert Darcey,* awarded by the
count palatine Sigismondo Capodilista. Elected candidate of College of
Physicians of London 1604, fellow 1607, Lumleian lecturer 1615–56, elect
1627, treasurer 1628 (London, Royal College of Physicians, Annals of the
College of Physicians of London 2, fols 129, 174, 176, 177, 193v, 194; 3, fols C,
76, 86v). Apptd with William Clement* 1620 to watch the surgeons' campaign
in parliament. Physician at St Bartholomew's Hospital London from 1609.
Royal physician from 1618. Wrote *De motu cordis* (Frankfurt, 1628); *De
circulatione sanguinis* (Cambridge, 1649); *De generatione animalium* (London,
1653). His anatomy lectures of 1616 are *Prelectiones anatomiae universalis*
(London, 1886).
   Andrich, 46. Rossetti, *Stemmi*, 164, 181, nos 736, 841. Rossetti, 'Nel quarto
centenario,' 239–43. *DNB*.

HASTINGS, John. See Thomas Hoby.*

HATTON, William. c. 1565–97.
Son of Sir Christopher. Educated Oxford. Paris early 1580s with Anthony
Ashley. Reported to be in Padua 1584 'pursuing his exercises and studying
bonnes lettres' by Arthur de Champernon in his letter to Francis Walsing-
ham* from Padua of that year. Kt 1586. MP same year and 1589. Married
Elizabeth, daughter of Thomas Cecil. A friend of Henry Unton,* with whom
he went to the Netherlands 1586 and fought at Zutphen.
   AO, II, 673; III, 1064. Hasler, II, 279–80.

HAWKINS, Henry. D. 1646.
Civilian and intelligencer. Son of John. Matr. pensioner Peterhouse, Cam-
bridge 1568, BA 1571–2, MA 1575, fellow 1575–9, proctor 1583–4, DCL 1591.
Adm. Gray's Inn 1584. Abroad with Lord Zouche* 1587, matr. Basle same
year, Prague 1589. Apparently studied civil law in Heidelburg, Altdorf, Pavia,
Bologna, Pisa, and Padua, where taught by Guido Panciroli. Warrant Doctors'

Commons 1591 but not fully admitted. Intelligence agent for earl of Essex in Venice 1590s, in contact with many English travellers to the Veneto, including Peregrine Bertie,* Francis Davison,* Edmund Bruce,* and Richard Willough-by.* Travelled to Padua July 1596 to help draw up will of Roger Manners,* who was seriously ill there. Manners* was recovering by the time Hawkins arrived (Birch, II, 59). Implicated in Essex rebellion.

Le Neve, III, 620. Wackernagel, II, 357. Levack, *The Civil Lawyers*, 237. Hammer, 'Uses of Scholarship,' 36–7. Hammer, 'Essex and Europe,' 361–4. See also Sir Griffin Markham.*

HEARNE, HERON, Thomas. B. c. 1574.
Brasenose College, Oxford matr. 1593, BA 1594–5, MA 1598. Archbishop Whitgift applied on his behalf for a licence for him to travel to Padua 1601 (HMC, *Hatfield*, XI, 146). MD Padua 1602, witnessed by Robert Darcey,* Anthony Fortescue,* Simeon Foxe,* Peter Mounsel,* Edward Silliard,* and Richard Willoughby.* Failed oral examination for admission to College of Physicians of London 1602 (London, Royal College of Physicians, Annals of the College of Physicians of London 2, fol. 165v). Formally admitted for a candidateship 1604 (ibid., fol. 175), fellow 1606 (ibid., fol. 190v).

Rossetti, 'Membri,' 181. *AO*, II, 685. Munk, I, 123. Rossetti, 'Nel quarto centenario.'

HERBERT (*alias* THOMSSEN), George.
Catholic exile. Native of Dorchester, apparently in service of Matthew Arundel until reign of Elizabeth, when left England for fear of persecution of Catholics. Visited various countries, pensionary of Philip II in 1590s, arrested in Middelburg 1595 on suspicion of plotting against English government with other English Catholic exiles. Claimed to have learned his Italian at Padua, having lived there for a year and a half at the age of eight or nine (i.e., late 1540s; cf. George Dudgeon*).

HMC, *Hatfield*, V, 225–6. Turnbull, 148. Loomie, 251.

HERSON, __.
Dined with Arthur Throckmorton* Venice 1581 (Canterbury, Canterbury Cathedral Archives, MS U. 85, Box 38, I, fol. 65). Encountered by Samuel Foxe* Padua c. 1585.

BL, MS Lansdowne 679, fols 44–5.

HOBY, Philip. c. 1504–58.
Diplomat and traveller. Son of William. Brother of Thomas.* Ambassador to Spain and Portugal and gentleman of the king's chamber under Henry VIII.

Imprisoned in Tower 1543 for Protestant views. Military service France c. 1544. MP 1547, envoy to Charles V next year. Privy councillor and master of the ordinance in the north 1552. Member of commission set up to assist masters of the Court of Requests same year. Ambassador to Charles V with Sir Richard Morison* next year. Received permission to travel abroad for health 1554. Brussels then Padua same year with his brother Thomas.* Shared house there with Wiliam Thomas,* Thomas Wrothe,* John Cheke,* Anthony Cooke.* All visited Mantua same year, then Caldiero and Venice 1555. Knew in Italy Titian and Pietro Aretino. Frankfurt with Thomas Hoby* same year, Wesel where encountered Richard Bertie,* Brussels where saw Edward Courtenay.* England 1556.

Bartlett, *English in Italy*, 269–71. *DNB*. Hoby, 116–26. Leadam, xci. T. Landoni, ed., *Lettere scritte a Pietro Aretino* (Bologna, 1873), I, 244.

HOBY, Thomas. 1530–66.

Traveller, diarist, and translator of Castiglione. Son of William. Brother of Sir Philip.* St John's College, Cambridge, matr. 1545, where was a friend of Roger Ascham and John Cheke.* Strasbourg 1547, where studied under Martin Bucer, resided at imperial court at Augsburg where brother was ambassador. Italy 1548. Resided with Edmund Harvel* at Venice same year, then moved to Padua where encountered Thomas Wyatt,* John Cotton,* Francis and Henry Williams,* John Arundle,* John Hastings,* Christopher Alen,* John Schiere,* John Handford,* 'and dyverse other' (cf. Venice, Archivio di Stato, Capi del Consiglio di X, Lettere di Rettori e di altre cariche: Padova, 1542–57, Busta no. 82). Studied Italian there and attended lectures of Lazzaro Bonamico. Gives an account of the university in journal, partly drawn from Leandro Alberti's *Descrittione di tutta l'Italia*. Left Padua with Henry Killigrew* and Edward Murphin* following year, then extensive travels in Italy, including visit to Rome with William Barker* and to Siena with Francis Peto.* England 1551. In service of marquis of Northampton, commenced translation of Castiglione's *Libro del Cortegiano* 1553, printed 1561 with a prefatory letter from Cheke.* Marian exile with his brother, arriving in Padua 1554, where encountered Thomas Wrothe,* John Cheke,* Henry Neville,* John Cutts,* Richard Bertie,* John Tamworth,* the three Denny* brothers, Henry Cornwallis,* John Ashley,* William Drury,* Henry Kingsmill,* Thomas Wyndham,* Thomas Fitzwilliams,* Anthony Cooke,* John Brooke,* John Orphinstrange,* Roger and Mathew Carew* 'and dyverse other.' With his brother, John Cheke,* Francis Russell,* and Thomas Wrothe,* he visited Frankfurt, Wesel, and Brussels next year. England 1556. Married Elizabeth, daughter of Sir Anthony Cooke* 1557. Apptd ambassador to France, kt 1566. An official of the Court of Requests.

Bartlett, *English in Italy*, 272–3. Leadam, cix. Hoby, esp. 8–11. Chaney, 4–7. *DNB*. P. Compton, *The Story of Bisham Abbey* (Bath, 1979), 57–88.

HOPTON, Rudolph.
Witness to Paduan DCnCL of John Hart* 1574 (ASP, AN 5007, fols 26–7v). See also Edward de Vere.*

HUSE, HUSSEY, Laurence.
Advocate. Son of Anthony (the patron of Hugh Turnbull*). Brother of William.* Tutored at Padua by Hugh Turnbull* and sent letter there by Roger Ascham (Ascham, *Epistolarum libri*, 278). Witness to doctoral examinations in theology at Padua of Hugh Turnbull* and George Dudgeon* 1550. DCL Bologna, incorp. Oxford. Advocate of the Arches, apptd 1556 (PRO, SP12 109, fol. 88; LPL, Register of Archbishop Pole, fol. 22). Member of Doctors' Commons same year. Master in Chancery 1560–1602, accused of accepting fees contrary to the rules (Heward, 41).
Squibb, 153. *AGA, 1501–50*, nos 3881, 3888 transcribes 'Hiusius' as 'Licusius.' The notary clearly had difficulties since in no. 3881 an illegible word, presumably his first attempt at the surname, has been crossed out and is followed by 'Hiusius.'

HUSE, HUSSEY, William.
Son of Anthony (the patron of Hugh Turnbull*). Brother of Laurence.* Tutored at Padua by Hugh Turnbull* and sent letter there by Roger Ascham (Ascham, *Epistolarum libri*, 278). *Consiliarius* of the English nation 1551–2, pressurized by bedel to purchase a copy of the newly printed university statutes (AAU 6, fols 162v, 178, 182, 190). Witness to DTh of George Dudgeon* 1550.
Andrich, 30. *AGA, 1501–50*, nos 3881, 3888. See also Laurence Huse.*

HYDE, Henry. c. 1563–1634.
MP. Son of Lawrence. Father of Edward Hyde, earl of Clarendon. Matr. Magdalen College, Oxford 1579, BA 1581, MA 1584. Middle Temple 1585. Abroad 1590 to 1594: Spa, Germany, Italy, Florence, Siena, Rome, where favoured by Cardinal Allen, though other English priests objected to this (*Life of Edward, Earl of Clarendon*, Oxford, 1827, I, 3–6). Matr. Padua 1594 (AAU 30, fol. 93v). MP 1588–9, 1601.
Andrich, 134. Hasler, II, 261. *AO*, II, 781.

JEWEL, John. 1522–71.
Bishop of Salisbury. Son of John of Baden. Merton College, Oxford adm. 1535, scholar of Corpus Christi College, Oxford 1539, BA 1540, fellow 1542,

MA 1545, college prelector in humanity and rhetoric. Marian exile mainly in Frankfurt and Zurich from 1555. A student in Padua 1556, where lived with Scipione Biondi. Returned to England by 1559. Made use of the works of Venetian historian Marc Antonio Sabellico in his *Apology of the Church of England.*

Garrett, 198–9. *DNB.* Chavasse, 336.

JORDAN, JORDEN, Edward. 1569–1632.
Physician. Probably student of Hart Hall, Oxford. Matr. Basle as student of medicine 1588. MD at Padua c. 1591. Granted verbal authority to practise medicine by the College of Physicians of London 1595 provided he read Galen's *De temperamentis, De elementis [ex Hippocrate], De [naturalibus] facultatibus, De [causis] morborum, De symptomatum causis, De symptomatum differentiis,* and *De locis affectis;* reexamined same year and licensed to practise (London, Royal College of Physicians, Annals of the College of Physicians of London 2, fols 112, 114v). Fellow of college 1597 (ibid., fol. 129v). Wrote *A brief discourse of a disease called the suffocation of the mother,* 1603 (which notes, sig. A3, that he once witnessed, in the Santo in Padua, people allegedly possessed by the devil and calmed by the sign of the cross of the preacher). Also wrote *A discourse of natural baths and mineral waters* (London, 1631).

Wackernagel, II, 360. Rossetti, 'Membri,' 181. *AO,* II, 833. Munk, I, 113.

JOSSELYN, Francis.
Son of Henry. Matr. pensioner Jesus College, Cambridge c. 1592. Adm. Middle Temple 1595. Witness to MD of Edward Benedict* Padua 1601.

Rossetti, 'Nel quarto centenario.' Venn, I, 490.

KAYH, KEYE? Robert.
Matr. Padua 1596 (AAU 30, fol. 94v). Probably the Robert Keye who was a sizar at Corpus Christi College, Cambridge 1589, BA 1593–4 and ordained deacon of Norwich.

Andrich, 136. Venn, III, 13.

KILLIGREW, Henry. c. 1528–1603.
Protestant conspirator, Marian exile, and diplomat. Son of John. Possibly educated Cambridge. Joined household of John Dudley 1545, possibly guardian of Charles Brandon. Padua 1549 where encountered by Thomas Hoby,* with whom he travelled for a time in Italy together with Edward Murphin.* Agent for Dudley in Italy 1546, attempted to convince Edward Courtenay* at Ferrara to come to France and join rebellion. Further political

travels in following two years in Germany and France. MP 1552, 1572. Envoy
to Protestant princes of Germany under Elizabeth, secretary to English
ambassador at Paris, then ambassador himself. Missions to Scotland and Low
Countries. Teller of the Exchequer 1561–99. Kt 1591. Married Catherine,
daughter of Anthony Cooke.*

   Bartlett, *English in Italy*, 209–10. Hoby, 11. A.C. Miller, *Sir Henry Killigrew,
Elizabethan Soldier and Diplomat* (Leicester, 1963). Hasler, II, 394–5. *DNB*. See
also George Cranmer* and Henry Neville.*

KINGSMILL, Henry. c. 1534–c. 1577.
Marian exile. Son of Sir John. Studied civil law. Shared house with Thomas
Hoby* Paris 1552. Encountered by Thomas Hoby* Padua 1554. Joined household of Francis Russell* in Venice following year. Member of royal household
in 1560. MP 1563.

   Bartlett, *English in Italy*, 210–11. Hoby, 116. Hasler, II, 399. R.H. Fritze, '"A
rare example of godlyness amongst genetlemen": The Role of the Kingsmill
and Gifford Families in Promoting the Reformation in Hampshire,' in *Protestantism and the National Church in Sixteenth-Century England*, ed. P. Lake and
M. Dowling (London, 1987), 150. Baker, *Reports*, 371. J.K. McConica and C.S.
Knighton, 'Some Sixteenth-Century Corpus Families: Kingsmills, Nappers,
Lancasters and Others,' *The Pelican* (1978–9), 6–7.

KIRTON, Thomas?
The 'Kirton' encountered by Nicholas Faunt* Padua 1581 was possibly
Thomas Kirton, resident in English hospice in Rome c. 1563–70 (*EH*, 224–5,
227, 270–1).

   LPL, MS 647, fol. 110.

KNIGHTLEY, Richard.
Travelled with Nicholas Faunt* from Germany to Padua 1581. Probably a
member of the Knightley family of Northamptonshire.

   LPL, MS 647, fol. 110.

KNIVET, Reginald. See John Le Rous.*

KNOLLES, Henry. c. 1521–83.
Son of Robert. Brother of Francis. Travelled with John Champernowne and
Peter Carew to Venice 1540. Champernowne and Carew sailed on to
Constantinople while Knolles remained in Venice. Friend of John Caius* in
Padua same year. Contributor of eulogies to Thomas Wilson's* *Vita et obitus*

duorum fratrum Suffolciensium Henrici et Caroli Brandoni (London, 1551). Frankfurt late 1550s. Diplomatic mission 1562. MP 1563, 1572, active on parliamentary committees.

J. Vowell, 'The Life of Peter Carew,' *Archaeologia* 28 (1840), 103. Hasler, II, 414–15.

KNYVETAN, KNIVETON? Syneloroe?
Matr. Padua 1593 (AAU 30, fol. 93v).
Andrich, 134.

LACY, Ralph.
Elizabethan Catholic. Suspected of conspiring against the government 1562 and described journey to Europe same year or year before. At Padua met 'young Mr Parry'* and 'Mr Foskewe' (Fortescue*).
Cal. SP For. Eliz., 1562, no. 203.

LANE, John. 1542–78.
Jesuit. Corpus Christi College, Oxford 1565, fellow 1568, BA same year, MA 1572. Travelled partly with Robert Persons* to Padua 1574 to study law. Followed Persons* to Rome following year where became Jesuit. Alcalà 1578 where died.
McCoog, II, 387. Pollen, 23–5. *AO*, 874.

LANGTON, Robert. D. 1524.
Pilgrim. Queen's College, Oxford, DCL 1501 and benefactor of the college. Various benefices. A pilgrim to Compostella, visiting Venice and Padua on journey.
DNB. E.M. Blackie, ed., *The Pilgrimage of Robert Langton* (Cambridge, 1924), 29.

LATIMER, William. c. 1460–c. 1545.
Humanist. Fellow of All Souls College, Oxford, 1489, vac. by 1497, when arrived in Padua, and associated there with Richard Pace* and Cuthbert Tunstall.* Taught there by Niccolò Leonico Tomeo. Rome 1510–11, borrowed works from Vatican library and registered at English hospice. Oxford 1513, incorp. MA same year, BTh by 1531. Ordained as a priest. Various benefices, including rectorship of Saintbury in Gloucestershire, where resident from 1520s. Knew Thomas More, John Fisher, Thomas Linacre,* and Erasmus.
CE, II, 302–3. Allen, 'Linacre and Latimer in Italy,' 514–17. See also Mauritius.*

LEONARD, LENNARD, Henry. 1569–1616.
Son of Sampson and Margaret *suo jure* Baroness Dacre. Matr. fellow commoner Queens' College, Cambridge 1586. Adm. Lincoln's Inn 1588. Matr. Padua 1592 (AAU 30, fol. 93). Kt 1596. MP 1597. Became twelfth Lord Dacre 1611. Married daughter of Sir Richard Baker.*
    Andrich, 133. Venn, III, 74. Hasler, II, 460.

LE ROUS, John. D. 1590.
Son of Anthony of Suffolk. Probably a member of the London family of printers originally from Rouen: one Jean Le Roux/Rouse was resident in London 1536 and denizened 1544. Not to be confused with Jean Le Roux, prior of the Benedictine house of St Martin in the diocese of Rouen, present in Padua in 1556 (ASP, AN 4849, fols 36–7). BCL, Oxford 1562, DCL 1564. Contributor to Doctors' Commons from 1562. Possibly in Padua as a result of implication in Catholic conspiracies against the queen. Contract with Richard Shelley* Padua 1571 (ASP, AN 4856, fol. 297). Named Henry Fitzalan* and John Lumley as his guarantors in his *procura* at Padua 1571 (ASP, AN 831, fol. 366). DCnCL Padua, August 1571, including profession of Catholic orthodoxy, witnessed by Anthony Fortescue,* Richard Shelley,* Gilbert Talbot,* Henry Cavendish,* Charles Cavendish,* Daniel Withipoole,* Iodoch Nittio(?),* Reginald Knivet,* and Richard Villers,* and promoted by Tiberio Deciani, Marco Mantova Benavides, Giovanni Cieffalo, and Jacobo Menochio (AAU 143, fol. 327; ACV, Diversorum 56, fol. 53).
    Squibb, 155.

LEWKENOR, George.
Physician. New College, Oxford, fellow 1560–70, BA 1564. Travelled with Luke Astlow* and Robert Persons* through Antwerp and Frankfurt to Padua 1574.
    Pollen, 23–5. *AO*, 911.

LEYGHT, Henry.
Matr. Padua 1592 (AAU 30, fol. 93).
    Andrich, 133.

LILY, George. After 1495–1559.
Catholic divine. Son of grammarian William. Commoner of Magdalen College, Oxford 1528. Scholar of the law university Padua and member of the English nation 1534, where associated with Henry Coles,* Richard Morison,* and Richard Notur* (AAU 4, fols 296, 301). Wrote to Thomas Starkey* from

Venice in 1535 that he was considering joining the order of Theatines, because he was now not going to inherit from his father. Domestic chaplain of Reginald Pole.* Administrator (with Pole*) of English hospice Rome from 1538. Wrote *Virorum aliquot in Britannia clari fuerunt elogia* (attached to Paolo Giovio's *Descriptio Britanniae*) and other histories of Britain. England 1556. Various benefices.

LP, IX, nos 292, 659, 673, X, no. 503. *DNB. EH*, passim.

LINACRE, Thomas. c. 1460–1524.
Humanist and physician. Oxford by 1481, fellow of All Souls College 1484. Italy 1487, probably with the papal envoy William Sellyng, studied in Florence with Chalcondylas and Poliziano until 1490. Adm. to English hospice in Rome same year, warden following year, remaining in Rome until 1492. Paduan MD 1496. Then associated with Aldine 'Academy' in Venice, where knew Ambrogio Leone di Nola, Girolamo Aleandro, and Andrea Torresani. Helped with Aldine *editio princeps* of Greek Aristotle and translated pseudo-Proclus's *De sphaera*. England 1499. Tutor of Prince Arthur c. 1501 and royal physician from 1509. Founded College of Physicians of London 1518, with John Chamber* and others, and was its first president. Bequeathed lectureships in medicine to Oxford and Cambridge. Friend of Budé, Colet, More, Erasmus, and Richard Pace.* Wrote Latin grammatical works and Latin translations of Galen.

Madison et al., passim. See also William Latimer* and Thomas Lupset.*

LISTER, Joseph. c. 1568–1622.
Physician. Son of William. Brother of Matthew.* Matr. pensioner Trinity College, Cambridge 1588, BA 1593–4, possibly MA 1596. Matr. Leiden as a student of medicine 1596, same day as William Clement.* Matr. Basle 1597, probably same day as William Clement,* MA same year, with a dissertation entitled 'De anima humana.' Possibly MD Basle same year. Matr. Padua 1597 (AAU 30, fol. 95, same day as William Clement*). MD incorp. Oxford 1599, when licensed to practice medicine, MD incorp. Cambridge 1603. Practised at York.

Andrich, 137. Venn, III, 90. Innes Smith, 142. Wackernagel, II, 449.

LISTER, Matthew. c. 1571–1656.
Physician. Son of William. Brother of Joseph.* Oriel College, Oxford, matr. 1588, BA 1591, fellow and MA 1595. Witness to MDs of Thomas Hearne* and William Harvey* Padua 1602. Matr. Basle 1604, MD of Basle, incorp. Oxford 1605, Cambridge 1608. Fellow of College of Physicians of London 1607 (Lon-

don, Royal College of Physicians, Annals of the College of Physicians of London 2, fols 193v, 194), censor 1608 (ibid., fol. 202), elect 1625 (ibid. 3, fol. 63v). Italy 1610 with William Cecil, Viscount Cranborne (ibid., fol. 7), where corresponded with Dudley Carleton, English ambassador in Venice (PRO SP99 6, fol. 108). Physician to Queen Anne and Charles I. Kt 1636.

Rossetti, 'Nel quarto centenario.' *AO*, III, 918. *DNB*. Munk, I, 123. Maladorno Hargraves, 'I Cecil,' 121. London, Royal College of Physicians, MS 307 (Baldwin Hamey's *Bustorum aliquot reliquiae*), no. 72. Whitteridge, 39.

LITELOR, John.
His *procura* at Padua witnessed by Richard White* and Jerome Sapcot* 1566 (ASP, AN 829, fol. 470).

LLWYD, LLOYD, Humphrey. 1527–68.
Welsh antiquarian. Oxford, BA 1547, MA 1551. Servant of Henry Fitzalan* and married sister of his son-in-law Lord Lumley. Travelled with Fitzalan* to Padua 1566. MP 1558–9, 1563, 1567. Acquainted, like William Soone,* with Abraham Ortelius (J.H. Hessels, *Ecclesiae Londino-Batavae Archivium*, Cambridge, 1887, I, 63–4).

DNB. T.M. Chotzen, 'Some Sidelights on Cambro-Dutch relations, 1100–1600,' *Transactions of the Honourable Society of Cymmrodorion* (1937), 118–20, 129–44. R. Geraint Gruffydd, 'Humphrey Llwyd of Denbigh: Some Documents and a Catalogue,' *Denbighshire Historical Society Transactions* 17 (1968), 54–107.

LOKE, LOK? __.
Encountered by Samuel Foxe* Padua c. 1585. Possibly the traveller and merchant Michael Lok, the son of Sir William; or his son Zachariah who was BA Magdalen College, Oxford 1580, MP 1593, 1601.

DNB. Hasler, II, 485.

LUPSET, Thomas. c. 1498–1530.
Humanist. Son of William of London. St Paul's School, entered household of founder John Colet by 1508. Pembroke Hall, Cambridge early 1510s. Knew Erasmus and Linacre,* and supervised printing of Linacre's* *De sanitate tuenda* and More's *Utopia* in Paris 1517, where also met Guillaume Budé. England 1519. Succeeded John Clement* as Wolsey's reader in humanity at Oxford 1520, residing in Corpus Christi College until 1522, when already MA. Padua 1523, where associated with Richard Pace,* Thomas Winter,* Thomas Starkey,* Nicholas Wilson,* Edward Wotton,* and John Clement,*

and was the special companion of Pole.* Assisted on Aldine *editio princeps* of Greek Galen in Venice 1525. Tutor to Thomas Winter* in Paris 1528. England 1529, then Paris again with Pole.* England 1530. Wrote a number of theological, pietistic, and moral works.

Gee, *passim*.

LUPUS, John.
Law student at Padua. Lent Nicholas Beysell of Liège money to take his doctorate 1505, contract witnessed by John Chamber* (ASP, AN 1811, fols 328–9v).

LYSTER, __.
A 'Mr Lyster' from Lancashire was reported to have just come from Padua in May 1569.

HMC, *Hatfield*, I, 410.

MADDOX, Griffin, Griffith.
Welsh. Travelling companion and amanuensis of Philip Sidney* and witness with him to doctoral examination of John Hart* Padua 1574.

Osborn, *passim*.

MALIM, William. 1533–94.
Headmaster of Eton College and St Paul's School and traveller. Schoolboy at Eton. Scholar of King's College, Cambridge, adm. 1548, fellow 1551, BA 1553, MA 1556. Commenced study of civil law 1559. Headmaster of Eton from c. 1560. His 'consuetudinarium' of the college, setting aside Fridays for punishments, written about this time. Escape of some scholars in fear of severe punishments during queen's visit to Windsor 1563 inspired Ascham's *Scholemaster*, and, despite Malim's presentation of dedicatory verses to the queen on behalf of the college (BL, MS Royal, 12 A. lxvii), may have been the cause of his departure from England. *Consiliarius* of English nation Padua 1564 (AAU 10, fol. 231v). Constantinople same year, and also visited Cyprus and Turkey, where he stayed for eight months. England c. 1567. Prebendary of Lincoln Cathedral from 1569. At Cyprus was acquainted with the Venetian officials Giovan Antonio Querini and Lorenzo Tiepolo. Seems to have been maintained abroad by earl of Leicester and thus may have been there in a semi-official capacity, and was supported by Leicester in England afterwards. Dedicated to him English translation (undertaken on the urging of Thomas Wilson* and printed by John Day, 1572) of Nestor Martinengo's *Relatione di tutto il successo di Famagosta* (Venice 1572), an account of the Venetian loss of

Famagosta in Cyprus to the Turks in 1571, in which Malim's acquaintances
Querini and Tiepolo had perished. Headmaster of St Paul's School 1573–81.
Author of various Latin verses and letters.

DNB. M. McDonnell, *The Annals of St Paul's School* (Cambridge, 1959),
94–108. L. Cust, *A History of Eton College* (London, 1909), 55–69. W. Sterry,
ed., *The Eton College Register, 1441–1698* (Eton, 1943), 222. Sir Edward Creasy,
Memoirs of Eminent Etonians (London, 1876), 87–96. E. Rosenberg, *Leicester,
Patron of Letters* (New York, 1955), 96–104. W. Malim, *The true report of all
the successe of Famagosta ... Englished out of Italian* (London 1572). N. Carr,
trans., *Demosthenis Olynthiacae orationes tres* (London, 1571), sig. ciii. Thomas
Chaloner, *De republica Anglorum instaurandi libri decem* (London, 1579), passim.
Ascham, *Schoolmaster*, 6–12. R. Whitney, *A Choice of Emblemes* (Leiden, 1586),
152. See also John Friar* and Jerome Sapcot.*

MANERINGE, __.
Encountered by Samuel Foxe* Padua in c. 1585.

For possible identifications see Venn, III, 127; *AO*, III, 959–60; J. Croston,
County Families of Lancashire and Cheshire (London, 1887), 376–9.

MANERS, Edward.
Master of Bolton College. Grace to study abroad granted at Cambridge 1504.
DCnL Padua 1505, witnessed by John Faber* and John Chamber.* Incorp. Cam-
bridge 1505. Ordained 1507. Master of Bolton College, Edlingham in 1507.

AGA, 1501–50, no. 377. *BRUO*, 387.

MANNERS, Francis. 1578–1632.
Courtier, privy councillor, and administrator. Son of John. Younger brother of
Roger.* Cousin of Gilbert Talbot.* Christ's College, Cambridge 1595. Padua
1599–1600, where probably associated with Humphrey Coningsby* and
received payments from his brother. Florence where wrote to his brother
1600, Venice same year (HMC, *Rutland*, IV, 424, 432). Matr. University College, Oxford, 1600–1. Implicated in Essex rebellion. Possibly Inner Temple
1602. Lord lieutenant of Lincolnshire 1612. Became sixth earl of Rutland same
year. Various offices under James I.

Maladorno Hargraves, 'From Padua to the Field of Edgehill,' 114. *AO*, III,
965. *DNB.*

MANNERS, Roger. 1576–1612.
Fifth earl of Rutland. Son of John. Brother of Francis.* Cousin of Gilbert
Talbot.* Queens' College Cambridge and Corpus Christi College, MA 1595.

1599 married Elizabeth Sidney, daughter of Sir Philip.* Sent advice on his travels by the earl of Essex. Licence to travel for three years 1595 (PRO, SO3 1, fol. 551). Padua 1596 with his servant Thomas Beest* (HMC, *Rutland*, IV, 411). Matr. Padua same year (AAU 30, fol. 94v), taken seriously ill there, and visited by Henry Hawkins* and Edmund Bruce* (LPL, MS 658, fol. 410; MS 659, fol. 51). Germany and France same year, England 1597. Involved in Essex rebellion in Ireland 1599. Various offices under James I.

Andrich, 135. Hammer, '"This bright Shininge Spark,"' 94–5. Maladorno Hargraves, 'From Padua to the Field of Edgehill,' 114. *DNB*. Birch, I, 428. See also Henry Cuffe,* Henry Farr,* and George Wood.*

MARBURY, John.
Consiliarius and *electionarius* of English nation Padua 1549 (AAU 8, fol. 3v). Adm. Gray's Inn 1554.

Andrich, 29. Foster, 24.

MARKHAM, Sir Griffin. c. 1564–c. 1644.
Soldier and conspirator. Son of Thomas. Soldier in Europe 1590s and early 1600s. Reported to have been in Padua May 1596 in letter from Dr Hawkins* in Venice to Anthony Bacon (Birch, II, 22). Implicated in Bye plot and exiled. *DNB*.

MARTIN, __.
Encountered by Samuel Foxe* Padua c. 1585. Possibly Thomas Martyn, the son of John, civilian and Catholic controversialist.

DNB.

MASON, Anthony.
Adopted son of Sir John Mason.* In France early 1550s until Sir John's* death 1566, when taken in by William Capelin at Winchester College. Padua same year where tutored by Robert Poyntz* and George Gattacre,* and friendly with Richard White.* Clerk of the parliament 1574.

White, 92–109. D. Rhodes, 'Richard White of Basingstoke: The Erudite Exile,' in *Across the Narrow Seas*, ed. S. Roach (London, 1991), 23–30. *DNB*.

MASON, John. 1503–66.
Henrician servant. Father of Anthony.* Oxford, BA 1521, MA 1524, King's Scholar at Paris 1529–32. Padua 1533, where knew Thomas Starkey* and Reginald Pole,* Spain following year, southern Italy 1535, Venice 1536. Secretary to English ambassador in Spain 1537–41, king's French secretary

following year, clerk of privy council following year. Extensive diplomatic missions. Dean of Winchester diocese 1549–54. MP 1551–66. Chancellor of Oxford University 1552–6, 1559–66. Knew John Caius* and John Cheke.*
    DNB. LP, VII, no. 945, IX, no. 981. Dowling, 159–60. Horne, III, 84.

MASSON, Anthony.
Travelled in Italy, including Padua c. 1592
    Cal. SP Dom. Eliz., 1591–4, 163, no. 151.

MAURITIUS, MORYS? MORRIS? Christopher?
English student at Padua in the mid-1520s, by whom Niccolò Leonico Tomeo sent a copy of his commentary on Aristotle's *Parva naturalia* to William Latimer* in England (BAV, MS Rossiano 997, fol. 37). Probably the Christopher Morys who was BA Cambridge 1520–1 or the Morris who was BA Cambridge 1522–3.
    Venn, III, 215–16. Cf. Erasmus, *Opus epistolarum*, V, no. 1256 (*CWE*, IX, 17).

MERIDE? Hercules.
Consiliarius and *electionarius* of English nation Padua 1568. Apparently an Englishman, as eight members of the nation present at his election (AAU 11, fols 224v, 236v).
    Andrich, 38.

MICHELL, Humphrey. 1526–98.
Elizabethan MP. Servant first of Sir Thomas Smith, then of Edward Courtenay.* Padua 1555 or 1556, in which year sought Courtenay's* forgiveness for some undisclosed offence. Entered service of Francis Russell* same year. MP in five Elizabethan parliaments. Various government offices. Expert in hydraulic engineering.
    Bartlett, *English in Italy*, 211–12. Hasler, II, 47–8. Lemon, 85.

MIDDLETON, Christopher?
Encountered by Nicholas Faunt* Padua 1581 and by Samuel Foxe* Padua c. 1585. Possibly the Christopher Middleton, translator and poet, who probably matr. Brasenose College, Oxford 1580, age 20.
    DNB.

MILLIEIS, MYLLES? Richard.
Witness to MD of Edward Benedict* Padua 1601. Probably the Richard Milles of London, matr. Magdalen College, Oxford 1591, age 16, BA 1595, MA 1598.
    AO, 1015. Rossetti, 'Nel quarto centenario.'

MOONE, William.
Scholar of the law university at Padua and member of the English nation 1556–7. Probably the William Moone adm. Lincoln's Inn 1559.
    Andrich, 131. *Records of the Honourable Society of Lincoln's Inn* (London, 1896), I, 65. Cf. alternative identifications in Garrett, 228–9.

MORISON, Richard. D. 1556.
Henrician propagandist and Tudor diplomat. Canon of Cardinal College, Oxford, adm. c. 1526, BA 1528. Cambridge c. 1531, where knew William Gonnell and Thomas Cranmer. Briefly attended Inn of Court c. 1532. Padua same year, where student of law. *Consiliarius* of the English nation 1534, when associated with George Lily,* Henry Coles,* and Richard Notur.* Also associated in Padua with Thomas Starkey,* Reginald Pole,* Thomas Winter,* Michael Throckmorton,* John Friar,* and Damião de Goes and, in Venice, Edmund Harvel.* Pleaded poverty in Padua 1535, but then entered Cromwell's service there, reporting for him on Italian reactions to executions of More and Fisher. Returned to England 1536, and became government propagandist and diplomat. Licensed to travel abroad 1554 with John Cheke* and Anthony Cooke.*
    PRO, SP1 103, fols 31–2; SP1 106, fol. 26; SP1 126, fol. 158; SP1 133, fols 243–4. BL, MS Cotton, Nero B vi, fol. 150. *LP*, IX, no. 292; XIII, pt. 2, no. 507; XVI, nos 154–5. Berkowitz, 19–60. See also Philip Hoby,* Richard Shelley,* and Thomas Wrothe.*

MORLEY, William. c. 1531–c. 1597.
Marian exile. Son of Thomas. Brother of John, a member of Francis Russell's* train in Italy. Queens' College, Cambridge, matr. 1545, BA 1549, fellow 1548–50. *Consiliarius* of English nation 1556 (AAU 9, fol. 162). Cousin of John Pelham,* with whom settled in Geneva and joined congregation of John Knox 1557, and whose sister Anne he later married. Various local government positions under Elizabeth. MP 1571.
    Andrich, 31. Bartlett, *English in Italy*, 213. Garrett, 231. Hasler, II, 103.

MORYSON, Fynes. 1566–1630.
Traveller. Son of Thomas. Matr. Peterhouse, Cambridge 1580, BA, MA 1587, licence to travel 1589. Commenced six years of travelling 1591, Prague, Germany, Low Countries. Leiden 1593. Denmark, Poland, Vienna, Italy October 1593. Matr. Padua same year (AAU 30, fol. 93v) where remained all winter to study Italian. Naples, Rome, northern Italy April 1594 to early 1595. Later 1595 Geneva, then France. England May 1595. December 1595 commenced second journey: Germany, Venice, Joppa, Jerusalem, Tripoli, Aleppo,

Antioch, Constantinople, Venice, London July 1597. Scotland 1598. Dublin as an administrator under Sir Charles Blount, lord deputy of Ireland, 1600–3. Detailed observations in *Itinerary* written 1606–17, published same year.

Moryson, *Shakespeare's Europe*, 430–4 and *An Itinerary*. Andrich, 134. *DNB*.

MOUNSEL, MUNSEL, Peter. D. 1615.
Physician. Brasenose College, Oxford 1587, BA 1591, MA 1594. Studied medicine at Oxford and Cambridge for about five years. Paris 1601. *Consiliarius* of English nation Padua 1602 (AAU 15, fols 1–3v) and witness to Thomas Hearne's* and William Harvey's* MDs same year. Matr. Basle 1605. Professor of Physic at Gresham College in London 1607–15. Basle, Strasbourg, Leiden 1607 where he was probably MD.

Andrich, 46. Rossetti, 'Nel quarto centenario.' Whitteridge, 39. Ward, *Lives of the Professors*, 265–6. Wackernagel, III, 55.

MUNDAY, Anthony. 1553–1633.
Poet and playwright. Son of Christopher. Apprentice to a stationer 1576. Rome 1578, where resided at English College. In dedicatory letter to Edward de Vere* in his *The Mirrour of Mutabilitie* (London, 1579), sig Ciiiv, remarks on his travels in Italy to Rome, Naples, Venice, Padua, and 'diverse of their excellent cities.' His *The English Romayne Life* (London, 1582) exposes English Catholic practices in Rome. An actor c. 1579–80. Wrote and acted in numerous plays 1584–1602. Scripted various London pageants 1605–33. Edited Stow's *Survey of London.*

DNB.

MURPHIN, Edward.
Left Padua with Thomas Hoby* and Henry Killigrew* 1549. Rome with Thomas Hoby,* Francis Freitto (Peto*), and other Englishmen same year.

Hoby, 11, 24.

MYLY, Anthony.
Servant of earl of Essex. Reported to him from Padua 1594, especially concerning Englishmen in Italy in trouble with the Inquisition (LPL, MS 652, fol. 178).

NEUROTUS? NUROHTUS? NUROTTUS? Robert.
Matr. Padua 1597 (AAU 30, fol. 95). *Consiliarius* of English nation 1599 (AAU 15, fol. 1v).

Andrich, 45, 136.

NEVILLE, Henry. c. 1520–c. 1593.
Marian exile and Elizabethan gentleman. Godson of Henry VIII. Son of Sir
Edward. Father of Henry.* Gentleman of the privy chamber 1551 when kt.
Encountered by Thomas Hoby* Padua 1554. Joined Edward Courtenay's*
household in Venice 1556. Paris then England same year. Various government offices under Elizabeth. MP 1553, 1559, 1563, 1571, 1584 and served on
parliamentary committees.
     Bartlett, *English in Italy*, 213–14. Hoby, 116. Hasler, III, 124–5.

NEVILLE, Henry. 1562–1615.
Courtier and diplomat. Son of Sir Henry.* Matr. Merton College, Oxford
1577, where knew Henry Savile* (cf. HMC, *Buccleuch and Queensberry*, I, 28),
MA 1605. Licence to travel abroad April 1578 (PRO, E157 1, fol. 3). Encountered by Arthur Throckmorton* in Nuremburg in September 1580 (Rowse,
84), together with Robert Sidney, Henry Savile,* and George Carew.* Met
Hugo Blotius at Vienna, together with Henry Savile* and Robert Sidney, and
also Andreas Dudith (Vienna, Österreichische Nationalbibliothek, MS 9737z[17],
fol. 22; Feingold, 126, 131; P. Costil, *André Dudith, humaniste hongrois, 1533–89*,
Paris, 1935, 202, 442, 444–5, 447). Venice and Padua 1581. MP 1585–6, 1589,
1593, 1597, 1604, 1614. Ambassador to France 1599–1600. Kt 1599. Implicated
in Essex rebellion. Married Anne, daughter of Sir Henry Killigrew.*
     DNB. E. Sawyer, *Memorials of Affairs of State in the Reigns of Elizabeth I and
James I* (London, 1725), passim. Hasler, III, 122–4. See also Henry Cuffe* and
Ralph Winwood.*

NEVILLE, Henry. c. 1575–1641.
Son of Edward. Queens' College, Cambridge 1586, BA 1589, incorp. Oxford
1594. Travels in Germany and Italy with tutor Paolo Lentolo and partly with
Thomas Sackville.* Matr. Leipzig 1591 and Genevan Academy 1592. Matr.
Padua 1592 (AAU 30, fol. 93). Venice July 1594, approached there by English
Catholics. By c. 1596 had married Mary, daughter of Thomas Sackville,* Lord
Buckhurst. Served under earl of Essex at Cadiz. Kt same year. MP 1601, 1604,
1621. Friend of Sir Robert Sidney.
     Andrich, 133. Hasler, III, 125. HMC, *Hatfield*, XVI, 299. G. Erler, ed., *Die
iiingere Matrikel der Universität Leipzig* (Leipzig, 1909), I, 316. S. Stelling-
Michaud, ed., *Le livre du recteur de l'Académie de Genève* (Geneva, 1976), V, 20.

NITTIO? Iodoch. See John Le Rous.*

NOEL, NOWELL? Alexander? Laurence?
A Mr Noel was reported to have been with Thomas Randolph in France and

the tutor of the Haringtons* in Padua in 1558. Probably one of the two
Nowell brothers, both Marian exiles: Alexander Nowell (1507–1602), recorded
in Strasbourg and Frankfurt c. 1556–8, dean of St Pauls; Laurence Nowell (d.
1576), not to be confused with his cousin Laurence Nowell,* documented
with his brother in Germany, dean of Lichfield.
  DNB.

NOTUR, Richard.
Scholar of law and member of English nation Padua 1534 (AAU 4, fols 296v,
301).
  Andrich, 130. See also George Lily* and Richard Morison.*

NOWELL, Laurence. D. c. 1583.
Cousin of Alexander and Laurence Noel.* MP 1559. 1568–70 Paris, Venice,
Padua, Vienna, Basle, Leipzig. Possibly died abroad.
  Hasler, II, 149.

ORPHINSTRANGE, John. D. 1589.
Advocate and equity lawyer. Matr. St John's College, Cambridge 1544.
Corpus Christi College, Cambridge BA 1546–7, MA 1549. *Consiliarius* and
electionarius of English nation Padua 1552–3 (AAU 8, fol. 227v). Encountered
by Thomas Hoby* at Padua, August 1554. DCL Padua 1555, promoted by
Marco Mantova Benavides (AAU 144, fols 102v–3), incorp. Cambridge.
Advocate of the Arches 1558, adm. Doctors' Commons same year. Official of
the Prerogative Court of Canterbury c. 1557. Active in the archidiaconal court
of the diocese of London 1562. Lent law books by Sir Thomas Smith 1573
(Cambridge, Queens' College, MS 49, fol. 97). Master in Chancery 1558–60,
1572–89.
  Andrich, 30. Hoby, 117. Squibb, 153. Heward, 80, 90. W.H. Hale, *A Series of
Precedents and Proceedings in Criminal Causes, 1475–1640* (London, 1847), 145.

PACE, Richard. c. 1482–1536.
Humanist and diplomat. Educated under care of Thomas Langton, bishop of
Winchester. Possibly a student of Queen's College, Oxford. Padua, Bologna,
Ferrara c. 1496–1509. Servant of Cardinal Bainbridge Rome 1509. Secretary to
Henry VIII from 1515. Various diplomatic missions to 1525. Dean of St Paul's
1519. Apptd reader of Greek Cambridge 1520 but never took up the position.
Friend of Erasmus, Thomas More, Cuthbert Tunstall,* William Latimer,*
Thomas Linacre,* Reginald Pole,* Thomas Lupset,* John Stokesley.* Author of
various works.
  DNB. Wegg. See also Robert Wingfield.*

PAGE, John.
Consiliarius of English nation Padua 1568, 1569 (AAU 11, fol. 234).
  Andrich, 38.

PAITONUS, PAITON? Augustinus.
Student of medicine at Padua.
  Leland, 63.

PARKINS, Christopher. 1574–1622.
Jesuit scholar. Oxford 1565. Became Jesuit at Rome 1566. Dillingen 1574.
Resident Venice 1580s. Rome 1585 when protected William Cecil* from
Inquisition, and escorted him back to Padua. Involved with alchemist
Edward Kelley in Prague c. 1587–9. Agent and ambassador in northern and
eastern Europe for English government from 1589. MP 1597, 1601, 1604–11.
Master of Requests 1617.
  HMC, *Hatfield*, III, 411. Bell, *Handlist*, passim. *DNB*. Ungerer, II, 176.
McCoog, II, 431.

PARRY, Edward.
Son of Sir Thomas, comptroller of the household to Elizabeth. Half-brother of
Thomas Parry.* Padua 1560–2. Sir Francis Englefield* met him and Thomas
Parry* there. Encountered by Ralph Lacy* there c. 1561.
  Cal. SP For. Eliz., 1560–1, no. 963. Baskerville, 315.

PARRY, Thomas.
Half-brother of Edward.* Padua c. 1560, where encountered Sir Francis
Englefield.* His *procura* at Padua witnessed by George Gattacre* and
Anthony Fortescue* 1561 (ASP, AN 4851, fol. 36).
  Cal. SP For. Eliz., 1560–1, no. 963. Baskerville, 315.

PAYTON, PEYTON, John. 1579–1635.
Traveller, soldier, and MP. Son of Sir John, the friend of Peregrine Bertie* and
Sir Philip Sidney.* Adm. fellow commoner Queens' College, Cambridge 1594.
Travels abroad 1598–1601: Germany, eastern Europe 1598, Basle same year
where sent his father relations of Germany and Bohemia (Cambridge, Cambridge University Library, MS 2044, Kk, v. 2). Padua 1599 where probably a
consiliarius of university (Rossetti, *Stemmi*, 211, no. 1034). MP 1601. Gentleman
of the privy chamber and kt 1603. Lieutenant governor of Jersey 1628–33.
  DNB. HMC *Hatfield*, IX, 237. Hasler, III, 214–15. History of Parliament draft
biography. Cf. Rossetti, *Stemmi*, 160, 430, nos 703, 2046. Brown, 144.

PECKHAM, Robert. c. 1515–69.
Privy councillor in reign of Mary and Catholic exile. Son of Sir Edmund.
Gray's Inn adm. 1533. Kt 1553. MP 1554. Privy councillor 1553–8. Abroad
from 1564. Friend of John Perpoint,* George Gattacre,* Jerome Sapcot,* and
Richard White.* Padua, c. 1564–6. Encouraged White* to write his history of
Britain. John David Rhys* dedicated to him his *De italica pronunciatione*
(Padua, 1569). Died at Rome.

White, 125. J.W. Binns, 'Richard White of Basingstoke and the Defence of
the Tudor Myth,' *Cahiers Elisabethains* 11 (1977), 23. Bindoff, III,
80–1.

PELHAM, PALEUS, PULEUS, John. 1537–80.
Marian exile and student of law. Son of Nicholas. Queens' College, Cambridge, matr. *impubes* 1549. Passports to travel abroad issued to him and his
brother Anthony 1552. Shared lodging in Padua with Francis Southwell,*
arranged by their tutor John Everard* 1553. *Consiliarius* of English nation
Padua 1556–7 (AAU 9, fol. 201v) and *syndicus* of the ultramontanes in the
university of law for same period (ibid., fol. 275v). DCnCL Bologna 1557
(Bologna, Archivio di Stato, Studio 129, fol. 45v; Studio 140, fol. 46). Geneva
with William Morley* same year, where joined congregation of John Knox.
Padua 1558, where witness next year to doctorate in arts and medicine of
Hermanus Siderius Frivius of Groeningen (ACV, Diversorum 55 bis, fol. 53).
Various local government positions under Elizabeth. MP 1571. Kt 1573.

Andrich, 31–2. Bartlett, *English in Italy*, 284. Hasler, III, 193–4.

PERORIUS, Ioannes Maria.
Consiliarius English nation Padua 1597. Possibly not English as elected
'substitutus' (AAU 15, fol. 4).

Andrich, 137.

PERPOINT, John. See Richard White,* Robert Peckham,* and Jerome
Sapcot.*

PERSONS, Robert. 1546–1610.
Jesuit. Travelled from Oxford to Padua 1574 to study medicine on advice of
Thomas Sackville,* Lord Buckhurst. Associated during travels with George
Lewkenor* and shared 'a very commodious house' in Padua with John Lane*
and Luke Astlow.* Rome following year where became Jesuit.

Pollen, 23–5, 39. F. Edwards, *Robert Persons: The Biography of an English
Jesuit, 1546–1610* (St Louis, 1995).

PETIERO, PETER? Richard.
Consiliarius and *electionarius* of English nation Padua 1560–1 (AAU 10, fols 98, 116v). Possibly the Mr Peter who was in Venice 1558, had been in France, and was planning to go to Rome same year for fear of Turkish invasion of Venice.
Andrich, 34. *Cal. SP For. Eliz.*, 1558–9, no. 68. Cf. Le Neve, I, 412.

PETO, FREITTO, Francis.
Traveller. Son of John. Awarded pension by Edward VI to study in Italy. Briefly *consiliarius* of English nation Padua 1547, but his surname is written as 'Freitto' (AAU 7, fol. 195; cf. Andrich, 28). Servant of the duke of Northumberland. Toured Italy and employed as government agent and intelligencer 1548–51. Attended dinner given by imperial ambassador Don Diego di Mendoza Siena 1549 together with Thomas Hoby,* Edward Stradling, and other Englishmen. Rome with Thomas Hoby* and Edward Murphin* same year, then Florence with Thomas Hoby* 1550. Secretary of the English ambassador to the emperor 1554–6. Lived in Italy, France, and Flanders 1561–76.
Baskerville, 244–60. Hoby, 19, 24, 61.

PETO, William. D. 1558.
Catholic exile. Opponent of Henry VIII's divorce. Antwerp mid-1530s, then Venice, Padua, Rome 1538. Apptd bishop of Salisbury by Paul III 1547.
DNB.

PHILPOT, John. 1516–55.
Catholic exile and divine. Son of Sir Peter. Winchester College. New College, Oxford 1534–41, BCL 1539. Abroad same year. Theological dispute with Franciscan friar between Venice and Padua same year. Archdeacon of Winchester, but involved in many conflicts with his bishop John Ponet. Convicted of heresy and burned at stake 1555. Author of theological works.
DNB. Binns, *Intellectual Culture*, 248, 674. *AO*, III, 1160.

POLE, Reginald. 1500–58.
Cardinal and archbishop of Canterbury. Educated Oxford, Padua, Avignon. Opponent of Henrician Reformation, writing *Pro ecclesiasticae unitatis defensione* against Royal Supremacy 1535–6. Cardinal same year and associated with Italian *spirituali*. Governor of Viterbo in Papal State 1540s, active in Council of Trent. Almost elected pope 1550. Archbishop of Canterbury from 1556 and oversaw English return to Catholicism. Author of many works.

T.F. Mayer, 'Reginald Pole,' in *Dictionary of Literary Biography*, ed. D.A. Richardson (Detroit, 1993), CXXXII, 245–50. See also John Clement,* Thomas Clement,* Henry Coles,* Edward Courtenay,* Thomas Friar,* Thomas Goldwell,* George Lily,* Thomas Lupset,* Richard Morison,* John Mason,* Richard Pace,* Thomas Theobald,* Michael Throckmorton,* Hugh Turnbull,* Marmaduke Waldby,* Thomas Winter,* Edward Wotton.*

POWLE, Stephen. 1553–1633.
Intelligence agent and Chancery clerk. Broadgates Hall, Oxford, adm. c. 1564. Middle Temple 1574–9. Travels in France, Switzerland, and Germany 1580–2. Matr. Basle 1580. Intelligence agent for English government Heidelberg, 1585–6 and Venice 1587–8 (travelling through Germany in 1587 with Edward Lord Zouche*), sending news reports to Francis Walsingham.* In a letter written at Venice 1587 he lists places visited in Italy including Padua. Subsequently apptd deputy clerk of the Crown in Chancery and one of the six clerks in Chancery. JP in Essex. Kt by James I. Member of the council of the Virginia Company of London 1609.

V.F. Stern, *Sir Stephen Powle of Court and Country* (Selinsgrove, London, and Toronto, 1992), 83 and passim. Wackernagel, II, 284. See also John Wroth.*

POYNTZ, Robert.
Catholic divine. Son of John. Nephew of Sir Francis Poyntz. Winchester College. Fellow New College, Oxford 1554, BA 1556, MA 1560. Scholar of the law university Padua 1560 and *consiliarius* of English nation 1563–4 (AAU 10, fol. 223). Witnessed *procura* of Anthony Fortescue* 1563. Tutor with George Gattacre* of Anthony Mason* in Padua and knew Richard White* there, who described him as 'philosophus' (White, 109). From 1568 planned pilgrimage to Jerusalem (from Venice) with Richard Smith,* fellow of Trinity College, Cambridge. Probably never undertaken due to death of Smith* 1570. Settled in Louvain and wrote *Testimonies for the Real Presence of Christ's Body* and *Miracles Performed by the Eucharist*.

DNB. Andrich, 36, 131. Rossetti, *Stemmi*, 241, no. 1181. J. Maclean, *Historical and Genealogical Memoir of the Family of Poyntz* (Exeter, 1886), 116.

PRICE, Matthew.
Matr. Padua 1591 (AAU 30, fol. 93, same day as Thomas Sackville*). Probably the Matthew Price of Middlesex matr. as gentleman Jesus College, Oxford 1581, age 13.

Andrich, 133. *AO*, III, 1206.

PYNE, Tertullian.
Archdeacon. Member of St John's College, Oxford in 1570s, BA 1577. *Consiliarius* of English nation Padua 1580 (AAU 13, fols 2–4). Probably the 'Mr Piyne' mentioned as delivering a letter from Edward Unton* in Milan to Francis Walsingham* June 1583. Possibly DCL Basle. Archdeacon of Sudbury 1591.
    Andrich, 40. *AO*, IV, 1224. *Cal. SP For. Eliz.*, 1583, no. 355.

RANDOLPH, Jacobus.
Witness to John Hart's* doctorate in law and to the Scotsman John Russell's in arts Padua 1574 (ASP, AN 5007, fols 26–7v; 2342, fol. 473). *Consiliarius* and *electionarius* of English nation 1576–8 (AAU 12, fols 155v, 177v, 193). Probably the James Randolph matr. Cambridge 1567, BA 1571. Possibly the 'Randall' encountered by Nicholas Faunt* at Padua 1581.
    Andrich, 39–40. Venn, III, 420.

RATCLIFFE, Edward?
Encountered by Arthur Throckmorton* and Nicholas Faunt* Padua 1581, coming from Rome (LPL, MS 647, fol. 113). Probably Edward Ratcliff, 1533–1631, son of Ralph, matr. sizar Trinity College, Cambridge 1570, BA 1573–4, MA Corpus Christi College, Cambridge 1577, MD incorp. 1584 from Orleans, MD incorp. Oxford 1600. Physician to James I. Kt 1605.
    Venn, III, 414.

REINELL, George.
Matr. Padua 1593 (AAU 30, fol. 93v). Possibly the George Reynell of Devon, b. c. 1563, matr. Broadgates Hall, Oxford 1587, who was kt 1603, MP 1614, d. 1628.
    Andrich, 134. *AO*, III, 1246. History of Parliament draft biography. Cf. HMC, *Hatfield*, XXIV, Addenda, 147.

RHYS, John David. 1534–1609.
Welsh grammarian and physician. Son of Dafydd. Christ Church, Oxford 1555. Probably MD of Siena. Witness to doctorate in philosophy and medicine of Haym the Jew Padua 1568. Author of *Perutilis exteris nationibus de italica pronunciatione & orthographia libellus* (Padua, 1569), dedicated to Robert Peckham*; and various other works on Latin and Welsh languages.
    DNB. Veronese Ceseracciu, 'Ebrei,' 161.

RUSSELL, Francis. 1527–85.
Son of John, first earl of Bedford and inherited title. King's Hall, Cambridge early 1540s. Served in France with his father 1544. MP 1547–53, 1572, 1584.

Protestant who declared for Queen Jane in 1553, imprisoned by Mary, then pardoned same year. Under house arrest following year, then permitted to travel abroad 1554. Brussels then Padua same year, where encountered by Thomas Hoby.* Venice same year. Permitted to carry arms in Venice 1555, together with fourteen Englishmen including John Brooke,* Thomas Fitzwilliams,* Thomas Wyndham,* and Henry Kingsmill* (Venice, Archivio di Stato, Consiglio di X, Parti Communi, Reg. 22, July 1555). Visits to Rome, Naples, Ferrara, and Zurich following year. England 1557. Elizabethan magnate and collector of Italian and Latin books and manuscripts.

Bartlett, *English in Italy*, 290–1. *DNB*. Hasler, III, 307–8. See also Humphrey Michell.*

RUTLAND, Paul. D. 1532.
Medical student. Cambridge BA 1525–6, MA 1528, fellow of St John's College same year. Paduan MD 1531, incorp. Cambridge 1532.

Parker, 'Catalogus Cancellariorum,' 8. Venn, III, 502. *AGA, 1501–50*, no. 1736.

SACKVILLE, Henry.
Son of Thomas, Lord Buckhurst.* Brother of Thomas.* Pont-à-Mousson 1599–1602 for the recovery of his health. Escorted to Padua same year by his brother Thomas* for treatment by Paduan physicians (HMC, *Hatfield*, XII, 309–10, 461).

C.J. Phillips, *History of the Sackville Family* (London, 1930), I, 242–4. P. Bacquet, *Un contemporain d'Elisabeth I: Thomas Sackville, l'homme et l'oeuvre* (Geneva, 1966), 100, 317.

SACKVILLE, Thomas. 1536–1608.
Statesman. Son of Sir Richard. Father of Henry* and Thomas.* Cousin of Francis Alford.* Inner Temple poet (wrote parts of *Gorboduc* and a commendatory sonnet for Thomas Hoby's* *Courtier*). MP 1557–9, 1563. France same year, then Italy, including Padua. Imprisoned briefly Rome 1564. England 1566. Numerous diplomatic missions. Chancellor of Oxford University from 1591. Lord Buckhurst.

P. Bacquet, *Un contemporain d'Elisabeth I: Thomas Sackville*, passim. C. Wilson, 'Thomas Sackville, an Elizabethan Poet as Citizen,' in *Ten Studies in Anglo-Dutch Relations*, ed. J. Van Dorsten (Leiden, 1974), 40–50. *DNB*. *EH*, 220–1. Hasler, III, 316–17. See also Robert Persons.*

SACKVILLE, Thomas. 1571–1646.
Son of Thomas.* Brother of Henry.* Travels 1591–7, 1602, 1615–16. Matr.

Leipzig 1951. Matr. Padua 1591 (AAU 30, fol. 93, same day as Matthew Price*). Reported by Henry Wotton* to be newly arrived in Venice 1592 in a letter to Lord Zouche* (Smith, *Henry Wotton*, I, 295; cf. 292). Venice 1595 (from where wrote to Sir Robert Cecil: PRO SP99 1, fol. 228), France, Vienna, and Padua 1597 (from where wrote to Lord Burghley: PRO SP85 2, fol. 58). Escorted his sick brother Henry* from Germany to Padua 1602, as reported in his father's letters to Sir Robert Cecil (HMC, *Hatfield*, XII, 309–10, 461). Returned to Padua 1615 as Catholic exile (*Calendar of State Papers, Domestic Series, James I, 1611–1618*, ed. M.A. Everett Green, London, 1858, 270). Rome 1616.

Andrich, 133. Erler, 384. See also Henry Neville.*

SANDS, Richard.
Matr. Padua 1592 (AAU 30, fol. 93). Possibly the Richard Sandes who was BA Oxford 1579.

Andrich, 133. *AO*, IV, 1310.

SANDYS, Edwin. c. 1561–1629.
Son of Archbishop Sandys. Brother of George. Merchant Taylors' School 1571. Corpus Christi College, Oxford, matr. 1577, BA 1579, MA 1583, BCL 1589, fellow 1580. Middle Temple 1590. Taught by Richard Hooker and became his assistant and friend. Italy 1593–9, partly with George Cranmer.* Matr. Padua 1597 (AAU 30, fol. 94v). Kt 1603. Author of *A relation of the state of religion used in the west parts of the world*, completed in Paris in 1599 (London, 1605, later reprinted as *Europae speculum*). Notes religious practices he saw in Padua (sigs B2v and B3). Knew Paolo Sarpi who translated it into Italian. MP 1589–1626 and leader of the early Stuart Commons (Hasler, III, 339–41). Endowed lectureships in 'metaphysic philosophy' at Oxford and Cambridge. A director of East India Company and involved in Virginia and Somers Islands companies.

W.M. Wallace, *Sir Edwin Sandys and the First Parliament of James I* (Philadelphia, 1940), passim. C. Vivian, *Some Notes for a History of the Sandys Family*, ed. T.M. Sandys (London, 1907), 152–65. Andrich, 136. *DNB*. History of Parliament draft biography.

SANSENUS? SAMMES? JANSENUS? JONSON? JENISON? William.
Matr. Padua 1597 (AAU 30, fol. 95).

Andrich, 136. For possible identifications see Levack, *The Civil Lawyers*, 267–8; *AO*, II, 816; Venn, II, 483; Hasler, II, 376.

SAPCOT, Jerome.
Probably the son of John, an MP in 1559 and recusant under Elizabeth.

Lincoln College, Oxford, BA 1556, BCL 1560. *Consiliarius* and *electionarius* of English nation Padua 1565–7, 1573–4 (AAU 11, fols 64v, 76, 80v–1, 133v; AAU 12, fol. 47v). Witness to John Litelor's* *procura* at Padua 1566. Another witness, Richard White,* wrote to him same year describing his doctoral examination at Pavia. Also knew John Perpoint,* George Gattacre,* and Robert Peckham* at Padua. Author of *Ad primas leges Digestorum de verborum et rerum significatione* (Venice, 1579) dedicated to Giovanni Grimani, patriarch of Aquileia, the acquaintance of William Malim.* Probably the father of Anthony Sapcot, who from Venice was involved in supplying Dudley Carleton with art objects 1618–20 (PRO SP84 86, fol. 10; SP84 96, fol. 168).

Andrich, 36–7, 39. White, 125, 145–6. *AO*, IV, 312. Hasler, III, 344. See also Simeon Cleregatus.*

SAVILE, Henry. 1549–1622.
Mathematician, astronomer, and Greek scholar. Son of Henry. Brother of Thomas.* Oxford, Brasenose College, matr. 1561, fellow Merton College 1565, BA 1566, MA 1570, junior proctor 1575–7, warden of Merton 1585, assisted in foundation of Bodleian Library, founded professorships in Oxford in geometry and astronomy 1619. European tour with Robert Sidney, Henry Neville,* George Carew,* Arthur Throckmorton* 1578–81. 1580 Nuremburg, Altdorf, Breslau where visited Andreas Dudith and knew Jacob Monau. 1581 Prague, Vienna where associated with imperial librarian Hugo Blotius (Vienna, Österreichische Nationalbibliothek, MS 9737 z[17], fol. 22), Venice where knew Wolfgan Zündelin (like Philip Sidney* earlier, whom he possibly knew: Feingold, 125), Alvise Lullini, probably Girolamo Donzellini, and received letter from Andreas Dudith (Costil, 447); Padua where worked with Giovan Vicenzo Pinelli on ancient Greek scientific works including Geminus, Dionysius of Halicarnassus, Pappus, Simplicius. Rome. Also knew abroad Jacques-Auguste de Thou (cf. de Thou's letter to Savile of 1607, Paris, Bibliothèque Nationale, MS Dupuy 632, fol. 105) and kept commonplace book. Tutor in Greek to the queen. Provost of Eton from 1596. Sent intellience from Italy by Henry Cuffe* 1596–7 (HMC, *Hatfield*, VII, 234–5, 524–5). Associated with earl of Essex and suspected of involvement in Essex rebellion. English translation of *Histories* of Tacitus published 1591. Involved in translation of King James Bible. Edition of Chrysostom printed Eton 1610–13. Kt 1604.

DNB. Feingold, 124–31. Todd, 439–44. R. Goulding, 'Henry Savile and the Tychonic World-System,' *Journal of the Warburg and Courtauld Institutes* 58 (1995), 152–79. Hammer, 'Uses of Scholarship,' 44–5. See also Ralph Winwood.*

SAVILE, Thomas. D. 1593.
Mathematician, astronomer, collaborator of William Camden. Son of Henry.

Brother of Henry.* Merton College, Oxford fellow, BA 1580, MA 1585, proctor 1592. Abroad 1588–91: Breslau 1589 where visited Andreas Dudith and Jacob Monau, Venice 1589 where knew Wolfgang Zündelin and purchased Greek Aristotelian commentaries for himself and for Merton library, Padua 1589, where knew Georgius Deitricius (Vienna, Österreichische Nationalbibliothek, MS 9737 z^{17}, fol. 69), transcribed MSS, worked with Pinelli (Rivolta, 132, 155), and corresponded with Hugo Blotius, informing him of his meeting with Wolfgang Zündelin in Venice and Pinelli in Padua (Vienna, Österreichische Nationalbibliothek, MS 9737 z^{17}, fols 55, 85; cf. Monau's letter of introduction for Savile to Blotius, ibid., fol. 48, and Zündelin's letter to Blotius, ibid., fol. 68). Rome 1590, Padua again same year (ibid., fol. 95). Also associated with Isaac Casaubon (HMC, *12th Report, Cowper*, 18).
    DNB. Feingold, 72, 130–3. Todd, 439–44.

SCHENEUS, Gilbert. See Richard White.*

SCHIERE, SCHIERES, SHERES, SHIRE, John.
Student and tutor. Studying at Cambridge 1540, licensed to go abroad with William Brooke* following year. Tutor of William Brooke,* possibly Padua and Venice with him 1543–5. Encountered by Thomas Hoby* at Padua 1548. Still in the Veneto 1560s. In a letter to William Cecil, he offers to buy for him antique or *all'antica* busts in Padua.
    Hoby, 8. *Cal. SP For. Eliz.*, 1560–1, no. 697; 1561–2, no. 75. Baskerville, 318.

SCORLEUS, Robert.
Matr. Padua 1594 (AAU 30, fol. 93v).
    Andrich, 134. Cf. Hasler, III, 353.

SCROPE, Henry. c. 1570–1625.
Younger son of Henry, Baron Scrope of Bolton. Matr. fellow commoner Emmanuel College, Cambridge 1585, MA 1588. Gray's Inn adm. same year. Matr. Padua 1593 (AAU 30, fol. 93v, same day as William Godolphin*). Wrote there to Anthony Bacon, praising Paduan learning, physicians, and its 'diverse gentlemen strangers' (LPL, MS 649, fols 268, 277). *Consiliarius* of English nation same year (AAU 14, fols 2, 6, 12, 15v, 23v). From Venice sent Horatio Pallavicino a letter for earl of Essex same year. MP 1589, 1593, 1597, 1601.
    Andrich, 43, 133. *DNB*. Venn, III, 35. Hasler, III, 360.

SEAGER, Francis.
Matr. Padua 1591 (AAU 30, fol. 93).
    Andrich, 133.

SELLEY, SHELLEY? Demit. See Robert Wingfield.*

SENTLO, SAINT CLOW, SAINTLOW? Clement. See George Dudgeon* and
Hugh Turnbull.*

SHELLEY, Richard. 1513–89.
Catholic exile. Son of Sir William. Cousin of Philip Sidney.* Italy, probably
Padua, c. 1535–8, where knew Richard Morison,* then Constantinople.
Various diplomatic missions to 1550s. Grand Prior of the Knights of St John
of Malta from 1566. *Consiliarius* of English nation Padua 1567 (AAU 11, fol.
138). Witness to DCnCL of John Le Rous* 1571 and involved in a contract
with him same year (ACV, Diversorum 56, fol. 53; ASP, AN 4856, fol. 297).
Sidney* saw much of him in Venice 1573–4. Active Rome 1570s and 1580s,
involved in English hospice and College. Wrote to Francis Walsingham* and
to the queen from Venice, 1582–4 (PRO, SP99 1, fols 11–13, 24–31). Noted as
resident in Venice c. 1585 by Samuel Foxe.*
    Andrich, 37. *EH*, passim. *DNB.*

SHIRLEY, Robert. c. 1581–1628.
Matr. Padua 1595 (AAU 30, fol. 94, same day as John Stackvoaellus,* John
Gibson,* Robert Baosony,* and John Frear*). Persia c. 1598–1608, Italy, Poland
1609, Bohemia, Madrid, Rome, Milan, and Spain 1609–19, England same year.
Persia 1613, Portugal and Spain 1617–22. England 1624. 1627 Russia where
died. Painted by Van Dyck 1622.
    Andrich, 135. *DNB.* Smith, *Henry Wotton*, I, 477.

SIDNEY, Philip. 1554–86.
Poet, courtier, soldier. Son of Sir Henry. Christ Church, Oxford 1568–71.
Foreign tour 1573–4. Friendly with Wolfgang Zündelin and Sebastian Brys-
kett* in Venice. Witness to Paduan DCnCL of John Hart* 1574.
    Osborn, passim. See also John Payton,* Henry Farr,* Griffin Maddox,*
Roger Manners,* Henry Savile,* Richard Shelley,* Henry Unton.*

SILLIARD, SILYARD, SULLYARD, Edward.
Son of Sir John. Probably brother of William.* Named as a supporter of Mary,
Queen of Scots 1574, and as a Catholic recusant 1592. Sent gifts to Sir Robert
Cecil 1598–1602, requesting a passport to travel to Italy 1601. Witness to MD
of Thomas Hearne* Padua 1602.
    Bannerman Wainwright, 90. HMC, *Hatfield*, VIII, 20, IX, 343, X, 304, XI, 26,
169–70, XII, 452.

SILLIARD, William.
Probably brother of Edward.* Matr. Padua 1593 (AAU 30, fol. 93v). Wrote to
Sir Robert Cecil from Padua same year (PRO, SP85 1, fol. 158).
  Andrich, 134. W.C. Metcalfe, ed., *The Visitation of Essex* (London, 1878), 523,
533.

SIMAM, SEAMAN? SIMON? Daniel.
Matr. Padua 1597 (AAU 30, fol. 95).
  Andrich, 136.

SMALMAN, Samuel. B. c. 1559.
Son of John. Witness to Edward Benedict's* MD Padua 1601. Adm. English
College Rome 1602, first tonsure 1603, reader and other offices same year.
England same year.
  Kelly, 126. Rossetti, 'Nel quarto centenario.'

SMITH, SMYTH? Richard.
Travelling companion in Italy of Edward Unton.* Kept diary of visit for him.
Padua 1563, where commented on the university, the house of Livy, and
tomb of Antenor. Possibly the friend of Robert Poyntz.*
  Maclean, *Historical and Genealogical Memoir*, 116. Yeames, 106.

SMITH, Roger. See Edward Wotton.*

SOEKLIN? SOCKLIN? John.
Matr. Padua 1595 (AAU 30, fol. 94).
  Andrich, 135.

SOONE, William. Fl. 1540–75.
Protestant exile, civilian, and cartographer. Cambridge, BA 1545, MA 1549,
resident Gonville Hall 1548–55. *Consiliarius* of English nation Padua 1558.
Regius Professor of Civil Law Cambridge following year. Left England same
year. Professor at Louvain, Rome, and Cologne. Assistant at Cologne to Abraham Ortelius, but fell out with him over alleged plagiarism in Ortelius's *De
situ orbis* of 1572 (Hessels, I, 63–4). Drew map of Cambridge and wrote fond
account of the city from Cologne in 1575 included in Braun and Hogenberg's
Civitates Orbis Terrarum (R. A. Skelton, ed., New York, 1966, II, i). Author of
De veteri et nova geographia (BAV, MS Ottobiano Lat. 1187). Auditor of English
hospice Rome 1578. Worked as an administrator in the Papal State.
  DNB. EH, 271. See also Humphrey Llwyd.*

SOTOR, Claudius.
Consiliarius of English nation Padua 1578 (AAU 12, fol. 205). Vice-rector of law university next year (AAU 12, fol. 153).
    Andrich, 40.

SOUTHWELL, Francis. D. after 1576.
Elizabethan Catholic. Son of Sir Robert. Reported by Peter Vannes to be in Padua January 1554, where his and John Pelham's* tutor was John Everard.* Orleans same year. Vannes reported that Southwell learned Latin and Italian and played the lute. His companions were 'worshipful gentlemen of England' and he was 'too studious than slack in Learning.' A devout Catholic and friend of Thomas Wilson.*
    Bartlett, *English in Italy*, 219–20.

SPENCER, Richard. c. 1553–1624.
Ambassador and MP. Son of Sir John. Magdalen College, Oxford, BA 1572, MA 1575, incorp. Gonville and Caius College, Cambridge 1575. Paris 1577, when wrote to Lord Burghley his patron. England by 1579. *Consiliarius* of English nation Padua 1581–2 (AAU 13, fol. 61v). Wrote to Burghley from Padua 1581 (*Cal. SP For. Eliz.*, 1581–2, no. 323). Encountered by Nicholas Faunt* in Padua same year. Delivered a letter from Arthur Throckmorton* in Padua to Hugo Blotius in Vienna same year (Canterbury, Canterbury Cathedral Archives, MS U. 85, Box 38, I, fols 66v, 67v). 1582 Augsburg, 1583 Paris. MP 1584, 1589, 1604 and active on parliamentary committees. Secretary to Lord Burghley 1586. Various diplomatic missions, 1588–1608. Kt 1603. Gentleman of privy chamber 1607–24. Various other government offices 1590s–1620s.
    Andrich, 40. Hasler, III, 245–6. History of Parliament draft biography.

SPENCER, Robert.
Scholar of the Paduan law university 1506 (AAU 2, fols 168v, 181). Witness to MD of John Chamber* 1505. Guarantor of Gamaliel Clifton* following year. *Consiliarius* and *electionarius* of English nation 1508. Adm. Doctors' Commons 1508 as a contributor where described as doctor, amended to scholar, of both laws. Presented Subscription Book to Doctors' Commons 1511. Prebendary of Milton in Lincoln Cathedral.
    Andrich, 20–1. Squibb, 8, 17, 21, 127. *AGA, 1501–50*, no. 418.

STACKVOAELLUS? STOCKWELL? STOCKWOOD? John.
Matr. Padua 1595 (AAU 30, fol. 94, same day as John Gibson,* Robert Shirley,* Robert Baosony,* and John Frear*). Possibly the divine John Stockwood, supported 1594–7 by earl of Essex.
    DNB. Andrich, 135.

STAFFERTON, William. D. 1588.
Priest. MA Oxford. English College Rome 1583, ordained following year.
Paduan doctorate 1585. England by 1588.
  Renold, 55, 58, 63, 159.

STAFFORD, Sir Robert.
Padua 1550, where encountered Francis Yaxley.*
  Baskerville, 324.

STARKEY, Thomas. c. 1500–38.
Humanist and political thinker. Son of Thomas. Magdalen College, Oxford,
BA 1516, MA 1521 and pro-proctor same year. Padua c. 1522 with Reginald
Pole* and Thomas Lupset.* Friend of Niccolò Leonico Tomeo, doctor of arts
by 1525. Paris with Pole* 1529, Avignon and Padua to 1534. Witness to
Paduan MD of Thomas Bill* 1533. England following year, Cromwellian
servant and royal chaplain. Author *of Dialogue betwen Pole and Lupset* and *An
Exhortation to Unity and Obedience.*
  DNB. Mayer, *Thomas Starkey,* passim. See also Michael Throckmorton,*
Thomas Lupset,* John Clement,* John Friar,* George Lily,* Richard Morison,*
John Mason.*

STOKESLEY, John. c. 1475–1539.
Bishop of London. Magdalen College, Oxford, fellow c. 1495, vice-president
1505–7. Borrowed books from Vatican library 1513. Royal chaplain 1518,
member of the council 1521, almoner 1523. Dean of Chapel Royal. Various
diplomatic missions. Active in Italy, including Padua, 1530, to gather opinions on royal divorce with Richard Croke.* Bishop of London same year. A
friend of Erasmus and Richard Pace.*
  DNB. CE, III, 289–90. Surtz, passim. Emden, III, 1785–6.

STYLE, Henry. B. c. 1486.
Advocate. Winchester College, adm. 1506, New College, Oxford 1511, fellow
1513, vac. by 1519. *Consiliarius* of English nation Padua 1518 ('D. Henricus
anglicus' in AAU 3, fol. 74v). DCL, possibly of Padua. Adm. Doctors' Commons as contributor 1522, as advocate 1523, where described as doctor of
foreign university. Possibly related to diplomat John Style.
  Andrich, 22. Squibb, 140. *BRUO,* 547.

TALBOT, George.
Encountered by Samuel Foxe* Padua c. 1585. Probably the George Talbot who
matr. sizar Jesus College, Cambridge 1582.
  Venn, IV, 197.

TALBOT, Gilbert. 1553–1616.
Elizabethan privy councillor. Son of George, earl of Shrewsbury. Cousin of Francis and Roger Manners.* Sent by father to Padua 1570 and wrote to him from there same year, announcing his arrival and that of his brother-in-law Henry Cavendish* (LPL, MS 3206, fol. 571). Witness to DCnCL of John Le Rous* Padua 1571. MP 1572. First Lord of the Treasury 1582. Inherited family title 1590. Disputes with family, gentle neighbours, tenants, and the queen for next five years. Knew Thomas Wilson* by 1572 and was a friend of Francis Southwell* and Francis Walsingham.* Privy councillor 1601.

E. Lodge, *Illustrations of British History, Biography and Manners* (London 1838), II, 19–20, 145. *DNB.*

TAMWORTH, John. c. 1524–c. 69.
Marian exile and Elizabethan offical. Son of Thomas. William Thomas* wrote his *Italian Grammar* at Tamworth's request while both were in Padua 1548. Associated with Anthony and Henry Denny* in Padua. Encountered by Thomas Hoby* Padua 1554. MP and many government offices under Elizabeth. Married Christian, sister of Francis Walsingham.*

Bartlett, *English in Italy*, 220–1. Hoby, 116. W. Thomas, *Principal Rules of the Italian Grammar* (London, 1562), verso of title page. Hasler, III, 474–5.

TEDDER, William.
Priest and vicar. Adm. English College Rome 1579. London 1583, where arrested and imprisoned. Italy 1585, where encountered by Samuel Foxe* in Padua. England same year, recanted his Catholicism 1588 and became a vicar.

EH, 255. Kelly, 10. Renold, 42–3, 67–70.

TEMPLE, William.
Marian exile. Eton, King's College Cambridge, MA 1533. Present at John Cheke's* disquisitions on Demosthenes' *Three Orations* in Padua 1554, as recounted in a letter of Temple's of that year, written 'in aedibus Titi Livii.' Basle 1555.

Wilson, *Arte of Rhetorique*, xxxi, cxxix. Garrett, 303.

THEOBALD, Thomas.
Cromwellian agent. Intelligencer for Thomas Cromwell Italy late 1530s. Padua 1538. Dealings with Reginald Pole,* Edmund Harvel,* and Michael Throckmorton.*

LP, XIII, nos 507–9. Robertson, pt 2, 576.

THOMAS, William. D. 1554.
Welsh writer. Clerk of the council under Edward VI. Implicated in Thomas Wyatt* conspiracy, arrested 1554, and executed same year.
   DNB. See also John Tamworth* and Philip Hoby.*

THROCKMORTON, Arthur. 1557–1626.
Courtier and diarist. Son of Sir Nicholas. Cousin of George Carew.* Magdalen College Oxford, matr. 1571. Travelled with Sir Amyas Paulet's embassy to France 1576–7. Fought in Netherlands 1578. European tour 1580–2: Netherlands, Germany, Italy, France, partly with Edward Ashby, Henry Neville,* Henry Savile,* George Carew,* Robert Sydney. Stayed with Hugo Blotius Vienna 1581. Padua same year, where encountered Fathers Fant* and Brookes,* Nicholas Faunt,* [Edward?] Ratcliffe,* Richard Spencer,* and in Venice Herson.* MP 1589, supported by Francis Walsingham.* JP from c. 1591. 1596 joined expedition to Cadiz where kt. Associated with Henry Wotton.*
   DNB. Hasler, III, 490–1. Throckmorton's diary covering 1578–95 and 1609–13 is in Canterbury, Canterbury Cathedral Archives, MS U. 85, Box 38, I–III, drawn on extensively in Rowse.

THROCKMORTON, Michael. D. 1558.
Catholic exile and servant of Cardinal Pole.* Son of Sir Robert. Witness to MD of Thomas Bill* Padua 1533, where described as scholar of law. Friendly with Thomas Starkey* (BL, MS Cotton, Nero B vii, fol. 112). Entered Pole's* service c. 1537; represented him to English government, delivering his *Pro ecclesiasticae unitate defensione* to the king. Escaped England by feigning disloyalty to Pole* and promising to spy on him for English government. Rome 1547–51, where active in English hospice. Visited by his nephew George 1552, who was warned by Peter Vannes not to be entrapped by him. Mantua 1555–8 (except for frequent meetings with Edward Courtenay* and a brief visit to England c. 1556). His son Francis remained in Italy. Credited with authorship of *A copy of a very fyne, wytty letter sent from the right reverend Lewis Lippomanus* (London, 1556).
   LP, XI, nos 129, 1363; XII, pt 1, nos 34, 430. Venice, Archivio di Stato, Consiglio di X, Parti Communi, Reg. 20, fol. 140. *AGA, 1501–50,* no. 1943. PRO, SP1 105, fol. 1. Bartlett, *English in Italy,* 84–5, 294–5. *EH,* passim. See also Henry Coles,* Richard Morison,* and Thomas Theobald.*

TOLIUS? TOLUS? TOOLY? Paulus.
Consiliarius of English nation Padua 1582 (AAU 13, fol. 101v). Probably the 'Tooly' encountered by Nicholas Faunt* in Padua 1581.
   Andrich, 41. Cf. Venn, IV, 252.

TORKINGTON, Sir Richard.
Priest. Pilgrimage to Holy Land 1517–18, visiting Venice and Padua on journey.
 DNB. W.J. Loftie, ed., *Ye Oldest Diarie of Englysshe Travell* (n.p., 1884), 8–9.

TOWNSHEND, Aurelian. Fl. 1601–43.
Poet. Son of John. Foreign tour c. 1600–3 financed by patron Sir Robert Cecil. Padua 1601. Gentleman of the privy chamber under Charles I, writer of court masques.
 Maladorno Hargraves, 'I Cecil,' 120. *DNB.* HMC, *Hatfield*, XI, 2, 180, 289, XII, 195, 454–5, XIV, 179–80.

TRACY, Anthony.
Matr. Padua 1595 (AAU 30, fol. 94). One Sir Anthony Tracy was in Florence in 1608, and was noted as having visited Rome at around that time in a list by Simon Willis.
 Andrich, 135. HMC, *Hatfield*, XXIV, Addenda, 147.

TRILLUS? TIRILLUS? Thomas.
Consiliarius of English nation Padua 1594–5 (AAU 14, fols 41, 50, 52v).
 Andrich, 43–4.

TRISTANUS, __.
Consiliarius of English nation Padua 1568 (AAU 11, fol. 248v). Apparently English, as elected by eight members of the nation.
 Andrich, 38.

TUKE, Peter.
Matr. Padua 1597 (AAU 30, fol. 95).
 Andrich, 136.

TUNSTALL, Cuthbert. 1474–1559.
Churchman and humanist. Son of Thomas. Oxford c. 1491. King's Hall, Cambridge 1496–7. Italy, including Padua, from 1497. DCnCL probably of Padua. Chancellor to Archbishop Warham 1508. Commissary general of Prerogative Court of Canterbury 1511. Master of the Rolls 1516. Bishop of London 1522. Bishop of Durham 1530. President council in the north same year. Imprisoned in Tower 1550. Deprived of see 1552, reinstated under Mary, deprived again 1559. Author of various works. A friend of Erasmus.
 CE, III, 349–54. Sturge, passim. See also Robert Fisher,* William Latimer,* Richard Pace,* Robert Wingfield.*

TURNBULL, Hugh. 1517–66.
Churchman. Scholar of Corpus Christi College, Oxford from 1532, fellow 1536, BA same year, MA 1539, BTh 1545, lecturer in logic 1535, bequeathed copy of Chrysostom to the college. Matr. Louvain 1547 and linked with others of the 'More circle' who left England at accession of Edward VI. Tutor of Laurence and William Huse* Padua c. 1550 (Ascham, *Epistolarum libri*, 278). DTh at Padua witnessed by Huse* brothers and Nicolaus Alenus* same year (ASP, AN 5026, fols 312–4v). Turnbull's doctorate (and that of George Dudgeon,* witnessed by Turnbull) reported to royal council in England by Peter Vannes, English agent in Venice, and presence of Clement Sentlo* and of one Herbert (George Herbert*?) noted. Wrote to Reginald Pole* from Padua 1555, seeking patronage and mentioning one of his patrons as Anthony Huse, father of Laurence and William Huse.* England by 1558, when created commissioner for heresy. Dean of Chichester diocese, 1558–66. Possibly an advocate in the Consistory Court of Canterbury.
   AGA, 1501–50, nos 3881, 3888. *BRUO*, 579–80. J. Loach, 'Reformation Controversies,' in McConica, *History*, 394. Turnbull, 148. Horne, II, 6. T.F. Mayer, 'When Maecenas was Broke: Cardinal Pole's "Spiritual" Patronage,' *Sixteenth Century Journal* 27 (1996), 422.

TURNER, William. c. 1509–68.
Physician and divine. Pembroke Hall, Cambridge 1526, BA 1530, MA 1533. Abroad from 1540–7: Italy 1540–1, including Padua, Bologna, and Ferrara where probably MD; Switzerland, Germany, Netherlands. Physician to duke of Somerset 1547–52. MP 1547. Marian exile in Germany. Author of naturalist and Protestant controversial works.
   Bindoff, III, 490–2.

TUSSER, Francis.
Intelligencer. Matr. Padua 1592 (AAU 30, fol. 93). His intelligence work noted by Lord Darcy in a letter from Venice to Lord Burghley same year.
   Andrich, 133. Smith, *Henry Wotton*, II, 467.

UMILLUS, Thomas.
Matr. Padua 1593 (AAU 30, fol. 93v, same day as Henry Hyde*).
   Andrich, 134.

UNTON, Sir Edward. 1534–82.
Son of Sir Alexander. Father of Edward* and Henry.* Inner Temple 1551. Venice and Padua 1563, diary of journey kept by companion Richard Smith.*

Bought Machiavelli's *Istorie fiorentine*. MP 1554, 1563, 1572. Apparently travelled abroad again with his son Edward* 1574 (PRO, E157 1, fol. 1).
  Yeames, 92–113. Hasler, III, 541–2.

UNTON, Edward. 1556–89.
Traveller. Son of Sir Edward.* Brother of Henry.* Oriel College, Oxford by 1572, BA 1573. Apparently travelled abroad with his father Edward* 1574 (PRO, E157 1, fol. 1). Encountered by Nicholas Faunt* Padua 1581. Arrested by Inquisition Milan 1583, released by ransom 1584, his brother Henry* raising much of the money. Suspected of Catholicism on return to England. MP 1584, 1586.
  Hasler, III, 540–1. See also Tertullian Pyne.*

UNTON, Henry. c. 1558–96.
Diplomat, soldier, and literary patron. Son of Sir Edward.* Brother of Edward.* Oriel College, Oxford BA 1573. Middle Temple 1575. Kt 1586. Travelled 1570s and 1580s, including Basle where matriculated 1577, and Padua. Captain under Leicester in Netherlands 1586, ambassador to Henry IV of France 1591–2, and 1595 to death. MP 1584, 1593. Friend of Philip Sidney,* Francis Walsingham,* William Hatton.*
  Funebria nobilissimi ac praestantissimi equitis D. Henricii Untoni ad Gallos bis legati regii, ibique nuper fato functi, charissimae memoriae ac desiderio, a musis Oxoniensibus apparata (Oxford, 1596). J. Stevenson, ed., *The Correspondence of Sir Henry Unton* (London, 1847). Hasler, III, 542–3. Hammer, 'Essex and Europe,' 359. Wackernagel, II, 246.

VALISESO? Richard. See John Hart.*

VAN DER STIGEN, Michael.
Described as 'anglus' in his payment as a doctoral candidate to the bedel of the law university Padua 1594 (AAU 54, fol. 331).

VASSEL? Vito? See John Hart.*

VERE, __.
Encountered by Samuel Foxe* Padua c. 1585. Possibly Horace Vere (later Baron of Tilbury) or Sir Francis Vere, both sons of Geoffrey Vere.
  The Complete Peerage (London, 1959), XII, 257.

VERE, Edward de. 1550–1604.
Son of John, earl of Oxford. Inherited title 1562. Oxford and Cambridge 1560s. Gray's Inn 1567. Licence to travel abroad for one year January 1575, renewed for one year March 1576 (PRO, E157 1, fols 2–3). Wrote from Padua to Lord Burghley, November 1575. Associated in the Veneto with Luke Astlow* and possibly Rudolph Hopton.* Wrote preface to Bartholomew Clerk's Latin translation of Castiglione's *Cortegiano* 1571. When Sir Henry Wotton* presented de Vere's son to the doge of Venice in 1617, he claimed that Edward de Vere, during his visit to Italy, was so impressed by Venice that he travelled no further but built a house there.
     HMC, *Hatfield*, II, 122. Ward, *Seventeenth Earl of Oxford. Cal. Ven.* 1615–17, XIV, no. 495. *DNB.* See also Anthony Munday* and Edward Webbe.*

VILLERS, Richard. See John Le Rous.*

VOLEY, John.
Consiliarius of English nation Padua 1559 (AAU 10, fols 60–2).
     Andrich, 34.

WALDBY, Marmaduke.
Chaplain of Cardinal Wolsey. BA Cambridge 1504–5, knew Erasmus there. Knew Reginald Pole,* Pietro Bembo, and Niccolò Leonico Tomeo in Padua from 1524 (Pole, I, 385). Still in Padua 1526 (Erasmus, *Opus epistolarum*, VI, no. 1675). By 1528 was Wolsey's chaplain and addressed as 'Doctor.' Canon resident at Ripon 1536, when refused to surrender books of Acts and Statutes, and then involved in Pilgrimage of Grace, for which imprisoned in Tower. Still living 1540.
     LP, IV, nos 3820, 3835, 4756. *Cal. Ven.* 1527–33, IV, no. 4756. *CE*, III, 424.

WALKER, __.
Doctor. Encountered by Samuel Foxe* Padua c. 1585.
     London, BL, MS Landsdowne 679, fols 44–5.

WALSINGHAM, Francis. c. 1530–90.
Elizabethan statesman. Scholar of King's College, Cambridge, adm. 1548. Probably abroad 1550–2. Adm. Gray's Inn 1552. Marian exile, first at Basle, where resided with Denny* brothers 1554–5. *Consiliarius* and *electionarius* of English nation Padua 1555–6 (AAU 9, fols 157, 163v, 201v). Receipt for his purchase of a clavichord and wine at Padua witnessed by Edmund Wyndham* 1556 (ASP, AN 1828, fols 239–40). Possibly heard the readings of John

Cheke* at Padua. Later drew up advice on educational travel for his nephew. England by 1560.

Andrich, 31. Read, esp. I, 17–27, II, 321, III, 438–42. Garrett, 319–20. See also Nicholas Faunt,* John Hart,* Richard Shelley,* William Hatton,* Stephen Powle,* Tertullian Pyne,* Gilbert Talbot,* John Tamworth,* Arthur Throckmorton,* Henry Unton,* John Wroth,* William Cecil,* Sebastian Bryskett,* Francis Alford,* Ralph Eure.*

WALTER, William. D. by 1523.
Welsh archdeacon of Brecon. Rector of ultramontane law university of Bologna 1492. *Consiliarius* of English nation Padua 1500–1 (AAU 2, fols 41, 66). DCnCL Bologna 1503. Adm. Doctors' Commons as contributor 1509. Archdeacon of Brecon in 1500 and 1520. Translator of Boccaccio's 'Titus and Gisippus' (London, 1523).

Andrich, 19. Parks, *English Traveller*, 625, 627 (Walter of England). Squibb, 15, 21, 128. C. Malagola, *Monagrafie storiche sullo Studio bolognese* (Bologna, 1888), 179. Le Neve, I, 311. L. Hutson, *The Usurer's Daughter: Male Friendship and Fictions of Women in Sixteenth-Century England* (London and New York, 1994), 84, 253.

WEBB, John.
Son of Robert. Brother of Joseph.* Witness to Edward Benedict's* MD Padua 1601 (ASP, AN 4105, fols 262–3).

WEBB, Joseph. Fl. 1612–33.
Grammarian and physician. Son of Robert. Brother of John.* Witness to Edward Benedict's* MD Padua 1601. Doctorate in arts and medicine Padua April 1603. England by 1616, when commenced, but apparently did not complete, process of admission by College of Physicians of London. Suspected of papistry by parliamentary commissioners 1626, fined for unlicensed medical practise by College of Physicians same year (London, Royal College of Physicians, Annals of the College of Physicians of London 3, fols 26v, 65v, 66). Matr. Leiden 1637. Author of *An appeale to truth in the controversie between art and use: about the best and most expedient course in languages* (London 1622) and various other works. Translator of Cicero's *Epistolae ad familiares* (London c. 1620).

Rossetti, 'Nel quarto centenario.' Innes Smith, 244. *DNB*. Munk, I, 169.

WEBBE, Edward. B. c. 1554.
Master gunner and traveller. Son of Richard. Travels in Mediterranean, Persia, Turkey, Egypt, Russia, and western Europe detailed in his *The Rare*

and most wonderful thinges (London, 1590). Padua late 1580s, where claimed to have encountered thirty Englishmen, one of whom reported him to the bishop as a heretic. Venice, Ferrara, Bologna, Florence, Rome, where met Cardinal Allen and stayed in English College; Naples, Palermo, where claimed to have met Edward de Vere.*

DNB. G. Capuano, *Viaggiatori britannici a Napoli tra '500 e '600* (Salerno, 1994), 55–7. Cf. Ward, *Seventeenth Earl of Oxford*, 111–12.

WENDON, Nicholas.

Civilian. Cambridge 1546, BA 1550, MA 1552, fellow of Trinity College same year. Adm. Doctors' Commons 1567 as a contributor, where described as DCL of a foreign university, possibly from Louvain c. 1567. Archdeacon of Suffolk 1559–75. Acquired licence to travel abroad for his health (PRO, E157 1, fol. 1: February 1573). Deprived of archdeaconry. A witness to doctorate of John Hart* Padua 1574. Listed as a fugitive living abroad in 1575, together with John Hart* and (Roger?) Fitzwilliams* (PRO, SP12 105, fol. 105). Emigrated to Rome, where ordained 1578.

Squibb, 157. Venn, III, 365. Horne, VII, 48. Le Neve, II, 489, 499.

WHITE, Richard. 1539–1611.

Catholic exile, jurist, and historian. Son of Henry. Adm. Winchester College 1553, New College, Oxford 1557, BA 1559. Met jurist Viglius Zwichem von Aytta in England. Abroad 1560 to study law on advice of John Boxall.* Louvain 1560, where delivered two orations 1563 ('De circulo artium et philosophiae' and 'De eloquentia et Cicerone,' printed in White's *Orationes*, 1596. Cf. *STC* 25403). Moved to Italy same year to avoid civil disturbances in France and was a witness to *procura* of Anthony Fortescue* Padua same year. Delivered an oration at Padua entitled 'Pro divitiis regum' same year, addressed to Anthony Mason,* occasioned by their respective reactions to the public display of the treasury of Venice (White, 92–110). *Consiliarius* and *electionarius* of English nation 1564–5, summoned to appear before the rector in December 1565, together with eight other *consiliarii*, for disobeying his rulings (AAU 11, fols 4, 61, 73v, 77v). Witness to *procura* of John Litelor* together with Jerome Sapcot* Padua 1566 where described as student of law. Also knew at Padua Thomas Even,* the medical student Gilbert Scheneus* – whom he also knew at Venice and Pavia – Robert Poyntz,* George Gattacre,* Jerome Sapcot,* John Perpoint,* Robert Peckham,* Donatus Rullus (a former *familius* of Reginald Pole*), and Giovan Vicenzo Pinelli; and, at Venice, Jacobo Foscareno. Medallion commemorates him at Padua. In his oration delivered at Pavia 1566, 'Pro doctoratu,' names his Paduan law teachers as Marco Mantova Benavides, Giudo Panciroli, Tiberio Deciani, and Giovanni Cieffalo, identifying Panciroli, with whom he still corresponded in the 1580s, and Mantova, to whom he dedicated part of his *Aelia Laelia Crispis epitaphium antiquum* (Padua, 1568), as particular friends. DCnCL of Pavia same year. Adm. as contributor to Doctors' Commons 1568, despite urgings of Thomas White, head of New College, Oxford, who advised that he could practise as an advocate without a doctorate incorporated in an English university. Emigrated to Douai 1570. Became first principal of Marchiennes College there same year, lectured publicly on law there from 1572, and became Regius Professor of Law, the rector of the university and count palatine. Wrote *Historiarum Britanniae insulae libri* (Douai, 1597–1607), apparently encouraged by Thomas Goldwell*; *Leges Decem virorum in duodecim tabulis, Institutiones Iuris Civilis in quattuor libris, Primam partem Digestorum in quattuor libris* (1597); *Brevis explicatio privilegiorum iuris, et consuetudinis, circa venerabile Sacramentum Eucharistiae* (Douai, 1609); and *Breves Explicatio Martyrii Sanctae Ursulae et undecim millum virginum Britannarum* (Douai, 1610).

Squibb, 157. Andrich, 36–7. Rhodes, 'Richard White of Basingstoke,' 23–30. Binns, 'Richard White of Basingstoke,' 17–29. Pollard, 93. White, *passim*. Rivolta, 33.

WHYTEHORNE, Thomas.
Musician. Travels in Italy 1554, including Padua. Published Italianate *Triplex of Songs*, 1571. Not to be confused with Peter Whytehorne, translator of Machiavelli's *Arte della guerra*.

Baskerville, 322. Chaney, 7–8. *DNB*. J.M. Osborn, ed., *The Autobiography of Thomas Whythorne* (Oxford, 1961), esp. 68.

WILLIAMS, Francis. See Thomas Hoby.*

WILLIAMS, Henry. See Thomas Hoby.*

WILLOUGHBY, Richard. D. 1617.
Son of George. Corpus Christi College, Cambridge, BA 1567–8, fellow 1569, proctor 1578. Left England next year and converted to Catholicism. *Consiliarius* of English nation Padua 1584, 1585, 1587–8, 1591, 1593, 1595 (AAU 13, fols 179v, 185v, 190v, 199, 201v; AAU 14, fols 1v, 35, 37, 57v, 59v, 61). Vicar of the law university's rector 1605. Witness to doctorates of Edward Benedict* 1601, Thomas Hearne* and William Harvey* 1602, John Moore 1605, John Frear* 1610, John Wedderburn 1615. Encountered by Samuel Foxe* in Padua c. 1585. Showed Thomas Coryat around Padua c. 1608 (Coryat, I, 299). A friend of Ralph Winwood* (cf. HMC, *Buccleuch and Queensberry*, I, 131) and supplied intelligence to Henry Hawkins* from Padua 1594 (HMC, *Hatfield*, V, 45–6; cf.

BL, MS Harley 288, fol. 242). A relative of Peregrine Bertie,* to whom he wrote from Venice in 1596 (LPL, MS 660, fol. 76). A friend at Padua of Galileo, Lorenzo Pignoria, Paolo Gualdo, and Marco Corner. Visited Jerusalem in 1612 with one 'Mr Bowes,' Nicholas Hare, and other Englishmen (PRO, SP99 10, fol. 190v).

Andrich, 41–4. A.W. Maladorno Hargraves, 'Un poeta inglese minore: Nicholas Hare (1582–1622),' *QSUP* 8 (1975), 94. A. Lytton Sells, *The Paradise of Travellers* (London 1964), 111. Smith, *Henry Wotton*, II, 114. HMC, *Hatfield*, V, 45–6. Rossetti, *Stemmi*, 208, no. 1002. C. Bellinati, 'Richard Willoughby, amico di Galileo, in una nota dell'obituario di S. Lorenzo (23 aprile 1617),' *Atti e memorie dell'Accademia Patavina di Scienze, Lettere ed Arti* 96 (1983–4), 137–141. Maladorno Hargraves, 'From Padua to the Field of Edgehill,' 113. A. Favaro, 'Riccardo Willoughby,' *Atti dell'Istituto Veneto* 71 (1911–12), 25–9. Maladorno Hargraves, 'Diplomi dottorali,' 172–3. London, BL, MS Harley 286, fol. 242; MS Harley 296, fol. 54.

WILSON, Nicholas. D. c. 1548.
Royal chaplain and almoner to Catherine of Aragon. Christ's College, Cambridge, BA 1509, MA 1512, BTh 1523, DTh 1524. Witness to MD of Edward Wotton* Padua 1525, where described as scholar of law. England from 1528, when appointed archdeacon of Oxford and to other benefices. Master of Michaelhouse from 1533. Wrote against Henry VIII's divorce. Refused oaths of succession and supremacy 1535, deprived of benefices, and imprisoned in Tower same year (where corresponded with Thomas More) until 1537. Recovered benefices. Imprisoned briefly again in 1540.

Dowling, 91. *AGA, 1501–50*, no. 1059. Venn, III, 430. See also Thomas Lupset.*

WILSON, Thomas. c. 1524–81.
Humanist and statesman. Son of Thomas. Uncle of Thomas.* Eton College, adm. 1537, scholar of King's College, Cambridge, adm. 1541, BA 1545–6. MA 1549. Friend of Roger Ascham and member of John Cheke* and Thomas Smith circle at Cambridge. Tutor to sons of duchess of Suffolk and wrote *Vita et obitus duorum fratrum Suffolciensium Henrici et Caroli Brandoni* (London, 1551) with Walter Haddon, which includes two eulogies by Henry Knolles.* Wrote logic manual *The Rule of Reason*, first printed 1551, and *Arte of Rhetorique*, first printed 1553. On the fall from power of duke of Northumberland sought refuge on continent. Attended Cheke's* disquisitions on the *Orations* of Demosthenes Padua 1555, and was inspired by them to produce his own English translation, printed in 1570, which parallels the dangers to liberty posed by Philip of Macedon and Philip II of Spain. Delivered funeral oration

at Padua for Edward Courtenay,* earl of Devon 1556 (text in Strype, III, Appendix, 191–5). Represented plaintiff in an English divorce suit in papal court 1557, to the annoyance of the English government who summoned him back to England. Remaining in Rome, was accused of heresy by Roman Inquisition for anti-Catholic comments in *Arte of Rhetorique* and imprisoned and tortured. Set free by Roman mob which destroyed Holy Office of Inquisition and its prison on death of Paul IV, 1559. Added some anti-papal jibes to second edition of *Arte of Rhetorique*, 1560. DCL or DCnCL Ferrara 1559 (HMC, *5th Report*, London, 1876, 304). England 1560. Adm. advocate of the Arches and member of Doctors' Commons 1561. Master of St Catherine's Hospital in the Tower and master of Requests same year. DCL incorp. Cambridge 1571 (Parker, 16). MP 1563–7 and 1572–81. Diplomatic mission to Portugal 1567. Wrote *Discourse uppon usurye by waye of Dialogue and Oracions*, 1572. Interrogator of prisoners suspected of involvement in Norfolk and Ridolfi plots 1571–2. Member of High Commission. Ambassador to Netherlands 1574–5 and 1576–7. Secretary of state in succession to Sir Thomas Smith, apptd 1577. A friend of Francis Southwell.* Owned portrait of 'a widow of Venice.'

DNB. Squibb, 154. Baskerville, 118–22. Wilson, *Arte of Rhetorique*. Wilson, *Three Orations*. A.J. Schmidt, 'Thomas Wilson, Tudor Scholar-Statesman,' *Huntington Library Quarterly* 3 (1957), 205–18. Leadam, cvii, cix. Usher, 360. See also William Malim* and Gilbert Talbot.*

WILSON, Thomas. c. 1565–1629.
Keeper of the records and author. Son of Humphrey. Nephew of Thomas Wilson.* St John's College, Cambridge 1581, BA 1584, MA Trinity Hall, Cambridge 1587. Italy and Germany 1596, during which translated Diana de Monte Mayor from the Spanish. Inner Temple 1598. Had studied civil law for fifteen years by 1600. Secretary for intelligence matters to Sir Robert Cecil, in which connection knew Simeon Foxe.* Venice, Padua, Florence, Pisa, France 1601–2 (HMC, *Hatfield*, XXIII, Addenda, 96; PRO, SP98 1, passim; PRO, SP99 2, passim). Consul Valladolid 1604–5. MP 1605. Keeper of records in the Tower 1606–29. Kt 1618. Author of 'The State of England in A.D. 1600.'
DNB. History of Parliament draft biography.

WINGFIELD, Robert. c. 1464–1539.
Diplomat. Brother of Sir Richard. Rome 1505, resident at English hospice. His *procura* at Padua dated 1506 names Thomas Knight (who is documented as present in Rome, same year) and Thomas Halsey (a student at Bologna in 1510 and a visitor to English hospice in Rome in 1512) as his guarantors, with Demit Selley* as a witness (ASP, AN 1812, fol. 260). *Consiliarius* of English nation 1508 (AAU 3, fol. 35). Various diplomatic missions from same year.

Endless squabbles with Richard Pace* on missions to the emperor in 1510s, and also worked as a diplomat with Cuthbert Tunstall.*

Andrich, 21. *DNB.* Parks, *English Traveller*, 375–6, 474, 627. Wegg, 34, 71–93, 96–112, 158. *LP*, II, nos 2176, 2177, 2178, 2277.

WINTER, Thomas. D. after 1537.
Illegitimate son of Cardinal Wolsey. Matr. Louvain 1518. Italy from 1522, probably with Thomas Lupset.* Acquainted with Reginald Pole* at Padua same year. Possibly in Louvain 1523–4, returned to England c. 1524–6, when travelled to Paris. Was joined there by Lupset* 1528. Supported by Thomas Cromwell after the fall of Wolsey. In Paris until c. 1530, Venice c. 1531, England same year. Paris 1532, then Padua under charge of Richard Morison* same year until 1534, Ferrara same year, returned to England same year.

Dowling, 157–8. Zeeveld, 51–65, 78–9, 92–4. PRO, SP1 70, fols 182–3; SP1 71, fols 126–7; SP1 82, fols 105, 213; SP1 85, fol. 43; SP1 96, fol. 134. BL, MSS Cotton, Nero B vi, fol. 126; Nero B. vii, fol. 198; Vitellius B v, fol. 273; MS Harley 6989, fol. 36. See also Richard Morison.*

WINWOOD, Ralph. c. 1563–1617.
Diplomat and secretary of state. Son of Richard. Matr. St John's College, Oxford 1571, probationer fellow of Magdalen College from 1582, BA same year, MA 1587, BCL 1590–1, proctor 1592. Matr. Padua 1594 (AAU 30, fol. 94). A friend of Henry Neville* and Henry Wotton* and knew Richard Willoughby* and Henry Savile.* Ambassador in France 1601–2, English agent in The Hague intermittently 1603–13. Secretary of state and MP 1614–17.

Andrich, 134. *DNB.* HMC, *Buccleuch and Queensberry*, I, 24–5, 28. Smith, *Henry Wotton*, passim. Sawyer, passim. History of Parliament draft biography. See also Samuel Foxe.*

WITHIPOOLE, Daniel. See John Le Rous.*

WOOD, George.
Matr. Padua 1596 (AAU 30, fol. 94v). Probably the Oxford student who was a servant of Roger Manners,* and who was with Manners* in France 1597 (HMC, *Rutland*, IV, 411).

Andrich, 153. *AO*, IV, 1670.

WOOD, Laurence.
Matr. Padua 1594 (AAU 30, fol. 94).

Andrich, 134. For probable identification see Venn, IV, 453.

WOTTON, Edward. 1492–1555.
Naturalist. Son of Richard. Magdalen College School, Magdalen College 1506, BA 1514, fellow 1516. First reader in Greek Corpus Christi College 1521. Padua 1520s. Paduan MD 1525 witnessed by Nicholas Wilson,* Thomas Starkey,* Robert Birch,* Roger Smith,* and Robert Chaloner* (ACV, Diversorum 55, fol. 38v). Worked on Aldine Galen same year with Thomas Lupset,* John Clement,* and Anthony Rose. Fellow of College of Physicians 1528, *consiliarius* 1531, 1547, 1549, elect 1531, censor 1552, 1553, 1555, president 1541–3. Physician to duke of Norfolk and Margaret, countess of Salisbury, mother of Reginald Pole.* His Galenica later used by John Caius.*
    DNB. See also Henry Coles.*

WOTTON, Henry. 1568–1639.
Writer and diplomat. Son of Thomas. Winchester College. New College Oxford, matr. 1584, Hart Hall c. 1585, Queen's College 1586–9, BA 1588. Abroad 1589–94: Heidelberg University 1589–90, Vienna where knew Hugo Blotius, Altdorf 1590, where became friendly with Edward, Lord Zouche,* Bologna, Venice, and Padua with Zouche* 1591–2, Rome by 1592, where met Cardinals Bellarmine and Allen, Naples, Genoa, Florence, Geneva 1593, where lodged with Isaac Casaubon, France 1594. Arrived at Padua with letters of introduction from Blotius to Giovan Vicenzo Pinelli, and stayed in Padua 'in casa di Sr. Marcantonio al Pozzo della Vacca appresso i Padri Gesuiti' (Vienna, Österreichische Nationalbibliothek, MS 9737 z^{17}, fol. 172. Cf. G. Saggiori, *Padova nella storia delle sue strade*, Padua, 1972, 289). Middle Temple 1595. Secretary of earl of Essex same year, and active as a foreign intelligencer for him in England and abroad to 1600. Abroad same year, partly in Florence. England 1603, kt 1604, and became English ambassador to Venice from 1604–12; 1616–19; 1621–4. A friend of Richard Baker.* Various other diplomatic positions. MP 1614, 1625. Provost of Eton 1624–39. Gentleman of the privy chamber by 1629. Author of *The Elements of Architecture, A Survey of Education* and other works, probably including *The State of Christendom.*
    Smith, *Henry Wotton*, passim. Hammer, ' "This bright Shininge Spark," ' 124–5, 128. Hammer, 'Uses of Scholarship,' passim. History of Parliament draft biography. See also Francis Davison,* Thomas Sackville,* Arthur Throckmorton,* Edward de Vere,* Ralph Winwood.*

WROTH, WROTHE, John. D. after July 1616.
Intelligencer. Son of Thomas.* Encountered by Samuel Foxe* in Padua c. 1585. A student at Padua c. 1588 but also supplied intelligence to* Sir Francis

Walsingham* same year and to Lord Burghley 1591–2 (Wernham, III (1591–2), 435; PRO, SP99 1, passim). Knew Stephen Powle* in the Veneto (*Cal. SP For. Eliz.*, 1588, 475–6). MP 1593.

Hasler, III, 658. History of Parliament draft biography. Cf. Davison, xxxix–xlii, and Smith, *Henry Wotton*, I, 279.

WROTHE, Thomas. 1518–73.
Marian exile. Son of Robert. Father of John.* St John's College, Cambridge. Gray's Inn adm. 1536. MP 1545. Gentleman of the privy chamber following year. Kt 1547. Protestant supporter of Northumberland, present at conference on the sacrament in house of Richard Morison* 1551. Supporter of Queen Jane, briefly imprisoned by Mary, then permitted to travel abroad. Travelled with John Cheke* to Padua 1554, where met Hoby* brothers and Anthony Cooke.* Visited Mantua same year, and Caldiero with Cheke,* where again met Hobys,* and Venice and Augsburg with these three. On to Strasbourg with Cheke* same year, where met John Brett. Remained there until return to England in 1558. MP and various government offices under Elizabeth.

Bartlett, *English in Italy*, 224–5. Hoby, 116–17. Hasler, III, 664–5. *DNB*.

WYATT, Thomas. c. 1521–54.
Marian rebel. Son of Henrician poet Thomas Wyatt. Abroad 1544–50, partly on military service. Encountered by Thomas Hoby* Padua 1548.

Hoby, 8. *DNB*. D. Loades, *Two Tudor Conspiracies* (London, 1965). See also William Thomas.*

WYNDHAM, Edmund.
Catholic recusant. Probably illegitimate son of Sir Edmund of Felbrigg and brother of Thomas Wyndham.* *Consiliarius* and *electionarius* of English nation Padua 1556 (AAU 9, fols 164, 201v). A witness to Francis Walsingham's* purchase of a clavichord and wine in Padua same year (ASP, AN 1828, fols 239–40). England c. 1557 and possibly ordained as a priest. Teaching civil law, probably at Cambridge, in 1559, when refused to swear to oath of supremacy. DCL by 1565 (possibly from Padua), when adm. Doctors' Commons as an advocate. Adm. advocate of the Arches same year. Imprisoned, then exiled, under Elizabeth but protected from more severe punishment by his brother-in-law Sir Nicholas Bacon. Paris 1580, but recalled same year. Eventually promised to swear obedience to Elizabeth. Involved in missionary priests' conflict at Wisbech Prison 1595, and particularly with Christopher Bagshaw.* Corresponded with earl of Essex 1596 (LPL, MS 654, fol. 244).

Hoby, 116. Andrich, 31–2. *Cal. Ven.* 1555–7, VI, no. 169. Squibb, 156. Frere, 447. H.A. Wyndham, *A Family History, 1410–1688* (Oxford, 1939), 122–4. Renold, *Wisbech Stirs*, xv, xxv, 22, 36–40, 41–5.

WYNDHAM, Thomas.
Encountered by Thomas Hoby* Padua 1554. Licensed to carry arms Venice 1555 (Venice, Archivio di Stato, Consiglio di X, Parti Communi, Reg. 22, July 1555).
  Bartlett, *English in Italy*, 226. See also Francis Russell* and Edmund Wyndham.*

YAXLEY, Francis. D. 1565.
Conspirator. Client of Sir William Cecil. Italy 1550. Met Robert Stafford* at Padua same year, and studied there Latin and Italian. England 1552, MP same year, and student of Gray's Inn. Diplomatic missions. Intrigued against Elizabeth early 1560s and imprisoned.
  Baskerville, 324. *DNB.*

ZOUCHE, Edward. c. 1556–1625.
Baron Zouche of Harringworth. Son of George. Travelled abroad from 1587: Germany with Stephen Powle,* Basle 1588, Altdorf with Henry Wotton* 1590, Vienna 1591, Padua with Wotton* 1592. Envoy to James VI of Scotland same year and 1594. Commercial mission to Denmark 1598. Guernsey 1600. England 1601. 1602 President of council in Wales. Active in colonial ventures from 1609. Lord Warden of the Cinque Ports. Interested in horticulture and a literary patron.
  DNB. Smith, *Henry Wotton*, II, 482–3. See also Thomas Sackville.*

... FIDIO? ... LFIDO? ... SSIDU? Jacobus.
Elected to the law university rector's syndicate at Padua in 1581 (AAU 13, fol. 64: 'Jacobus Anglus'). *Consiliarius* of English nation 1582 (AAU 13, fol. 92v, where first part of surname illegible; cf. Andrich, 41: 'Delfidio').

... SILDUS? ... FILDUS? Anthony.
Matr. Padua 1592 same day as Henry Neville* (AAU 30, fol 93, where first part of surname illegible; cf. Andrich, 133: 'Crevelsidus').

__, Adrianus.
MD Padua 1525, where described as 'Britanus' (*AGA, 1501–50*, no. 1053).

Select Bibliography

Primary Sources: Manuscript and Archival

Basle
Universitätsbibliothek
MS KI4

Bologna
Archivio di Stato
Studio   129, 140, 379

Cambridge
Cambridge University Library
MS Baker 37 (Mm I 48)
MS 2044 Kk. V. 2

Queens' College
MS 49

Canterbury
Canterbury Cathedral Archives
MS U. 85, Box 38, I–III

London
British Library
Additional   1938, 10268, 19061, 28035, 29549, 40676
Cotton   Cleopatra E vi
                                    Faustina C ii

3

	Nero B vi–vii
	Vespasian D xviii, Vespasian F xiii
	Vitellius B iv, Vitellius B v, Vitellius B xiii
Egerton	837, 1998, 2262, 2604
Hargrave	225
Harley	283, 288, 296, 1327, 3829, 4888, 6265, 6989
Lansdowne	43–4, 978
Royal	11 A xvi, 12 A. lxvii, 17 A ix, 17 C x, 17 D ix, 18 A i
Sloane	1047, 3280

Lambeth Palace Library
MSS 647, 649, 652–5, 658–60, 3206
Register of Archbishop Pole
Register of Archbishop Whitgift

Public Record Office

C 38	1–3
E 36	216
E157	1, 26
SO 3	1
SP 1	16, 18, 47, 55, 70–1, 81–2, 85–6, 90, 92, 95–6, 99, 102–3, 105–6, 126–7, 131, 133
SP 12	105, 109, 184, 265
SP 98	1–2
SP 99	1–2

Royal College of Physicians

Annals of the College of Physicians of London	2–3
MS 307	

University of London Library
MS 187

Milan
Biblioteca Ambrosiana
MS Q. 122 sup.

Munich
Bayerische Staatsbibliothek
MS Lat. 28128

Oxford
Bodleian Library
MS Carte 205
MS Rawlinson D 400

Padua
Archivio Antico dell'Università
MSS 2–15, 30, 54, 143, 144, 316,
    333, 459, 652, 675–6

Archivio della Curia Vescovile
Diversorum 42, 47, 54, 55, 55 bis, 56

Archivio di Stato
Archivio Notarile   829, 831, 1809–12, 1828, 2333, 2337, 2342,
                                     4104–5, 4848–9, 4851–2, 4856, 5007, 5026

Biblioteca del Seminario
MSS 71, 634

Paris
Bibliothèque Nationale
MS Dupuy 632

Vatican City
Biblioteca Apostolica Vaticana
MS Ottob. Lat. 1187
MS Regin. Lat. 1291
MS Ross. Lat. 997
MS Urb. Lat. 1044

Venice
Archivio di Stato
Capi del Consiglio di X, Lettere
    di Rettori e di altre cariche:
    Padova, 1542–57, Busta 82

Consiglio di X	Lettere ai Capi 14
Consiglio di X	Misti 45–6
Consiglio di X	Parti Communi, Reg. 15, 20, 22,
Senato Terra	23, 34

Biblioteca Correr
MS Correr 1349

Biblioteca Nazionale Marciana

MS Ital. VII	1934 (9013)
MS Ital. IX	364 (7167)
MS Ital. X	24 (6527)
MS Ital. X	91 (6606)
MS Gr. Z.	225 (307)
MS Lat. VI	272 (2883)
MS Lat. XIV	61 (4241)
MS Lat. XIV	171 (4665)

Vienna
Österreichische Nationalbibliothek
MS 9737z[17]
MS 9737z[14–18]

Primary Printed Works

Agricola, G. *Bermannus: Un dialogue sur les mines*, ed. R. Halleux and A. Yans. Paris, 1990.

Allen, P.S. and H.M. Allen, eds. *Letters of Richard Fox*. Oxford, 1929.

Anglo, S., ed. 'An Early Tudor Programme for Plays and Other Demonstrations against the Pope.' *Journal of the Warburg and Courtand Institutes* 20 (1957), 176–9.

Ascham, R. *Epistolarum libri*. Oxford, 1703.

– *The Schoolmaster (1570)*, ed. L.V. Ryan. Ithaca, NY, 1967.

Bannerman Wainwright, J., ed. 'Two Lists of Supposed Adherents of Mary Queen of Scots, 1574 and 1582.' Catholic Record Society Publications, *Miscellanea* VIII, 86–142. London, 1913.

Beccadelli, L. *Monumenti di varia letteratura*. Bologna, 1797.

Bembo, P. *Lettere*, ed. E. Travi. Bologna, 1987–93.

Birch, T. *Memoirs of the Reign of Queen Elizabeth*. London, 1754.

Botfield, B., ed. *Prefaces to the First Editions of the Greek and Roman Classics and the Sacred Scripture*. London, 1861.

Brugi, B., ed. *Atti della nazione germanica dei legisti nello Studio di Padova*. Venice, 1912.

–, ed. 'Una descrizione dello Studio di Padova in un ms del secolo XVI nel Museo Britannico.' *Nuovo Archivio Veneto* 15 (1907), 72–88.

Caius, J. *Works*, ed. E.S. Roberts. Cambridge, 1912.

Carew, G. 'A Treatise of the Maisters in Chauncerie.' In *A Collection of Tracts Relative to the Law of England*, ed. F. Hargrave, I, 293–319. London, 1787.

Chambers, D.S., ed. *Faculty Office Registers*. Oxford, 1966.

Coryat, T. *Coryat's Crudities*. Glasgow, 1905.

Croke, R. *Orationes duae*. n.p., 1520.

Cuffe, H. *The differences in the ages of man's life*. London, 1607.

Davison, F. *The Poetical Rapsody*, ed. N.H. Nicolas. London, 1826.

Deciani, T. 'Apologia pro iurisprudentibus.' In T. Deciani, *Responsa*, III, fols 1–36. Venice, 1579.

Denifle, H., ed. 'Die Statuten der Juristen-Universität Padua vom Jahre 1331,' *Archiv für Literatur- und Kirchengeschichte des Mittelalters* 6 (1892), 308–562.

Erasmus, Desiderius. *Ciceronianus*. Toronto, 1986.

– *Opus epistolarum*, ed. P.S. Allen. Oxford, 1906–58.

Erler, G., ed. *Die iüngere Matrikel der Universität Leipzig*, I. Leipzig, 1909.

Favaro, A., ed. *Atti della natione germanica artista nello Studi di Padova*. Venice, 1911.

Foster, J., ed. *The Register of Admissions to Gray's Inn, 1521–1889*. London, 1889.

Foxe, J. *Acts and Monuments*, ed. S.R. Cattley. London, 1839.

Frere, W.H., ed. *Registrum Matthei Parker Diocensis Cantuariensis A.D. 1559–75*. Oxford, 1928.

Frimmel, T., ed. *Der Anonimo Morelliano*. Vienna, 1888.

Gallo, R., ed. 'Due informazioni sullo Studio di Padova della metà del Cinquecento.' *Nuovo Archivio Veneto* 72 (1963), 17–100.

Gribaldi Mofa, M. *Epistolae Patavinae*, Basle, 1922.

Herendeen, W.H., and K. Bartlett. 'The Library of Cuthbert Tunstall, Bishop of Durham.' *Papers of the Bibliographical Society of America* 85 (1989), 235–96.

Herrtage, S.J. *England in the Reign of King Henry the Eighth*. London, 1878.

Hessels, J.H., ed. *Ecclesiae Londino-Batavae Archivium*. Cambridge, 1887.

Historical Manuscripts Commission. *Calendar of the MSS of the Most Honourable the Marquis of Salisbury preserved at Hatfield House*. London, 1883–1967.

– *Fifth Report*. London, 1876.

- *The MSS of his Grace the Duke of Rutland preserved at Belvoir Castle.* London, 1905.
- *Report of the MSS of the Duke of Buccleuch and Queensberry preserved at Montague House, Whitehall.* London, 1899.
- *Twelfth Report,* Appendix, I: *MSS of the Earl Cowper preserved at Melbourne Hall, Derbyshire.* London, 1888.
Hoby, T. 'A Booke of the Travaile and Life of Me Thomas Hoby,' *Camden Society* 10. London, 1902.
Kelly, W., ed. *The* Liber Ruber *of the English College, Rome,* I. London, 1940.
Leland, J. *Principum ac illustrium aliquot et eruditorum in Anglia virorum encomia.* London, 1589.
Lemon, R., ed. *Calendar of State Papers, Domestic Series, of the Reigns of Edward VI, Mary, Elizabeth, 1547–80.* London, 1856.
Leonico Tomeo, N. *De varia historia libri tres.* Basle, 1531.
- *Dialogi.* Venice, 1524.
- *Opuscula.* Venice, 1525.
Longolius, C. *Opera.* Florence, 1524.
McCann, J., and H. Connolly, eds. *Memorials of Father Augustine Baker.* London, 1933.
Mitchell, W.T., ed. *Epistolae academicae, 1508–96.* Oxford, 1980.
Moryson, F. *An Itinerary.* Glasgow, 1907.
- *Shakespeare's Europe: Unpublished Chapters of Fynes Moryson's Itinerary.* London, 1903.
Oates, J.C.T., and H.L. Pink, eds. 'Three Sixteenth-century Catalogues of the University Library.' *Transactions of the Cambridge Bibliographical Society* 1 (1949–53), 310–40.
Pace, R. *De fructu qui ex doctrina percipitur,* ed. F. Manley and R.S. Sylvester. New York, 1967.
Parker, M. 'Catalogus Cancellariorum.' In M. Parker, *De antiquitate Britanniae ecclesiae.* London, 1572.
Pole, R. *Epistolarum collectio,* ed. A.M. Quirinus. 1744–58. Reprint Farnborough, 1967.
Pollen, J.H., ed. *Memoirs of Father Robert Persons.* London, 1906.
Profitable Instructions. N.p., 1633.
Reed, A.W. 'John Clement and His Books.' *The Library* 6 (1925–6), 329–39
Relazioni dei rettori veneti in terraferma, IV: *Podestaria e capitanato di Padova.* Milan, 1975.
Renold, P., ed. *Letters of William Allen and Richard Barrett, 1572–1598.* London, 1967.
- , ed. *The Wisbech Stirs.* London, 1958.

Riccoboni, A. *De Gymnasio Patavino*. Padua, 1598.

Robinson, R. *A brief collection of the queenes majesties most high and most honourable courtes of record*, ed. R.L. Rickard. London, 1953.

Rogers, E.F., ed. *The Correspondence of Sir Thomas More*. Princeton, 1947.

Rossetti, L., ed. *Gli stemmi dello Studio di Padova*. Trieste, 1983.

– , ed. *Matricula Nationis Germanicae Artistarum in Gymnasio Patavino, 1553–1721*. Padua, 1986.

– , ed. 'Un documento del 1493 degli scolari tedeschi nello Studio di Padova.' *Atti memorie dell'Academia Patavina di Scienze, Lettere ed Arti* 70 (1959–60), 65–72.

St German, C. *Doctor and Student*, ed. T.F. Plucknett and J.L. Barton. London, 1974.

Salter, H.E., ed. *Registrum Annalium Collegii Mertonensis, 1483–1521*. Oxford, 1923.

Sanuto, M. *I diarii*. Venice, 1893.

Sawyer, E., ed. *Memorials of Affairs of State in the Reigns of Elizabeth I and James I*. London, 1725.

Scardeone, B. *De antiquitate urbis Patavii*. Basle, 1560.

Smith, L.P., ed. *Life and Letters of Sir Henry Wotton*. Oxford, 1907.

Smith, T. *De republica Anglorum*, ed. M. Dewar. Cambridge, 1982.

Spedding, J., ed. *Letters and Life of Francis Bacon*. London, 1861–74.

Starkey, T. *A Dialogue between Pole and Lupset*, ed. T.F. Mayer. London, 1989.

Statuta artistarum Patavini Gymnasii. Padua, 1607.

Statuta spectabilis et almae Universitatis Iuristarum Patavini Gymnasii. Venice, 1551.

Strype, J. *Ecclesiastical Memorials*. Oxford, 1822.

Thomas, W. *The History of Italy*, ed. G.B. Parks. London, 1963.

Thorndike, L., ed. *University Records and Life in the Middle Ages*. New York, 1971.

Turnbull, W.B., ed. *Calendar of State Papers, Foreign, of the Reign of Edward VI, 1547–53*. London, 1861.

Ungerer, G., ed. *A Spaniard in Elizabethan England: The Correspondence of Antonio Pérez's Exile*. London, 1976.

Wackernagel, H.G., ed. *Die Matrikel der Universität Basel*. Basle, 1951–80.

Weaver, F.W., ed. *Somerset Medieval Wills, 1531–58*. Somerset Record Society 21. London, 1905.

Wernham, R.B., ed. *Lists and Analyses of State Papers, Foreign Series, Elizabeth I*. London, 1964–93.

White, R. *Orationes*. Arras, 1596.

Wilson, T. *Arte of Rhetorique*, ed. J. Derrick. New York and London, 1982.

– (trans.) *The Three Orations of Demosthenes*. London, 1570.

Wood, A. *Athenae oxonienses*. London, 1641.
– *Athenae oxonienses*, ed. P. Bliss. London, 1813.
Yeames, A.H.S., ed. 'The Grand Tour of an Elizabethan.' *Papers of the British School at Rome* 7 (1914), 92–113.

Secondary Printed Works

Allen, P.S. 'Linacre and Latimer in Italy.' *English Historical Review* 18 (1903), 514–17.
Andrich, G. *De natione Anglica et Scota iuristarum Universitatis Patavinae ab a. 1222 p. Ch. n. usque ad a. 1738*. Padua, 1892.
Bacquet, P. *Un contemporain d'Elisabeth I: Thomas Sackville, l'homme et l'oeuvre*. Geneva, 1966.
Baker, J.H. 'English Law and the Renaissance.' *Cambridge Law Journal* 44 (1985), 46–61.
– *An Introduction to English Legal History*. London, 1979.
– *The Reports of Sir John Spelman*, II. London, 1978.
Bartlett, K.R. *The English in Italy, 1525–1558*. Geneva, 1991.
– 'English Students at Padua, 1521–58.' *Proceedings of the PMR Conference* 4 (1979), 88–107.
– '"The misfortune that is wished for him": The Exile and Death of Edward Courtenay, Earl of Devon.' *Canadian Journal of History* 14 (1979), 1–28.
Baskerville, J. 'The English Traveller to Italy, 1547–60.' PhD dissertation, University of Columbia, 1967.
Bedouelle, G., and P. Le Gal. *Le Divorce du roi Henry VIII*. Geneva, 1987.
Bell, G. 'Elizabethan Diplomacy: The Subtle Revolution.' In *Politics, Religion and Diplomacy in Early Modern Europe: Essays in Honour of De Lamar Jensen*, ed. M.R. Thorp and A.J. Slavin, 267–87. Kirksville, MO, 1994.
– *A Handlist of British Diplomatic Representatives*. London, 1990.
Berkowitz, D.S. *Humanist Scholarship and Public Order*. Washington DC, 1984.
Bertolaso, B. 'Ricerche d'archivio su alcuni aspetti dell'insegnamento medico presso l'Università di Padova nel Cinque e Seicento.' *Acta medicae historiae patavina* 6 (1959–60), 17–37.
Bindoff, S.T., ed. *The House of Commons, 1509–58*. London, 1982.
Binns, J.W. *Intellectual Culture in Elizabethan and Jacobean England*. Leeds, 1990.
– 'Richard White of Basingstoke and the Defence of the Tudor Myth.' *Cahiers Elisabethains* 11 (1977), 17–29.
Brotto, A.G., and G. Zonta. *La facolta teologica dell'Università di Padova*. Padua, 1922.

Brown, H.F. 'Inglesi e Scozzesi all'Università di Padova dall'anno 1618 sino al 1765.' In *Monografie storiche sullo Studio di Padova*, 137–213. Venice, 1922.

Brugi, B. 'Gli studenti tedeschi e la S. Inquisizione a Padova nella seconda metà del secolo XVI.' In B. Brugi, *Gli scolari dello Studio di Padova nel Cinquecento*, 71–100. Padua, 1905.

– *La scuola padovana di diritto romano nel secolo XVI.* Padua, 1888.

– 'L'Università dei giuristi in Padova nel Cinquecento,' *Archivio Veneto Tridentino* 1 (1922), 1–92.

Buxton, J., and P. Williams, eds. *New College, Oxford.* Oxford, 1979.

Chaney, E. '*Quo vadis?* Travel as Education and the Impact of Italy in the Sixteenth Century.' In *International Currents in Educational Ideas and Practices*, ed. P. Cunningham and C. Brock, 1–28. London, 1988.

Chavasse, R. 'The Reception of Humanist Historiography in Northern Europe: M.A. Sabellico and John Jewel.' *Renaissance Studies* 2 (1988), 327–38.

Churchill, I.J. *Canterbury Administration.* London, 1933.

Cobban, A.B. 'Medieval Student Power.' *Past and Present* 53 (1971), 28–66.

Conway Davies, J. *Catalogue of Manuscripts in the Library of the Honourable Society of the Inner Temple.* Oxford, 1972.

Costil, P. *André Dudith, humaniste hongrois, 1533–1589.* Paris, 1935.

Dalton, C. *A Life of Edward Cecil Viscount Wimbledon.* London, 1885.

De Bellis, D. 'La vita e l'ambiente di Niccolò Leonico Tomeo.' *QSUP* 18 (1980), 36–75.

– 'Niccolò Leonico Tomeo interprete di Aristotele naturalista.' *Physis* 17 (1975), 71–93.

De Lazzari Bumbaca, A. 'Schede per scolari francesi a Padova, 1532–6.' *QSUP* 3 (1970), 137–44.

De Sandre, G. 'Dottori, università, commune a Padova nel Quattrocento.' *QSUP* 1 (1968), 15–45.

Dizionario biografico degli italiani. Rome, 1960– .

Donaldson, P.S. *Machiavelli and Mystery of State.* Cambridge, 1988.

Dowling, M. *Humanism in England in the Reign of Henry VIII.* London, 1986.

Dupuigrenet Desroussilles, F. 'L'Università di Padova dal 1405 al Concilio di Trento.' In *Storia della cultura veneta*, ed. G. Arnaldi and M. Pastore Stocchi, III, pt 2, 607–47. Vicenza, 1980.

Elton, G.R. *Studies in Tudor and Stuart Politics and Government*, II. Cambridge, 1974.

– *The Tudor Constitution.* Cambridge, 1982.

Emden, A.B. *A Biographical Register of the University of Oxford to A.D. 1500.* Oxford, 1965–9.

Facciolati, F. *Fasti Gymnasii Patavini.* Padua, 1757.

Fedalto, G. 'Stranieri a Venezia e a Padova.' In *Storia della cultura veneta*, ed. G. Arnaldi and M. Pastore Stocchi, III, pt 1, 499–535. Vicenza, 1980.

Feingold, M. *The Mathematicians' Apprenticeship: Science, Universities and Society in England, 1560–1640*. Cambridge, 1984.

Fenlon, D. *Heresy and Obedience in Tridentine Italy: Cardinal Pole and the Counter-Reformation*. Cambridge, 1972.

Fowler, T. *The History of Corpus Christi College*. Oxford, 1893.

Fox, A., and J. Guy. *Reassessing the Henrician Age: Humanism, Politics and Reform, 1500–1550*. Oxford, 1986.

French, R. *William Harvey's Natural Philosophy*. Cambridge, 1994.

Garrett, C.H. *The Marian Exiles*. Cambridge, 1938.

Gee, J.A. *The Life and Works of Thomas Lupset*. New Haven, 1928.

Gillow, J. *Bibliographical Dictionary of the English Catholics*. London and New York, n.d.

Gottfried, R.S. 'English Medical Practitioners, 1340–1530.' *Bulletin of the History of Medicine* 58 (1984), 164–82.

Grafton, A., and T. Jardine. 'Studied for Action: How Gabriel Harvey Read His Livy.' *Past and Present* 128 (1990), 30–78.

Guy, J.A. *The Cardinal's Court: The Impact of Wolsey in Star Chamber*. Hassocks, 1977.

– *The Public Career of Thomas More*. Brighton, 1980.

– , ed. *The Reign of Elizabeth I: Court and Culture in the Last Decade*. Cambridge, 1995.

Hammer, P. 'Essex and Europe: Evidence from Confidential Instructions by the Earl of Essex, 1595–6.' *English Historical Review* 111 (1996), 357–81.

– 'The Uses of Scholarship: The Secretariat of Robert Devereux, Second Earl of Essex, c. 1585–1601.' *English Historical Review* 109 (1994), 26–51.

– '"This bright Shinine Spark": the Political Career of Robert Devereux, Second Earl of Essex, c. 1585–c.1597.' PhD thesis, University of Cambridge, 1991.

Handover, P.M. *The Second Cecil*. London, 1959.

Harris, B.J. *Edward Stafford, Third Duke of Buckingham*. Stanford, 1986.

Hasler, P.W., ed. *The House of Commons, 1558–1603*. London, 1981.

Heal, F., and R. O'Day, eds. *Continuity and Change: Personnel and Administration of the Church of England, 1500–1642*. Leicester, 1976.

Helgerson, R. *Forms of Nationhood*. Chicago, 1992.

Helmholz, R.H. *Roman Canon Law in Reformation England*. Cambridge, 1990.

Heward, E. *Masters in Ordinary*. Chichester, 1990.

Horne, J.M., ed. *Fasti ecclesiae Anglicanae, 1541–1857*. London, 1969– .

Horton-Smith, L.G.H. *George Acworth*. N.p., 1953.

Hutter, I. 'Cardinal Pole's Greek Manuscripts in Oxford.' In *Manuscripts at Oxford: An Exhibition in Memory of R.W. Hunt*, 108–14. Oxford, 1980.

Innes Smith, R.W. *English-Speaking Students of Medicine at the University of Leyden*. Edinburgh and London, 1932.

Jardine, L. *Erasmus, Man of Letters*. Princeton, 1993.

Jardine, L., and W. Sherman. 'Pragmatic Readers: Knowledge Transactions and Scholarly Services in Late Elizabethan England.' In *Religion, Culture and Society in Early Modern Britain: Essays in Honour of Patrick Collinson*, ed. A. Fletcher and P. Roberts, 113–24. Cambridge, 1994.

Jones, W.J. *The Elizabethan Court of Chancery*. Oxford, 1967.

Katz, D. *The Jews in the History of England, 1485–1850*. Oxford, 1994.

Kelley, D. 'Civil Science in the Renaissance: Jurisprudence Italian Style.' *The Historical Journal* 22 (1979), 777–94.

– 'History, English Law and the Renaissance.' *Past and Present* 65 (1974), 24–51.

– 'Law.' In *The Cambridge History of Political Thought, 1450–1700*, ed. J.H. Burns, 66–94. Cambridge, 1991.

Keynes, J. *The Life of William Harvey*. Oxford, 1966.

Kibre, P. *The Nations in the Medieval Universities*. Cambridge, MA, 1948.

– *Scholarly Privileges in the Middle Ages*. London, 1961.

Kraye, J., ed. *The Cambridge Companion to Renaissance Humanism*. Cambridge, 1996.

Labowsky, L. 'Manuscripts from Bessarion's Library Found in Milan.' *Medieval and Renaissance Studies* 5 (1961), 108–31.

Leadam, I.S. *Select Cases in the Court of Requests, 1497–1569*. London, 1898.

Leader, D.R. *A History of the University of Cambridge*, I. Cambridge, 1988.

Lee, R.W. *The Elements of Roman Law*. London, 1956.

Le Neve, J. *Fasti ecclesiae Anglicanae*. Oxford, 1854.

Levack, B.P. *The Civil Lawyers in England, 1603–41*. Oxford, 1973.

– 'The English Civilians, 1500–1750.' In *Lawyers in Early Modern Europe and America*, ed. W. Prest, 108–28. London, 1981.

Loomie, A.J. *The Spanish Elizabethans*. New York, 1963.

Lowry, M. *The World of Aldus Manutius*. Oxford, 1979.

McCain, R. 'English Travellers in Italy during the Renaissance.' *Bulletin of Bibliography* 19 (1947–8), 68–9, 93–5, 117–19.

McConica, J.K. 'The Catholic Experience in Tudor Oxford.' In *The Reckoned Expense: Edmund Campion and the Early English Jesuits*, ed. T.M. McCoog, 39–66. Woodbridge, 1996.

– *English Humanists and Reformation Politics*. Oxford, 1965.

– 'The Social Relations of Tudor Oxford.' *Transactions of the Royal Historical Society* 27 (1977), 115–34.

– , ed. *The History of the University of Oxford*, III: *The Collegiate University*. Oxford, 1986.

McCoog, T.M. *Monumenta Angliae*. Rome, 1992.

McCuaig, W. *Carlo Sigonio: The Changing World of the Late Renaissance*. Princeton, 1989.

MacCullogh, D., ed. *The Reign of Henry VIII: Politics, Policy and Piety*. London, 1995.

Maclean, I. *Interpretation and Meaning in the Renaissance: The Case of Law*. Cambridge, 1992.

Maclean, J. *Historical and Genealogical Memoir of the Family of Poyntz*. Exeter, 1886.

Madison, F., M. Pelling, and C. Webster, eds. *Linacre Studies: Essays on the Life and Works of Thomas Linacre, c.1460–1524*. Oxford, 1977.

Maladorno Hargraves, A. 'From Padua to the Field of Edgehill: An Outline of the Career of Robert Bertie, Thirteenth Baron Willoughby d'Eresby.' *Atti e memorie dell'Accademia Patavina di Scienze, Lettere ed Arti* 87 (1974–5), 109–29.

– 'I Cecil e lo Studio Patavino.' *QSUP* 16 (1983), 119–26.

– 'I diplomi dottorali di John Frear (1610) e di Samuel Turner (1611) al British Museum.' *QSUP* 13 (1980), 169–77.

– 'Un dottore di Padova alla berlina: John Bastwick.' *QSUP* 3 (1970), 101–12.

Martellozzo Forin, E., and E. Veronese. 'Studenti e dottori tedeschi a Padova nei secoli XV e XVI.' *QSUP* 4 (1971), 49–102.

Mayer, T.F. 'Marco Mantova and the Paduan Religious Crisis of the Early Sixteenth Century.' *Cristianesimo nella Storia* 7 (1986), 41–61.

– *Thomas Starkey and the Common Weal: Humanist Politics and Religion in the Reign of Henry VIII*. Cambridge, 1989.

Mugnai Carrara, D. 'Profilo di Niccolò Leoniceno.' *Interpres* 2 (1978), 169–212.

Munk, W. *The Roll of the Royal College of Physicians of London*, I. London, 1878.

Nicholson, G. 'The Nature and Function of Historical Argument in the Henrician Reformation.' PhD thesis, University of Cambridge, 1977.

Nutton, V. 'John Caius and the Linacre Tradition.' *Medical History* 23 (1979), 373–91.

– *John Caius and the Manuscripts of Galen*. Cambridge, 1987.

O'Day, R. *Education and Society, 1500–1800: The Social Foundations of Education in Early Modern Britain*. London, 1982.

Ohl, R.E. 'The University of Padua, 1405–1509: An International Community of Students and Professors.' PhD dissertation, University of Pennsylvania, 1980.

Osborn, J. *Young Philip Sydney*. London, 1972.

Pagel, W. 'Harvey Revisited (Part I).' *History of Science* 8 (1969), 1–31.

– 'Harvey Revisited (Part II).' *History of Science* 9 (1970), 1–52.
– *William Harvey's Biological Ideas*. Basle and New York, 1967.
Parks, G.B. 'Did Pole Write the "Vita Longolii?"' *Renaissance Quarterly* 26 (1973), 274–85.
– *The English Traveller in Italy*. Rome, 1954.
Parmiter, G. de C. *The King's Great Matter: A Study of Anglo-Papal Relations, 1527–34*. London, 1967.
Plochmann, K. 'William Harvey and his Methods.' *Studies in the Renaissance* 10 (1963), 192–210.
Pollard, G. *Medals of the Renaissance*. London, 1978.
Rashdall, H. *The Universities of Europe in the Middle Ages*, ed. F.M. Powicke and A.B. Emden. Oxford, 1936.
Read, C. *Mr Secretary Walsingham and the Policy of Queen Elizabeth*. Oxford, 1925.
Reid, R.R. *The King's Council in the North*. London, 1921.
Relazioni tra Padova e la Polonia: Studi in onore dell' Università di Cracovia nel VI centenario della sua fondazione. Padua, 1964.
Rhodes, D. 'Richard White of Basingstoke: The Erudite Exile.' In *Across the Narrow Seas*, ed. S. Roach, 23–30. London, 1991.
– 'Some English, Welsh, Scottish and Irish Book-Collectors in Italy, 1467–1850.' *Bookbinding and Other Bibliophily* (1994), 247–76.
Ridder-Symoens, H. de, ed. *A History of the University in Europe*, I. Cambridge, 1992.
Rivolta, A. *Catalogo dei codici pinelliani dell'Ambrosiana*. Milan, 1933.
Roberti, M. 'Il collegio padovano dei dottori giuristi.' *Rivista italiana per le scienze giuridiche* 35 (1903), 171–249.
Robertson, M.L. 'Thomas Cromwell's Servants: The Ministerial Household in Early Tudor Government and Society.' PhD dissertation, University of California, 1975.
Rose, P.L., and S. Drake. 'The Pseudo-Aristotelian *Questions of Mechanics* in Renaissance Culture.' *Studies in the Renaissance* 18 (1971), 65–104.
Rossetti, L. 'I collegi per i dottorati *auctoritate veneta*.' In *Viridarium floridum: Studi di storia veneta offerti dagli allievi di Paolo Sambin*, ed. M.C. Billanovich, G. Cracco, and A. Rigon, 365–86. Padua, 1984.
– 'Membri del "Royal College of Physicians" di Londra laureati nell'Università di Padova.' *Atti e memorie dell'Accademia Patavina di Scienze, Lettere ed Arti* 75 (1963), 175–201.
– 'Nel quarto centenario della nascita di William Harvey.' *QSUP* 9–10 (1977), 239–43.
– *The University of Padua: An Outline of Its History*. Milan, 1972.

Rowse, A.L. *Ralegh and the Throckmortons.* London, 1962.

Scarisbrick, J.J. *Henry VIII.* London, 1981.

Schenk, W. *Reginald Pole, Cardinal of England.* London, 1950.

Schmitt, C. 'William Harvey and Renaissance Aristotelianism.' In *Humanismus und Medizin,* ed. G. Keil and R. Schmitz, 117–38. Weinheim, 1984.

Siraisi, N.G. *Arts and Sciences at Padua.* Toronto, 1973.

Sorbelli, A. 'La nazione nelle antiche università italiane e straniere.' *Studi e memorie per la storia dell'Università di Bologna* 16 (1943), 93–232.

Squibb, G.D. *Doctors' Commons: A History of the College of Advocates and Doctors of Law.* Oxford, 1977.

Stein, P. *The Character and Influence of the Roman Civil Law: Historical Essays.* London, 1988.

Stella, A. 'Tentativi controriformistici nell'Università di Padova e il rettorato di Andrea Gostynski.' In *Relazioni tra Padova e la Polonia: Studi in onore dell' Università di Cracovia nel VI centenario della sua fondazione,* 75–87. Padua, 1964.

Stone, L. *The Crisis of the Aristocracy, 1558–1641.* Oxford, 1965.

Sturge, C. *Cuthbert Tunstall: Churchman, Scholar, Statesman and Administrator.* London, 1938.

Surtz, E. *Henry VIII's Great Matter in Italy: An Introduction to Representative Italians in the King's Divorce, Mainly 1527–35.* Ann Arbor, 1975.

Todd, R.B. 'Henry and Thomas Savile in Italy.' *Bibliothèque d'Humanisme et Renaissance* 58 (1996), 439–44.

Tomasini, J.P. *Gymnasium Patavinum.* Udine, 1654.

Toso Rodonis, G. *Scolari francesi a Padova agli albori della Controriforma.* Padua, 1970.

Trapp, J.B., and H. Schulte Herbrüggen, eds. *'The King's Good Servant': Sir Thomas More, 1477/8–1535.* London, 1978.

Usher, R.G. *The Rise and Fall of the High Commission.* Oxford, 1913.

Van Caenegem, R.C. *Judges, Legislators and Professors: Chapters in European Legal History.* Cambridge, 1987.

Venn, J., and J.A. Venn. *Alumni Cantabrigienes,* pt 1. Cambridge, 1922.

Veronese Ceseracciu, E. 'Ebrei laureati a Padova nel Cinquecento.' *QSUP* 13 (1980), 151–6.

Vos, V. 'The "Vita Longolii": Additional Considerations about Reginald Pole's Authorship.' *Renaissance Quarterly* 30 (1977), 324–33.

Ward, B.M. *The Seventeenth Earl of Oxford, 1550–1604.* London, 1928.

Ward, J. *The Lives of the Professors of Gresham College.* London, 1740.

Wear, A., R. French, and I.M. Lonie, eds. *The Medical Renaissance of the Sixteenth Century.* Cambridge, 1985.

Webster, C., ed. *Health, Medicine and Mortality in the Sixteenth Century.*
  Cambridge, 1979.

Wegg, J. *Richard Pace, a Tudor Diplomatist.* New York, 1971.

Whitteridge, G. *William Harvey and the Circulation of the Blood.* London, 1971.

Woolfson, J.M. 'John Claymond, Pliny the Elder, and the Early History of
  Corpus Christi College, Oxford.' *English Historical Review* 112 (1997),
  882–903.

Zeeveld, G.W. *Foundations of Tudor Policy.* Cambridge, MA, 1948.

Index